AN INTRODUCTION TO CRITICAL CRIMINOLOGY

Pamela Ugwudike

First published in Great Britain in 2015 by

Policy Press
University of Bristol
1-9 Old Park Hill
Bristol BS2 8BB
UK
t: +44 (0)117 954 5940
e: pp-info@bristol.ac.uk
www.policypress.co.uk

North American office:
Policy Press
c/o The University of Chicago Press
1427 East 60th Street
Chicago, IL 60637, USA
t: +1 773 702 7700
f: +1 773-702-9756
e:sales@press.uchicago.edu
www.press.uchicago.edu

© Policy Press 2015

Reprinted 2016

British Library Cataloguing in Publication Data
A catalogue record for this book is available from the British Library.

Library of Congress Cataloging-in-Publication Data
A catalog record for this book has been requested.

ISBN 978-1-4473-0942-0 paperback
ISBN 978-1-4473-0940-6 hardcover

Cover design by Double Dagger
Front cover: image kindly supplied by Photodisc
Printed and bound in Great Britain by by CMP, Poole
Policy Press uses environmentally responsible print partners

Contents

Introduction

An Introduction to Critical Criminology introduces students to key perspectives in critical criminology. As a field of study within criminology, critical criminology comprises several perspectives that emphasise disparate themes. Collectively the perspectives criticise mainstream criminological theories on several grounds. In addition, most of the perspectives assert that the origins[1] of crime and deviance[2] can be traced to unequal power dynamics, and other inequalities in society, which can expose the less powerful to criminalisation, and sometimes to victimisation.

Many criminology textbooks do not pay sufficient attention to critical criminological perspectives. In the UK, textbooks that include sections on critical criminology often confine themselves to descriptions of dated perspectives. Thus the textbooks typically discuss the foundations of critical criminology peremptorily, alongside other criminological theories. In the US, the situation appears to be the same. As DeKeseredy (2010: 18) rightly observes:

> one area that is consistently given poor treatment is critical criminology. Some texts simply ignore this side of the field. Others give extensive coverage, perhaps an entire chapter, but limit themselves to ancient intellectual battles and detailed coverage of long-discredited leftist theories.

An Introduction to Critical Criminology aims to address the paucity of accessible introductory texts on the subject. The text seeks to provide a reliable analysis of the foundational perspectives[3] in critical criminology that emerged in the 1960s and the 1970s. It also explores additional critical criminological perspectives that have emerged since the 1970s.

The UK and the US are often cited as the 'birthplaces of contemporary critical criminology' (Sparks, 1980, cited in DeKeseredy and Dragiewicz, 2012: 3). Other writers dispute this claim. For example, van Swaaningen (1999: 6) points out that 'if we are to believe the handbooks, criminology is a discipline of dead Europeans and living North Americans'. Most texts on the subject do, indeed, focus on insights from the UK and the US. *An Introduction to Critical Criminology* deviates from this trend. The text presents insights from jurisdictions across Western Europe and America. This is because it is important to acknowledge that the work of writers in Europe influenced some of the foundational theorists in the field (van Swaaningen, 1997). Furthermore, contemporary critical criminological perspectives have emerged across Europe. As Schwendinger and colleagues (2008: 55) correctly observe, perspectives that are underpinned by ideas that are associated with critical criminological perspectives exist not only in the UK and in North American jurisdictions such as the US and Canada, but also in Australia, Norway, Italy and Germany (see also DeKeseredy and Dragiewicz, 2012).

Therefore, *An Introduction to Critical Criminology* introduces readers to the work of key scholars from other jurisdictions, including: the Dutch sociologist Willem Bonger (1916), who some describe as the 'founding father of critical criminology' (van Swaaningen, 1999: 9); the German penal theorists Georg Rusche and Otto Kirchheimer (1939) who charted the political economy of punishment[4] in industrial capitalist societies; the Italian writers Dario Melossi and Massimo Pavarini (1981), and Alessandro DeGiorgi (2007), who have more recently explored the political economy of punishment in advanced capitalist jurisdictions. The text also introduces readers to critical perspectives that have emerged from the work of European scholars even if they do not necessarily identify themselves as critical criminologists. These scholars include the French (post-)structuralist Michel Foucault (1977), the Norwegian penal abolitionists Nils Christie (1981; 2000; 2004) and Thomas Mathiesen (1974; 1990), and the Dutch abolitionist Willem de Haan (1991; 2010).

Critical criminology is now an essential component of criminology, criminal justice and sociology courses in many universities in the Western world and beyond. Many students of law, social policy, and other social science subjects also undertake modules on critical criminology. It is hoped that *An Introduction to Critical Criminology* will serve as a useful learning and teaching resource for students and academics in diverse disciplines.

Indeed, *An Introduction to Critical Criminology* has an avowedly pedagogical agenda. At the end of each chapter, there is a list of key points that summarise the themes covered. Each chapter also contains questions that can serve as guides for essay preparation. In addition, some of the chapters contain boxed-off sections that help illustrate the issues covered by the chapter more vividly. In sum, *An Introduction to Critical Criminology* aims to serve as an accessible text that introduces undergraduate students to key foundational and contemporary debates in critical criminology.

Outline of chapters

It is impossible to cover every critical criminological perspective in any one text. It is a field of study that is expanding quite rapidly. As DeKeseredy and Dragiewicz (2012: 6) note: 'critical criminologists have attended to a legion of topics and it is impossible to do them all justice in one book'. Therefore, *An Introduction to Critical Criminology* confines itself to key perspectives that tend to populate module booklets designed for undergraduate critical criminology modules, and also the module booklets for theoretical criminology modules.

An Introduction to Critical Criminology comprises 13 chapters, which are divided into four thematic parts. Part One of the text focuses on foundational perspectives in critical criminology. It begins with Chapter One, which is an introductory chapter. The chapter attempts to define critical criminology and sets out the features that unite most critical criminological perspectives. Its primary aim is to guide readers through the key themes that separate critical criminology from mainstream criminology. Chapter Two introduces readers to the labelling perspective. The labelling tradition has been described as one of the foundational perspectives that launched critical criminology as a field of study. The chapter analyses the work of key proponents of the tradition, particularly the US sociologist Howard Becker (1963, 1967).

Chapter Three introduces conflict perspectives in criminology, with particular reference to the work of its key proponents, including Thorsten Sellin (1938a; 1938b), George Vold (1958), Austin Turk (1966, 1969) and Richard Quinney (2008 [1970]). Other key writers include William Chambliss and Robert Seidman (1971). These scholars have explored how the diversity of norms, values and/or cultures in any one society can create conflict between groups. The scholars argue that, ultimately, the group or groups that are able to assert their norms, values and/or cultures determine definitions of crime in that society.

In Chapter Four, there is a review of Marxist criminology. The chapter describes the work of early writers in the field, such as Willem Bonger (1916), who described capitalism as criminogenic. In the 1970s, Marx-inspired criminologists on both sides of the Atlantic contributed to a turn in criminology towards more radical analyses of crime and deviance. Primarily, Marx-inspired criminologists trace crime and deviance, and responses to both, to the social, political and economic structures of capitalist societies. Chapter Four introduces the work of these criminologists, including the US-based scholars Richard Quinney (2008 [1970]) and William Chambliss (1975), and the British-based scholars Ian Taylor, Paul Walton and Jock Young (1973). There are detailed analyses of two key strands of British Marxist criminology that emerged from the National Deviancy Conferences (NDCs) of the 1960s. These strands are 'the New Criminology' and 'the Birmingham School'. Chapter Four also explores anarchist criminology. Like the Marxist criminologists, anarchist criminologists trace the origins of crime to what they perceive to be an unjust and unequal social order. They propose radical transformations of the status quo.

Part Two of the text reviews the criticisms that the key foundational perspectives in critical criminology received in the 1970s and 1980s. In that period, criminologists and others on the Left and Right of criminology[5] launched formidable attacks on the foundational perspectives. Indeed, the foundational perspectives experienced something of a decline in the 1980s. Part Two describes several factors that contributed to this decline. It comprises three chapters. First, Chapter Five reviews the neo-conservative criminological perspectives that emerged in the 1970s and the 1980s. These perspectives rejected the search for fundamental causes. They de-emphasised the impact of structural factors and focused instead on proposing crime control strategies. Chapter Six details the criticisms that the foundational perspectives received from writers in Britain who went on to develop an approach that came to be known as left realism in the 1980s. This is an ideological stance that has also informed the work of scholars in North America, such as Elliot Currie and Walter DeKeseredy. Chapter Six explores the origins of left realism and its key ideas about crime and its control.

Feminist criminology is an important strand of critical criminology. It has criticised not only the mainstream criminological theories, but also the foundational critical criminological perspectives. It has accused criminology in general of gender-blindness and androcentrism. Chapter Seven reviews the work of the key writers, including Carol Smart, who is a pioneer of this field of study. The chapter also explores advances in the field. A key example is the study of masculinities.

Critical criminology has expanded into several different strands since its popularity within criminology waned in the 1970s. Part Three of the text explores more contemporary perspectives in critical criminology. It begins with Chapter Eight, which sets out the work of contemporary scholars who have expanded on ideas put forward by the foundational perspectives, particularly Marxist criminology. These contemporary scholars assert that power[6] is an important factor that shapes constructions of crime and the operation of criminal justice. Far from the traditional focus of mainstream criminological theories, which has been traditionally on the behaviour of those who possess low socio-economic status, these scholars study the crimes of the powerful. Some (but by no means all) of the scholars who study the crimes of the powerful echo the views of the Marxist criminologists, who argued that the powerful (those who possess material wealth and political influence) are able to influence the operation of the law, and can escape law enforcement when they violate the law or cause others harm. As we shall see in Chapter Four, Marxist criminologists emphasised this theme. Downes and Rock (2011: 269) observe that: 'The "crimes of the powerful" and their relative immunity from prosecution and penal sanction, with all due allowance for the occasional exemplary sentence, was a central theme for Marxist criminology'.

Thus, some criminologists who have gone on to study the crimes of the powerful have been influenced by insights from Marxist criminology. A notable exception is the neo-Chicagoan Edwin Sutherland (1949), who, in the 1940s, drew attention to crimes of higher-status individuals and corporations, which he described as 'white-collar crimes'. Nevertheless, Downes and Rock (2011: 258) maintain that it was the advent of Marxist criminology that provided the impetus for subsequent studies of the crimes of the powerful. They argue that: 'None of the theories in vogue in the 1950s and 1960s addressed white-collar crime and crimes of corporations at all satisfactorily' (Downes and Rock, 2011: 258). Since the 1980s, several criminologists have turned their attention to the crimes of the powerful. These criminologists have built on the themes of power and wealth inequality in capitalist societies, which were central to Marxist criminology. They have drawn attention to the impunity that the powerful enjoy when they commit crime. The criminologists have also highlighted the relative vulnerability of the less powerful to criminal justice interventions. Key proponents of this area of study include the late Steven Box (1987) and Steve Tombs (2007).[7] Closely aligned with the work of these criminologists is the ideological position of other scholars who also draw attention to the interrelatedness of power, crime and criminal justice. Described as Zemiologists, these writers assert that criminology and criminal justice should expand their parameters to incorporate not only acts that the criminal law defines as 'crime', but also acts that cause social harm and undermine social justice. These include the harmful actions of the powerful, particularly the state and large corporations. Zemiologists point out that the definition of crime by the criminal law focuses attention on the issues that are selected by those who have the power to influence how laws are created. Consequently, according to the Zemiologists, the definition or construction of crime offered by the criminal law diverts attention from the harmful activities of the powerful (see also Lynch, 2011). Chapter Eight explores these arguments and introduces readers to the work of key writers in this field including Paddy Hillyard and Steve Tombs (2005, 2007).

Chapter Nine maintains the theme of power and its relationship to constructions of crime. The chapter explores an emerging field of study that illuminates, *inter alia*, how power shapes the constructions of, and responses to, activities that harm the physical environment. This field of study is often described as 'green criminology'. The chapter introduces readers to perspectives in the field by drawing on the work of its proponents, including Vincenzo Ruggiero and Nigel South (2013a; 2013b), Rob White (2010a; 2010b; 2013) and Michael Lynch (1990, 2011).

Cultural criminology is another relatively recent development in critical criminology. Cultural criminologists study the cultural and structural contexts of crime and crime control. Unlike other criminological theories, cultural criminologists focus not only on the background factors that they believe may contribute to crime (such as socio-economic disadvantage), but also on what they describe as foreground factors. These factors include the emotions and thrills that, in their view, can motivate and sustain criminality. Chapter Ten describes the work of pioneers in this field, including Jeff Ferrell and Mike Presdee.

Chapter Eleven explores Critical Race Theory (CRT). CRT emerged from the work of scholars in the field of critical legal studies, and has very much been oriented towards developments in the US. Nevertheless, it comprises themes that are relevant to critical criminology. For example, it critiques the existing legal order in some Western jurisdictions and argues that the legal order disadvantages people of colour. As such, CRT identifies itself as a scholarly endeavour that seeks to align itself with movements that seek to transform unjust legal systems. It is useful to acknowledge that, with its roots in critical legal studies, CRT sits on the outside of critical criminological orthodoxy. However, its focus on the impact of unequal social structures on definitions of crime, and on criminal justice policies, suggests that CRT and critical criminology share sufficiently complementary ideals. Therefore, although CRT is not commonly viewed as a critical criminological tradition, it deserves consideration in any text that concerns itself with critical perspectives on crime and criminal justice. Key writers in this field include Richard Delgado and Jean Stefancic (2012). Chapter Eleven analyses CRT's central themes alongside the work of other criminologists who have explored similar themes in their evaluation of the racial dynamics of criminal justice in UK contexts.

Part Four focuses on critical perspectives on punishment. It comprises Chapter Twelve, which examines the work of penal theorists, who have offered critical perspectives on punishment. Their work falls within the critical tradition because they contextualise their analyses of punishment within the social, economic and political arrangements that prevail in society. Scholars who have contributed to this field of study include the German penal theorists Georg Rusche and Otto Kirchheimer (1939). Contemporary writers in the field include the Italian writers Dario Melossi and Massimo Pavarini (1981) and Alessandro DeGiorgi (2007), to name but a few. In addition, Chapter Twelve examines ideas put forward by penal theorists who have drawn attention to the use of punishment as a mechanism of surveillance or panoptic penal regulation and control in capitalist societies. The French (post-)structuralist Michel Foucault (1977) can be described as a key writer in this field. Additional critical perspectives on punishment explored in the chapter include the work of Stanley Cohen, David Garland, Loic Wacquant, Malcolm Feeley and Jonathan Simon. Abolitionism represents yet another critical perspective on punishment. Therefore, Chapter Twelve examines the work of writers in the abolitionist tradition, including the Norwegian abolitionist Nils Christie (2000) and the Dutch abolitionist Willem de Haan (1991; 2010). Chapter Twelve also presents key ideas from convict criminology, which is a critical criminological perspective that explores the impact of penal sanctions, particularly imprisonment. It is a critical criminological tradition that focuses exclusively on the experiences of convicts as described mainly by the convicts and ex-convicts themselves. Pioneers in the field include Stephen Richards and Jeffrey Ross (2001). Individually, criminologists who offer critical perspectives on punishment present substantively different accounts of punishment. Together, they focus their analysis (to varying degrees) on links between social, political and economic arrangements, and the use of punishment in advanced Western societies.

The final chapter explores future directions in the field of critical criminology. It examines the social, political and economical changes that have occurred in many Western societies in recent decades. It argues that the changes have opened up new areas of study for critical criminologists.

I hope that *An Introduction to Critical Criminology* will provide a reliable review of the main priorities of critical criminology. Scholars in the field challenge dominant ideas about crime and deviance. They present persuasive arguments to support their contention that social, economic and political dynamics shape definitions of crime and deviance, and the operation of criminal justice systems. In their view, it is futile to view crime and deviance as static concepts, or to ignore the wider structural dynamics that appear to configure crime, deviance, and societal responses to both phenomena.

Notes

[1] Bernard (1981: 374) defines mainstream criminology, which is also sometimes described as orthodox criminology or conventional criminology, as: 'criminology which is approved by the established power groups [it] will tend to function as a tool of those groups in their

attempt to control out-of-power groups'. Chapter One explores the criticisms critical criminologists have levelled at mainstream criminology in more detail.

[2] 'Deviance' is typically defined as any act that deviates from the norms of society (or from what many people in any society consider 'normal' acceptable behaviour). As Kai Erikson (1962) argues:

> it is common practice in sociology to picture deviant behaviour as an alien element of society. Deviance is considered a vagrant form of human activity, which has somehow broken away from the orderly currents of social life and needs to be controlled.

Reinforcing this, Stanley Cohen (1971: 9) defines deviance as 'behaviour which somehow departs from what a group expects to be done or what it considers the desirable way of doing things'. Crime on the other hand is behaviour that is prohibited by the criminal law. That said, as Becker (1963: 9) observers: 'deviant behaviour is often proscribed by law – labelled criminal'.

[3] The book will use the term 'foundational perspectives' to describe the parent theories in critical criminology. These theories became popular in the 1960s and 1970s. They provided the impetus or, indeed, the basis for the emergence of critical criminology.

[4] A number of definitions have been proffered for the term 'political economy', and the term is employed within several disciplines, from economics and sociology to criminology (Reiner, 2012b). According to De Giorgi (2007: 17), 'the label "political economy of punishment" refers to a neo-Marxist critique of penality'. Thus defined, the political economy of punishment refers to a critique of the political and socio-economic structures that shape criminal justice in capitalist societies.

[5] Criminologists on the Left of criminology integrate in their analysis of crime, considerations about the possible influence of how structural factors, such as class inequality, might impact on crime and deviance. The less radical criminologists on the Left cite socio-economic disadvantage and other social factors. Criminologists on the Right trace the causes of crime to the individual. They typically overlook wider structural or socio-economic influences.

[6] 'Power' is a multidimensional concept that may be subject to several possible definitions. Critical criminological perspectives appear to view power as the ability of an individual, group, institution or body to impose their will on others.

[7] As we shall see in Chapter Eight, Steve Tombs has also contributed to the development of the field of study described by some as Zemiology.

Part One
Foundational critical criminology

ONE

What is critical criminology?

Introduction

Critical criminology has no standard definition. DeKeseredy and Dragiewicz (2012: 1) point out that 'The definition of critical criminology is subject to much debate and there is no widely accepted precise formulation'. Perhaps this is because it comprises several variants. It is a fluid and vast field of study. It encompasses perspectives that sometimes emphasise divergent themes, use diverse methodologies and espouse different ideologies.

Its origin has also been the subject of much contention. As noted in the introductory chapter, some cite the UK and US as the 'birthplaces of critical criminology' (DeKeseredy and Dragiewicz, 2012: 6). Others, notably, van Swaaningen (1999: 6), trace its origins to several Western European countries. Van Swaaningen (1999) provides a useful overview of the development of critical criminology in Europe. He sets out the work of those he describes as the 'European precursors of critical criminology'. For example he cites the work of the scholars Colajanni, Merlino and Turati, who, as far back as the 19th century, when Lombroso founded the positivist school, critiqued Lombroso's work for failing to account for the role of social class and the exploitation of the lower classes in crime causation. This is consistent with subsequent arguments that were put forward by the Marxist criminologists from the 1970s onwards. Van Swaaningen (1999) also draws attention to the work of the French scholar Manouvrier, who presented arguments in the 19th century that are similar to the position of the Zemiologists.[1] As noted earlier, Zemiologists propose that the label of 'crime' should be discarded because it does not sufficiently accommodate the harmful activities of the powerful in society. Others cited by van Swaaningen include the Dutch penal scientist Clara Wichmann and the German scholars Julius Vargha and Theodor Reik, who tendered arguments in the early 20th century that are similar to contemporary abolitionism.[2] In the period after the Second World War, van Swaaningen writes that others, ranging from the Utrecht scholar Ger Kempe to the Leiden criminologist Willem Nagel, introduced conflict perspectives. Van Swaaningen (1999: 10) describes them as the much-overlooked 'continental precursors of critical criminology in the 1950s'. In addition, van Swaaningen points to the influence of critical scholars in the Frankfurt school, and the French structuralists Michel Foucault and Louis Althusser. Also worthy of mention are the Italian neo-Marxists, including Antonio Gramsci, who heavily influenced the work of scholars in the Birmingham School. For example, Stuart Hall and

his colleagues drew on Gramsci's ideas about the ideological strategies that states employ to legitimise authoritarian policies.[3]

An important reason why the US and the UK are identified as the birthplaces of critical criminology is that much of the work that is described as critical criminology today has been influenced to varying degrees by critical perspectives on crime and social control that became popular in the 1970s. Key examples are the interactionist sociology of deviance[4] (Becker, 1963, 1967) and Marxist criminology (Taylor et al, 1973; Chambliss, 1975). However, van Swaaningen reminds us that, added to the early European critical criminologists, others who have not been particularly influenced by the critical tradition that dominated the field in the US and the UK in the 1970s include scholars from Europe whose work in the 1980s can be categorised as critical criminology because of their critique of criminal laws and penal practices. Examples include the work of the Italians Alessandro Baratta and Luigi Ferrajoli, the Spanish writer Perfecto Andres Ibanez, the Dutchman Antonie Peters, and the German texts edited by Klaus Luderssen and Fritz Sack (see generally, van Swaaningen 1999).

The foregoing suggests that the term 'critical criminology' can be, and has been, applied rather inconsistently to a diverse range of theories and perspectives from various jurisdictions. To complicate matters, textbooks in the field describe these theories and perspectives (often interchangeably) as radical, socialist, Marxist, New or Theoretical criminology (see, eg, Russell, 2002; Downes and Rock, 2011). However, it is perhaps intellectually unproductive to delve into arguments over what should constitute the universal descriptor for the field. It is perhaps more important to focus (as this text intends to do) on key insights that have emerged from the foundational and contemporary perspectives in the field. Therefore, in this text, I have used the term 'critical criminology' as it is now commonly used in critical criminological texts and journals. The term encompasses an array of theoretical traditions that trace the origins of crime, deviance and several social problems, such as gender and racial inequality, to an unequal social order.

Given its varied and contested history, and also given that it comprises somewhat diverse perspectives, trying to define critical criminology is likely to be, at best, a mammoth task, and, at worst, a fruitless one. Nevertheless, it is possible to identify key features that critical criminological perspectives share in common. Although the perspectives invariably focus on differing explanatory and methodological themes, most of the perspectives share some or all of the following features in common:

- a critique of orthodox or mainstream criminological theories;
- an anti-essentialist conception of human identity, including deviant identity;
- a description of deviance as the product of social construction; and
- an ideological view that deviance and its control are inextricably linked to power dynamics in society.

What I have just outlined above are some of the main features that distinguish most critical criminological perspectives from mainstream or orthodox criminology. It is worth adding that, as mentioned earlier, although critical criminological perspectives share some features in common, they emphasise different explanatory themes. Below, there is a more detailed exploration of the three features just listed. Subsequent chapters in the text reveal the occasionally divergent explanatory themes that the critical criminological perspectives covered emphasise.

Deviance as a problematic concept: critiquing mainstream criminology

Downes and Rock (2011: 346) observe that, in the 1960s, there was a 'shift from criminology to the sociology of deviance'. Central to this shift was a fundamental critique of mainstream criminology and the idea that human conduct, such as crime and deviance, has immanent proprieties by which it can be identified. A key development in this context is the interactionist sociology of deviance that became popular through the work of Howard Becker in the 1960s, and the other critical criminological perspectives that drew on aspects of Becker's work. These perspectives, including Marxist criminology, went on to dominate the field through much of the early to mid-1970s.

Critical criminology is *critical* of mainstream criminological theories. Its main criticism is that the mainstream theories do not view crime and deviance as problematic concepts. Rather, they accept unquestioningly that behaviour defined as deviance has immanent deviant properties (Downes and Rock, 2011). Equally, critical criminologists criticise mainstream theories for accepting without question the definition of crime offered by the criminal law. How does the criminal law define crime? Broadly, it defines crime as an act or omission that violates the law and is punishable by law. The two main elements of a crime or offence are: *mens rea*, which is the mental element (the guilty mind); and *actus reus*, which is the act or the omission (the guilty act).[5] Critical criminologists criticise mainstream theories for accepting this definition without question. They are accused of: taking the criminal law's definition for granted; focusing on street crimes and other crimes that are typically committed by less-powerful individuals; tracing the causes of crime to the individual involved in crime; and portraying the individual either as a rational actor or as a victim of predisposing factors, or both. They are also accused of assisting the state in the pursuit of its social and other policy agendas. The definition of critical criminology offered by David Friedrichs (2009: 10, emphasis in original), who is a key writer in the field and has written extensively about the crimes of the powerful, encapsulates these themes:

> Critical criminology is an umbrella term for a variety of criminological theories and perspectives that challenge core assumptions of mainstream (or conventional) criminology in some substantial way and provide alternative approaches to understanding crime and its

control. Mainstream criminology is sometimes referred to by critical criminologists as *establishment, administrative, managerial, correctional, or positivistic* criminology. Its focus is regarded as excessively narrow and predominately directed toward individual offenders, street crime and social engineering on behalf of the state.

Before we explore critical criminology's critique of mainstream criminology in more detail, it is perhaps useful to briefly explore the tenets of the mainstream theories. The mainstream theories that have attracted the ire of critical criminologists are classicism, positivism (in particular) and variants of both theories.

The classical school of criminology: a brief review

Although philosophers and theologians began to think and write about crime as far back as the medieval period (Carrabine et al, 2009), many criminological texts identify classicism as the first established theory of crime in modern society. It emerged in the mid-18th century. In that period, religious views dominated explanations of human behaviour, including crime. The penal system was capricious and punishments were barbaric. The system appeared to protect the property, pecuniary and other interests of the ruling class. Minor offences, particularly property offences, were punishable by death in an economic system that was rooted in the historic legacy of the aristocracy. A feudal system of production prevailed, and the aristocrats were the main owners of property, particularly landed property. They were powerful and they ruled much of ancient Europe. They appointed magistrates and police to regulate the behaviour of the masses and maintain social order. Whatever judicial system existed was not centralised and was, as such, characterised by widespread judicial discretion. Judicial rulings were often arbitrary, disproportionately punitive and designed to protect the interests of the ruling class.

Cesare Beccaria (1738–94) is widely regarded as the founding father of the classical school of criminology. He was a reformer and he advocated an equitable legal system that would recognise that human beings are rational beings who deserve rational responses to their actions. He proposed penal codes that would ensure clarity of punishment. Jeremy Bentham (1748–1832) is also considered to be a key proponent of the classical school of criminology. He began to write in the late 18th century, and he also advocated a more rational penal system. Bentham proposed a system that promotes the doctrine of 'utilitarianism'. This doctrine states that moral actions are actions that produce maximum utility, benefit or consequences for the majority of people. From Bentham's utilitarian perspective, actions should be judged by their outcomes. Those that produce the greatest utility are moral actions. As long as an action produces maximum benefit for the greatest number of people, it is morally justifiable even if it occasionally causes hardship for a few. For example, utilitarian theorists believe that punishing a few innocent people may be necessary if the greatest benefit for the greatest number of people can be achieved. According to Bentham (1776, quoted in Burns and Hart, 2008: 393)): 'it is the greatest happiness of the greatest number that is the measure of right and wrong'. The moral worth of punishment should therefore be judged on the basis of its consequences.

Bentham may be described as a 'reductivist' because he proposed that punishments should also reduce crime (Cavadino and Dignan, 2007). He designed the 'panopticon', which he envisaged would be a prison that would facilitate the covert observation of prisoners. Although such observation would not be constant, the prisoners would believe that they are under constant surveillance, and this presumption should achieve the dual objectives of punishment and reform. The prisoners would complete the tasks that they are given and would also exhibit good behaviour if they believe that they are under constant observation. This highlights Bentham's commitment to reductivism. He believed that a penal sanction should produce an outcome – it should also reform the offender. As a reductivist, Bentham also argued that deterrent punishment represents a rational response to crime. Broadly conceived, deterrent punishment is based on the notion that human beings are rational beings who calculate the costs and benefits of an action. Where the benefits appear to outweigh the costs, an individual is likely to engage in that action. Therefore, deterrent punishment is required to ensure that the costs of crime outweigh its benefits. Studies have since challenged the validity of key presumptions that underpin deterrence theory, particularly the notion that the cost of crime, such as the increased severity of punishment, is an effective deterrent (Blumstein et al, 1978; Cook, 1980; Nagin, 1998; Doob and Webster, 2003).[6]

The foregoing suggests that classical criminology sought to develop a legal system that is cognisant of the nature of human beings as rational beings. It grew out of the Enlightenment and the emergence of the 'modern world' or of 'modernist society' (Milovanovic, 2011a: 150) in the mid-17th century. In this period there was a shift away from spiritual explanations of crime and the use of barbaric and chaotic punishment systems, towards more rational explanations of crime and responses to crime across Western Europe (Carrabine et al, 2009: 81; Sherman, 2011). Sherman (2011: 423, emphasis in original) defines the Enlightenment as:

> an intellectual movement encouraging people to think for themselves, rather than accepting the opinions of church and state authorities … it was also an effort to apply intellectual *reasoning* to the analysis of complex problems long seen as matters of faith or emotion. (See also Gay, 1996, cited in Sherman, 2011: 423)

Pratt and colleagues (2011: 7) observe that:

> at the heart of the Enlightenment was the use of reason and logic to improve political systems, enhance social justice, and generally better

> the lot of humanity.... All Enlightenment devotees sought to bolster justice in social and political institutions; the criminal justice system was therefore a primary target of reformers' writings and commentaries.

A broad intellectual development accompanied the Enlightenment era, particularly the view that the social actor is a rational being who is capable of responding to a rational system of punishment (Cohen, 1988). Such a rational system would incorporate punishments that are celeritous, certain, proportionate and enshrined in the law. These Enlightenment ideals influenced the early classicists. Indeed, the advent of the Enlightenment and the intellectual change it brought in its wake influenced the early proponents of the classical school and their search for more humane legal and penal systems. As Cohen (1988: 3) put it, the early classicists, like Beccaria (1738–94) and Bentham (1748–1832), were 'Enlightenment thinkers' who sought to reform the existing penal system by replacing the 'archaic, barbaric, repressive or arbitrary' criminal law system with a system that would draw on the liberal values or ideals that emerged with the Enlightenment. Added to its origins in the age of the Enlightenment, classicism also emerged when broader shifts were occurring within other disciplines. These disciplines sought to align themselves with new scientific approaches to studying the natural world. There was an effort to develop scientific understandings of human beings as rational beings.

Classicism has been criticised on several grounds. The presumption that human behaviour is predicated upon rational decision-making has attracted criticism from those who point to situations where the presumption of rationality is perhaps untenable. Children and the mentally disabled are examples of people who may not always be capable of rational decision-making. Furthermore, as critical criminologists would argue, classicists focus on the offence and overlook wider structural factors, such as power and wealth inequality and socio-economic disadvantage. According to critical criminologists, structural factors may circumscribe the choices available to individuals. As Downes and Rock (2011: 259) observe: '"classical criminology" and its neo-classical variants are viewed as incapable of reconciling forms of inequality ... and the extension of rationality ... to those who offend against the law'.

Having set out a skeletal description of the classical school, I now turn to a description of the second mainstream theory that critical criminologists criticise, namely, positivism. Quite unlike extreme variants of classicism, which overlook differences between individuals and focus narrowly on the offence committed and how best to respond to it, positivism focuses on the individual who committed the offence and how best to respond to, or treat, the individual. In other words, while classicists focus on the response that crime deserves, positivists emphasises the treatment that the perpetrator requires. Positivists believe that we can apply scientific techniques associated with other disciplines, such as psychiatry, to the study of the social world in order to identify causal relationships between different aspects of it. Thus, we can study individuals and identify the factors that cause them to offend, and the treatment that can address those factors.

Positivist criminology: an overview

Positivism emerged in the 19th century at a time when scientific explanations of natural phenomena were gaining ascendancy. Positivists formed the view that with scientific diagnostic methods, they could identify the causes of crime and prescribe the appropriate treatment. From this perspective, treatment, not punishment, is considered to be the most effective response to crime. This view of the causes of crime and strategies for responding to crime underpinned the rehabilitative penal ideal that some argue emerged in the late 19th century, reached its epoch in the post-war years and suffered a decline in the 1970s (see, generally, Garland, 2001). The circumstances of its decline have been explored and contested at length elsewhere (see Garland, 2001; Matthews, 2005). Meanwhile, for much of the late 19th century to the 1970s, the positivistic approach to explaining crime and responding to crime dominated criminology and criminal justice. Some argue that it has since resurfaced as the prevailing orthodoxy (Muncie, 2000; Young, 2010).

Unlike the voluntarism that is implicit in classicist explanations of crime, the doctrine of determinism underpins positivism. According to this doctrine, predisposing factors explain human behaviour. Positivists believe that scientific methods of experimental discovery can be used to identify these causal factors. The early positivists offered deterministic explanations of crime and challenged the classicists' belief that the social actor is rational and able to exercise his or her free will. Taylor and colleagues (1973: 38) note that 'The positivists rejected outright the Classicists' notion of a rational man capable of exercising free will'.

A useful taxonomy of determinist perspectives on crime causation may be presented here as the biological approach, the psychological approach and the sociological approach (see also Burke, 2009). It is argued that these variants of positivism may sometimes exist interactively rather than independently. The origin of the biological variant is often traced to the work of Cesare Lombroso in late 19th century. Indeed, many texts describe Lombroso as 'the founder of modern criminology' (Carrabine et al, 2009: 86). Reiner (2012a: 32) observes that 'The term "criminology" was specifically coined to describe the Lombrosian version of the quest for theoretical understanding of the aetiology of crime'.

Lombroso founded the Italian School of Criminology, which is now associated with the view that a 'criminal type' exists. He is identified as the chief architect of a strand of positivism that is described as biological positivism. This approach to the study of crime traces crime causation to physical human attributes. The focus of analysis is the body of the individual. There is a presumption that individuals lack rational choice and are constrained by their physical attributes. Thus, according to biological positivism, the typical criminal has distinct physical features (Gibson, 2002). These features enable us to separate the criminal from the non–criminal. The primary methodology of biological positivism is the scientific method of empirical enquiry. Lombroso developed his idea of the 'born criminal' through experiments in which he compared the physical features of Italian prisoners with the features of Italian soldiers. He sought to highlight the physical features of the so-called 'born criminal'. In Lombroso's view, the 'born criminal' is atavistic or a throwback to pre-human beings or savages, who, in turn, lack the essential qualities (including the intellectual and moral capacity) of the fully developed human being. Subsequent empirical work challenged the validity of these claims. According to Goring (1972 [1913], cited in Carrabine et al, 2009: 86):

> Lombroso's work was flawed, had he looked beyond prison walls, he would have realised that the physical features he attributed exclusively to prisoners were actually found throughout the entire population. We now know that no physical attributes, of any kind described by Lombroso, simply distinguish criminals from non-criminals.

Indeed, Lombroso himself went on to revise some of his original ideas. However, other writers have elaborated Lombroso's ideas further with their views that offenders possess specific identifiable physical characteristics (Kretschmer, 1936). Some of these writers highlight what they describe as the genetic dimension of crime or the heritability of behaviour, including criminal behaviour (Klinefelter et al, 1942; Glueck and Glueck, 1950; Mednick, 1987).

The psychological variant of positivism comprises several perspectives. Following Freud, psychoanalytic perspectives assert that crime is the product of inadequate socialisation and the failure to address negative behavioural impulses during childhood development. Learning theories emphasise that crime, like other human behaviour, is learned behaviour. For example, Edwin Sutherland (1939) introduced differential association theory, which traces the origins of crime to culturally transmitted criminogenic techniques and attitudes during social interaction. Individuals who are exposed to relationships and other forms of social interaction where explanations and ideas that are supportive of crime exceed explanations that are supportive of law-abiding behaviour are more likely to become lawbreakers.

Some learning theorists draw on Ian Pavlov's classical conditioning theory, which suggests that external stimuli can be used to condition human behaviour. Therefore, psychological positivists influenced by Pavlov's classical conditioning theory would argue that external stimuli, including the environment that an individual is socialised in, can condition that individual to engage in crime. From this perspective, behaviour is the product of conditioning.

There are also psychological positivists who draw on the US psychologist B.F. Skinner's (1938) operant conditioning perspective. Operant conditioning is based on the idea that behaviour is dependent on the response it receives. It is a form of conditioning that involves responding to behaviour with reinforcements in order to ensure that the behaviour will be repeated. The objective is to ensure that the person exhibiting the behaviour is able to learn the link between the behaviour and its consequences. This perspective suggests that human behaviour is the product of external influences, primarily reinforcements. For example, incentives offered for specific behaviour can serve as positive reinforcements which can in turn, encourage that behaviour. Thus, if an individual is rewarded for criminal behaviour, that individual learns to repeat that behaviour. Equally, the proponents of operant conditioning believe that negative reinforcements can be used to ensure that if an individual is confronted with a negative situation, that individual can learn how to adopt a new behaviour that will help him or her avoid the situation in future. It is generally believed that reinforced behaviour is repeated behaviour. People learn how to exhibit a form of behaviour if they are conditioned or taught to exhibit that behaviour.

These psychological perspectives are considered to be deterministic because they suggest that immutable external factors, such as reinforcements that emerge from the external environment, explain criminal behaviour. Indeed, psychological theories, particularly those that draw on Pavlov's classical conditioning and B.F. Skinner's operant conditioning, which are, as such, rooted in behaviourism – a psychological theory of learning that was developed by John B. Watson (1913) – have been criticised for being deterministic. It is argued that they overlook human agency and the ability of human beings to interpret their observations and experiences, and to act on the basis of their interpretations. They depict human behaviour as the product of conditioning. However, it is worth noting that there are psychological perspectives that reject the deterministic view of crime causation. For example, social learning theory asserts that human behaviour originates from observing the behaviour of others and the arising consequences, *and then* making the choice to emulate the observed behaviour and consequences (Bandura, 1977; Akers and Jennings, 2009). Proponents of social learning theory argue that human behaviour can be shaped not simply by conditioning or experience, but by observation and choice – people can learn through observing others, and can decide whether or not to emulate the behaviour that they have observed (Bandura, 1977). This approach adds a cognitive dimension and moves away from the determinism implied by learning theories that emphasise the impact of external factors on human behaviour.

Other psychological theories have also sought to distance themselves from primarily deterministic explanations by claiming that there are cognitive, intellectual, impulsivity, reasoning or thinking patterns that explain human behaviour, including criminal behaviour (see, eg, Gottfredson and Hirschi, 1990). These theories have also been criticised, not least because: they lack sufficiently robust empirical support; the studies they rely on do not address cultural specificity; the studies tend to generalise their findings beyond the scope of the samples employed (unrepresentative samples); and the definitions of key terms, such as 'impulsivity', lack precision and tend to vary one from study to the next (Hollin, 1989). For this reason, it is perhaps difficult to draw convincing conclusions from these theories and the studies that underpin them.

Sociological perspectives in positivism include the work of the French sociologist Emile Durkheim (1952; 1964). Durkheim espoused a functionalist view of crime. For example, he highlighted the role of crime as a unifying event because when it responds to crime, society is able to collectively identify and adapt to new normative principles. Society is also able to collectively reassess its boundaries of acceptable behaviour. In addition, Durkheim traced crime and disorder in society to inadequate cultural and social controls. For Durkheim, significant changes in a society, which may be for example, the product of rapid economic change, can loosen established societal controls that regulate norms, values and aspirations. Lack of normative controls can create anomie. The latter can be described as 'normlessness' (Rock 2012: 45). It manifests itself as widespread discontentment, frustration and other conditions that can in turn, trigger deviant behaviour (see also, Reiner 2012). Another key contributor to sociological positivism is Enrico Ferri (1856–1928), who has been described as 'one of the three central figures of the "positive school"' (Taylor et al, 1973: 27). Ferri (1901) argued that alongside biological factors, sociological variables can also contribute to crime. According to Ferri, factors that may cause crime include the social and cultural environment that provides the context for the socialisation of the individual offender, and even the physical environment the offender inhabits.

In the early 20th century, some sociologists of deviance contributed to the development of sociological positivism. The sociologists include Robert Ezra Park and his student Ernest W. Burgess (1966 [1921]), who explored links between urban ecology and crime. Their work is described as social disorganisation theory (see also Reckless, 1933; Shaw and Mackay, 1942).

Social disorganisation theory explores how human beings interact with their built (urban) environment. The theory posits that rapid social changes, such as increased immigration, cause changes to the urban environment, weaken social bonds and lead to social disorganisation, which causes crime. Thomas and Znaniecki (1918–1920) provided the earliest rendition of social disorganisation theory. Contemporary versions of the theory emerged from the work of sociologists such as Robert Ezra Park and Ernest W. Burgess in the 1920s and the 1930s, who, like Thomas and Znaniecki before them, were also based in the University of Chicago Sociology Department. These sociologists were pivotal to the growth of US sociology. Park and his student Burgess conducted ecological studies of crime (or studies of crime in urban areas – particularly in urban Chicago and its environs). Unlike the biological positivists, who claimed that the causes of crime could be traced to the individual, this group of sociologists traced the origins of crime to ecological factors to do with the social and cultural environment or neighbourhoods in which crime occurs. They took stock of the rapid social, cultural and ecological changes that were occurring in the US as it moved towards industrialisation and the urbanisation of some of its cities, of which Chicago was a notable example. Park and Burgess used anthropological methods, particularly ethnography, to study the social constitution of urban areas in Chicago. They observed the movement of populations of different cultural and social backgrounds into urban areas where industries were located, in search of employment. These populations tended to be transient, unlike the close-knit farming communities of the pre-industrial era. According to the Chicago sociologists, the rapid changes, which saw the concentration of what they described as transient, culturally diverse and typically socio-economically deprived populations in deprived urban areas, created sociocultural conflict, social disorganisation and crime. They averred that those areas lacked the strong community ties that had hitherto served as sources of informal social control.

In his study of the urbanisation of Chicago, Ernest Burgess (1925) pointed out that urban areas expand outwardly. He maintained that industries and businesses tend to be located in the centre of urban areas. According to Burgess, located close to this central area is the 'zone in transition'. Migrants in search of employment gravitate to this zone because of its proximity to industries and businesses that provide employment. As people become more economically secure, they move to the outer zones that surround the zone in transition. The further away a zone is from the zone in transition, the more economically buoyant the area and its residents are. Burgess maintained that the greatest concentration of migrants, unconventional social arrangements and deviant lifestyles are found in the zone in transition. In view, this explains the higher rate of crime and deviance in that zone.

Other University of Chicago sociologists who contributed to this field of study include Shaw and Mackay (1942), who drew on Burgess's (1925) work on the urban ecology of Chicago. They argued that delinquency is culturally transmitted through generations of socio-economically deprived groups. These groups tend to live in the zone closest to the centre of a city (what Burgess referred to as the 'zone in transition'). The zone in transition was said to be an area populated by poor, culturally diverse, transient groups with limited bonds that can serve as informal sources of social control, and with differing cultures and values. These groups were said to be in conflict with each other, causing social disharmony and disorder and destabilising social institutions in the community, including the family, the Church and schools, which traditionally act as informal sources of control. These factors were identified as the causes of social disorganisation, crime and deviance in those communities.

Social disorganisation theorists maintained that in affected communities, the impact of social disorganisation and weakened social control mechanisms were such that criminality became socially acceptable and even actively encouraged (Cullen and Agnew, 2011). It was argued that in order to control crime, it was necessary to change not the individual, as the biological and psychological positivists believe, but the environment or neighbourhood in which crime occurs (Shaw and Mackay, 1942).

Other Chicago School sociologists were influenced by Shaw and Mackay's work. For example, Edwin Sutherland (1949) drew on their work when he introduced differential association theory. As we saw earlier, this theory holds that criminal behaviour is learned behaviour. The theory traces the causes of crime to culturally transmitted criminogenic techniques and attitudes that are said to abound in areas that are steeped in social disorganisation. Sutherland maintained that these areas tend to be the highest crime areas. Additional examples of the work that have been done in this field include Reckless's (1961) and Reiss's (1951) work on the link between weakened social bonds in a community and crime. Their work paved the way for the emergence of contemporary control theory (see also Cullen and Agnew, 2011).

The early social disorganisation theorists highlighted migration and ethnicity as a major explanatory factor. Indeed, implicit in accounts that trace crime to social disorganisation in urban areas is the notion that migrant groups, and others who reside in these areas, lack traditional forms of social control because they are dislocated from their homes, and from the social control mechanisms that used to regulate their behaviour. As such, they are deemed likely to exist on the margins of conventionality and to engage in unconventional behaviour, including crime.

Proponents of the first Chicago School are by no means the only writers to make these claims. Other writers on the Right of the political spectrum (an example is Charles Murray[7]) have also traced crime causation to urban ecology, and particularly to the constitution of families residing in deprived urban areas. A high proportion of these families tend to belong to ethnic minority groups. Charles Murray and others who espouse these views, offer racialised accounts of crime causation. They locate the causes of crime within the structure and culture of socioeconomically deprived families, particularly African-American families (in the US) and Afro-Caribbean families (in the UK). As we shall see in Chapter Six, it is argued that Murray's accounts lack sufficient empirical validation.

Carrabine and colleagues (2009: 557) point out in Britain that the tendency to offer racialised accounts of crime causation can be traced back to the 19th century, when notions of 'deviant foreigners' were applied to migrants including: 'Irish, East European Jewish, Malay and Chinese migrants'. Furthermore, according to Carrabine and colleagues (2009), in the 1970s, media-generated moral panics about young male West Indians (particularly of Jamaican origin), who migrated with their families to the UK in the post-war period of the 1940s and settled mainly in deprived urban/inner-city areas, replaced historical moral panics about the criminal activities of the so-called white underclass. There were moral panics about the purported contribution of these groups to novel forms of crime and disorder in these communities, including the crime of mugging (Hall et al, 1978). More recently, similar accounts have been offered in the UK in respect of Eastern European migrants from countries that include Romania and Bulgaria.

Several studies undermine the veracity of social disorganisation theory and its claims about the link between migrants, weakened social control, social disorganisation and crime (Stretesky et al, 2013). The studies cast considerable doubt on the contention of the social disorganisation theorists that migration and ethnicity are important dimensions of social disorganisation and crime. These studies highlight structural disadvantage and disenfranchisement (rather than migration and ethnicity) as key factors that explain the concentration of crime in the areas mapped out by the social disorganisation theorists (Sampson and Wilson, 1995). For example, in their large-scale study of socio-economic inequality and crime in inner-city areas in the US, Blau and Blau (1982: 114) concluded that:

socioeconomic inequalities between races, as well as economic inequality generally, increases rates of criminal violence, but once economic inequalities are controlled poverty no longer influences these rates ... and the proportion of Blacks in the population hardly does. These results imply that if there is a culture of violence, its roots are pronounced economic inequalities, especially if associated with ascribed position.

Similarly, Stretesky and colleagues (2013: 91) reinforce this by pointing out that:

research has shown that social disorganisation occurs regardless of ethnicity, therefore leading scholars to conclude that it is not individual characteristics that lead one to commit crimes; rather, economic status and the anomie that is created lead to social disorganisation and crime.

In the 1940s and the 1950s, the work of functionalist theorists such as Thomas Merton, who developed strain theory (also described as anomie theory), overshadowed the work of the Chicago sociologists (Downes and Rock, 2011). Merton drew on the work of the French sociologist Emile Durkheim (1897). Durkheim had attributed the causes of crime and disorder in societies to inadequate cultural and social controls. For Durkheim, significant change in a society such as rapid economic change can loosen established societal controls that regulate human aspirations. Lack of societal controls can create anomie. The latter manifests itself as widespread discontentment, frustration and other conditions that can in turn, trigger deviant behaviour (see also, Reiner 2012).

Echoing these ideas, Mertonian strain theory comprises two strands. One strand traces the origins of crime in capitalist societies such as the US to the dissonance between cultural norms or accepted beliefs about the goals citizens should strive for to attain success (primarily material success), and cultural beliefs about what constitutes legitimate means of attaining these goals.[8] Those who are able to attain material success through deviant means are sometimes admired and respected. Material success is considered to be more valuable than moral rectitude. Greater attention is paid to attaining the goals that lead to success than to the importance of using appropriate means to attain those goals. Merton believed that this amounts to anomie, which he described as a concept that explains why the US had a higher rate of deviance than other societies. The second strand of Mertonian anomie seeks to explain why deviance appears to be more prevalent among specific groups, particularly marginalised groups. In terms of the concentration of deviance among such marginalised groups to anomie, which may arise not only from the effort of all in society to acquire material success using any means possible, but also from the effort of the structurally marginalised in particular to attain culturally defined goals using illegitimate means mainly because they have been denied access to legitimate routes to success such as useful jobs and material resources.

Scholars who believe that Merton's work was a fundamental critique of capitalism and the structural conditions is creates, even if he chose not to make this explicit, have described Merton as 'a cautious rebel' (Taylor et al, 1973, quoted in Young, 2013: xix). This is because as they point out, although he was critical of capitalism, Merton did not once cite the word 'capitalism' in his description of anomie and its role in crime causation (Young, 2013: xix). In addition, Merton did not explore the factors that contribute to the structural inequalities he described. These inequalities include class inequality and the existence of a socio-economically marginalised group that is particularly vulnerable to criminal justice intervention (Young, 2013). Therefore, his work has been described as 'a critique of capitalism that does not mention capital, a Marxism that does not once mention Marx' (Young, 2013: xix).

Quite unlike Merton's anomie or strain theory, which views the resort to illegitimate routes to success as an individual endeavour, Albert Cohen's subcultural theory (another theory within sociological positivism) holds that this process is a collective one that is played out in the youth subcultures that the disenfranchised migrate to. As mentioned earlier, structural-functionalist theories, including the work of Thomas Merton, his student Albert Cohen and others, emerged in the 1940s and 1950s and overshadowed social disorganisation theory. Furthermore, in the 1960s, interactionist sociologists of deviance, including Howard Becker (1963, 1967), whose work contributed to the emergence of critical criminology, rejected the claims of the social disorganisation theorists. Becker maintained that *social reaction to deviance* (not *social disorganisation* in urban areas) causes crime and deviance. We shall examine Becker's work in Chapter Two.

Positivism, particularly biological positivism, has been criticised for being deterministic. It is argued that positivists generally overlook human agency and rationality. In addition, its reliance on scientific methods of enquiry leaves it unable to recognise that the meanings with which research participants describe the social phenomena that affect them are valid sources of knowledge. Thus, it has been described as a determinist theory that overlooks 'the meanings of crime in people's lives' (Carrabine et al, 2009: 65).

For reasons that we shall now explore, critical criminologists criticise the mainstream theories – classicism and positivism – for accepting without question the definition of crime given by the criminal law. The mainstream theories are also criticised for focusing their explanations of the causes of crime and deviance on the individual offender. They are accused of ignoring the social, economic and political structures that shape the definitions of crime and deviance. Critical criminologists do not accept that the definition of crime given by the criminal law is straightforward and unproblematic (see Box 1.1; see also Schwendinger and Schwendinger, 1970). Equally, they do not view deviance as an unproblematic dimension of behaviour. In the search for the causes of crime and deviance, critical criminologists focus their exploratory lens not on flaws within the individual, but on flaws within the social, economic and political structures of society. They accuse the mainstream theories of overlooking these flaws. Herein lies the main division in criminology between the critical and mainstream traditions. As van Swanningen (1999) points out, mainstream criminologists view criminology as a scientific project that should focus on helping the state to develop an efficient criminal justice system in order to maintain the existing social order. By contrast, critical criminologists would rather view criminology as a critique of the existing order (van Swaaningen, 1999).

Thus, critical criminologists accuse mainstream theories of furnishing the state with the intellectual or academic knowledge required for controlling target populations whose actions are deemed inimical to the interests of the powerful in society (including the state). In their view, mainstream theories are conformist and uncritical because they view crime and deviance as unproblematic concepts. They are accused of seeking to maintain the established (albeit oppressive) social order by assisting in the control and repression of those who are labelled as deviants because their actions threaten the status quo (Taylor et al, 1973).

Box 1.1: Taylor, Walton and Young (1973): critiquing mainstream criminological theories

Ian Taylor, Paul Walton and Paul Young are criminologists whose work served as the platform that launched Marxist criminology in Britain in the 1960s and 1970s. Marxist criminology is an important approach within critical criminology, and Chapter Four provides a detailed analysis of the approach. Meanwhile, it will suffice to state here that, broadly, Marxist criminologists trace crime and deviance to class inequality in capitalist societies. They argue that class and power are inextricably linked in such societies. The powerful enjoy socio-economic and political advantage and are less vulnerable to criminalisation. The Marxist criminologists criticise mainstream criminology. They describe classicism and positivism as state-sponsored theories. They criticise positivism, in particular, for what they describe as its determinism, its spurious claims to scientific knowledge about crime and its failure to countenance structural factors that, according to the Marxist criminologists, render the lower classes in capitalist societies more vulnerable to criminalisation. From the perspective of the Marxist criminologists, the mainstream theories are wrong to accept the legal definition of crime. The Marxist criminologists describe crime and deviance as socially constructed labels to which the lower classes are particularly vulnerable. In the following extract from the text *The New Criminology*, Taylor and his colleagues outline some of the critiques critical criminologists level against mainstream criminological theories:

> The NDC [National Deviancy Conference] was deconstructionist to a person, anti-essentialist in its stance ... it dwelt on the social construction of gender, sexual proclivity, crime, suicide, drugs and mental state. And beneath all this was an underlying critique of both strands of state intervention: positivism and classicism. For the twin metanarratives of progress – social engineering and the rule of law – were consistently subject to criticism. Positivism was perhaps the main enemy; its ontology was seen to take human creativity out of deviant action, its sociology erected a false edifice from which deviants were bereft of culture and meaning, its

> methodology elevated experts to the role of fake scientists discovering 'laws' of social action ... but the rule of law also came under scrutiny. The NDC was concerned about how the criminal justice system was selective and ineffective. That is, how crime occurred endemically yet the justice system focused on the working class and youth. Crimes of the powerful were ignored, middle class deviance tolerated ... the mass media were seen to select out deviant groups. (Taylor et al, 1973: 23–4)

Critical criminologists, particularly the more radical theorists among them, such as the Marxist criminologists, would argue that effective crime prevention can be achieved, not by transforming legal and penal strategies (as the classicists would have it) or by transforming individuals who have been labelled as criminals (as the positivists would have it), but by transforming societal structures to achieve social justice. For critical criminologists, the aetiology of crime and deviance is located not in the constitution of the individual, but in the constitution of society.

Critical criminology's anti-essentialism

Another feature that unites most critical criminologists is their anti-essentialist stance. Critical criminological perspectives, particularly foundational perspectives, like the labelling perspective, embrace anti-essentialism. The latter is philosophical position that rejects the idea that the categories with which we make sense of human identity (categories such as deviant–normal, criminal–non-criminal and so forth) have identifiable traits, properties or characteristics that make the categories what they are. Anti-essentialists do not accept that there are essential characteristics (or essences) by which these categories and other entities of their kind may be identified and defined, and which differentiate them from other entities. The categories cited earlier, and other social categories, are said to be socially constructed. Social categories are created by those who have the power to create them, and impose them on others. According to Patel and Tyrer (2011: 117–18):

> Anti-essentialism focuses on the social construction of categories ... and the role of power, language and discourses in constructing identities ... for example, the things that make up human identities, such as masculinity/femininity, hetero-/homosexual, sane/insane, black/white, working-middle-class and so on ... may be seen as socially bestowed identities rather than essences of the person.

Thus, anti-essentialism is a useful tool that critical criminologists have used to unpick essentialist ideas about human identities and behaviour. Anti-essentialists argue that a danger of essentialism is that essentialist ideas about social categories are usually manifestations of the interests, prejudices and sometimes the ignorant views of the people who create such ideas. However, over time, these ideas may evolve into stereotypes that can stigmatise and exclude the groups affected. Individuals might find themselves subject to discriminatory and other disadvantageous treatment because of socially constructed ideas about their behaviour, race, gender, sexuality and so forth. It follows that essentialism can give rise to ideas that are held out as the universal 'truth' about target groups that include racial minorities, women and other groups, even where such ideas are, in essence, mere fabrications and myths.

The concept of hegemonic ideology[9] illustrates how states may present myths about target populations as reality to mobilise public support for potentially unpopular or contentious policies. Extreme examples of this include the propaganda campaign of Nazi Germany. Another example is the rhetoric and catalogue of myths that helped legitimise the enslavement and oppression of Africans in several US jurisdictions over more than three centuries. Over time, the myths propagated by the state may be considered to be perfectly legitimate and an inevitable feature of normality. As Snider (1998: 27) puts it, hegemony exists where 'acceptance of the status quo rests heavily on notions that it constitutes the necessary and inevitable ordering of the world'.

Sociologists of deviance such as Howard Becker, who, as already noted, contributed to the emergence of critical criminology, also acknowledge that essentialist ideas about an individual or group can trigger a 'self-fulfilling prophecy'. According to Robert Merton (1968: 477), who coined the concept, a self-fulfilling prophecy is 'a false definition of the situation evoking a new behavior which makes the originally false conception come true'. Those who create rules and define the norms of society may create a false but stigmatising concept that is based on their prejudices or subjective beliefs, and apply it to an individual. If others view that concept in essentialist terms, they may react to that individual on the basis of the false concept and they may exclude the individual.

People may also expect the individual to whom the concept is applied to behave according to that concept and may unwittingly foreclose opportunities for that individual to behave in any other way. Interactionist sociologists of deviance[10] believe that, over time, the individual may internalise the concept and revise their behaviour (see, eg, Becker, 1963). The fabricated concept thus evokes new behaviour. The new behaviour validates the fabrication and makes those who acted on the basis of the fabrication believe that they were right all along. They will not realise that it was their actions that produced the new behaviour. If they did not react on the basis of the fabrication, the new behaviour would not have occurred. As such, the fabrication becomes a self-fulfilling prophesy in line with Robert Merton's definition.

Some feminist criminologists reject essentialist ideas about gender. Instead, they advocate anti-essentialist definitions of gender. They argue that gender is a social construction and not a biological fact (unlike sex), and that in settings such as criminal justice contexts or in the workplace, notions of difference bolster stereotypes and discriminatory treatment that can disadvantage women (Adler, 1975).[11] The same can be said about essentialist ideas that revolve around race and other human attributes. These ideas have been historically used to separate and categorise human beings.

Indeed, historical sociological debates about gender difference and racial difference clearly illustrate the dangers of essentialism. Like Robert Merton, William Isaac Thomas (1863–1947), the American sociologist who made significant contributions to sociology in the early to mid twentieth century also emphasised the remarkable ease with which fabrications can transform into 'truth' or reality. Thomas observed that 'If Men define situations as real, they are real in their consequences' (Thomas and Thomas, 1928: 572). This mantra, known as the *Thomas Theorem*, suggests that subjective interpretations, rather than the objective reality of phenomena, shape our behaviour. This means that we react to things not as they are, but as we perceive them to be. William Isaac Thomas's (1907) observation was very informative. He highlighted how fabrications about demographic attributes such as gender and race can evolve into truth claims. These truth claims may then provide the basis for the oppression of a specific gender or ethnic group. Thomas's work is quite remarkable because he was writing at a point in US history when what many now consider to be fabricated essentialist ideas about gender difference and racial difference were considered to be the universal 'truth'. Women and black people were deemed to possess inferior intelligence and were generally considered to be inferior to white men. Those who sought to endorse these truth claims drew on dubious biological and psychological 'theories' to support their position that biologically determined gender and ethnic differences exist.

Thomas wrote extensively about the fallacy of gender difference and ethnic difference. For example, in response to ideas about purported gender and ethnic differences in levels of intelligence, Thomas pointed out that intelligence is the product of 'accumulated knowledge'. It is not attributable to genetic factors. External factors such as availability of opportunity and cultural expectations are some of the factors that help explain levels of knowledge and intelligence, not genetic factors. He stated that when it comes to matters of intelligence, 'The real variable is the individual, not the race' (p 456). At a point in history when many black people in the US were illiterate because they had emerged from a system of slavery that outlawed their education, it was quite easy to overlook this limiting factor and to attribute their illiteracy to biologically determined inferiority or lack of intelligence. Thomas argued instead that black people and others who have been deprived of the opportunity to acquire intelligence and knowledge are not 'intellectual' not because of any biological or physical features, but because, unlike others, they had not received tuition on how to 'manipulate the materials of knowledge' (p 465).

Caesarea Lombroso, who, as mentioned earlier, is recognised as the founding father of criminology, presented essentialist ideas about those he described as the 'born criminal'. He proposed that a criminal type exists. Indeed, the entire positivist project has been criticised for its essentialism, which is manifest in its search for defining characteristics that differentiate the criminal from the non-criminal. Such an enterprise can lead to spurious claims about normality and abnormality, with devastating consequences for those who do not meet socially constructed standards of normality. The foregoing suggests that essentialist ideas about human identity are typically dubious at best, and generally unfounded at worst. Nevertheless, they have held sway at different points in history, and it is possible that they have provided the basis for the stigmatisation, marginalisation, disenfranchisement and even the dehumanisation of target populations. These are some of the dangers of essentialism, of assuming that we can define individuals according to immanent qualities. Sometimes, prejudice, self-interest or ignorance may cloud our judgement and lead us to ascribe false definitions to others, and to react to them according to those definitions, with profound implications. Recognising this, critical criminologists emphasise the implications of labels, including deviant labels. In short, as mentioned earlier, critical criminological perspectives, particularly the foundational perspectives, reject essentialist ideas about deviant identity on ontological grounds, and also on the basis that universal claims about crime and other similar concepts are typically based on unsound or distorted ideas. Indeed, the foundational perspectives and even some contemporary variants acknowledge the dangers of essentialist ideas about crime and deviance. Howard Becker (1963: 193–4), for example, points to the importance of problematising 'commonplace' beliefs about those who are labelled as deviants, and emphasises that 'it is easier to construct mythical wrongdoers, and give them whatever qualities go best with our hypothesised explanations'.

The social construction of deviance

The idea that crime and deviance are social constructions is another feature that several critical criminological perspectives share in common. The perspectives assert that crime and deviance have no inherent or intrinsic qualities. They have no objective existence. It is argued that crime, for example, does not automatically appear in criminal codes. It is socially constructed. It has no identifiable ontological, fixed or immutable reality. Therefore, the meaning of crime resides not in any inherent quality it might have (because it has none), but in the way that it is constructed or defined by those (the individuals or groups) who have the power to define actions as crime or to influence law marking processes. In a similar fashion, individuals or groups such as the police interpret and enforce the laws these people create. The human factor is always present. Laws are not created or enforced in a vacuum.

To substantiate their ideas about the contingent and mutable nature of crime, critical criminologists who describe crime as a social construction draw attention to legal acts that have been defined as 'crime' in the past but which are now legal. A commonly cited example is homosexuality, which was illegal in the UK until 1967, in Scotland until 1980 and in Northern Ireland until 1982. If, as the essentialists would have it, the acts or forms of behaviour that are defined as crimes have unique features that make them criminal, then acts that are defined as crimes cannot subsequently become anything other than crimes. However, as the aforementioned example indicates, acts that are defined as crimes may be redefined as legal.

Some critical criminologists also argue that it is not the *moral* quality of an act that makes the act a crime. These critical criminologists typically adopt a pluralistic view of society (Young, 2009). They maintain that advanced Western societies such as the UK and US are quite diverse and do not necessarily have a set of consensually agreed moral codes or values. Consequently, contested ideas about social phenomena (including crime), and about norms and values, prevail in these societies. Indeed, this pluralistic view of Western societies such as the US and UK underpins much critical criminological theorising. Some critical criminological perspectives go beyond a pluralistic view of society to emphasise that society is characterised by conflict. To cite one example, criminologists who write from a conflict perspective (see Chapter Three) argue that advanced Western societies, particularly the US and UK, comprise diverse groups in conflict with each other. There are divisions along business, faith, cultural and ethnic lines. These differences are said to be the product of increased migration. In such societies, conflict between the different groups stems from competition between the groups for social, cultural, economic and political advantage. The group or groups who are able to assert their will on other groups define the norms, values, laws and other rules of behaviour. Crime is, as such, a social construct, and the law does not reflect consensually agreed norms, values, morals and so forth. We shall explore conflict perspectives in Chapter Three. For now, it is worth noting that critical criminologists generally hold a pluralistic view of advanced Western societies. In his description of the emergence of critical criminology in the 1960s and 1970s, Jock Young (2009: 7, emphasis in original), who was one of the early proponents of Marxist criminology in Britain, noted that:

> the new deviance revolution involved the rejection of absolutist notions of value.... We live in a pluralistic society with a magical cubism of perspectives, where one's deviancy is another persons' normality.... *Deviance is not inherent in an action but a quality bestowed upon it....* Furthermore, the definitions of those in power are proclaimed as absolutist standards of normality and are given top ranking ... orthodox criminology, together with cognate disciplines, especially psychiatry, has a key role in *explaining away* deviancy as a lack of values rather than alternative norms and realities ... in this, the *label* criminal or deviant carries with it essentialist connotations of undersocialisation, irrationality, mindlessness, impulsiveness, etc., often caricatured in positivist terms.

To further substantiate their claim that it is not the moral quality of an act that makes it a crime, some critical criminologists draw attention to acts that are defined as crime or offences even where those acts do not appear to violate dominant moral codes or standards. An example is spitting on the street. This has become illegal in the London Borough Council of Enfield in England. At the present time, spitting anywhere else in London is perfectly legal! While offences such as spitting on the street might help prevent incidents that cause public nuisance, we might be reluctant to define them as actions that violate moral codes. Indeed, it is generally accepted that there is no inextricable link between morality and legality.

Furthermore, some critical criminologists would point out that it is not the *harmfulness* of an act that makes the act a crime. Spitting on the street in Enfield is not necessarily harmful *per se*, but, as we have seen, the law prohibits it. Similarly, although killing a human being is quite harmful, it is the circumstances of the killing and not the act of killing that determines whether or not it will be described as a crime. There are circumstances in which killing may be described as perfectly legal and even acceptable. Killing an enemy combatant in a war situation[12] represents one such example but killing a human being in many other situations is considered to be a very serious crime. Jock Young (2002: 254) summed up this irony aptly with the following statement: 'Crime has no ontological reality ... the "same" behaviour can be constructed totally differently. Thus, for example, a serial killer could be either a psychopathic monster or a hero if dropping bombs daily in the Afghan War.'

As the foregoing suggests, critical criminologists adopt the view that it is not the harmfulness of an act that makes it a crime. Indeed, many harmful acts are not regulated by the criminal law. For example, criminologists who study crimes of the powerful present statistics which suggest that although large corporations engage in activities that place members of the public in dangerous situations and even cost lives, the activities of these large corporations are regulated mainly by regulatory organisations and not by criminal justice agencies. To illustrate their position, some critical criminologists question why police enforcement typically focuses on specific types of crimes such as street crimes and burglary. These are the so-called conventional crimes that are associated with the poorer and less-powerful groups in society, and these crimes dominate official crime statistics (Chambliss, 1975; Hillyard and Tombs, 2005, 2007). By contrast, the more harmful activities of powerful groups (such as those who run large corporations or who hold senior positions in government) tend to be minimised or even redefined as lawful activities, even where these activities produce more significant harm and victimisation than crimes of the less powerful (see also Box, 1987). According to Jock Young (2002: 254) another 'irony' that the radical criminologists sought to confront is 'That criminal law, although phrased in a language of formal equality, is targeted in a way that is selective and substantially unequal'. In putting forward these arguments, critical criminologists highlight the concept of power as an important factor in the social construction of crime and criminality. They explore the link between power, crime and criminal justice by examining how the powerful in different contexts of social interaction appear to enjoy greater impunity than the less powerful.

Deviance as the product of power dynamics

As the foregoing suggests, the idea that the definition of crime and deviance, and responses to both, are shaped by power dynamics represents yet another feature that characterises several critical criminological perspectives. Critical criminologists generally agree that society comprises powerful groups who can influence the creation of rules and laws. Howard Becker (1963), whose work on the labelling approach laid the foundation for the development of critical criminology in the UK and US from the 1970s onwards, identified powerful interest groups as key rule creators (see Box 1.2). He described them as 'moral entrepreneurs' who occupy positions of authority and have the power to create rules and also to label those who violate the rules as deviants.

It is worth noting that critical criminologists differ in their views about the specific groups who create rules and impose them on others, or who can influence the construction of crime and deviance. For example, Marxist criminologists focus their analysis on the structural dynamics of capitalist societies. It is therefore not surprising that they identify wealthy, ruling-class capitalists (and, for some, both the wealthy capitalists and the state) as the group that can influence the way in which laws are created and enforced (Chambliss, 1975). For some feminist criminologists, particularly the radical feminists, the power to shape constructions of crime and responses to crime resides in men. They argue that patriarchy or male domination is interwoven in the fabric of society and impacts on women as victims of crime or as perpetrators of crime. I shall have more to say about radical feminism in Chapter Eight. For now, it will suffice to say that just as the ruling class is the powerful group in Marxist criminological analyses, and interest groups are the powerful groups in Becker's rendition of the labelling approach, men represent the powerful in feminist analyses of crime causation and control.

Box 1.2: Power dynamics and the construction of deviance

Howard Becker's work laid the foundation for the development of critical criminology. Becker was born in 1928. He studied at the University of Chicago's Sociology Department, where he later taught as a member of faculty. He developed his work at a time of rapid social and political change in the US, and particularly in the city of Chicago, where he was based. In that period, academics in the US began to espouse views that are positioned on the Left of the political spectrum. The liberal views that informed Becker's work are quite evident in his seminal text, titled *Outsiders: Studies in the Sociology of Deviance* (Becker, 1963), which set out the tenets of an area of study that later came to be known as the labelling perspective, or labelling theory. This area of study highlighted the socially constructed nature of crime and deviance. It emphasised the power dynamics that underpin the social construction of deviance. Downes and Rock (2011: 175) note that 'Becker's *Outsiders*, was to become one of the two most frequently cited of all American criminological writings in the period between 1945 and 1972'.

Here, I reproduce extracts from Becker's text. The extracts illustrate his views about the role of power in the creation and regulation of deviance. He argues that there are groups who have the power to make rules for others (the moral entrepreneurs). According to Becker (1963: 162), the 'moral entrepreneur' is the person or group 'at whose instance the rule is made'. They typically occupy positions of power and advantage in society.

> Who can, in fact, force others to accept their rules and what are the causes of their success? That is of course, a question of political and economic power. Later we will consider the political and economic process through which rules are created and enforced. Here it is enough to note that people are in fact always forcing their rules on others, applying them more or less against the will and without the consent of those others. (Becker, 1963: 191)

> Differences in the ability to make rules and apply them to other people are essentially power differentials (either legal or extra-legal). Those groups whose social position gives them weapons and power are best able to enforce their rules. (Becker, 1963: 191)

> Under what circumstances do we make and enforce *ex post facto* rules? I think empirical investigation will show that it occurs when one party to a relationship is disproportionately powerful so that he can enforce his will over others' objections but wishes to maintain an appearance of justice and rationality. (Becker, 1963: 191)

> We see that social rules, far from being fixed and immutable, are continually constructed anew in every situation, to suit the convenience, will, and power position of various participants. (Becker, 1963: 191)

> Interactionist theorists of deviance pay particular attention to the differentials in the power to define; in the way one group achieves and uses power to define how other groups will be regarded, understood, and treated. Elites, ruling classes, bosses, adults, men, Caucasians – superordinate groups generally – maintain their power as much by controlling how people define the world, its components, and its possibilities, as by the use of more primitive forms of control. (Becker, 1963: 204)

Becker and other labelling theorists were later criticised by some Marxist criminologists for focusing on the labelling activities of agents of social control (such as interest groups, elites etc) who do not necessarily possess political and economic power (Taylor et al, 1973). Marxist criminologists argued that Becker should have acknowledged more specifically the role of the state and ruling–class capitalists, who, according to Marxist criminologists, wield considerable political and economic power (Taylor et al, 1973). In other words, labelling theorists were criticised for not being radical enough in their analysis of the power dynamics that shape definitions of crime and deviance. It is argued that they did not sufficiently challenge the existing capitalist order, which, in the view of Marxist criminologists, creates structural inequalities that give rise to crime and deviance. Marxist criminologists went on to develop radical analyses of the political economy of crime and deviance.[13]

Conclusion

Critical criminology has no standard definition and its origin is contested. Nevertheless, critical criminological perspectives share several features in common. They reject mainstream criminological theories. In addition, they subscribe to anti-essentialism, which asserts that concepts such as crime and deviance have no inherent qualities; rather, they are socially constructed labels. Critical criminologists also emphasise the interrelatedness of power and constructions of crime and deviance. They aver that groups in society who occupy positions of power can influence the enactment and enforcement of laws. These groups are also typically immune from law-enforcement activities. Although critical criminological perspectives differ somewhat in the areas of enquiry that they choose to focus on, they agree, unlike mainstream criminology, that power invariably informs definitions of crime and deviance, and also the operation of the criminal law. The latter does not reflect consensually agreed norms and values. Those who occupy positions of power influence how laws are made and how they are enforced, and they are relatively immune from law-enforcement activities. Lynch (2011: 6) notes that:

> Despite growing specialisation, the field of critical criminology is united in its emphasis on addressing power differentials, hierarchies and inequalities as explanations of crime as these impact the distribution of crime over time and place, and in relation to crime and justice, and processes of doing justice as these impact the making and enforcing of laws ... it is [the] commitment to the powerless and marginalised that distinguishes critical from orthodox criminology.

In addition, critical criminologists argue that the power to create laws and avoid law enforcement resides in those who enjoy racial, gender and class advantage. Therefore, crime is the product of structural inequalities that disadvantage minority ethnic groups, women and the lower classes. Reinforcing this, DeKeseredy and Dragiewicz (2012: 1) observe that 'critical criminologists view hierarchical social stratification and inequality along class, racial/ethnic, and gender lines as the major sources of crime'.

In sum, added to the unifying features described earlier, critical criminological perspectives are more likely to commit themselves to developing insights that can help humanise rather than harden the impact of penal policy. This suggests that they share a political motive that situates them firmly on the side of those who are typically vulnerable to deviant and criminal labels (Becker, 1967).

These are the 'underdogs': the people or groups they describe as the victims of unequal and unjust socio-economic arrangements that render them vulnerable to criminalisation.

SUMMARY

- Critical criminology has no standard definition. This may be because it comprises several variants.
- Although critical criminological perspectives focus on differing explanatory themes, they share several features in common.
- A key theme that critical criminological perspectives share in common is their critique of mainstream criminology. The mainstream theories may be broadly classified as classicism, positivism or variants of both theories.
- The foundational critical criminologists maintained that crime and deviance are social constructions. In their view, acts that are defined as crime and deviance have no inherent properties that make them criminal.
- Critical criminologists argue that power differentials in society explain the construction of, and responses to, crime and deviance.

SAMPLE QUESTIONS

1. Assess the tensions between critical criminological perspectives and mainstream criminological theories.
2. Voluntarism, determinism and anti-essentialism are doctrines that underpin explanations of crime. Critically examine the differences between these doctrines.

Notes

[1] See Chapter Nine.

[2] See Chapter Fifteen.

[3] In Chapter Four, which explores Marxist criminology, there is a discussion of the work of Stuart Hall and his colleagues.

[4] In this context, the 'sociology of deviance' includes the work of the generation of sociologists of deviance, who produced work in the 1950s and 1960s that greatly popularised the interactionist/labelling approach to the study of deviance. A notable example is Howard Becker (1963), whose work is described in Chapter Two.

[5] The rule that prosecutors must prove beyond reasonable doubt that the two main elements of an offence concurred does not apply to offences that are defined as strict liability offences. For these offences, prosecutors do not have to establish *mens rea* in order to prove that an offence has been committed.

[6] More evidence exists in support of the deterrent effect of the certainty of punishment (Von Hirsch et al, 1999).

[7] See Chapter Six.

[8] Merton based his work on conditions in the US.

[9] As we shall see in Chapter Three, the neo-Marxist Antonio Gramsci argues that the concept of hegemony can be described as control or domination through ideology (Hoare and Nowell-Smith, 2005).

[10] The work of the interactionist sociologists of deviance (particularly Howard Becker) is explored in more detail in Chapter Two.

[11] Other feminists (including some who believe that gender is socially constructed) oppose this argument. They argue that male-defined norms and values shape the social status, treatment and overall experience of women in society. Therefore, women could be disadvantaged when gender difference is not taken into account (see, generally, Daly and Chesney-Lind, 1988; Burgess-Proctor, 2006). For example, in criminal justice settings, women might be judged and treated according to rules that are defined for, and by, men. Consequently, these feminists propose that it is perhaps more useful to acknowledge that women possess universally distinct qualities. These issues are dealt with in Chapter Eight.

[12] This is legal provided that the killing conforms to the provisions of the Geneva Conventions of 1949, and the accompanying protocols that legislate against barbarity during armed conflict/warfare in order to protect civilians and other non-combatants.

[13] Chapter Four sets out in detail the key arguments within Marxist criminology.

TWO

The labelling perspective

Introduction

The idea that social reaction creates deviance was central to a field of study in criminology that became popular in the 1960s and 1970s, and is now described as labelling theory. A commonly held view is that the US sociologist Howard Becker (1963) initiated this tradition, which emphasises that social reaction to behaviour (in the form of attaching a deviant label to that behaviour, and to the individual responsible for the behaviour) can create further acts of deviance. According to Becker, two factors explain why social reaction creates deviance. One factor is that those who violate the rules that are created by the groups in society who have the power to create rules for others may have the label of deviant conferred on them (Becker, 1963). Another reason why social reaction creates deviance is that once the label of deviant is publicly attached to an individual, the label may produce a social impact: the individual may experience public stigmatisation and exclusion. The label may also produce a psychological impact – it can alter the individual's self-identity – the individual may start to view himself or herself as a deviant and may also start to act according to the label. The social and psychological implications of deviant labels are discussed in more detail later on in the chapter (see also Tierney, 2009). Meanwhile, it is clear that the labelling theorists attached quite a significant amount of importance to the impact of deviant labels. Writing about the labelling tradition, Downes and Rock (2011: 177) note that: 'For a while, the naming associated with deviance was held to be so important … that the entire approach was generally, if misleadingly, termed "labelling theory"'.

Origins of the labelling tradition

The labelling approach may be described as an approach to the study of deviance that, in the 1970s, challenged the fundamental assumptions of mainstream criminology. Until the 1970s, the accepted view within the discipline was that deviance is an unproblematic concept. It was generally accepted that criminal behaviour creates or attracts social control from informal forces of control, such as parents and teachers, or from formal control agents. By contrast, the labelling theorists made what must have appeared to be a startling claim at the time: they rejected the prevailing idea that deviance activates social control, and argued instead that social control activates or creates deviance! Indeed, they maintained that social reaction is the key variable in the creation of deviance, not individual pathology, the exercise of free will and rational choice, or the other factors emphasised by mainstream criminology.

Earlier writers, such as the historian and anarchist Frank Tannenbaum (1938) and Edwin Lemert (1951), suggested that social reaction in the form of applying deviant labels could generate further acts of deviance long before Howard Becker developed his ideas. They stated that deviance can be conceived as a reaction to the stigma and marginalisation that may accompany social reaction. Therefore, social control can, in fact, be quite counterproductive.

That said, the work of sociologists based in the University of Chicago Sociology Department in the 1960s was fundamental to the development of the labelling tradition from the 1960s onwards on both sides of the Atlantic. As mentioned earlier, most criminological texts identify Howard Becker (1963) – who was a sociologist in the University of Chicago Sociology Department – as the original proponent of the labelling tradition (Downes and Rock, 2007). Others rightly note that the labelling approach paved the way for the development of critical criminology as a distinct field of study within criminology (Taylor et al, 1973; van Swaaningen, 1997). Indeed, Jock Young (1988: 163), who, alongside other Marxist criminologists in Britain, critiqued the labelling perspective in the 1970s, later acknowledged that 'It was the impact of the West Coast labelling theory centring around Howard Becker which set the creaking chariot of radical criminology off on its course'.

In the 1960s, when the labelling tradition became popular, social and cultural conditions were changing in several Western countries. In the US, where Howard Becker developed his ideas about the social construction of crime and deviance, social and cultural norms were in a state of flux. It was a time when, on both sides of the Atlantic, 'the world seemed turned upside down' (Young, 2009: 7). There was growing recognition that the increasing diversity in society had created a pluralistic society made up of diverse populations with equally diverse norms and values. This meant that it was no longer tenable to presume, as mainstream criminology was said to have done, that society is characterised by norms and values that are consensually agreed upon, or to assert that the law reflects this consensus. In his description of the wider contexts from which the labelling perspective emerged, Jock Young (2009: 7) put it that, as one of several traditions that revolutionised the field of deviancy studies, the labelling tradition emphasised 'the rejection of absolutist notions of value.... We live in a pluralistic society with a magical cubism of perspectives, where one person's deviancy is another person's normality and where there are numerous audiences.'

Added to the increasing diversity of values, questions were also being asked about the veracity of psychiatric interventions, policing activities, mass media reports, the behaviour of politicians and the workings of the middle classes (Young, 2009). In the US, social activism flourished in the shape of the Civil Rights Movement, the struggle of black people for social equality, feminism, anti-war activism (channelled towards the Vietnam war) and environmental activism. On both sides of the Atlantic, the period witnessed change:

the emergence of dramatic expressive youth cultures, the challenge of new bohemianism and a strident second wave of feminism all raised questions of the status quo, reversing the traditional questions of criminology and the sociology of deviance.... A whole stratum of middle-class youth came into collision with the police on demonstrations, on civil rights marches, and in the policing of their everyday lives.... The new deviancy theory and the new criminology that came close after it were organically linked to this. (Young, 2009: 7)

Thus, in the 1960s, more liberal ideas about moral issues were emerging, and there was growing recognition that it is wrong to presume that a moral consensus can emerge from societies that are becoming increasingly characterised by ethnic and cultural diversity. It became difficult not to dispute the right of any one group to impose its moral ideals on other groups. Power was recognised as the key variable that made it possible for one group to promote its moral, or, indeed, its social, agenda and to label others whose activities threatened that agenda as 'deviants'. In that period, Howard Becker and others began to argue that because there is no consensus on what constitutes acceptable norms and values, definitions of deviance and crime do not reflect consensual agreement in society about what is moral or immoral behaviour. They do not reflect consensual norms and values. As society is not sufficiently homogeneous, there can be no consensus, moral or otherwise, on what constitutes deviance or crime. For this reason, definitions of deviance and crime are not consensually agreed definitions; rather, they are definitions that are constructed by those who have the power to construct such definitions. They reflect the norms and values of those who have the power to create the law or to influence its creation. Therefore, it is not the moral, harmful or other quality of an act that makes it crime or deviance; rather, an act becomes crime or deviance when it is defined as such by those who can impose such labels on others. Meanwhile, those who are most susceptible to these labels are those 'in lower structural positions' (Young, 2009: 7). Thus, a primary theme that underpins the labelling tradition is that crime and deviance are socially constructed categories. Jock Young (2009: 7) did go on to remark that the tradition is 'social constructionist in [its] orientation, stressing that deviance is a constructed category rather than some fixed essence'.

The influence of symbolic interactionism

Key writers in the labelling tradition, particularly Howard Becker, drew on the sociological theoretical perspective that is known as symbolic interactionism. More specifically, they drew on the brand of interactionism that has its origins in the posthumously organised work of George Herbert Mead (1863–1931). Mead's students organised his work after he died in 1931, and one of his pupils, the sociologist Hebert Blumer (1969), elaborated his work further and coined the term 'symbolic interactionism'. Unsurprisingly, George Herbert Mead has been described as 'the chief architect of symbolic interactionism' (Manis and Meltzer, 1972: xi) and as 'the founding father of interactionism' (Downes and Rock, 2011: 79). Mead's ontological view of the nature of human behaviour influenced the work of prominent neo-Chicagoans or theorists of the University of Chicago School of Sociology (Downes and Rock, 2011), including Blumer (1969) and Howard Becker (1963). These theorists and others developed Meadian interactionism, which has since evolved in several directions. The ontological basis of symbolic interactionism can be summarised as follows:

- There is a focus on the impact of social interaction on human behaviour.
- Symbolic interactionists also emphasise the introspective quality of behaviour because they believe that individuals interpret and ascribe meaning to their encounters or 'what confronts them' in the social world (Blumer, 1966: 536), including the symbols, language and other media of communication others use when they interact with them.
- Symbolic interactionists believe individuals that interpret these media of communication introspectively by conversing with the self: a process that has been variously described as 'self-interaction' (Blumer, 1966: 535) or 'internal gyrations of the self' (Downes and Rock, 2011: 178).
- The objective of 'self-interaction' is to assess the self on the basis of encounters in the world including other people's views and definitions, real and imagined. In this context, the self becomes a socially constructed object that comprises two dimensions: the 'I' and the 'me'. The 'I' is the individual's creative interpretation of 'what confronts him [or her]' in the world (Blumer 1966. 536), including the symbols, language and the various signs other people use to communicate with them during social interaction. The 'me' is the individual's response to his or her creative interpretations.
- Symbolic interactionists believe that, ultimately, human action is the product of the creative interpretations that occur during self-interaction. Therefore, human action is socially constructed.
- According to Blumer (1966: 537), in deciding on which line to action to pursue, the individual takes into account *inter alia*: '…the actions of others, the expectations and demands of others, the rules of his group, his situation, his conceptions of himself, his recollections, and his images of prospective lines of conduct'.
- Thus, the individual might adopt the views and attitudes of others, and may subsequently align his or her behaviour accordingly (Denzin, 1992; Plummer, 2000).

It is important to recognise that an individual's interpretations of the views and expectations of others do not necessarily have to mirror actual reality; the meanings we attach to our experiences or to other people's actions or definitions during social interaction are based on our interpretations – our constructions of reality – and not on actual reality. As Blumer points out, Mead insisted that:

In non-symbolic interaction human beings respond directly to one another's gestures or actions; in symbolic interaction they interpret each other's gestures and act on the basis of the meaning yielded by interpretation (Blumer, 1966: 527).

It is therefore not surprising that writers within the labelling tradition are also influenced by phenomenology (Rock, 2012). They are particularly influenced by the version of phenomenology that was developed by Alfred Schutz, albeit 'to a lesser extent' than symbolic interactionism (Spencer, 2011: 199).

The influence of phenomenology

Phenomenology is a theoretical framework in sociology that emphasises the socially constructed nature of social phenomena, including crime. A key difference between phenomenology and interactionism is that while interactionists believe that human actors tend to derive knowledge of themselves from internal interpretations of the signs and symbols they receive from the people they interact with, phenomenologists assert that human actors are the primary arbiters of knowledge about themselves and their capabilities. Thus, from a phenomenological perspective, to understand the nature of deviance, the task of the social scientist is to generate information from the actors involved in creating deviance (the labellers and the labelled) about what the labels mean to them. Their interpretation of the reality of deviance is the most accurate interpretation. The concept – 'deviance' – has no objective reality; it is a social construction. For this reason, the study of social phenomena is only valid in so far as it helps us generate information from social actors about how they interpret things or the meanings they ascribe to things. As we shall see, labelling theorists such as Becker adopted these views and conducted studies that explored how labelled deviants interpret the labels attached to them, and how their interpretations affect their behaviour. That said, the influence of symbolic interactionism is more evident in Becker's work. As we shall also see later in this chapter, he studied how deviant labels affect the labelled deviant's perception of self, with implications for the deviant's future behaviour.

The influence of ethnomethodology

Labelling theorists drew on yet another theoretical tradition, known as ethnomethodology. This sociological approach builds on the earlier work of Erving Goffman (1959, 1961), and was developed by Harold Garfinkel (1991). According to Goffman (1961), in US society, established cultural norms govern social interaction, and people try to adapt their identity and behaviour to these norms during social interaction. Garfinkel (1991) built on Goffman's work and argued that in order to understand human behaviour, one needs to take into account the rules and methods that govern people's perception of the things they observe or the things that happen to them. Therefore, to understand how behaviour comes to be defined as crime or deviance, one needs to examine the rules and methods with which people label the behaviour of others. It is also necessary to examine the rules and methods with which the labelled make sense of their situation and adapt to the label imposed. Therefore, crime has no objective existence; it arises from the rules and methods people employ when they define/ label certain behaviour during their interactions with others. Ethnomethodology is the study of these rules and methods.

In sum, the influence of symbolic interactionism (and, to a minor degree, phenomenology and ethnomethodology) is evident in the empirical work that the labelling theorists, including Becker, undertook. The influence of phenomenology manifests itself in Becker's view that deviance is a social construction. He argues that in order to understand the impact of deviant labels, it is necessary to study the meanings that both the labellers and the labelled deviants attach to the label. The influence of ethnomethodology is evident in Becker's interest in the micro-contexts, or small words, of social interaction in which labels are attached. Importantly, the influence of symbolic interaction manifests itself not only in Becker's focus on the contexts of symbolic interaction in which signs and symbols are used to communicate and act upon deviant labels, but also (as we shall see later on in this chapter) in Becker's study of the psychological impact of a deviant label on the labelled deviant's perception of self.

Given the aforementioned theoretical antecedents, it is perhaps not surprising that Becker and other labelling theorists studied the micro-contexts of social interaction to examine the origins and implications of deviant labels. According to Downes and Rock (2011: 175), symbolic interactionists provide a 'formal description of little social worlds that constitute a society. Schools, gangs, families, pubs and hospitals are not unlike the natural areas of the Chicago school'.

Key arguments

Here, I shall expand on key themes that underpin the labelling perspective. These themes may be broadly classified as follows:

- social reaction creates deviance; and
- deviance is a label that can create further deviance.

Social reaction (labelling) creates deviance

Labelling theorists employ the term 'social reaction' to explain the act of naming or labelling behaviour as deviant. Social reaction also involves attaching the negative connotations of the label to the individual who is believed to be responsible for that behaviour. Labelling theorists argue that the acts or omissions that are labelled as deviance have no intrinsic quality or qualities. They are not different from other acts or omissions; the only quality they share in common is the label of deviance. The label of deviance gives an act or omission its meaning. In addition, the labeller and the labelled act upon that meaning, with profound implications, as examined later. We have also seen that scholars in the labelling tradition espouse anti-essentialist views about deviant identity.

Deviance is a label that can create further deviance

As mentioned earlier, labelling theorists, such as Howard Becker, were heavily influenced by symbolic interactionism when they claimed that a deviant label can pose implications for the labelled deviant's perception of self, which may, in turn, affect subsequent behaviour. According to Becker and other writers in the field, two factors contribute to this. First, the label may pose psychological implications. As an interactionist, Becker (1963) believes that this is because the names or labels others use to define us affect how we view ourselves and our status in society, and how others treat us. As Rock (2012: 66) notes: 'Naming can create a self'. In other words, the self can be altered by our interpretation of other people's perceptions of us. We learn about people's perceptions of us through the symbols (names, signs and language) they use to communicate with us during social interaction. Becker's analysis of how the names, signs and symbols that emerge during social interaction affect perceptions of self, and subsequent behaviour, reveals the influence of symbolic interactionism in his study of deviance.

Second, writers in the labelling tradition assert that the label may produce a social implication (see also Tierney, 2009). They argue that once an individual has been labelled, the deviant label may alter not only the individual's perception of self, but also the individual's public identity – the way other people view and react to the labelled deviant. It becomes the individual's master status. Therefore, whatever status the individual enjoyed in the past becomes irrelevant.

Admittedly, this is a rather crude rendition of the labelling approach because it overlooks Becker's subsequent claim that the impact of labelling is not automatic. In a revised edition of his text *Outsiders: Studies in the Sociology of Deviance*, Becker (1963) went on to acknowledge the possibility of human agency. He recognised that some labelled deviants may choose to reject the label. Nevertheless, as we shall see further later, critics have taken Becker and other labelling theorists to task for proffering what the critics consider to be a rather deterministic account, which presupposes that deviant labels inexorably propel those who are labelled towards a deviant lifestyle.

An important reason why Becker emphasised that deviant labels pose social implications is that, in his view, once the label is conferred on an individual, it is assumed that the individual is inherently deviant and will permanently conform to the negative connotations of the label. Irrespective of that individual's subsequent behaviour, over time, this assumption morphs into a 'self-fulfilling prophesy', mainly because the assumption triggers events and circumstances that, in turn, conspire to confirm the individual in the deviant label. This is the likely outcome of labelling even if the label is spurious. The label sets in motion a series of events that encourage the labelled deviant to adopt the deviant label and act according to the label. Jock Young (2009: 7) observed that this insight about the metamorphoses of projected behaviour into a self-fulfilling prophecy[1]:

> runs through the critical tradition in criminology; it is at the heart of its intellectual enterprise ... over time such stigmatization can become self-fulfilling. For, in certain circumstances, people become like the label. The folk devils conjured up out of moral indignation and prejudice are actually constructed by the forces of social control. Fantasy is translated into reality.

In the book *Outsiders: Studies in the Sociology of Deviance*, Becker (1963) sought to illustrate his position that social reaction, in the form of labelling an individual a deviant, creates circumstances that may conspire to confirm the labelled deviant in the deviant label, and may consequently trigger further acts of deviance. He argued that social reaction can create deviants who may be straitjacketed into a deviant label and denied the opportunity to escape the negative connotations of the label. According to Becker, the deviant label can foreclose opportunities for a legitimate lifestyle. For example, if an individual is labelled a shoplifter or a violent criminal, the label becomes that individual's master status. It does not matter if the individual is a teacher or a doctor. He or she assumes a new master status, which may pose adverse implications for gaining access to legitimate routes to mainstream lifestyles, such as employment and education. Thus, labelled deviants may be denied access to employment, good accommodation and legitimate forms of recreation. Such marginalisation or exclusion is likely to 'worsen their situation' and compel them to live their lives in line with the already-entrenched view (no matter how spurious such a presupposition may be) that they are 'essentially' deviant (Downes and Rock, 2011: 145). As Jock Young (2013: xx) remarks: 'ideas, however misconceived, may very well self-fulfil in reality'.

Rock (2012) provides additional examples of how the deviant label can constrain choices and compel the labelled deviant to act according to the label. Some may become subject to undercover policing and enhanced surveillance, which places them at greater risk of police intervention. Others might find themselves entrapped through undercover police work into offences that they may not have committed in the absence of such entrapment. Some who are convicted of sexual offences may have their names publicly advertised. While this may reduce the risk of reoffending, it has the effect of 'certainly freezing the criminal as a secondary deviant' (Rock, 2012: 67). Rock (2012: 67) writes that:

> Once a person is publicly identified as a deviant, moreover, it may become difficult for him or her to slip back into the conventional world, and measures are being taken with increasing frequency to enlarge the visibility of the rule-breaker.

Consequently, the expectation that the labelled individual will commit further acts of deviance becomes a prediction that fulfils itself because events conspire to confirm the labelled in that position. The individual may be stigmatised, may be excluded from mainstream society and may find it difficult to maintain a lifestyle that is inconsistent with the false expectations of the label. Having been denied access to legitimate means of survival within mainstream society, the labelled deviant may resort to a deviant subculture of similarly marginalised people, where he or she may adopt illegitimate means of survival. Becker (1963: 81) defined 'subculture' as a culture that 'operates within and in distinction to, the culture of the larger society'. He described marginalised groups of labelled deviants as 'outsiders'. These groups also come to view mainstream society as outsiders. According to Becker, involvement in these subcultures increases the likelihood that the labelled deviant will go on to establish a deviant career. Thus, the act of labelling triggers a series of events that may ultimately culminate in the development of a deviant career: 'One of the most crucial steps in the process of building a stable pattern of deviant behaviour is likely to be the experience of being caught and publicly labelled as a deviant' (Becker, 1963: 31). The following often-cited quotation encapsulates Becker's views about the aetiology of deviance:

> ... *social groups create deviance by making the rules whose infraction constitutes deviance,* and by applying those rules to particular people and labelling them as outsiders. From this point of view, deviance is not a quality of the act the person commits, but rather a consequence of the application by others of rules and sanctions to an 'offender'. The deviant is one to whom the label is successfully applied; deviant behaviour is behaviour that people so label. (Becker, 1963: 9; emphasis in original)

Secret/primary deviance and labelled/secondary deviance

To explain the mechanisms through which labelling creates further acts of deviance, Becker (1963) argued that deviance comprises two different components, namely: secret deviance and labelled deviance. Lemert (1972) classified these two components as primary and secondary deviation. Secret deviance is deviance that is undetected and, as such, does not attract public censure. According to Lemert (1972: 48), primary deviance occurs in 'a wide variety of social, cultural and psychological contexts ... has only marginal implications for the psychic structure of the individual; it does not lead to symbolic reorganization at the level of self-regarding attitudes and social roles'. Therefore, primary deviance is a form of deviance that has limited implications for the primary deviant's perception of self.

Secondary deviance, on the other hand, is quite different. Lemert (1951: 76) notes that 'When a person begins to employ his deviant behavior or a role based upon it as a means of defense, attack, or adjustment to the overt and covert problems created by the consequent social reaction to him, his deviation is secondary'. Lemert also stated that:

> Secondary deviation is deviant behaviour, or social roles based upon it, which becomes a means of defense, attack, or adaptation to the overt and covert problems created by the societal reaction to primary deviation. In effect, the original causes of the deviation recede and give way to the central importance of the disapproving, degradational, and isolating reactions of society. (1972: 48)

Secondary deviation comprises two stages: the first stage occurs when social control agents publicly label an individual as a deviant; and the second stage is activated when the labelled deviant revises his or her perception of self and accepts or internalises the label as a master status. As noted earlier, a master status is the main attribute, trait or characteristic people expect an individual to possess over other attributes, and 'people are surprised and find it anomalous' if that individual does not possess that trait (Becker, 1963: 115). The labelled deviant internalises the master status, and it informs that individual's perception of self. Writers in the labelling tradition believed that, contrary to popular belief, criminogenic motives do not give rise to criminal acts. Rather, labelling triggers a series of events that may ultimately give rise to the criminogenic motives with which the labelled individual may go on to build a criminal career. By differentiating between primary and secondary deviance, labelling theorists sought to emphasise that there are clear demarcations between the origins of behaviour and the effects of other people's reactions to that behaviour.

Studying the origins of deviance

Becker and other interactionist theorists of deviance conducted studies that explored the origins of deviance. They did not engage in the 'armchair theorising' they ascribed to mainstream criminology, particularly functionalism. As noted earlier, they sought to explore the micro-contexts, or sites of social interaction, from which deviance emerges. To this end, they used ethnographic methods, including participant observation, to immerse themselves in the social worlds of their research participants.[2]

Becker conducted studies that examined the activities of two groups: marijuana users and dance musicians.[3] He studied the creation of the Marijuana Tax Act of 1937, which criminalised the use of marijuana. According to Becker, those he described as moral entrepreneurs[4] contributed significantly to the creation of the Act. The moral entrepreneurs in this context were members of the Federal Bureau of Narcotics, who launched a moral crusade against marijuana use. The Bureau embarked upon a media campaign to portray the drug as harmful for the users and for the wider public. This media campaign contributed to the successful prohibition of the drug. The campaign also generated quite a lot of money for the Bureau and increased its powers.

The new law prohibiting marijuana use created a new group of outsiders – those who went on to engage in marijuana use. Those who were caught were labelled as deviants. Becker drew on his study of marijuana users (after the prohibition of the drug) to illustrate his view that labelling can create further acts of deviance. According to Becker, marijuana use has three stages. The stages are: the beginner, who uses the drug for the first time; the occasional user, whose use is quite sporadic; and the regular user, who uses the drug systematically. Social control mechanisms can either precipitate or foreclose progression from one stage to the other. Ultimately, those who go on to become entrenched users are those who can overcome constraining social control mechanisms, such as: limited supply to discourage use; pressure on users to conceal use in order to avoid censure; and the tendency of social control agents to portray marijuana use as immoral. Social control agents portray marijuana use in this way in order to create a moral obligation to comply with the rules prohibiting marijuana use, and substance use in general. Those who cannot overlook the immoral quality that has been ascribed to substance use desist from such activity. As Becker (1963: 77) put it: 'Certain morally toned conceptions about the nature of drug use and drug users thus influence the marijuana user. If unable to ignore these conceptions, use will not occur at all'.

Therefore, altering the potential user's moral outlook so that they are unable to ignore conventional values about the use of the drug may help deter use. That said, for those who are able to rationalise and justify their use of the drug, moral imperatives lose their deterrent effect and they become more entrenched users of the drug. According to Becker, users in this category may retreat to subcultures that comprise other users. Within these subcultures, they learn how to replace the negative connotations attached to the drug by mainstream society (the outsiders) with alternative values acquired during interactions with the other users (the insiders):

> the degree of use appears to be related to the degree to which the conceptions are no longer influential, having been replaced by rationalizations and justifications current among users. In short, a person will feel free to use marijuana to the degree that he comes to regard conventional conceptions of it as uninformed views of outsiders and replaced those conceptions with the 'inside' view he has acquired through his experience with the drug in the company of other users. (Becker, 1963: 77)

Becker's study of marijuana users helps illustrate his key arguments about the creation of outsiders who retreat into subcultures of other outsiders and consequently go on to establish a deviant career. As a member of a deviant subculture, the labelled deviant (in this case, the labelled marijuana user) learns through differential association[5] (the act of learning the behaviour of the people one interacts with socially) to justify and rationalise deviant acts. Thus, Becker suggests that, ultimately, creating rules creates deviance. This is because rules create rule violators, who are then labelled as deviants. Labelled deviants may join deviant subcultures, where they may learn to rationalise their deviant activities. We have seen earlier that Becker also suggested that the stigma attached to deviant labels might undermine the ability of labelled deviants to lead legitimate lifestyles in mainstream society. This may also prompt them to join deviant subcultures made up of other marginalised 'outsiders'. In those subcultures, they may go on to establish deviant careers, and to view members of mainstream society as 'outsiders'.

Becker also drew on his study of dance musicians[3] to demonstrate how deviant identities and subcultures are created, and the role the subcultures perform. He argued that subcultures exist outside the mainstream culture. The subcultures enable people who share a specific lifestyle that is considered by outsiders to be unconventional, to come together and devise a culture that addresses the problems they encounter. The problems are caused by incompatibilities between their perception of their lifestyle and society's perceptions. In these subcultures, the members establish their identity. To illustrate these arguments, Becker (1963) examined the factors that explain why dance musicians create subcultures. He suggested that the subcutures formed by dance musicians serve as a means of responding to perceived threats to artistic autonomy. The perceived threats stem from the efforts of customers and employers to control the type of music the dance musicians play. Becker argued that dance musicians, and others who belong to the service industry typically resist the efforts of their clients and employers to control aspects of their work, and undermine their autonomy. But, dance musicians who resist customer demands that are inconsistent with their views about the type of music they should play, may suffer repercussions that include loss of patronage. Nevertheless, as Becker observed, the dance musicians (such as 'the extreme "Jazz" musicians', p 82) who resist the intrusion of outsiders, try to resolve the conflict between 'artistic integrity' (p 108) and commercial success by retreating to subcultures of like-minded musicians who shun conventional music, and indeed conventional society. In these circumstances, subcultures serve as a means of responding to the problem posed by perceived threats to autonomy.

Like the deviants who are able to adopt techniques that help them to neutralise or justify their deviant activities, the dance musicians who choose 'artistic integrity' over 'conventional success', and who then retreat into subcultures of like-minded musicians also adopt techniques that help them to justify their decision to remain faithful to their choice of music (p 82). For this reason, Becker believes that the experiences of those who retreat into subcultures of marginalised dancehall musicians and are, as such, viewed as unconventional musicians reflect the experiences of those who retreat into subcultures of labelled and marginalised deviants:

> The problems arising out of the difference between the musician's definition of his work and those of the people he works for [the customer and the employers] may be taken as a prototype of the problems deviants have in dealing with outsiders who take a different view of their deviant activities. (Becker, 1963: 83)

Becker's empirical examples serve as useful heuristic devices for understanding his views about the impact of labels on identity, perception of self and subsequent behaviour. By labelling individuals as deviants and denying them the opportunity to engage in mainstream activities, mainstream society might push them into deviant subcultures where their unconventional activities are more likely to become entrenched forms of behaviour.

Impact of social reaction (labelling) on group behaviour: deviancy amplification

Other scholars have applied the labelling argument to group behaviour. For example, the social statistician Leslie Wilkins demonstrated how social reaction to the 'deviant identities' of target groups can create further acts of deviance by those groups (Muncie, 2010: 143). Leslie Wilkins (1964) used the concept of 'deviancy amplification' or 'deviation amplification' to demonstrate how this can happen.

Deviancy amplification is the product of several distinct stages of social reaction. Wilkins argues that, first, because deviant groups are socially and spatially isolated from mainstream society, information about their activities travels quite a distance through several media before it reaches the majority (see also Downes and Rock, 2011). This information is typically exaggerated and sensationalised in transit so that by the time it reaches mainstream society, it incorporates fabricated elements. Nevertheless, the information tends to elicit a negative response from the public in the form of moral outrage and demands for law enforcement. The public's response to exaggerated reports about the deviant group's behaviour creates new deviant identities and new contexts for further deviant acts. This is because the group might respond to the outrage and the growing publicity that they are attracting with further acts of deviance. Muncie (2010) remarks that: 'The further an individual is defined as having moved away from the cultural norm the more likely they actually behave in a non-conformist fashion'. The group's acts of deviance are again fed back to the public in distorted and sensationalised format, which again stimulates outrage and demands for greater law enforcement. Ultimately, a vicious circle ensues in which social reaction to distorted and exaggerated reports about the group's activities create even further deviant identities and further contexts for further deviant acts! Ironically, the publicity generated by sensationalised media reports about the group's activities might glamorise or eventually normalise the activities. Consequently, social reaction in the form of intolerance and censure can trigger the very behaviour that is not tolerated. Asserting this view, Wilkins (1964) argues that social reaction can set in motion a 'vicious circle, where a negative social reaction to certain forms of behaviour reinforces, rather than undermines, the deviant activities concerned'. Although his explanatory framework is quite different, Wilkins's deviancy amplification theory very much echoes the views of labelling theorists who argue that social reaction to deviance can quite counterproductively create further acts of deviance.

Social reaction and group behaviour: the creation and consequences of moral panics

Scholars such as Jock Young, Stanley Cohen and others expanded on amplification theory in their description of how social reaction to the activities of a group can create moral panics and further acts of deviance (Downes and Rock, 2011). Jock Young coined the term 'moral panics' (Young 1971a: 182; 1971b: 50). To a significant degree, the theoretical foundation of moral panics can be traced to the labelling approach, which emphasises that social reaction to behaviour can create further acts of deviance. Young (1971a) defined moral panics as 'heightened concerns about some behaviour or group and this also involves or results in increased hostility toward the group concerned'. In *The Drugtakers* Young (1971a) presented the findings of his study of drug use in inner-city London. In the study, Young (1971a) explored how the media amplifies the activities of young drug users and how media amplification creates public fear and indignation. It fuels calls for criminal justice interventions and, in the process, creates 'fantasy crime waves' (Young, 2009: 6). It may also create further acts of deviance by the target group. He described these processes as 'deviancy amplification'. As we have seen earlier, Wilkins also suggested that deviancy amplification occurs when negative social reaction to exaggerated reports about the activities of a group is fed back to the group, which then responds with further acts of deviance that are fed back to the public in exaggerated format, fuelling a cyclical process in which social reaction creates further deviance. As Young (2009: 6) puts it:

> the mass media carry a narrative that both titillates and condemns ...
> it both amplifies the problem and provides explanations and outcomes
> (particularly 'the nemesis effect') ... such a media amplification creates
> a spiral of public fear and indignation, pressurizing control agencies
> such as the police and magistrates and creating fantasy crime waves ...
> this process of deviancy amplification, however fantastic in its premises,
> is real in its consequences, including, in some instances, self-fulfillment
> of stereotypes.

In sum, Young's (1971) study found that the public's reaction to drug use among young people can create a moral panic that is targeted not 'against drugs per se', but against the young people and the culture that supposedly encourages drug use and hedonism (Young, 2009: 5). Just as the labelling theorists argued, Young found in his study that social reaction to drug use among young people (in this case, in the form of a moral panic) ultimately fuelled even further drug use among this group.

Other scholars in the field of critical criminology who also applied the labelling argument (that social reaction creates deviance) to group behaviour include Stanley Cohen (1973) and Stuart Hall and colleagues (1978). These scholars elaborated on the concepts of deviancy amplification and moral panics. In the text *Folk Devils and Moral Panics: The Creation of the Mods and Rockers*, Stanley

Cohen (1973) explored how social reaction to the activities of a group can create moral panics and further acts of deviance (see Box 2.1). In the text, Cohen set out a paradigm for understanding the origins and nature of moral panics. The text demonstrates how exaggerated media reports about clashes between rival groups of young people (the Mods and the Rockers) in Clacton on an Easter bank holiday weekend created a moral panic about a purported rise in youth crime. Ultimately, the public's reaction to the reports exacerbated the young people's deviant activities. Media reports about the young people's styles, including their style of dressing, modes of transport and hairstyles, appeared to suggest that these were somehow symbolic of the young people's deviant traits. The news media predicted even more serious acts of deviance. It is argued that the exaggerated reports inflamed public fears by creating the impression that there had been a decline in moral standards and a rise in delinquent subculture activities and general delinquency. Thus, the media reports fuelled a moral panic, which evoked punitive sentiments among the public and successfully transformed the young people involved into 'folk devils'.

Ultimately, although the moral panic evoked punitive sentiments and triggered law-enforcement activity, the moral panic might have also created further acts of deviance. This is because the impact of sensationalised media reports might have been to spur on other young people to engage in gang activities even when they might not have been otherwise attracted to such activities (Cohen, 1973; Muncie, 2010). Cohen (1973) argued that the media attention might have encouraged some of the gang members involved in the conflict to engage in more expressive acts of deviance. It is also worth noting that moral panic can also create further acts of deviance if, as a consequence of the increased law enforcement that accompanies the moral panic, more activities associated with the folk devils become labelled as deviance. This, in turn, creates the impression that the deviant activities of the folk devils have increased.

Cohen and Young (1973) explored these themes further in the edited text *The Manufacture of News*. Together, they highlighted the role of the media in shaping understandings of crime and deviance through exaggerated reports that incite public fear and mobilise support for whatever agenda the media seeks to promote. They argued that an important consequence is that social reaction orchestrated by the media goes on to create further acts of deviance.

Box 2.1: The impact of labelling on group behaviour

Stanley Cohen's (1973) text *Folk Devils and Moral Panics: The Creation of the Mods and Rockers* is considered to be the seminal text on moral panics. Published in 1973 about events that occurred in the 1960s, it has been reprinted over the years and is currently in its third edition. In the text, Cohen described in detail the processes and conditions that give rise to moral panics and the creation of 'folk devils'. The latter are the target population that is held responsible for the event or behaviour that is the object of the moral panic. In the following extract, Cohen sets out some of the key features of a moral panic:

Societies appear to be subject, every now and then, to periods of moral panic. A condition, episode, person or group of persons emerges to become defined as a threat to societal values and interests; its nature is presented in a stylised and stereotypical fashion by the mass media; the moral barricades are manned by editors, bishops, politicians and other right-thinking people; socially accredited experts pronounce their diagnoses and solutions; ways of coping are evolved or (more often) resorted to; the condition then disappears, submerges or deteriorates and becomes more visible. Sometimes that object of the panic is quite novel and at other times it is something which has been in existence long enough, but suddenly appears in the limelight. Sometimes the panic passes over and is forgotten, except in folklore and collective memory; at other times it has more serious and long-lasting repercussions and might produce such changes as those in legal and social policy or even in the way society conceives itself. One of the most recurrent types of moral panic in Britain since the war has been associated with the emergence of various forms of youth culture ... whose behaviour is deviant or delinquent.... The Teddy boys, the Mods and Rockers, the Hells Angels, the skinheads and the hippies have all been phenomena of this kind.... Groups such as the Teddy boys and the Mods and Rockers have been distinctive in being identified not just in terms of particular events (such as demonstrations) or particular disapproved forms of behaviour (such as drug-taking or violence) but as distinguishable social types. In the Gallery of types that society erects to show its members which roles should be avoided and which should be emulated, these groups have occupied a constant position as folk devils: visible reminders of what should not be. (Cohen, 1973: 1–2)

Every moral panic has a folk devil (see Box 2.1). The latter is the person or group that is held to be responsible for the event or behaviour that is the object of the moral panic. The folk devil is the outsider who is portrayed as a threat to dominant moral values, is demonised and is targeted for punishment. Public outrage effectively legitimises the creation of law-enforcement policies that are targeted at the group. They become subject to tighter controls and close surveillance.

As noted earlier, other writers have also theorised the concept of moral panics and its role in the creation of deviance. In the text *Policing the Crisis*, Stuart Hall and his colleagues (1978) offered a more radical rendition of the concept of moral panics. They described how in the 1970s, the state, through its agents of social control, such as the media and the police, magnified the activities of a target population – young black men – in order to mobilise political, social and cultural support for a crime control agenda. In the text, the authors describe the strategies that social control agents employ to consolidate understandings of crime around specific themes. For example, media-generated images of crime may converge around the activities of groups who traditionally represent the typical folk devils. These groups include young people, minority ethnic groups, immigrants and other vulnerable groups. The work of Stuart Hall and his colleagues is considered in more detail in Chapter Three.

In recent years, instances of moral panics abound. Sporadic moral panics about immigration represent a prime example. In the 1990s, some sections of the British media created a moral panic about immigration and identified asylum seekers from war-torn regions around the world as the folk devils. Asylum seekers were held responsible for many problems, including crime in deprived neighbourhoods. More recently, the focus has been on migrants from some countries in the European Union. A more contemporary example of a media–orchestrated moral panic is the recent portrayal (by some sections of the British media) of young Muslim males as potential terrorists. This is a very harmful portrayal that can potentially impact on the public consciousness, and on criminal justice policy and practice, with adverse consequences for the target population.

Other key writers in the labelling tradition

Although Becker is regarded as the founding father of the labelling tradition, as mentioned earlier, there are other writers who contributed to the development of the tradition. Indeed, some of these writers published their work many years before Becker's (1963) *Outsiders* was published. Becker himself acknowledges that early proponents of the labelling tradition include: Frank Tannenbaum (1938), Edwin Lemert (1951), John Kitsuse (1962), Kai Erikson (1962) and Erving Goffman (1968). These writers averred that social reaction creates deviance.

Frank Tannenbaum's (1938) work, now considered 'a precursor to modern labelling theory' (Muzzatti, 2012: 158), employed several concepts including 'the dramatization of evil' to demonstrate how social reaction to the actions of youth subcultures can stigmatise the members of these subcultures, and establish their identity as deviants. Tannenbaum drew on his experiences in prison to construct an analysis of how formal social sanctions consolidate deviant labels. As we saw earlier, these ideas underpin the position of labelling theorists. We have also seen that Downes and Rock (2011: 174) described Edwin Lemert (1951) as a key interactionist and 'a vital forerunner of the interactionist sociology of deviance'.. Another key contributor to the labelling tradition is John Kitsuse, whose statement in the following encapsulates his position on the aetiology of deviance:

> Deviance may be conceived as a process by which the members of a group, community, or society (1) interpret behaviour as deviant (2) define persons who so behave as a certain kind of deviant, and (3) accord them the treatment considered appropriate to such deviants. (Kitsuse, 1962: 248)

Kai T. Erikson, who is also another contributor to the tradition, put it that:

> Deviance is not a property *inherent in* certain forms of behaviour; it is a property *conferred upon* these forms by the audiences which directly or indirectly witness them. Sociologically then, the critical variable in

the study of deviance is the social *audience* rather than the individual *person*, since it is the audience which eventually decides whether or not any given action or actions will become a visible case of deviation. (Erikson, 1962: 308, emphases in original)

Becker, Kitsuse and Erikson all recommended that studies of deviance should primarily focus on the impact of naming or labelling (see also Downes and Rock, 2011).

Criticisms

The labelling tradition has attracted several criticisms. Writers on the Right argue that it appears to be more concerned with the plight of the criminal (the labelled deviant) than the victim. Those on the Left (as we shall see further later and in Chapter Three) believe that it does not provide a full account of the structural factors that help us understand crime and criminal justice (see, eg, Taylor et al, 1973).

It has also been argued that although deviancy theorists, including writers in the labelling tradition, claim that their objective is to 'humanise and normalise the "deviant", to show that he is essentially no different from us' (Liazos, 1972: 104), they continually highlight the experiences of the 'deviant', and they employ the term 'deviant' to describe the people they focus on in their analyses. For Liazos (1972: 105), 'The continued use of the word "deviant" (and its variants), despite its invidious distinctions and connotations', suggests that the deviancy theorists are not as committed to an anti-essentialist conceptualisation of deviant identity as they claim to be. Indeed, Liazos argues that the deviancy theorists made statements that appeared to reinforce the popular belief that those who are labelled as deviants are different from others in society. According to Liazos (1972), this reveals a certain degree of prejudice towards those labelled as deviants. It indicates that despite their claims to the contrary, deviancy theorists, including Becker, really did believe that labelled deviants are essentially 'inferior', and different from others. It calls into question the sincerity of their professed commitment to challenging the longstanding depiction of labelled deviants as inherently different and inferior individuals. In addition, Liazos believes that the writers reinforced officially endorsed, or indeed, officially formulated, stereotypical notions of the deviant as someone who commits crimes of a 'dramatic predatory nature', such as 'robbery, burglary or rape' (Dinitz et al, 1969, cited in Liazos, 1972). They did this by focusing on predatory crimes of the kind just mentioned and by focusing 'on perverts' or people who are engaged in behaviour and activities that are deemed socially unacceptable, such as addiction, prostitution, predatory crimes and behaviour associated with mental illness.

Some insist that the labelling tradition is not a theory and it comprises numerous perspectives that are sometimes contradictory. Indeed, Becker (1963: 178) himself finds it unfortunate that the tradition came to be described as 'labelling theory'.

He states that 'a number of people ... contributed to the development of what has rather unfortunately been called "labelling theory"'. He also refutes the claim made by critics that he tried to propound a labelling 'theory':

> I never thought the original statements by myself and others warranted being called theories of the fully articulated kind they are now criticised for *not* being ... sometimes critics suggest that a theory was proposed, but that it was wrong. (Becker, 1963: 178, emphasis in original)

Thus, he emphasises his 'dissatisfaction with the expression "labelling theory"' and argues that his work is best described as 'an interactionist theory of deviance'. In his view, 'Labelling theory, then, is neither a theory, with all the achievements and obligation that go with the title, nor focused so exclusively on the act of labelling as some would have thought' (Becker, 1963: 181).

Some also point out that in the focus on the impact of deviant labels, the perspective does not explain secret or primary deviance, and even appears to suggest that deviant behaviour before it is labelled is 'unimportant' (Akers, 1968: 463). According to Akers, the priority given to the impact of deviant labels could lead one to conclude that:

> people go about minding their own business, and then – 'wham' – bad society comes along and slaps them with a stigmatized label. Forced into the role of deviant the individual has little choice but to be deviant (1968: 463).

Rejecting what he describes as the tendency of labelling theorists to overlook the initial act of deviance before it is labelled, Akers (1968) argues that deviant labels do not cause the initial behaviour that subsequently becomes labelled. In some instances 'the behaviour creates the label' (p 464). Others have echoed these criticisms, pointing out that if as the labelling theorists claim, an act becomes deviant when the label of deviant is attached to it, how, then, can secret deviance exist? As Taylor and colleagues (1973) observe, a consequence of the failure to define the causes of primary deviance is that the labelling scholars appear to overlook unlabelled deviance, and the unlabelled deviant (Taylor et al, 1973).

In response, Becker (1963) argues that this criticism reveals a misinterpretation of the aims of the labelling perspective. He emphasises that the perspective did not set out to establish the cause/s of deviance. According to Becker (1963: 179), writers in the labelling tradition had 'more modest aims' than that. They sought to expand understandings of the nature of deviance by directing attention away from the typical focus on the offender. Their aim was to refocus attention on the activities of other parties who also contribute to the creation of deviance. Reinforcing this, Downes and Rock (2011: 144) note that 'Labelling theorists do not particularly address themselves to the "cause" of delinquency, since they are far more concerned to develop a missing dimension in previous theorising: the impact of social reactions to deviance'.

Becker also maintains that it was never the intention of labelling theorists to claim that the action of moral entrepreneurs in labelling individuals as deviants is the *sole* factor that causes deviance. However, the proponents of the tradition did successfully demonstrate that the act of labelling can foreclose opportunities (eg job opportunities) and make it difficult for the labelled deviant to lead a legitimate lifestyle:

> One of the most important contributions of this [labelling] approach has been to focus attention on the way labelling places the actor in circumstances which make it harder for him to continue the normal routines of everyday life and thus provoke him to 'abnormal' actions (as when a prison record makes it harder to earn a living at a conventional occupation and so disposes its possessor to move to an illegal one). (Becker, 1963: 179)

Some critics contend that the labelling perspective does not explain why some labelled deviants commit deviant acts while others in their group or community do not (Gibbs, 1966). There is also the argument that the perspective is deterministic because it appears to suggest that the deviant label propels the recipient into an unavoidable deviant career (Pfohl, 1994). For some critics, this overlooks the ability of the social actor to reject a deviant label. In a scathing criticism of the labelling approach, Alvin Gouldner (1973: 38–9) famously remarked that the perspective portrays the deviant as a victim who can be said to be more 'sinned against than sinning' and who is 'man-on-his-back', not 'man-fighting-back'. In response to this often-cited criticism, Becker points out that he did not claim that a deviant label always channels the labelled deviant into a life of deviance. As Becker (1963: 179) put it:

> The act of labelling, as carried out by moral entrepreneurs, while important, cannot possibly be conceived as the sole explanation of what alleged deviants actually do. It would be foolish to propose that stick-up men stick people up simply because someone has labelled them stick-up men.

Becker (1963: 180) also maintains that:

> To suggest that defining someone as deviant may under certain circumstances dispose him to a particular line of action is not the same as saying that mental hospitals always drive people crazy or that jails always turn people into habitual criminals.

Notwithstanding these rebuttals by Becker, several commentators, including the British Marxist criminologists of the 1970s, argue that the labelling perspective casts the labelled deviant as a passive underdog who is incapable of escaping the unfortunate impact of the label (Taylor et al, 1973). Although they emphasise the socially constructed nature of crime and deviance, Marxist criminologists describe the deviant as an active being. Indeed, Marxist criminologists describe deviance as a conscious act of defiance by the labelled deviant in the face of oppressive and exploitative socio-economic conditions. Thus, for Marxist criminologists, deviance is not a condition that constrains the deviant. Indeed, van Swaaningen (1999: 11) comments that Marxist criminologists sought to replace 'the image of a deprived underdog by that of an underclass fighting back and interactionist analyses of labelling processes by a political economy of criminalisation'.

As already mentioned, Marxist criminologists and others also formed the view that the labelling perspective does not pay sufficient attention to the unequal power structures that may also explain crime and deviance, such as the power to make laws and impose deviant labels (Taylor et al, 1973). The labelling tradition, it is argued, focuses unduly on the interactional micro-contexts from which labelling (criminalisation) emerge, while ignoring wider societal structures or macro-level factors that, in their view, create inequalities of wealth and power, and expose the less powerful to deviant labels. Writing about the general field of the sociology of deviance, Liazos (1972: 104) remarked that deviancy theorists such as Becker did not 'try to relate the phenomena of "deviance" to larger social, historical, political, and economic contexts'. He also argues that the labelling perspective focused on the 'dramatic' aspects of activities or forms of behaviour that are typically described as deviant, such as juvenile delinquency (Liazos, 1972: 104). Liazos goes on to state that by focusing on labelled deviants, or those he described as 'nuts, sluts and perverts', the deviancy theorists were unable to explore the acts and forms of behaviour that produce significant victimisation but are not labelled because the perpetrators are so powerful that they can shield themselves from deviant labels and their negative implications. According to Liazos (1972: 110), in these cases: 'people are not powerful enough to make the "deviant" label stick' Examples include crimes committed by powerful individuals and large corporations. Liazos (1972: 111) insists that: 'the corporate economy kills and maims more, is more violent, than any violence committed by the poor (the usual subjects of studies of violence)'. The critics assert that by failing to study the violent and other harmful acts perpetrated by the powerful, the deviancy theorists (including writers in the labelling tradition) overlooked harmful activities of the more powerful members of society. As Liazos (1972: 104–5) put it:

> Despite explicit statements by these authors of the importance of power in the designation of what is 'deviant', in their substantive analyses they show a profound unconcern with power and its implications. The really powerful, the upper classes and the power elite, those Gouldner

(1968) calls the 'top dogs', are left essentially unexamined by these sociologist of deviance.

Liazos also criticised the labelling tradition for emphasising the activities of those he described as 'lower and middle level agents of social control' (1972: 115). These agents include the police, prison officials, mental hospital staff and also the moral entrepreneurs who called for the introduction of the Marijuana Act. According to Liazos, the tradition overlooked the most powerful who exercise political and economic power, and are able to create rules that protect their interests. They also punish those whose actions threaten the status quo. For Liazos (1972: 115-16), the powerful are: 'the ruling institutions and groups', such as 'the political manipulators who pass laws to defend their interests and persecute dissenters' (Liazos, 1972: 115–16). Indeed, it is argued (particularly by Marxist criminologists) that the labelling perspective draws more on symbolic interactionism and other micro-level sociological traditions than political economy (Reiner, 2012b).

It is worth noting, however, that Becker (1967) did go on to write an article in which he posed the question: '*Whose side are we on?*'. The article proposed that it is incumbent on sociologists to clearly explicate their political bias towards the underdogs of criminal justice. These are the structurally marginalised, who tend to be more vulnerable to criminal justice interventions. He also believed that it is practically impossible to identify and study those who are at the very top of the social hierarchy because the rungs of the social hierarchy extend almost to infinity. Liazos (1972: 116) dismissed this supposition that 'Everyone has somebody over him, so there is no one at the top' as a 'clever point without substance'. He argued that some, particularly the ruling class, have far more power than others. According to Liazos, the ruling class employs the label of deviant as an instrument for discrediting and silencing those who challenge the status quo. Therefore, it is necessary to study the actions of this class. Writers who applied the labelling argument (that social reaction creates deviance) to group behaviour have also encountered several criticisms. In particular, the concept of moral panics has been subjected to extensive criticism. More recent adaptations of the concept have emerged in the work of Goode and Ben-Yehuda (1994). These writers question the idea that moral panics originate from the actions of the more-powerful groups in society. Instead, they point out that other sections of society, including the less-powerful groups, can also initiate moral panics. They offer a threefold categorisation of moral panics, or models of moral panics. With the interest group model, people who can create rules for others in society orchestrate the moral panic to further their interests. The elite engineered model of moral panics emerges from the actions of the more-powerful groups and has as its underlying objective the effort to incite public fear and anxiety where such fear and anxiety may bolster a given political imperative. Finally, the grassroots model of moral panics is generated by the public in response to activities that are believed to threaten public well-being. Such moral panics may be indicative of a sense of social insecurity.

Additional writers have also criticised the concept of moral panics. McRobbie and Thornton (1995), for example, cite several factors that have, in their view, converged to undermine the relevance of moral panics as a core feature of contemporary societies. These include the rise in the frequency of moral panics and the corresponding decline in their noteworthiness. McRobbie and Thornton maintain that in contemporary societies, there is growing social and cultural diversity. Therefore, the degree of moral consensus required for a successful moral panic, in which a target population is designated as folk devils or outsiders who threaten consensual moral standards, does not exist. Left realists (whose work is described in Chapter Seven) reject the central idea that underpins the concept of moral panics – this is the idea that crime is a social construction and the fear of crime is the irrational product of exaggerated media reports about crime. The left realists argue that crime is a real problem; it requires realistic interventions and should not be dismissed as a social construction, or as the product of moral panics that create irrational public fear and anxiety (Lea and Young, 1984, 1993). According to Young (1997a: 474): 'It [left realism] emerged as a critique of a predominant tendency in left wing and liberal commentaries which downplayed the problem of crime, talking about media instigated moral panics and irrational fears of crime.'

Conclusions

The labelling perspective made significant contributions to criminology. It expanded the study of crime and deviance to include greater appreciation of the impact of social reaction to both phenomena. Indeed, its major contribution to criminological theory was to shift explanations about the causes of crime away from the crime itself (the focus of classicist criminology) and from the criminal (the focus of positivist criminology). Instead, labelling theorists drew attention to social mechanisms that, in their view, create crime and deviance. For labelling theorists, these social mechanisms are set in motion when those who have the power to create rules for others create a new rule. Some people violate the new rule, and the label of 'deviant' is attached to them. Events may subsequently conspire to constrain the labelled deviants within the deviant identity and the deviant roles associated with the label.

The same applies when the label of 'criminal' is attached to an individual. A criminal record can affect the convicted offender's chances of gaining access to the resources that are required to pursue a legitimate lifestyle in mainstream society. It can affect the labelled individual's chances of gaining employment. The label/conviction is stored in official records and, in many instances, the individual has to declare the conviction to potential employers. Such a declaration may limit access to jobs, accommodation and even further education in mainstream institutions of learning. In the UK, higher education institutions require that students should declare any criminal convictions they have received. Thus, a criminal label can stigmatise the labelled individual, foreclose opportunities for legitimate endeavour and push the deviant to the margins of society, where the main sources of support are likely to come from similarly marginalised deviants.

As an antidote that might neutralise the counterproductive implications of labelling, some jurisdictions have adopted restorative justice principles (Rock, 2012). These principles are based on John Braithwaite's (1989) notion of 'reintegrative shaming', which involves labelling (or public naming) but has the added dimension of giving the labelled deviant the opportunity to make amends to the victim or to wider society. Once the deviant has made the requisite reparations, he/she is able to re-enter society.

Edwin Schur's (1973) text, aptly titled *Radical Non-Intervention*, emphasised the negative impact of deviant labels, particularly on young people, and the importance of non-intervention. In practical terms, this entails diverting them away from the criminal justice system and its institutions. He viewed penal institutions for young people as schools of crime. He also considered treatment or reform programmes to be particularly ineffective and, indeed, harmful. For Schur (1973: 155), radical non-intervention simply means: 'leave kids alone wherever possible'. According to Schur, youth offending is transitory is often an aspect of to normal human development. Non-intervention takes this into account. Importantly, non-intervention might help shield young people from the impact of potentially stigmatising and exclusionary labels that might propel them towards developing deviant careers. Indeed, Schur believed that the only difference between young people who are labelled as delinquents and other young people is that labelled delinquents have been exposed to youth justice intervention, or to 'the juvenile justice system' as it is described in the US.

Several studies have assessed the veracity of the labelling argument that social reaction can create further deviance. We have seen that in the text *Outsiders*, Becker (1963) drew on two studies (of marijuana users and dancehall musicians) to illuminate his views about the impact of social reaction. Additional studies provide ample empirical support for the labelling tradition. The studies suggest that the tradition offers a useful framework for understanding the experiences of a wide range of individuals and groups who are classed as deviants. These groups include young people whose demeanour or other demographic attributes appear unacceptable to some police officers (Piliavin and Briar, 1964), male homosexuals (Hooker, 1957; 1963), drug users (Schur, 1963; 1965) and the mentally ill (Scheff, 1974). The studies suggest that these groups often find themselves almost constrained to adapt their behaviour to the expectations or stereotypes that accompany the label imposed on them. The label assumes a self-fulfilling prophecy and poses adverse implications for their well-being or for their ability to thrive in mainstream society. In a more recent study, Bernburg and colleagues (2006) explored the short-term impact of formal criminal justice labelling on the likelihood of subsequent offending. They examined the impact of early contact with the youth justice system and found that young people who receive youth justice labels tend to join subcultures and become involved in further offending.

Debates about the negative impact of deviant labels influenced youth justice policy in the 1970s in the UK quite significantly. Attempts were made to reduce police intervention in the lives of young people and to reduce the negative impact of criminal records on job opportunities. The introduction of the Offender Rehabilitation Act in 1974 represents an example of the effort to reduce the impact of criminal convictions on future employment prospects. The Act provides that after a period of time, or after the rehabilitation period has elapsed, offenders convicted of some criminal offences may consider any conviction (and, since 2008, any caution) spent. This means that they do not have to disclose the convictions in job or insurance applications. Some professions are exempt from the provisions of the Act. These include professions that involve working with vulnerable groups, including children, and professions within the criminal justice system and the health service. However, in many cases, the Act does ameliorate the adverse impact of criminal labels. In an article that critiques cultural criminology, which is one of the recent critical criminological perspectives that trace their intellectual heritage to the labelling tradition, Spencer (2011: 198) aptly sums up the contributions of the labelling perspective as follows:

> Labelling theorists rapidly became current and widely influential in political and social debate and their interrogations of the stigmatization of the powerless and criticisms of total institutions worked to create policies of de-institutionalization.... In terms of its world-changing impact, labelling theory is one of the best measuring rods for which subsequent critical criminologists should be judged.

Nevertheless, some commentators have stated that efforts at 'delabeling and decarceration' did not produce projected outcomes: official crime rates continued to rise in the 1970s and the 1980s (Downes and Rock, 2011: 351). Labelling theorists might argue that this outcome suggests that the labelling activities of the forces of social control were not curtailed to a suitable degree. By contrast, mainstream criminologists would reject this view and assert the rise in crime rates can be attributed to one key factor which is an increase in levels of criminality, and not to the impact of social control or social reaction.

The ideas espoused by labelling theorists heavily influenced the critical criminological perspectives that became popular in the 1970s. As noted earlier, it has been argued that the labelling tradition laid the foundations of critical criminology. Van Swaaningen (1999: 10) rightly observes that: 'North American scholars such as Howard Becker, Ed Lemert and Erving Goffman indeed prepared the ground for critical criminology in the late 1950s'.

SUMMARY

- The idea that social reaction to human action can create deviance was central to the labelling perspective that became popular in the US in the 1960s.
- Most criminological theories identify Howard Becker (1963) as the founding father of the labelling tradition.
- A key theme that underpins the labelling perspective is that deviance is a label that can create further deviance because:
  - A deviant label might pose psychological implications; it can alter an individual's perception of self. This is because the labelled individual might start to view him- or herself as deviant, and may go on to establish a deviant lifestyle.
  - A deviant label might also pose social implications because it is typically accompanied by social stigmatisation, which might foreclose opportunities for the labelled individual to pursue a legitimate lifestyle in mainstream society. The individual might then gravitate towards deviant subcultures, where it becomes likely that he or she will establish a deviant career.
- Other writers developed the labelling approach by demonstrating how social reaction to the activities or 'deviant identities' of target groups can create further acts of deviance (Wilkins, 1964; Young, 1971; Cohen, 1973; Muncie, 2010: 143). These writers went on to introduce the key concepts of deviancy amplification and moral panics in their effort to demonstrate how social reaction creates further acts of deviance.

SAMPLE QUESTIONS

1. Critically assess the view that: 'social groups create deviance by making the rules whose infraction constitutes deviance, and by applying those rules to particular people and labelling them as outsiders' (Becker, 1963: 9; emphasis in original).
2. To what extent do the concepts of deviancy amplification and moral panics reinforce the proposition that social reaction creates deviance?

Notes

[1] As we saw in Chapter One, Robert Merton (1968: 477), who coined the concept, describes a self-fulfilling prophecy as 'a false definition of the situation evoking a new behavior which makes the originally false conception come true'.

[2] Interactionists assert the primacy of ethnographic methods. Ethnography is a scientific research approach that is employed by researchers across several social science disciplines, from anthropology to sociology and criminology. It is used to study the nature, culture and other features of human societies. It involves the use of qualitative data collection methods, such as participant observation and semi-structured interviews, to explore micro-level interactions between social actors. Labelling theorists employ ethnography as a research strategy because they believe that the objective of social research should be to understand rather than explain the social world. Social researchers should seek to uncover the meaning that informs social interaction and action and, should therefore, stay as close as possible to the lived experiences of research participants.

Significant meaning is that employed by the social actors themselves, not by the sociologist, because it is that meaning which structures behaviour. Interactionism is consequently designed to take the observer and audience as far as is practicable inside the actors' own perspectives on selves, acts and environments. (Downes and Rock, 2011: 176)

[3] Becker (1963: 82) defines the dance musician as 'someone who plays popular music for money'.

[4] Becker describes those who have the power to create rules for others as 'moral entrepreneurs'. According to Becker, the creation of deviance begins when moral entrepreneurs embark upon a moral crusade to create a rule and to label those who violate the rule as deviants. The rule creators may be motivated by several factors. It may be that they intend to promote a specific moral agenda, or it could be that they believe the new rule will protect their own interests. Some may be motivated by humanitarian concerns. Becker also argues that a successful moral crusade is one that gains public support or legitimacy for the new rule and creates groups of outsiders who violate the rule. It also creates a social control (law-enforcement) machinery.

[5] Edwin Sutherland founded differential association theory (see Chapter One).

[6] Chapter Nine explores criminological perspectives on crimes of the powerful crimes of the powerful in more detail.

THREE

Conflict perspectives in criminology

Introduction

Some writers have offered critical perspectives on the study of crime by arguing that societies that are characterised by diversity rather than homogeneity are typically conflict–ridden. The writers trace that the origins of crime to the conflict in these societies. It is therefore perhaps not surprising that the writers are described as conflict theorists.[1]

The early conflict theorists drew distinctions between industrial societies (of the modern era) and traditional societies. They argued that traditional societies comprise homogeneous groups with consensual views about cultural issues, norms, values, morals and so forth. By contrast, industrial societies are characterised by conflict. In these societies, there is no consensus on what constitutes acceptable or unacceptable behaviour (norms and values). While the mainstream criminological theories took it for granted that modern industrial societies are characterised by moral consensus or that laws reflect consensually accepted norms and values, the early conflict theorists (and indeed conflict criminologists in general) maintained that these societies are characterised by conflict between diverse groups who differ along social, political, ethnic, religious and other lines. In addition, the conflict theorists argued that some groups are endowed with greater resources compared with other groups. They also possess political, social and economic power . Conflict between the groups manifests itself in the struggle for domination. Ultimately, the group or groups in society that are able to assert their will are also able to create dominant norms, values or culture. They are able to define crime and influence law enforcement in ways that protect their interests, and control the activities of other groups. Key writers in this field include Thorsten Sellin, George Vold, Austin Turk, Richard Quinney and William Chambliss.[2]

Origins of the conflict perspectives

The origins of conflict perspectives of law and criminal behaviour date back to the work of Thorsten Sellin, who first suggested that culture conflict can create violations of laws and norms (Sellin, 1938a: 98). According to Sellin (1938a: 98), culture conflict may be defined as 'a conflict of conduct norms … [that] may arise as a process of group differentiation within a cultural system or area, or as a result of contact between norms drawn from different cultural systems or areas'.

Sellin believed that conflict can arise when migrants settle in a society and the society becomes culturally diverse. From Sellin's perspective, in a society with a dominant culture and accompanying norms that are the product of consensus, the members of that society internalise the dominant norms during socialisation and accept them as legitimate norms. Culture conflict is more likely to occur in societies that are heterogeneous and comprise not only a mainstream group, but also subgroups that have broken away from the mainstream. These subgroups will create their 'conduct norms', and there is typically conflict between the different groups over which norms should prevail when both cultures interact. Selling (1938b: 66) remarked that 'The transformation of a culture from a homogeneous and well-integrated type to a heterogeneous and disintegrated type is therefore accompanied by an increase in conflict situations'. According to Sellin (1938b), the influx of migrants can set these processes in motion. Culture conflict in such societies arises from differences in the 'conduct norms' (values, lifestyles, accepted forms of behaviour) of the migrant populations and the indigenous populations. As Sellin (1938b: 63) put it: 'Conflicts of cultures are inevitable when the norms of one cultural or subcultural area migrate to or come in contact with those of another'.

Criminal behaviour emerges from the conflict in these societies through a variety of means. Groups with political, social and other societal advantage are eventually able to transform their norms into dominant norms. Other groups without such advantage have their norms criminalised (defined as criminal). In addition, these other groups, for example, migrants to that society, would tend to engage in behaviours that are acceptable within the religious, cultural and social ideals of the places that they have migrated from, but which violate the conduct norms of the area that they have settled in. The clash between the behaviour of the migrants and the dominant norms would typically expose the migrants to criminalisation. There are several examples of how culture conflict can create crime when the conduct norms of migrant populations clash with dominant norms and become criminalised. Cases of female circumcision and so-called 'honour' crimes[3] have been uncovered in Western jurisdictions where such practices are illegal. From this perspective, laws, including the criminal law, can be defined as the conduct norms of those who have the power to transform their norms into dominant norms that others are required to conform to. Crime is the product of the conflict between the conduct norms of a dominant group in a society, and the conduct norms of other groups in that society.

George Vold (1958) is another conflict theorist. He focused on group conflict and explored how different groups in society, keen to protect their interests, compete with each other. He argued that conflict arises from this competition between groups. The law represents an important area of conflict. But, the more powerful groups are able to influence the enactment of laws, and the laws tend to protect their interests. The less powerful groups lack the power to influence the creation of laws and law-enforcement activities. Therefore, their interests are not protected by the law have no vested interest in complying with the law. They would tend to violate the law and have their actions criminalised. Thus, crime can be defined as the behaviour of less-powerful groups that threatens the interests of the powerful.

In his description of the nature of crime in contemporary societies, Vold focused mainly on the types of behaviour that may be described as forms of resistance to an unequal and unfair social order. They are the behaviours tend to be criminalised (they tend to be identified as criminal behaviour) and they typically include political protests, industrial disputes and forms of activism that are motivated by the quest to end racial domination and discrimination. From Vold's perspective crime is 'the normal, natural response of normal, natural human beings struggling in understandably normal and natural situations for the maintenance of the way of life to which they stand committed' (Vold and Bernard, 1979: 296).

Unlike the earlier conflict theorists, such as Thorsten Sellin and George Vold, who described crime as behaviour that is inconsistent with dominant norms, subsequent conflict theorists drew on the labelling tradition and described crime as the product of definitions that are attached to behaviour. Austin Turk (1966), for example, argued that crime is a label that is applied to behaviour by those who belong to the group he described as 'the authorities' or the 'political authorities' (p 345). This group can compel others in society to comply with the legal norms they create. Turk (1966: 346) defined a legal norm as 'a cultural norm officially announced by the political authorities in a collectivity'. According to Turk (1966: 345), legal norms or 'authoritative norms' (p 346) are accepted and considered to be legal by the masses not because the masses internalise or accept the norms, but because of social conditioning; 'they have learned to defer to the decisions of the powerful subset, i.e., to view the subset as "authorities".[4] Deference to norms may arise after failed attempts at conflicts or challenges to authority, or after an internalisation process through which individuals learn to defer to the established 'authority structure'. As Turk (1966: 345) puts it, deference arises after the masses are 'socialised into the authority structure'. The norms created by the powerful do not always reflect the social norms of a society. However, they are viewed as legal because those who are subject to authority (those who lack authority, in other words, those who are denied participation in law-making) have learned to defer to them: 'most legal norms will be seen by members of the collectivity as "legal" only to the extent that the norm of deference to authority has been established.... Legality is ... dependent upon recognition of the *superior power* of norm-announcers' (1966: 346, emphasis in original). Where no group with overarching authority exists, the legality of enacted legal norms may be disputed, and the dispute can only be resolved if a powerful group of individuals who are able to compel others to defer to their authority emerges (1966: 346).

In sum, Turk held the view that groups are socialised into a value framework that endorses a hierarchical societal structure. This structure comprises those in authority (who have the power to create and enforce laws) and those who are subject to authority. Conflict between both groups threatens this status quo and results in the criminalisation of the less-powerful groups – those who are subject to authority. As mentioned earlier, in developing his conflict perspective, Turk was influenced by the labelling tradition. He argued that the acts that are labelled as crime have no intrinsic qualities. For Turk (1966: 341), 'official labelling behaviour on the part of legal authorities, rather than the behaviour of the individual, is the actual source of his criminality'. Labelling infuses behaviour with its deviant status.

Apart from George Vold and Austin Turk, there are other conflict criminologists, such as Richard Quinney (2008 [1970]) and William Chambliss (Chambliss and Seidman, 1971).[5] In *Social Reality of Crime*, Richard Quinney (2008 [1970]) set out arguments that are consistent with conflict perspectives on crime and criminal justice. The text was first published in 1970, but has been reprinted several times. The latest edition published was in 2008. In the text, Quinney defined crime as a label. He argued that the less powerful are more vulnerable to this label if their acts violate the criminal law. By contrast, the more powerful enjoy impunity because they are able to influence the political process, and also criminal law administration and enforcement processes. Like the earlier conflict theorists, Quinney (2008 [1970]: 9) formed the view that heterogeneous societies, that is, societies that are characterised by 'diverse value systems and normative groups', are conflict-ridden. There is no consensus on values and norms in these societies. That said, subgroups within such societies have stable cultural and consensual values. The subgroups with an agenda organise themselves effectively and assume high positions in the political power structure. They become able to ensure that laws and policies protect their interests (Quinney, 2008 [1970]). Given their ability to influence government decisions, including decisions to do with the creation of laws and policies, they can control other groups in society. As Quinney (2008 [1970]): 16, emphasis in original) put it:

> Criminal definitions are formulated according to the interests of those segments (types of social groupings) of society which have the power to translate their interest into *public policy*. The interests – based on desires, values, and norms – which are ultimately incorporated into the criminal law are those which are treasured by the dominant interest groups in society. In other words, those who have the ability to have their interests represented in public policy regulate the formulation of criminal definitions.

As the foregoing indicates, from Quinney's perspective, there is an uneven distribution of power in conflict-ridden societies. Some subgroups assume the power to control others, and they promulgate laws that protect their interests. For Quinney (2008 [1970]: 11, 39): 'power ... is the ability of persons and groups to determine the conduct of other persons and groups'; 'and shape public policy'. Clearly, like writers in the labelling tradition, Quinney views crime as the product of definitions. In other words, he considers crime to be a social construction. He states that 'Crime is not inherent in behaviour, but it is a judgment made by some about the actions and characteristics of others, (2008 [1970]: 16). He acknowledges that scholars in the labelling tradition, such as Howard Becker,

Kai T. Erickson and John I. Kitsuse, developed this view of crime. In addition, Quinney echoes the views of these scholars when he argues that the lower classes are more vulnerable to deviant labels compared with the dominant class. He believes that those (among the lower classes) whose behavioural patterns are not taken into account when laws are created are more vulnerable to the label of crime than those who create and apply the law.

For Quinney, the very idea that criminal definitions are formulated or constructed indicates that there is conflict in society. According to Quinney (2008 [1970]: 17): 'Criminal definitions exist, therefore, because some segments of society are in conflict with others. By formulating criminal definitions, these segments are able to control the behaviour of persons in other segments.'

From Quinney's perspective, the criminal law and, indeed, public policy are created primarily because subgroups in society are in conflict with others. It is by creating criminal law and other aspects of public policy that powerful groups protect and maintain their interests. He insists that: 'Public policy itself is a manifestation of an interest structure in politically organised society' (2008 [1970]: 39).

Box 3.1 sets out Quinney's theoretical position on the link between conflict and crime.

Box 3.1: Quinney (2008 [1970]) *The Social Reality of Crime*

An important dimension of Quinney's argument is the view that the dominant group in society is able to construct not only 'crime', but also 'the reality of crime', which is eventually accepted by the masses. The powerful, keen to shape the world in a certain way, create ideas and provide information that influence people's views. For example, information and images that do not necessarily mirror actual reality may be communicated to the masses through media outlets. The objective is typically to shape public perception of the nature of crime, the characteristics of the typical offender and the best strategies for responding to crime. This is the process of constructing a 'social reality of crime' that fails to capture the true reality of crime. In the quotations below, Quinney outlines these arguments:

Conflict is especially prevalent in societies with diverse value systems and normative groups. Experience teaches us we cannot expect to find consensus on all or most values and norms in such societies. (Quinney, 2008 [1970]: 9)

Conflict and power are inextricably linked in the conception of society presented here. The differential distribution of power produces conflict between competing groups, and conflict, in turn, is rooted in the competition for power. (Quinney, 2008 [1970]: 11)

Groups that have the power to gain access to the decision-making process also inevitably control the lives of others. A major assumption in my conception of society, therefore, is the importance of interest groups in shaping public policy.

Public policy is formed so as to represent the interests and values of groups that are in positions of power... (Quinney, 2008 [1970]: 12)

Law is made by men, representing special interests, who have the power to translate their interests into public policy. (Quinney, 2008 [1970]: 35)

Quinney (2008 [1970]: 15-23) summed up his conflict theory of crime in the following six propositions. The first defines crime and the sixth combines the features of the first five propositions. Therefore, the four middle propositions present a theory that describes the phenomena that heighten the likelihood of crime. The propositions are interrelated and they illumine the processes and conditions that converge to create the social reality of crime in capitalist societies:

1. DEFINITION OF CRIME: Crime is a definition of human conduct that is created by authorised agents in a politically organised society (p 15).
2. FORMULATION OF CRIMINAL DEFINITIONS: Criminal definitions describe behaviours that conflict with the interests of segments of society that have the power to shape public policy (p 16).
3. APPLICATION OF CRIMINAL DEFINITIONS: Criminal definitions are applied by the segments of society that have the power to shape the enforcement and administration of criminal law (p 18).
4. DEVELOPMENT OF BEHAVIOUR PATTERNS IN RELATION TO CRIMINAL DEFINITIONS: Behaviour patterns are structured in segmentally organised society in relation to criminal definitions, and within this context, persons engage in actions that have relative probabilities of being defined as criminal (p 20).
5. CONSTRUCTION OF CRIMINAL CONCEPTIONS: Conceptions of crime are constructed and diffused in the segments of society by various means of communication (p 22).
6. 6. THE SOCIAL REALITY OF CRIME: The social reality of crime is constructed by the formulation and application of criminal definitions, the development of behaviour patterns related to criminal definitions, and the construction of criminal conceptions (p 23).

Thus, Quinney (2008 [1970]) believes that the propensity of the powerful to formulate laws corresponds directly with the level of conflict in society. Together, the very definition of the terms 'crime' and 'criminal' and the types of punishment inflicted, all reflect the interests of the powerful. The law changes in line with the changing interests of the powerful. Where the law reflects interests that are no longer relevant to the powerful, the law is changed to bring it in line accordingly. In all these arrangements, those who have interests in, or who engage in, behaviours that are inconsistent with the interests of the powerful (that are enshrined in the law) have two options. Either they change their behaviour or they do nothing and have their behaviour defined as 'criminal'. Crime is a definition that is applied mainly to the behaviour of the powerless if such behaviour is considered to be in conflict with the interests of the powerful. In addition, the actions, prejudices and interpretations of those charged with administering law enforcement also influence the application of criminal labels.

In *Law, Order, and Power*, Chambliss and Seidman (1971) also argued that society is divided into diverse groups that are in conflict with each other. They described the law is the product of conflict and compromise between groups who are engaged in a struggle to promote their values and interests. According to Chambliss and Seidman, ultimately, the law comes to reflect the values and interests of groups with superior political and economic standing. As such, these groups are less likely than other groups to have their behaviour and activities labelled as legal violations or crime. It follows that therefore, the law is an instrument of power that is used to protect the interests of the powerful in a conflict-ridden society. Criminal justice officials, including the police and the courts, implement the law using strategies that work to the advantage of those with superior political and economic power, but which disadvantage others. Those with superior power can conceal their violation, or manoeuvre themselves out of the law-enforcement process, through covert negotiations or the robust legal defence facilities available to them. Indeed, Chambliss and Seidman argued that the historical function of the law has been to control the behaviour of the less powerful and to protect the financial and other interests of the powerful.

The foregoing discussion about conflict perspectives reveals the diversity of perspectives in that tradition. That said, some unifying themes can be identified. For example, conflict theorists appear to share the view that what is defined as criminal behaviour is really behaviour that is consistent with the values and interests of groups that do not conform to dominant values (see also Bernard, 1981). Ultimately, what makes behaviour 'criminal' is the ability of some groups to influence the creation of laws in ways that represent their values and interests and also criminalise other groups.

Criticisms

Conflict perspectives have been criticised for several reasons. Some reject the view that conflict in societies shapes the creation of laws and definitions of criminal behaviour. The critics argue that such a view does not account for crimes that are included in criminal codes not as a result of conflict in society or the struggle for control, but because these crimes are consensually recognised as deserving of their criminal status because it is beneficial to society to view them as such (Chambliss, 1975). In addition, some point out that the perspectives do no acknowledge that many crimes are not the product of political struggle between groups struggling for dominance. People who belong to the same group may victimise each other. There is also the argument that conflict theorists portray the labelled deviant as passive victims of inequitable social, economic and political conditions. Furthermore, conflict theory has been criticised by those who argue that it does not explain why those whose interests are marginalised accept unfair conditions that do not serve their interests (see, generally, Burke, 2009). Bernard (1981) identifies additional limitations of the conflict perspective. He points out that those who consider the prevailing order to be perfectly acceptable would disagree with the view of the conflict theorists that crime is the product of power arrangements that inhere in the social order. There is also the criticism that conflict theorists are unable to challenge the unequal status quo that they themselves allude to. This is because any attempt to do so will (in line with their own explanatory framework) amount to a struggle to promote their own interests, and assert their will on others.

Bernard (1981) also points out that conflict theorists do not align themselves with any moral position on the constitution of society or the composition of the criminal law. It is also argued that conflict theorists do not proffer any views about the quality and impact of crimes. For example, they do not consider the social harms that are caused by the activities of the powerful, or the revolutionary activities of the oppressed that tend to be criminalised. From a conflict perspective, ideas about what constitutes the ideal society and morally acceptable criminal laws would be relative to each group's views about the moral values and interests that should shape the criminal law. The latter will also influence levels of conformity. Those whose interests are enshrined in the law are more likely to comply with the law compared with those whose interests are not represented. The foregoing indicates that conflict criminologists adopt an objective stance. They do not prescribe what the dominant values of interests in society should be or which values or interests should shape the criminal law. Critics reject this position and the suggestion that objectivity and non-partisanship can be features of criminological theorising. They argue that criminological perspectives that claim to be value-free and do not explicitly align themselves with the powerless, are in fact, supportive of ruling class interests. Indeed, conflict theorists such as Austin Turk, have been criticised for espousing conservative ideals. Richard Quinney injects a degree of radicalism into his account of the nature of crime when he avers that those who are labelled as criminals are not victims of inadequate socialisation, but, rather, rational actors, and their actions (which are labelled as crime) are actions that express their feelings about the unequal order that disadvantages them. By contrast, Turk, for example, argues that marginalised or 'subordinate groups' create deviant subcultures to counter the exclusionary mainstream culture. According to Turk, those he describes as 'subordinate groups' lack adequate socialisation. Therefore, authorities should somehow coerce them into accepting the dominant consensus (Burke, 2009).

Some radical criminologists, such as Marxist criminologists (whose work we shall encounter in Chapter Four), who emphasise the role of structural factors, including exploitative production relations, would argue that Turk's analysis is limited because it overlooks the impact of wider structural factors. Indeed, conflict theorists have been criticised for offering what the critics consider to be ahistorical and decontextualised accounts of the purported link between the culture of marginal groups and crime (Hayward and Young 2012). Conflict theorists, such as Turk and Quinney, have been criticised for not strongly articulating that deviance is a manifestation of conflict in structurally unequal societies (Taylor et al, 1973). Although Quinney did mention that crime might be a rational reaction to conditions created by an unequal and unfair social order, the Marxist criminologists Taylor and colleagues (2013: 276) went on to state that Quinney did not pay sufficient attention to 'structural analysis', which would have illuminated the impact of structural factors on the creation of deviance.

SUMMARY
- The origins of conflict perspectives of law and criminal behaviour date back to the work of Thorsten Sellin, who first suggested that culture conflict might create 'legal violations' or 'norm violations' (Sellin, 1938a: 98).
- Conflict theorists trace the origins of crime to conflict in societies that comprise opposing groups.
- The group or groups that are able to assert their will are able to infuse formal laws with their norms, values or culture.
- The dominant groups are also able to influence law enforcement in ways that protect their interests and control the activities of other groups.
- Therefore, conflict theorists suggest that conflict is an inevitable feature of every society and the law settles the conflict in ways that benefit the dominant group or groups.
- Crime can be described as deviation from formal laws that reflect the norms, values, culture and overall interests of the dominant group.

SAMPLE QUESTIONS
1. Is crime the product of definitions that are attached to the behaviour of less-powerful groups in conflict-ridden societies?
2. Do laws reflect the interests of dominant groups in society?

Notes
[1] Although Marxist criminology is sometimes described as the radical dimension of conflict criminology, this chapter on conflict criminology does not explore Marxist criminology. Marxist criminologists certainly argue that society is characterised by conflict, but they trace the source of conflict primarily to structural factors, such as the capitalist economic system, which, in their view, creates class conflict and crime. Chapter Four explores Marxist criminology in detail.

[2] Quinney and Chambliss later went on to incorporate Marxist themes in their analysis of crime causation and control.

[3] 'Honour' crime is the practice of harming or even murdering a female member of a family for failing to abide by traditional, cultural and/or religious injunctions about how women should conduct themselves. A family member either commits or incites the 'honour' crime (sometimes in collusion with other family members).

[4] By 'authoritative' norms, Turk means legally enacted laws (1966: 346). The 'authorities' are 'political authorities' that enact and enforce laws (1966: 346).

[5] As noted earlier, both Quinney and Chambliss went on to produce work that is now more accurately described as Marxist criminology.

FOUR

Marxist criminology

Introduction

It is clear from the previous chapters that the labelling approach influenced some (but not all) conflict theorists, including Richard Quinney. The perspective also influenced Marxist criminologists. Marxist criminology became popular in the US and UK in the early 1970s. There are diverse Marxist perspectives in criminology, but, in general, compared with the labelling theorists and the conflict theorists, Marxist criminologists espouse more radical views about the origins of crime and deviance. This means that they trace the origins of crime and deviance, and, indeed, other social problems, such as class and racial inequality, to what they consider to be an unequal and unjust social and economic order that should be dismantled (Taylor et al, 1973; Young, 2013).

For Marxist criminologists, a key objective is to demonstrate that capitalism[1] is a mode of production that is riddled with contradictions that create class conflict and crime (Chambliss, 1975). A wider objective is to shift the focus of criminological analysis away from positivistic theories of crime that trace causality to the individual (particularly individuals who are located on the lowest levels of the social strata). According to the criminologists who introduced Marxist criminology in Britain, Ian Taylor, Paul Walton and Jock Young (1975: 234):

> What many radical deviancy theorists, Marxist or otherwise are attempting to do is to move criminology away from a focus on the 'criminality' of the poor, the pathologising of 'deviant' behaviour into categories derived from biology, psychology or positivist sociology, and to abolish the distinction between the study of human deviation and the study of the functioning of States, and ruling-class ideologies as a whole.

Origins of Marxist criminology

As mentioned in Chapter Two, the foundational perspectives in critical criminology grew out of a period in 1960s and early to mid-1970s when social activism proliferated on both sides of the Atlantic (but mainly in the US) and produced several radicalised scholars (Downes and Rock, 2011). The socio-economic structures of several jurisdictions across Europe and America were also undergoing significant transformation. In the latest revision of *The New Criminology*, which is the seminal text that launched Marxist criminology in

Britain, Jock Young (2013) pointed out that *The New Criminology* was written when Fordism[2] was undergoing a decline, alongside its accompanying features of stable employment buffered by a strong manufacturing economy, family stability and more homogeneous communities (Young, 2013). This period was marked by rising unemployment and crime rates (particularly property crime). Some trace these developments to the adverse economic conditions of post-industrialism, which disenfranchised the unskilled population (Reiner, 2012b). In that period, some Marx-inspired scholars began to articulate what they described as growing socio-economic inequality in capitalist societies, typified by an unequal distribution of power and wealth. These scholars also pointed to the conflict that arose from this inequality of power and wealth, and the limited ability of capitalism to address the conflict (Downes and Rock, 2011). The Marx-inspired scholars emphasised the relevance of the labelling approach, which had (albeit only to a limited extent in the view of the Marx-inspired scholars) drawn attention to how power shapes the construction of deviance and responses to it. According to Marxist criminologists, the labelling perspective provided the basis for a more extensive exploration of what they considered to be the inextricable link between the structural conditions of capitalist society and the origins of crime and deviance. Marxist criminologists were, as such, heavily influenced by the labelling approach.

Despite these antecedents, as we have seen in Chapter Two, Marxist criminologists in Britain accused the labelling theorists and mainstream criminologists of overlooking the wider structural factors that cause crime and deviance. They argued that the labelling perspective did not provide a suitably radical account of the origins of crime and deviance. In their view, the labelling perspective did not pay sufficient attention to wider societal structures that create power differentials in capitalist societies and render the less powerful more vulnerable to deviant labels and criminalisation compared with the powerful.

Early Marxist criminologists drew on diverse theoretical and intellectual traditions, from the labelling tradition to versions of Marxist theory. They also share some ideas in common with the conflict perspectives described in Chapter Three. For example, like the conflict theorists cited in Chapter Three, Marxist criminologists argue that society is not characterised by consensus, but by conflict. Thus, Marxist criminologists maintain that capitalist societies comprise different groups who are keen to protect their interests, and who are therefore in conflict with each other. However, while conflict theorists believe that society comprises diverse subgroups, early Marxist criminologists maintained that society primarily comprises ruling-class capitalists, who own the means of production, and an exploited working class, who are employed by the ruling class to maintain the production processes that sustain capitalism. The working class have to sell their labour for the wages they need for their survival. The conflict between both groups produces crime and deviance. We shall examine this contention later on in this chapter. For now, it is worth noting that unlike the labelling perspective, and the conflict perspective, Marxist criminologists trace the causes of crime and deviance to the unequal distribution of power and material wealth in capitalist societies.

They believe that crime and deviance originate from the conflict between groups over the distribution of societal wealth and resources. Indeed, as mentioned earlier, conflict theorists such as Quinney and Chambliss revised their ideas in the late 1970s and began to integrate Marx-inspired ideas about the struggle for societal resources into their views about the links between conflict and crime. Quinney (1974; 1975, 1980 [1977]), for example, viewed the criminal law as an instrument that the state uses to control groups whose actions threaten the capitalist social order. Chambliss (1975) traced the origins of crime to the unequal distribution of wealth, and the exploitation of the working class in capitalist societies by the ruling class (the capitalists).

Thus, unlike the labelling perspective and the conflict perspective, Marxist criminologists were more explicit in their critique of the status quo (the prevailing social, economic and political order) of capitalist societies. They described the status quo as inherently unjust. They argued that in capitalist societies, social, economic and political structures and institutions operate to the advantage of the ruling class. The activities of the lower classes – the proletariat – which threaten the status quo are defined as crime. Therefore, the state is considered by Marxist criminologists to be far from neutral in the creation of crime and deviance.

Added to the influence of the labelling perspective, it goes without saying that Marxist criminologists were heavily influenced by aspects of Marxist theory. Karl Mark, the founder of Marxism, did not develop a systematic theory of crime and criminal law. Taylor and colleagues (2013: 222; see also Taylor et al, 1973), the pioneers of Marxist criminology in the UK, did acknowledge that:

> Karl Marx, concentrating on problems of political economy and the relationships of capital and labour, did not write a great deal specifically on the subject of crime and deviance. There is little evidence that Marx had anything more than a passing interest in crime as an aspect of human behaviour.

However, as the conflict theorist (and later Marxist theorist) William Chambliss (1975: 149) notes, 'the logic of Marxian theory' or the fundamental tenet of Marxism lends itself to critical analysis of established institutions in capitalist societies, including the criminal justice system. Moreover, Karl Marx himself believed that ruling-class capitalists use the law and other means to protect their interests and repress the activities of the working class. This implies that the law is not a set of objective and consensually agreed norms, but an instrument that is used to protect capitalist imperatives. Indeed, Marx's position on the Factory Acts of 19th-century England illustrates his instrumental view of the law. Marx was of the view that the Factory Acts of 1833 were created to fulfil specific economic and political objectives (see, eg, Reiner, 2012b). Although he did acknowledge that the regulations provided several advantages for workers – for example, it imposed limits on the working day – the regulations were put in place to ensure the steady supply of labour and, ultimately, to ensure that the British economy could enjoy sustained growth and stability (Booth, 1978). According to Reiner (2012b), Marx's analysis of the English Factory Acts demonstrates that, like Marxist criminologists, Marx did consider the impact of structural factors, such as the prevailing economic system (or the prevailing mode of production), on the creation of laws and policies.

Marx and Engels also recognised that a capitalist economic system could potentially generate conflict and crime. They argued that industrial capitalism was characterised by exploitive and oppressive working conditions. In their view, the capitalists who own the means of production oversaw these conditions. The adverse conditions disadvantaged the working class, and gave rise to an even more marginalised 'unproductive' and 'dangerous class' or the 'lumpenproletariat'[3] with no role in production, or the struggle between the classes for control of resources in capitalist societies (Taylor et al, 1973, 2013: 31; Matthews, 2012: 94). Engels argued that the exploitation and oppression of workers in industrial capitalist societies created a sense of hopelessness, that rendered the workers more likely to commit specific types of offences, such as stealing from the wealthy. Engels (1845) also maintained that the crimes of the working class could, indeed, represent individual acts of rebellion against their demoralisation under capitalist exploitation. The crimes serve as a means of expressing their contempt for those who exploit them (see also Taylor et al, 1973, 2013; Lynch, 2011). For Marx and Engels, property crime appeared to be prevalent in capitalist societies. However, both theorists insisted that the equitable distribution of wealth should ensure that everyone has access to the resources they need. This should, in turn, reduce property crime (Marx 1842/1975; Engels 1845/1975).

As Matthews (2012) notes, although Marx and Engels provided informative (albeit limited) accounts of how the crimes of the working class (and those they described as the lumpenproletariat) might emerge from contradictions inherent in capitalist societies, their analysis was limited because they did not consider how capitalism might also create opportunities for the crimes of the ruling or dominant class. Matthews (2012: 94) asserts rightly points out that the working class and the so-called lumpenproletariat are not responsible for all crimes.

Willem Adrian Bonger (1876–1940) was the first to apply Marxist views to the study of crime. He has been described as the 'first Marxist criminologist' because he sought to demonstrate how the social, political and economic structures of capitalist societies create crime (Matthews, 2012: 94). Reiner (2012b: 310–11) describes Bonger as 'an ethically inspiring figure, who pioneered many themes of subsequent radical (and indeed liberal) criminology … a pioneer of the political economy of crime and control'.

Bonger (1916; 1969) argued that capitalism is criminogenic because it gives rise to values and conditions that create crime. This is because, in Bonger's view, capitalism creates egoism (or self-interest), which is the pursuit of selfish interests at the expense of others. By its nature, capitalism discourages altruism and encourages the values of competition and consumerism across all sections of society. Competition as a prevailing societal value manifests itself in the struggle for societal resources – particularly material resources. Consumerism as another prevailing value promotes the acquisition of material resources above other values. It encourages people to become preoccupied with acquiring material things that they do not need. Bonger insisted that consumerism triggers an inordinate desire to consume goods and services irrespective of affordability. People sometimes resort to extreme measures to acquire these goods and services, including excessive work, indebtedness and criminal activity. Bonger also argued that capitalist marketing strategies boost consumerism, which affects all sections of society. Thus, capitalism heightens competition and material aspiration, or consumerism, and, in turn, makes people unable to resist the urges of predation in the event of economic hardship (see also Reiner, 2012b; Matthews, 2012). That said, Bonger believed that because the bourgeoisie or the dominant class control the operation of the law, the proletariat are more vulnerable to criminalisation for the adverse forms of behaviour that capitalism engenders (see also Akers and Sellers, 2009).

Bonger did go on to describe crime as the product of multi-causal factors. He identified psychological factors and situational factors, also contribute to crime. Nevertheless, his instrumental view of the law as a system that operates to the advantage of the more powerful anticipated the work of the labelling theorists (Reiner, 2012b) and other critical criminologists.

The Marxist criminologists of the 1970s and 1980s criticised Bonger's work for being eclectic, mainly because he described crime as the product of multi-causal factors. Ironically, some Marist criminologists subsequently went ahead to advocate a 'fully social theory' of crime, which, in itself, reads like a catalogue of multiple causal factors (Taylor et al, 1973; Reiner, 2012b). They also criticised him for his alleged 'failure to "appreciate" crime as diversity', and for being a 'correctionalist' who was motivated by his aversion for disorder (Reiner, 2012b: 311; see also Taylor et al, 1973: 232, 235).

Despite earlier work by the likes of Bonger, it is argued that radical criminology did not become popular in the UK and US until the 1960s and 1970s. As Reiner (2012b: 209) notes: 'Until the flowering of radical criminology in the 1960s and 1970s little systematic attention was given by Marxists or others on the Left to crime or criminal justice'. An overview of the emergence and key tenets of Marxist criminology on both sides of the Atlantic is provided below.

Key arguments in Marxist criminology

There are diverse Marxist perspectives in criminology and they draw on vastly different variants of Marxism (Greenberg, 1993). However, they share specific features in common. These can be described as: a conflict view of contemporary societies, including Western societies such as the US and the UK; an emphasis on the political economy of crime in capitalist societies; and a rejection of mainstream criminology for accepting without question the legal definition of crime. In the 1960s and the 1970s, Marxist criminologists began to argue that contrary to the presumptions of mainstream criminologists, crime is not the product of defects within the individual. Instead, they maintained that crime is the product of defects within the structure of capitalist societies, which ultimately render marginalised groups more vulnerable to criminalisation than powerful groups. Therefore, criminology should focus on identifying the causes of criminalisation, not the causes of crime. There are two broad perspectives within Marxist criminology. Both perspectives share in common key ideas about the political economy of crime, but they differ markedly in their description of the state's role in the creation of crime and the administration of crime control in capitalist societies. The two perspectives are classified as instrumental Marxism and structural Marxism.

Instrumental Marxists (Quinney, 1974; 1975; 1977; Chambliss, 1975) cite the ruling class (the wealthy capitalists) as the more powerful group in capitalist societies. According to the instrumental Marxists, the ruling class exerts pressure on the state to criminalise those (the less powerful) whose actions threaten the capitalist social order. Thus, the ruling class are able to ensure that the criminal law and the criminal justice system operate to their advantage and criminalises those whose actions jeopardise their interests (Henry and Einstadter, 2006). The state complies because the ruling class control the means of production and, by implication, the wealth of society. Chambliss (1975: 230) remarks that in capitalist societies, 'The state becomes an instrument of the ruling class enforcing laws here not there, according to the realities of political power and economic conditions'.

Some Marxist criminologists reject this conceptualisation of the state's role. They argue that the ruling class are not as cohesive or as able to manipulate the state as the instrumental Marxists suggest (Chambliss and Seidman, 1971; Greenberg, 1993, cited in Matthews, 2012; Spitzer, 1975). Structural Marxists insist that the state plays a more autonomous role in the criminalisation of less–powerful groups whose actions threaten capitalist interests. It uses its power proactively to maintain the power structures and the dynamics of production that sustain the unequal capitalist order (Lynch and Groves, 1986). Indeed, it may control the excesses of capitalism by also criminalising those capitalists whose actions expose the deleteriousness of capitalism. However, its primary agenda is to criminalise the disenfranchised whose actions threaten capitalist interests. From this perspective, the criminal law and the criminal justice system are mechanisms for preserving the interests of the ruling class (Quinney, 1974; 1975; 1980 [1977]).

Marxist criminology in the US

In the 1970s in the US, some criminologists expanded on the idea that societies are characterised by conflict. These criminologists assumed a more radical stance by incorporating versions of Marxism into their analysis of crime and crime control. For example, in his article titled 'Toward a Political Economy of Crime', William Chambliss (1975) traced crime to the conflict that inheres in capitalist societies. He emphasised that capitalism is a mode of production that is characterised by specific contradictions that give rise to class conflict and crime. According to Chambliss, one such contradiction is that capitalism is sustained by creating in the masses the irrational desire to consume the goods and services produced by the capitalist system. The system also relies on ensuring that some members of the working class are kept almost impoverished. This sharpens their desire to earn more in order to consume more. The capitalists ensure that the ever-looming presence of a reserve labour force incentivises people to work at demoralising jobs. These economic relations amount to another contradiction of capitalism, namely, the masses are unable to earn enough money to purchase the goods and services that they have been conditioned to irrationally desire. This is a contradiction that also gives rise to perceived exploitation and violent reactions by the masses. Chambliss maintained that the state labels the violent reactions of the exploited classes as crime.

For Chambliss, another contradiction that gives rise to crime in capitalist societies stems from the class division in such societies. Capitalist societies are divided into a 'ruling class that owns the means of production [the resources that are used to produce goods and services], and a subservient class that works for wages' (Chambliss, 1975: 150–1). This class division in capitalist societies creates conflict between the classes. As mentioned earlier, there are also exploitative social and economic relations in such societies: the capitalists/ruling class exploit the subservient class. The latter group is variously described as the proletariat, the working class or the subservient class (Taylor et al, 1973; Chambliss, 1975). Chambliss argued that the exploitative social and economic relations deepen the conflict between the classes, and the conflict ultimately manifests itself in the form of rebellions and riots among the exploited class. Crime emerges from this class warfare or from 'the struggle between classes' (Chambliss, 1975: 151), and the state uses its power to create laws that define the rebellious acts of the exploited class as criminal. Chambliss therefore espoused an instrumental view of the role of the state in the creation of crime. He went on to comment that, in response to acts of rebellion:

> the state, acting in the interests of the owners of the means of production will pass laws designed to control, through the application of state sanctioned force, those acts of the proletariat which threaten the interests of the bourgeoisie. In this way, then, acts come to be defined as criminal.... The criminal law is thus *not* a reflection of custom (as other theorists have argued) but is a set of rules laid down by the state in the interests of the ruling class, and resulting from the conflicts that inhere in class structured societies; criminal behaviour is, then, the inevitable expression of class conflict resulting from the inherently exploitative nature of economic relations. What makes the behaviour of some criminal is the coercive power of the state to enforce the will of the ruling class. (Chambliss, 1975: 151; emphasis in original)

This suggests that criminal behaviour is an expression of resistance by the subservient classes against exploitative social relations. These views are consistent with Marx's 'primitive rebellion thesis', which refers to the revolution of the oppressed classes (Bernard, 1981).

Chambliss set out a series of propositions which, in his view, illuminate a Marxian analysis of the nature of crime and the operation of the criminal law. He stated that: acts that are defined as crime are defined as such to serve the interests of the ruling class; the ruling class can violate laws without repercussions while the subservient classes are more vulnerable to punishment if their acts violate the law; and greater industrialisation in capitalist societies will exacerbate the differences between the bourgeoisie and the proletariat and precipitate the expansion of penal law to ensure that it can be used to control of the proletariat.

Chambliss also wrote about the role that crime plays in society. In doing so, he again revealed an instrumental view of crime. He believed that crime serves several purposes. For example, it lowers the availability of surplus labour because it provides employment opportunities for many including criminologists, law-enforcement agents and others. The criminal law also serves the function of masking the problems caused by the oppressive economic conditions and the machinations of the capitalist class who oversee the exploitative economic order. It redirects the attention of the lower classes to the members of their own class. The criminal law achieves this because the actions of this class tend to be defined as crime. They, not the capitalist class, are often portrayed as the source of crime and other social problems. Chambliss thus proposed that crime is a social construction: it becomes a 'reality' when those who use it to serve their own interests create it (1975: 152).

Another issue Chambliss addressed is the aetiology or causes of criminal behaviour. In his view, people of all classes commit crime for reasons that are rational within their position in the class structure. According to Chambliss (1975: 152), the type of crime an individual commits is consistent with that individual's 'class position' or 'life conditions'. For example, in Chambliss's view, the ruling class, 'who control the political or economic resources of society', commit crimes of exploitation, including bribery, racketeering and other white-collar crimes. The lower class commit street crimes or acts of public disorder, and they lack the resources to pay their way out of law enforcement (Chambliss, 1975: 158). Therefore, Chambliss formed the view that there is no difference among the classes regarding their propensity to commit crime. However, the lower classes dominate official crime statistics because the ruling class have the power and resources to avoid law enforcement. They can bribe officials and/or employ expensive lawyers to help them escape law enforcement. Moreover, the state defines acts of resistance by the exploited classes as crime in an effort to protect the interests of the ruling class. By contrast, the harmful actions of the ruling class are usually not labelled as crimes by law-enforcement agents. Thus, as Chambliss (1974: 165) put it:

> criminal behaviour by any reasonable definition is not concentrated
> in the lower classes. Thus, to the extent that a theory of the causes of
> criminal behaviour depends on the assumption that there is a higher

rate of criminality in the lower classes, to that extent, the theory is suspect … criminality is simply not something that people have or don't have; crime is not something some people so and others don't. Crime is a matter of who can pin the label of crime on whom.

In addition, Chambliss pointed out that crime is not a static phenomenon: it varies across societies and its causes can be traced to societal structures, namely, 'the political and economic structures of society' (Chambliss, 1975: 152). Like some other Marxist criminologists, Chambliss maintained that socialist[4] societies, where the masses and the state control the means of production (not private individuals), are less likely to have intense class struggle.

Like Chambliss, Quinney (1974; 1975; 1980 [1977]) is another US-based writer who also contributed to the development of Marxist criminology. Quinney (1974: 53) argued that capitalist societies comprise diverse social groups that include: 'professionals, small business men, office workers and cultural workmen'. But, Quinney (1974: 53) described the main classes in these societies as: the ruling (dominant) class and the subordinate class. Adverse relations between the two classes shape the political, economic and social conditions that exist in these societies. Thus, like Chambliss, Quinney (1974: 53) maintained that there is division in capitalist societies because they comprise two classes that are in conflict with each other. According to Quinney (1974: 53), members of the ruling class generally share the same interests. The ruling class is: 'that class which owns and controls the means of production and which is able, by virtue of the economic power thus conferred upon it, to use the state as its instrument for the domination of society'. Here, again, we can observe an instrumental view of the role of the state. Quinney argued that the state criminalises those whose activities threaten the interests of the ruling class. The state has to protect the interests of the ruling class so that capitalism can thrive unabated. Indeed, Quinney described that the state as a creation of the ruling class in capitalist societies, and serves as an instrument that can be used to control the subordinate classes.

In US contexts specifically, Quinney identified the ruling class/capitalists as those who control large businesses and financial institutions in the US. He described them as the people who:

> make the decisions that affect the lives of those who are subordinate to this [ruling] class … it is according to the interests of the ruling class that American society is governed … in general they share common interests, and they exclude members of the other classes from the political process entirely. (Quinney, 1974: 54)

Quinney maintained that the ruling class has a fundamental goal, which is to sustain the existing capitalist order in order to protect its interests, including its financial interests and general wellbeing. In a bid to protect its interest, the ruling class uses the legal system to respond to internal 'threats to the established order'. The ruling class uses the criminal law to 'maintain domestic order'. Members of the ruling class hold the 'weapons of crime control' and they control the operation of the law (Quinney, 1975: 195). They also use military power to respond to external threats from abroad that upset the equilibrium of US capitalism internationally. Thus, the legal system in a capitalist state, like the US, exists and operates to protect the interests of the ruling class.

However, the state[5] is the agent that acts on behalf of the ruling class since the ruling class cannot control the legal system directly, but must do so through the state. For Quinney, the workings of the state is therefore of fundamental concern. He argued that the role of the state in a capitalist society is to protect the interests of the ruling class capitalists who control the means of production. Crime control according to Quinney is the key mechanism the state uses to promote the interests of capitalists and capitalism. Thus, from Quinney's point of view, the capitalist state is not an impartial unit. It does not represent the interests of the diverse and competing groups that make up civil society. Rather, the capitalist state operates as an instrument of coercion that protects the interests of the ruling class or the 'dominant economic class' (Quinney, 1974: 16).

Quinney (1980 [1977]) went on to argue that given the foregoing premises, crime is best described as a response to the particular conditions of capitalism. From Quinney's point of view, crimes of the subordinate class can be described as 'crimes of accommodation'. These are conventional crimes that are committed for survival, and examples include acquisitive predatory crimes like burglary and robbery. Additional examples are interpersonal crimes, such as the violent crimes that are perpetrated by the members of subordinate class against other members of their class. These crimes can be described as the product of the material inequality and exploitation that capitalism fosters (Quinney, 1980 [1977]: 47). 'Crimes of resistance' are acts of rebellion by the subordinate class or their reactions against the oppressive conditions of capitalism (Quinney, 1980 [1977]: 47). The crimes are targeted at the dominant class. Quinney also identified 'crimes of domination' as the crimes the ruling capitalist class commit to further their economic interests and to maintain the capitalist order. Examples of such crimes include organised crime and corporate crimes like 'price fixing'. Quinney described these crimes as 'crimes of economic domination'. 'Crimes of control' are the crimes criminal justice officials commit against accused persons, and 'crimes of government' are the crimes committed by elected and appointed state officials. Social harms are acts or omissions that are not necessarily defined as crime by the criminal law. Examples include discrimination on the basis of ethnicity and/or gender. For Quinney (1980 [1977]), then, capitalism is an economic system that creates criminogenic conditions, and the appropriate response is to replace capitalism with socialism. Quinney (2000: 107) put it that: 'only with the collapse of capitalist society and the creation of a new society, based on socialist principles, will there be a solution to the crime problem'. Quinney (2000: 170) also argued that:

> The only lasting solution to the crisis of capitalism is socialism. Under late, advanced capitalism, socialism will be achieved in the struggle of all people who are oppressed by the capitalist mode of production....

Other writers who contributed to Marxist criminology in the US and elsewhere include: Gordon (1973), who traced crime to the US economic system; Spitzer (1975), who argued that capitalism creates a class of economic outcasts who sometimes engage in deviant activities; and Greenberg (1993), who also wrote extensively in the field (see also Russell, 2002).

Marxist criminology in Britain: the new criminology

Marxist criminology gained ascendancy in Britain following a series of discussions by a group of young sociologists in the 1960s and early 1970s. As mentioned in Chapter One, the discussions took place during 14 conferences that were held between 1968 and 1973. These conferences were themed National Deviancy Conferences (NDCs). Jock Young (1988: 163), one of the original proponents of Marxist criminology in Britain, notes that 'The birth of radical criminology in this country in an organisational form was the National Deviancy Conference (NDC) formed in July 1968'. The first meeting was held at the University of York in 1968 (Young, 2009).

The conferences provided a forum for radical academics to challenge what they described as the orthodox (mainstream) criminological theories of the Institute of Criminology at Cambridge University and the Home Office Research Unit in England (Rock, 2012). In their view, the institute focused narrowly on the technocratic function of assisting the state in controlling the members of working class to ensure their compliance with ruling–class values and interests. Mainstream theorists were also accused of overlooking the role of the powerful and the state in constructing deviance and in using the criminal law to control those whose actions appeared to threaten the established capitalist social order. The institute's strategies were, as such, deemed to be primarily conservative and consistent with the agenda and priorities of the Home Office in England.[6]

The early proponents of Marxist theory in Britain described mainstream criminological theories as 'establishment theories' and traced the roots of these theories to positivist determinism, particularly the notion that a link exists between individual pathology and crime. Marxist criminologists in Britain rejected positivism, which was the prevailing orthodoxy within criminal justice policy and practice at the time. Jock Young observes that 'Positivism was perhaps the worst enemy' (Taylor et al, 2013: 23). The 'new criminologists' described the positivists' explanations as deterministic. This is because, in their view, the positivists overlooked individual agency and traced the aetiology of crime to factors beyond the control of the offender. Positivists were also criticised for ignoring what the Marxist criminologists described as the inequitable economic conditions in capitalist societies, and for giving intellectual legitimacy to self-styled 'experts' or 'fake scientists' who claimed that they could use scientific methods to identify universal causes of human behaviour. These 'experts' presided over decision-making in various institutions of control, from criminal justice agencies and mental hospitals to social work agencies and drug clinics (Taylor et al, 1973, 2013: 23).

Marxist criminologists in Britain criticised the so-called 'experts', including criminal justice practitioners and those they disparagingly described as 'administrative criminologists'.[7] They criticised these criminologists for accepting without question that crime is the product of defects within the individual 'criminal' and not defects within the structure of the prevailing capitalist order. They also criticised the labelling perspective and the conflict perspectives for failing to problematise the social, economic and political structures of capitalism. According to Marxist criminologists, these structures provided the impetus for the criminalisation of those whose actions appeared to be inimical to the interests of the ruling class/capitalists. In addition, as we shall see below, although the Marxist criminologists drew on aspects of labeling theory, they criticised labelling theorists for their deterministic portrayal of the labelled deviant as a passive victim who accepts the label without resistance (Downes and Rock, 2011; Taylor et al, 1973, 2013).

Marxist criminologists in Britain, like their US counterparts, sought to shift the focus of criminological theorising away from the individual who is labelled as an offender. A key objective was to direct attention to the role of structural factors such as the capitalist economic system. They drew on labelling theory and Marxist ideas, and they described capitalism as criminogenic. They argued that capitalism creates the 'power and need to criminalise' (Taylor et al, 1973, 2013). A key difference in the approach of the early Marxist criminologists in Britain was the shift away from what they described as the economic determinism of earlier Marxist approaches to the study of crime. Economic determinism is the view that economic inequality or poverty is the sole factor that creates conflict and crime (Reiner, 2012b). The British Marxist criminologists argued instead that crime and deviance can be described as the rational response of exploited groups to exploitative and adverse social conditions in capitalist societies. Marxists criminologists also drew attention to what they considered to be the complicity of the state in preserving an unfair status quo in which classism, racism, sexism and heterosexism are embedded in institutions and policy agendas (Walklate, 2011).

The NDC produced seminal work in the field of criminology. Two key pieces of work are the seminal text referred to earlier, titled *The New Criminology* (Taylor et al, 1973), and the writings that emerged from the University of Birmingham's Centre for Contemporary Cultural Studies (CCCS), led by Stuart Hall. Jock Young, who was one of the key proponents of Marxist criminology at the time (from the late 1960s to the mid-1970s), noted that *The New Criminology* was very much a product of the socio-political conditions of the late 1960s. The text set out what has been described as a 'neo-Marxist' account of crime and crime control (Downes and Rock, 2011: 258). Marxist criminology in Britain emerged amid a shift in criminology and politics to the Left.

Indeed, as noted earlier, the foundational perspectives in critical criminology grew out of a period in the 1960s and early to mid-1970s amid the rise of social activism on both sides of the Atlantic and changes to the structures of Western societies such as the US and the UK.

Marxist criminologists believed that to understand the origins of crime and deviance, it is important to examine, *inter alia*, the structure of capitalist societies. To this end, Marxist criminologists in Britain proposed a 'fully social theory of deviance' that would integrate diverse theoretical traditions. They borrowed from dimensions of ethnomethodology and phenomenology, but they drew mainly on aspects of Marxism and symbolic interactionism to propound their 'fully social theory' of deviance.

The 'fully social theory' of deviance states that to understand the nature of deviance, we must examine its seven dimensions of deviance, namely: its wider origins (its structural conditions); its immediate origins (its social-psychological basis); the act itself; the immediate origins of social reaction (its social-psychological basis); the wider origins of social reaction (its structural conditions); the outcomes of social reaction on the deviant's future behaviour; and the 'nature of the deviant process itself' (Taylor et al, 1973: 270-8; Reiner, 2012b).

Added to their effort to articulate a 'fully social theory of deviance', the Marxist criminologists also sought to redefine the image of the labelled deviant. As already noted, they distanced themselves from what they considered to be the determinism of some Marxist criminologists who portrayed the deviant as a passive victim of adverse socio-economic conditions. They also sought to distance themselves from the determinism they ascribed to the labelling theorists, who, in their view, portrayed the deviant as the passive victim of the deviant label. Therefore, Marxist criminologists in Britain described crime and deviance as acts of resistance by the exploited working class. Some members of the exploited working class engage in acts of resistance. Crime occurs when the state labels their acts of resistance as crime. The deviant is, as such, a fully rational actor with political motives. Crime is a rational response to socio-economic exploitation. It is a means of expressing dissatisfaction with the adverse conditions capitalism generates. The new criminologists also redefined the image of deviance itself. For Marxist criminologists, deviance is not objectively immoral and illegal, but a socially constructed label that the state and its agents attach to acts of rebellion against oppression; crime, then, is a political act. Therefore, the primary concern of criminology should not be to do what the 'administrative criminologists' do, which is to help the state control crime and punish criminals effectively, but to question the origins of crime and criminalisation (Young, 1988: 176). Criminologists should question why the actions of some groups are more likely to be labelled as crime and deviance. It should be acknowledged that individuals who react against exploitative economic conditions, unequal wealth distribution and class conflict in capitalist societies are criminalised to protect the interests of the powerful. Therefore, the best strategy for eradicating crime is to transform society and restore equality. Like the US-based Marxist criminologists, Taylor and colleagues proposed socialism and eventually communism as alternatives to capitalism. They believed that these modes of production would facilitate more equitable wealth distribution, which should, in turn, improve social relations and reduce crime.

Marxist criminology in Britain: the Birmingham school

As mentioned earlier, scholars based in the Birmingham School participated in the NDC and also produced seminal work in the field of Marxist criminology. In *Policing the Crisis: Mugging, the State and Law and Order*, Stuart Hall and his colleagues (1978) developed a more radical articulation of the concept of 'moral panics'[8] (see Box 4.1). They emphasised the structural contexts of moral panics in which the capitalist state, through its social control machinery (from the police to the courts) creates a moral panic as part of the effort to use ideological means to mobilise public support for its agenda. The media plays a significant role (albeit a secondary role) in attuning the public to the ideas that the state and the powerful ruling class wish seek to transmit through the moral panic. Thus, Hall and colleagues averred that the state can achieve popular support for its policies by setting in motion the hallmarks of a classic moral panic, which are: exaggerating the activities of a target population; fuelling public fear and anxiety; and securing legitimacy for draconian sanctions aimed at working-class groups and others who have been marginalised by the unfair capitalist order.

In *Policing the Crisis*, Stuart Hall and his colleagues (1978) described how, in the UK in the 1970s, the state along with the media, created a moral panic about the crime of 'mugging' in order to reassert its hegemony. It promoted the ideology that the social and economic problems of that period could be attributed to the crime of mugging and its perpetrators. Therefore, authoritarian policies were required to address both factors. According to Hall and colleagues, the state employed this strategy because it was undergoing a 'crisis of hegemony'; it was losing public support. In other words, it was losing its ability to govern by consent and it needed to reassert its legitimacy.

In developing these arguments, Hall and colleagues drew on the Italian neo-Marxist Gramsci's conceptualisation of hegemony. They sought to theorise the ideological strategies a state uses to secure public legitimacy and support for its exercise of power and control. For Gramsci, the concept of hegemony can be described as control or domination through ideology. In times of crisis and reduced public acceptance, states may reassert their hegemony by indoctrinating the public with the unquestionable belief that the state is a legitimate entity that deserves public support and legitimacy because it is committed to protecting the interests of all its citizens. In doing so, states seek to secure public support for state power, authority and dominance by consent – not by force. Therefore in the 1970s in response to the crisis of hegemony it faced, the state sought to regain its legitimacy. This crisis occurred because of social and economic developments in that period. There was declining welfare provision, increased acts of resistance by marginalised groups, perceived increases in rates of crime and disorder, and other social problems. Public acceptance of the state's responses to these problems was on the decline. Therefore, the state was losing its legitimacy. Creating a moral panic about the activities of a target group and convincing the public that the group deserved authoritarian responses served as a useful strategy that the state could employ to reassert its hegemony while also mobilising public support (primarily the support of the lower classes) for its authoritarian policies through consent and not by 'overt coercion' (Hall et al, 1978: 59).

Box 4.1: A radical analysis of 'moral panics'

In the text *Policing the Crisis: Mugging, the State and Law and Order*, Hall and colleagues (1978: 18) provided a radical account of the nature and role of moral panics. As mentioned above, they described the British state, through its agents of social control (mainly the police) and the media, created a moral panic about a street crime that was given the label of 'mugging' in the 1970s. Mugging involves using violent means to rob the victim. The objective of the moral panic was to reassert the state's authority and secure legitimacy for its authoritarian policies. In the UK, some sections of the media portrayed the crime of mugging (already a longstanding source of considerable fear in the US) as a new phenomenon. Hall and colleagues described how the police and sections of the media capitalised on deep-rooted negative sentiments about, in particular, young black West Indian men residing in inner-city areas. They capitalised on these sentiments and created a moral panic about the purportedly dangerous activities of this group. They created the impression that the group was largely responsible for most social problems including the rising rates of officially recorded street crimes, particularly mugging. They sought to legitimise the ideology that the crime of mugging is a new and threatening phenomenon that symbolises a general decline of order in society and requires authoritarian responses. It was described as the product of the interactive effect of age (being young), race (being black), gender (being male) and class (deprived, inner-city youths). It has been noted that: 'Though "mugging" was not exclusively a black crime, it was closely associated, in the media and the public mind, with black youth. During 1972–3, there was a major "moral panic" about the growth of mugging' (Critcher, 1993: 167). An extract from the text is presented below.

> We want to know what the social causes of 'mugging' are.... More important is why British society reacts to mugging, in the extreme way it does, at that precise historical conjuncture – the early 1970s. If it is true that muggers suddenly appear on British streets – a fact which, in that stark simplicity, we contest – it is also true that the society enters a moral panic about 'mugging'. And this relates to the larger 'panic' about the 'steadily rising rate of violent crime' which has been growing through the 1960s. And both these panics are about other things than crime, per se. The society comes to perceive crime in general, and 'mugging' in particular, as an index of the disintegration of the social order, as a sign that the 'British way of life' is coming apart at the seams. So the book is also about a society which is slipping into a certain kind of crisis. It tries to examine why and how the themes

> of race, crime and youth – condensed into the image of 'mugging' – come to serve as the articulator of the crisis, as its ideological conductor. It is also about how these themes have functioned as a mechanism for the construction of an authoritarian consensus, a conservative backlash.... How has the 'law-and-order' ideology been constructed? What social forces are constrained and contained by its construction? What forces stand to benefit from it? What role has the state played in its construction? What real fears and anxieties is it mobilising? These are some of the things we mean by 'mugging' as a social phenomenon. It is why a study of 'mugging' has led us inevitably to the general 'crisis of hegemony' in the Britain of the 1970s. This is the ground taken in this book.

Hall and colleagues (1978) argued that as part of the effort to create the impression that the crime of mugging is a new and threatening phenomenon that requires authoritarian responses, official crime statistics depicted qualitatively different offences as street crimes. This skewed the statistics at the time and created the impression that there had been a significant rise in rates of violent street crimes. Consequently, public anxiety and intolerance for these crimes intensified in that period. When three mixed-ethnicity young men – Paul Storey, James Duigan and Mustapha Fuat – were convicted of stealing from a man in a street in Birmingham, in the process causing serious injury to the victim, the crime attracted significant media attention. Most of the news reports cited the word 'mugging' in their headline. This must have exacerbated public anxiety about the crime. Perhaps unsurprisingly, the boys received exceptionally harsh sentences. Paul Story received a 20-year sentence, while James Duigan and Mustapha Fuat received 10 years each. Critcher (1993: 167) observes that:

> The sentences passed ... were the climaxes of a process of 'moral panic', which found its need for vengeance fulfilled in the victimisation of three juveniles. The sentences bore no relation to the nature of the crime committed as we understand it, nor did they reflect the relatively limited and wholly non-violent previous records of the three boys.

In the wake of these and other developments, which, according to Hall and colleagues, saw state agents such as the police and sections of the media continue to heighten public anxieties about mugging and the role of young black inner-city young men in the crime, the word 'mugging' came to symbolise the supposed threat posed by young black men living in inner-city 'urban' areas. They were portrayed as the folk-devils; the group responsible not only for mugging but also for the supposed decline in law and order.[9] Mugging itself became emblematic of 'general social crisis and "rising crime" *first*, a particular kind of robbery occurring in British streets second, and later' (Hall et al, 1978: 23, emphasis in original). In other words, anxieties about diverse social problems (including the perceived decline in law and order) evolved into a campaign against the street crime of mugging. As mentioned earlier, Hall and colleagues maintained that the objective of the moral panic was to mobilise public support and legitimacy for state authority, and the exercise of repressive state power, through consent, and not by coercion.

Criticisms

Marxist perspectives have received several criticisms. For example, some believe that by tracing crime to the structure of capitalist societies, Marxist criminologists reify structure and provide a rather deterministic account of crime causation (Downes and Rock, 2011). Feminist criminologists, who began to criticise mainstream criminology and critical criminology in the 1970s, pointed out that the Marxist criminologists of the 1970s overlooked the gender dimension of crime and criminal justice. The feminists argued that Marxist criminologists paid no attention to female offending and victimisation and ignored the impact of gender relations on crime and criminal justice (Mooney 2012). In fairness, it is necessary to point out that this criticism can be (and has been) extended to mainstream criminological theories.

Marxist criminologists and writers in the conflict tradition have also been criticised for failing to explicitly acknowledge that the criminal law and other legislations are not solely designed to criminalise and oppress the less powerful. Critics insist that the law protects all citizens from repression and crime. Some also point out that lawmakers strive to secure public legitimacy and support for the law by taking steps to demonstrate that the law represents the interests of everyone. Thus, the actions of the powerful are occasionally criminalised, and the interests of the powerless may also be taken into account when certain laws are created (Lynch and Stretesky, 2003).

Some critics insist that Marxist criminologists have been unable to explain why several capitalist countries have higher rates of violent crime than others. According to Schichor (1980: 195):

> Taking the United States as the embodiment of capitalist society does not contribute to the understanding of the crime problem either. It does not explain why in countries like England, France, Sweden, Norway, or New Zealand violent crimes are not as frequent as in the United States.

Marxist criminologists have also been taken to task for focusing almost one-dimensionally on crime in capitalist societies while overlooking the crimes that are committed in societies that do not operate a capitalist economy (Shichor, 1980)). They are accused of espousing utopic views because they believe that overthrowing capitalism and replacing it with socialism will significantly reduce crime. Indeed some Marxist criminologists assert that there is no class conflict in socialist societies. Therefore, there is no need to create laws that protect these interests and criminalise those whose actions are considered to be inimical to ruling-class interests. The Marxist criminologist William Chambliss (1975: 153) for example, stated that 'Socialist societies should have much lower rates of crime because the less intense class struggle should reduce the forces leading to and the functions of crime'. We have seen that Richard Quinney, who is another Marxist criminologist, also shared this view about the nature of socialist societies.

Critics reject these ideas as utopian and point out that several socialist societies have high rates of crime. They cite the example of Sweden, which witnessed a steep rise in crime shortly after it replaced its primarily capitalist system with a social-democratic system that is more consistent with socialist ideals (Felson, 1994, cited in Akers and Sellers, 2009). According to Shichor (1980: 196), 'so far in socialist countries the abolition of crime has not become a reality. This fact is obviously a disturbing one for radical criminologists ...'.

There is also the argument that some socialist states operate oppressive regimes (Cohen, 1979). Indeed, several critics emphasise that the oppressive activities that Marxist criminologists attribute to capitalists and to the state can be found in socialist and communist regimes (see, generally, Akers and Sellers, 2009). Reinforcing this, Bernard (1981: 375) states that 'in those societies where capitalism has been overthrown, crime has not been eliminated. In addition, any reduction of crime in these societies appears to be more a function of severely repressive enforcement practices than of the reduction of conflict'.

In response to the foregoing, Marxist criminologists point out that some of the socialist countries the critics cite as examples of oppressive socialist societies[10] cannot be described as 'truly socialist' states. Rather, they are best described as 'state capitalism', 'collectivism' or other systems that aimed to be, but fell short of being, truly socialist states (Greenberg, 1981, cited in Akers and Sellers, 2009: 249).

Marxist criminologists have also been accused of idealism because they believe that revolutionary action by the oppressed working classes is required to overthrow capitalism in order to replace it with socialism. They posit revolutionary transformation as the solution to the problem of crime. Critics insist that these ideas have limited practical value. As Lynch and Groves (1986: 105) observe, Marxist criminology has been described as 'a utopian realm of thought with no relevant policy implications except revolution'.

Some point out that although the 'new criminologists' proposed a fully social theory of deviance, they focused unduly on structural explanations while overlooking the micro-contexts of crime and crime control (Reiner, 2012b). Others, particularly cultural criminologists,[11] believe Marxist criminology provides an account of crime causation that is limited because it overlooks foreground factors that are linked to crime. These factors, according to cultural criminologists, include the thrills, excitement and other emotions of crime (Hayward and Young, 2012).

Another criticism is that Marxist criminologists do not accurately represent the ideas of the pioneers of Marxist theory – Karl Marx and Engels – accurately. As mentioned earlier, Marx and Engels did not write about the causes of crime in much detail. Hirst (1975) reinforces this, and points out that Marxist theory does not address crime and deviance. He states that:

> There is no 'Marxist theory of deviance' either in existence, or which can be developed within orthodox Marxism. Crime and deviance vanish into the general theoretical concerns and specific scientific object of Marxism. Crime and deviance are no more a scientific field of Marxism than education, the family or sport. The objects of Marxist theory are specified by its own concepts: the mode of production, the class struggle, the state, ideology etc. (Hirst, 1975: 204)

Some Marxist criminologists accept the premise of this criticism. For example, the Marxist criminologists who wrote the *New Criminology* refer to themselves as neo-Marxists because they recognise that they revised some of Marx's ideas about the structure of capitalist societies (Taylor et al, 1973). In addition, as Brown (2002) points out, the *New Criminology* drew not only on selected Marxist ideas, but also on an eclectic range of theoretical influences. As noted earlier, Taylor and colleagues (1973: 234) did state that their aim, just like the other 'radical deviancy theorists, Marxist or otherwise', was to, *inter alia*, alter the focus of criminology by moving the discipline away from its focus on the poor, and from the tendency to emphasise biological, psychological or 'positivistic' sociological concepts that depict behaviour as pathological. They also sought to embed the study of deviance within the study of state activity and the ideologies of the ruling class (Taylor et al, 1973: 234).

Another criticism that was levelled at the Marxist perspectives of the 1960s and 1970s is that Marxist criminologists adopted definitions of deviance that appeared to imply that the concept has intrinsic qualities (see also Bernard, 1981). Critics suggest that Marxist criminologists should have explicitly described deviance as nothing more than rules and ideas that are created by the powerful in society (see also Sumner, 1976; Tierney, 2009). There is also the criticism that Marxist criminologists placed class at the centre of their analysis of crime and deviance. Critics assert that the class distinctions that the Marxists referred to, and the idea that there is a ruling class who own the means of production and who oppress the working class, are now rather obsolete ideas. This is because class is no longer considered to be the key factor that divides groups in advanced capitalist societies. In addition, class difference or even 'class' is no longer as clear-cut as it used to be because of the increased diversity that characterises contemporary several Western capitalist societies (Bernard, 1981). Thus, the relationship between class and ownership of the means of production is far more tenuous than it may have been in the past (Bernard, 1981).

In the 1980s, Marxist criminology came under sustained attack from criminologists whose work we will encounter in Chapter Six. These criminologists are now described as left realists. Perhaps ironically, Jock Young, who was instrumental to the emergence and development of Marxist criminology in Britain in the 1970s, contributed to the emergence of left realism (Lea and Young, 1984, 1993). The left realists criticised their former colleagues in Marxist criminology for ignoring the real victims of crime and for supposedly romanticising or idealising those who commit offences (particularly the members of the working class who commit street crimes, such as property offences). Marxist criminologists were criticised for portraying working-class offenders as the victims of oppressive material conditions who are engaged in equitable wealth redistribution, or, in other words, as 'amateur Robin Hoods' involved in 'righteous attempts to redistribute wealth' (Lea and Young, 1984: 262; see also Rock, 2012). In short, Marxist criminologists were criticised for defining offending behaviour as a form of political activism or political resistance by the oppressed proletariat against the bourgeoisie (see also Jones et al, 1986).

The left realists went on to describe their former colleagues as 'Left Idealists', and to accuse them of espousing idealistic ideas that overlooked the reality of crime, particularly for disadvantaged working-class victims (Lea and Young, 1984). They also criticised their former colleagues within Marxist criminology for dismissing crime, criminal statistics and the fear of crime as social constructions, and for failing to provide useful insights into how best to reduce crime and the fear of crime in a climate of rising crime rates and heightened fear of crime. Instead, Marxist criminologists, in the view of the left realists, seemed content to proffer idealistic and impractical ideas about how best to respond to crime. For example, Marxist criminologists proposed a revolution to overthrow capitalism and replace it with a socialist system. Thus, according to Jock Young and his left realist colleagues, Marxists criminologists placed themselves in a position where they were unable to proffer practical short-term crime control strategies. The left realists argued that this provided the impetus for the rise of neo-conservative criminology, and its harsh 'law and order' ideology, in the 1970s. Additional radical perspectives also emerged in the 1970s alongside Marxist criminology. Anarchist criminology and Peacemaking criminology are two key examples.

Anarchist criminology

Apart from Marxist criminology, other radical perspectives that emerged in the 1970s include anarchist criminology and peacemaking criminology. Anarchist criminology is a radical tradition that critiques the law and the legal authority of nation-states and their institutions, including criminal justice institutions (Ferrell, 1998). It traces the origins of crime to an unequal social order, just as Marxist criminologists do. Like the Marxist criminologists, anarchist criminologists propose radical transformations to the structures of society and societal institutions, including the criminal justice system. However, unlike Marxist criminologists, who propose that the capitalist system and its unequal class structure should be replaced with a socialist system, anarchists reject centralised societal systems and hierarchical structures of power and authority (Henry and Einstadter, 2006). They insist that there should be dismantled because they are destructive to individuals and communities (Tifft and Sullivan, 1980; Barak, 2009). Anarchist criminologists advocate egalitarian social arrangements instead. In their analysis of the legal system they propose an anti-authoritarian model of justice in which the law ceases to protect the powerful, and prioritises principles such as tolerance and diversity (Ferrell, 1996, cited in Welch, 2004).

Peacemaking criminology

Peacemaking criminology is a critical criminological perspective that can be described as an offshoot of anarchist criminology. It emerged from Harold Pepinsky's (1978) work in an article titled 'Communist Anarchism as an Alternative to the Rule of Criminal Law'. The article contained anarchist critiques of the rule of law. In the article, Pepinsky called for the rule of law to be replaced with communist anarchism. He later went on to develop peacemaking criminology as a non-violent response to crime, unlike the violence that, in his view, underlines established state law and existing systems of justice (see also Pepinsky, 2012; 2013).

Perhaps reflecting their roots in anarchist assumptions, peacemaking criminologists propose decentralised models of law and justice. They also reject formal authority or formally constituted government, and advocate instead the freedom of the individual, the benefits of diversity and a society that is organised on the basis of the voluntary cooperation of its citizens. In short, peacemaking criminologists explore how to develop criminal justice systems that would complement anarchist ideals (Pepinsky and Quinney, 1991).

Added to its roots in anarchism, peacemaking criminology draws on a wide range of theoretical, philosophical and religious traditions. As Pepinsky indicates in the following extract, some writers in this field are influenced by:

> 'the great wisdom traditions' – specifically Christianity, Hinduism, Buddhism, Islam, Judaism, and Native American, that 'teach us that the way to liberation is through love, compassion, and peace while the way to remaining in our inner prison ["being held hostage to fear and anger"] is through attachment to such things as accumulation of wealth, the attainment of success, and the grasping for power'. (Braswell et al, 2001: 24, quoted in Pepinsky, 2013: 321)

Peacemaking criminologists are also influenced by humanism, Christian socialism, liberation theory, Eastern meditative thought, feminism, Marxism and penal abolitionism (DeKeseredy, 2010). Peacemaking criminologists draw on these traditions as part of their effort to develop alternative strategies that can replace traditional penal responses. They call for an end to retributive punishments – they believe that such punishments are ineffective (Pepinsky, 2013). According to peacemaking criminologists, retributive punishments appeal more to negative emotions, such as anger and hate, which should be contained not maintained (Groves, 1991). Indeed, Pepinsky (2013: 322) points out '"Penal abolition" also overlaps with "peacemaking criminology'" (see also Morris and West, cited in Pepinsky, 2013). There is a view that the criminal justice system, through its use of violence to respond to crime, has failed because according to the peacemaking criminologists, violent strategies trigger violent responses (Pepinsky, 2012; 2013). It follows that peacemaking criminologists believe that existing justice systems produce violence rather than crime reduction. Consequently, scholars in this field advocate instead what they describe as peacemaking strategies. They aver that peacemaking strategies are more positive and compassionate strategies. Examples are voluntary mediations that could help secure victim and offender reconciliation. In their view, these are preferable to violent responses, such as punishment (Friedrichs, 1991).

Peacemaking criminologists seek to overcome the limitations that are associated with the perspectives that trace the origins of crime to individual factors while overlooking structural factors and the perspectives that prioritise the latter. Thus, the peacemaking criminologists propose responses to crime that into account the role of individual responsibility in crime causation alongside measures that are designed to alleviate social disadvantage. In terms of the former, they endorse what they describe as 'socially just' and restorative strategies as alternative and more effective responses to crime (Pepinsky, 2013: 321). They cite several examples of restorative justice practices in diverse settings. For example, Boyes-Watson (2008, cited in Pepinsky, 2013) refers to the 'peacemaking circles' that some communities in North America convene to address the problems that confront members of the community. These circles serve as alternatives to formal systems, including the criminal justice system. They provide the opportunity for aggrieved parties to resolve their differences in community settings that are more supportive than vindictive. Peacemaking circles are said to be similar to restorative justice approaches. Pepinsky (2013: 322) acknowledges that 'writers on peacemaking circles see their work as falling under the heading of "restorative justice"'. In this context, restorative justice can be traced to Christian ideas of seeking to repair the social harm caused by crime, rather than trying to excise the crime from the criminal (Eglash, 1977, cited in Pepinsky, 2013). It is a response to crime that is quite different from 'retributive justice' (punishment of offenders) and 'distributive justice' (treatment of offenders) (Pepinsky, 2013).

Conclusions

It is important not to overlook the contributions that the radical perspectives, particularly Marxist criminology, made to criminology. Marxist criminologists presented persuasive arguments to support the view that power and wealth are distributed unevenly in some capitalist societies (particularly in the UK and the US). They also drew attention to the impact of power on criminalisation processes, and also to the relative impunity that the powerful enjoy when they break the law. They maintained that crime and deviance are not endemic in any social class.

The key issue is that those who have political and economic power in capitalist societies can avoid law enforcement.

In addition, by the 1980s, other scholars who were apparently influenced by the work of the radical theorists began to amass a wealth of intellectual and empirical material that they have subsequently used to reinforce Marxist criminologists' ideas about the harmful activities of those who control political and economic resources and the impunity that they enjoy (see, eg, Box, 1983; Hillyard and Tombs, 2005, 2007). These scholars do not necessarily place capitalism at the centre of their analysis as the Marxist criminologists did. Some have replaced the terms 'the ruling class' and 'the working class' with the terms 'the powerful' and 'the less powerful' (see also Tierney, 2009). Marxist criminology began to lose its popularity in the late 1970s. Key factors that contributed to its declining popularity in that period include the criticisms it sustained, the declining influence of Marxist theory in the 1970s and the emergence of criminological realism, (see Chapters Six and Seven).

SUMMARY

- Marxist criminologists argue that capitalism gives rise to contradictions that create conflict and crime. Although they differ somewhat in the themes they emphasise, Marxist criminologists generally believe that crime is very much linked to structural inequalities that, in their view, shape class relations in capitalist societies. Some criticise mainstream criminology and the labelling perspective for overlooking the wider social structures that cause crime.
- Unlike the labelling perspective and the conflict perspectives, Marxist perspectives are more explicit in their criticism of the status quo (the prevailing social, economic and political order) of capitalist societies.
- According to Marxist criminologists, in capitalist societies, the ruling class exploit the working classes. Acts of rebellion by members of the working class are labelled as crime.
- Instrumental Marxists argue that the ruling class (the capitalists) exert pressure on the state to criminalise those (the less powerful) whose actions threaten the established capitalist order. By contrast, structural Marxists maintain that the state plays a more autonomous role in the criminalisation of less-powerful groups whose actions threaten capitalist interests.
- Additional perspectives in criminology that offer radical accounts of crime and justice include anarchist criminology and peacemaking criminology.

SAMPLE QUESTIONS

1. How do conflict criminologists describe the causes of crime?
2. 'Capitalist societies ... create substantial amounts of crime' (William Chambliss, 1975: 150). Discuss.

Notes

[1] Broadly conceived, capitalism is a mode of production where private individuals own the means of production. This means that the capitalists own the capital and other resources that are used to produce the goods and services we consume in society. The capitalists produce goods and services for profit, and they employ workers who sell their labour to the capitalists for wages but often have no share in the profit of their labour.

[2] Fordism is the term used to refer to the period in the early 20th century when the economic structure of several Western societies was characterised by industrialisation and mass production. The system of production in that era was reliant on low-skilled labour.

[3] Taylor and colleagues (1973; 2013) note that before the advent of Marxist criminology, Marxism did not concern itself with explaining crime and deviance. There was a general belief that crime and deviance are primarily perpetrated by the lumpenproletariat. The lumpenproletariat were deemed to have no useful role in the class or political struggle between the proletariat (working classes) and the bourgeoisie (dominant class), or in the revolution that would overthrow capitalism and, with it, bourgeoisie domination. As such, the activities of the lumpenproletariat (of which crime and deviance were considered to be central) were not deemed worthy of consideration. More effort had to be devoted to the analyses of capital and labour, and how both factors define the struggle between the dominant class, who control capital, and the working classes, who provide the labour required to sustain capitalism.

[4] Bonger (1916; 1969: 198) defines socialism as an economic system where 'the means of production [are] held in common'. Marxist criminologists argue that such societies are not likely to be characterised by the level of conflict found in capitalist societies, which give rise to crime and to the functions crime fulfils in capitalist societies.

[5] Quinney describes the capitalist state as a group of institutions that interact with each other to orchestrate the political organisation of civil society. These institutions include the government, the administration (which comprises departments that manage the economic and other activities of the state), the military, the police, the judiciary and local governments (Miliband, 1969, cited in Quinney, 1974). For Quinney, state power resides in these institutions. The interests of the ruling class penetrate the decision-making processes of some of the people who lead these institutions – the 'state elites' (Quinney, 1974: 97) or the governing elites (p 27). Thus, the ruling class is able to use state institutions, such as the police, courts and prisons, to control the subordinate classes and coerce them into submission.

[6] In 2007, the Ministry of Justice became responsible for key services and agencies that used to be managed by the Home Office. Examples include the courts service and the key penal services (the prison and probation services).

[7] Administrative criminologists suggest that the origins or causes of crime are not important questions for criminology and are, in any event, intractable issues. For administrative criminologists, it is more important to explore how to control crime cost-effectively by, for example, reducing opportunities for crime (Young, 1988).

[8] As we have seen in Chapter Two, criminologists who contributed to the emergence of radical perspectives in criminology (in Britain) introduced the concept of moral panics. Jock Young created the concept, and Stan Cohen developed it.

[9] Hall and colleagues (1978) acknowledged that the neo-Marxist Nicos Poulantzas's work 'greatly stimulated and informed' their work. For example, Hall (1988) highlighted the relevance of Poulantzas's concept of 'authoritarian statism'. Poulantzas defined this concept as intensive and extensive state control accompanied by the swift decimation of institutions that protect citizens' rights. This manifests itself through the criminalisation and control of politically motivated targets and socio-economically marginalised groups. However, Hall and colleagues identified what they considered to be a weakness in Poulantzas's authoritarian statism. This pertains to the failure to acknowledge strategies states employ to mobilise 'popular consent'. One such strategy might be to fuel perceived insecurity and widespread anxieties in order to reassert state hegemony. We have seen earlier that Hall and colleagues drew on Gramsci's conceptualisation of hegemony to explore these themes. Hall and colleagues also noted that another limitation of the concept of authoritarian statism is that it could not account for the effort of the state in that period (the 1970s) to portray itself as 'anti-statist' (or as a liberal state with limited interest in interfering the lives of ordinary citizens) in order to mobilise public support (Hall, 1988; see also Coleman et al, 2009: 3).

[10] Examples are the former states of the Soviet Union and Eastern Europe.

[11] Chapter Twelve focuses on cultural criminology.

Part Two
Critiquing foundational critical criminology: challenges from Left and Right

FIVE

The advent of neo-conservative criminology

Introduction

An important factor that contributed to the decline of radical perspectives in criminology, including Marxist criminology, is the rise of perspectives on the Right of criminology in the 1970s. These perspectives have been described as 'the new administrative criminology' (Young, 1988: 176). They have also been described as 'neo-conservative' perspectives or 'neo-liberal' criminology.[1] This is because they are said to promote ideas about crime and its control that are associated with neo-conservative ideology of the political Right regarding, *inter alia*, the importance of pursuing economic advancement that benefits a few, preserving traditional values, maintaining order, reinvigorating traditional institutions of control (for example, the family, educational institutions and penal institutions), reducing the role of the state, overlooking socio-economic causes and focusing instead on rationalising penal policies and practice to improve efficiency. Given their commitment to conservative ideals, it is perhaps not surprising that the neo-conservative perspectives of the 1970s and the 1980s went on to have a profound impact on the criminal justice policies of Conservative and Republican governments in the UK and the US, respectively. Rigakos (1996: 76) observes that, 'in the 1970s, neoconservatism enjoyed a dramatic rejuvenation. Since that time, critical criminologists have remained vigilant against a neoconservative onslaught that first materialised in the United States, travelled to England, and has now hit home in Canada.'

According to Jock Young (1988: 176), neo-conservative criminology or the 'new administrative criminology' emerged in the 1970s in the midst of an aetiological crisis.[2] This occurred because existing explanations about the causes of crime appeared to be invalid for reasons we shall explore later. The aetiological crisis erupted alongside a crisis of penality[3]. It was generally believed at the time that existing police enforcement practices were ineffective (Young, 1988, 1994). As Young (1988: 176) put it: 'If there was a crisis in aetiology there was also a crisis in penalty. Conventional police work simply did not seem effective against crime.'

In terms of the aetiological crisis, positivism, which was the prevailing orthodoxy at the time, appeared to have failed in its effort to define the causes of crime. Indeed, sociological or 'socio-democratic' positivism suffered a decline in that period. The sustained rise in crime rates in the 1980s, despite improved economic conditions, appeared to invalidate positivistic explanations that attributed crime causation to social and economic disadvantage. According to Young (1988: 159), 'The central problem for social democratic or Fabian positivism was that a wholesale improvement in social conditions resulted, not in a drop in crime, but the reverse. I have termed this the aetiological crisis.'

The aetiological crisis also occurred within Left criminology. In particular, Marxist criminology's focus on the political economy of crime had led it to assert that crime is the product of adverse economic conditions. This view, in Jock Young's (1988) estimation, amounted to economic determinism. The difficulty that Marxist criminology encountered was that welfarist policies had been introduced to alleviate socio-economic and other disadvantages but official statistics appeared to suggest that these did not result in a fall in crime rates, as existing theorists (including some positivists and the Marxist criminologists) had expected (Young, 1988). Young summarises the features of what he described as 'the crisis of aetiology and penality in late modern societies':

> … This was a world where there was a consensus stretching across a large section of informed opinion that the major cause of crime was impoverished social conditions (social positivism) and that crime was a minority phenomenon, which could be contained by the judicious intervention of the criminal justice system (neo-classicism). Anti-social conditions led to anti-social behaviour, political intervention, and economic reconstruction which improved conditions would, therefore inevitably lead to a drop in the crime rate. Yet precisely the opposite happened … the highest affluence in the history of humanity [was] achieved, yet crime increased. … Furthermore, the response of shoring up the criminal justice system, increasing the size of the police force and the capacity of prisons, did not seem to work either. (1997: 418–82)

Another development in the 1970s that contributed to the rise of neo-conservative perspectives, and the decline of the positivistic rehabilitation enterprise that had prevailed since the postwar period is the pessimistic belief that rehabilitation is an ineffective penal strategy. This belief can be traced to publications that emerged in that period. The publications purported to show that the positivist-inspired rehabilitative efforts that informed the treatment of individuals serving prison or community-based sentences were ineffective, suggesting that 'nothing works' (Brody, 1976; Martinson, 1974). The publications provided the impetus for an assault on penal modernism and its rehabilitative ethos[4] from several quarters. Neo-conservative criminologists, such as James Q. Wilson (1975), whom we shall encounter later in this chapter, cited Martinson's publication to support their contention that punitive strategies should replace rehabilitative strategies. Indeed the publications heralded the so-called 'nothing works' era, and served as a launch pad for the emergence of neo-conservative criminology. However, it is now widely accepted that the reports were exaggerated, perhaps to shore up the neo-conservative political ideology that was emerging in that period. Rigakos

(1996: 83) notes that, 'In 1974, Robert Martinson published his now famous meta-analysis of rehabilitation programs in the United States. The credo "nothing works" resonated with conservatives in search of ammunition with which to attack and dismantle liberal policies'.

In addition, US based liberal professionals and penal theorists began to advocate the justice model of sentencing, and they proposed the 'just deserts' approach (American Friends Service Committee, 1971; von Hirsch, 1976). This is an approach that emphasises proportionality in sentencing. Advocates of the approach sought to promote inter alia: the use of proportionate and determinant sentences. They proposed that limits should be placed on the wide levels of discretion available to so-called 'experts' within the criminal justice system. These 'experts', it was argued, invariably based much of their decisions about the diagnosis and treatment of offenders on questionable positivistic 'scientific' evidence. There was a call for proportionate sentencing, which would ensure that offenders receive their 'just deserts' but would also protect offenders from the disproportionate, and sometimes indeterminate sentences that were being imposed because the prevailing belief at the time was that sentences should be tailored to suit the rehabilitation or treatment needs of the individual. Proportionality in sentencing was not given due consideration. As Cavadino (2010: 449) notes:

> The Justice model was a liberal approach steadfastly opposed to key features of positivism such as indeterminate sentences and individualised sentencing aimed at reforming offenders. Committed to the twin principles of due process in procedure and proportionate 'just deserts' in punishment (with the severity of penalties calibrated to the degree of seriousness of the offence, but favouring an overall reduction in levels of punishment).

Cavadino (2010: 449) also observes that the justice model played 'a significant role in the downfall of the rehabilitative ideal'.

Neo-conservative criminology: rational choice and routine activities theories

In the 1970s and the 1980s, amid the developments described earlier, neo-conservative perspectives emerged in criminology. These perspectives proposed offence-focused crime prevention strategies as more effective alternatives to the offender-focused rehabilitative strategies that prevailed at the time. The offence-focused prevention strategies were underpinned by the idea that crime is the product of opportunity and rational choice. These are ideas associated with the classical school of criminology, and with neo-classical economics. Therefore, the neo-conservative perspectives have also been described as neo-classical perspectives. However, the early classicists promoted the idea of a fair legal system that would safeguard rights and protect citizens from arbitrary decision-making. By contrast, the neo-classicists focused on crime prevention, and proposed strategies that, in their view, could be used to alter the setting in which crime occurs. The neo-classical perspectives came to be known as rational choice theory and routine activities theory.

Rational choice theory has its origins in the work of Ronald V. Clarke and his colleagues, who worked as senior researchers with the Home Office, while routine activity theory emerged from the work of writers based in the University of Illinois in the US – Lawrence Cohen and Marcus Felson (Cohen and Felson, 1979). These writers emphasise that crime is the product of opportunity (see also Felson and Clarke, 1998). They insist that effective crime prevention strategies are strategies that reduce opportunities for crime. Rational choice theorists, in particular, maintain that the potential offender is a rational being who calculates the costs and benefits of his or her actions, and chooses to engage in behaviour that provides greater benefits than costs. Therefore, increasing the costs of crime (in terms of the time, resources or effort required to commit crime) will encourage the potential criminal to make the rational choice not to commit crime (Clarke, 1980).[5] Rooted as they are in classical criminology's notion of the rational offender, these theories have attracted criticisms that are quite similar to those levelled at other classical theories that emphasise the primacy of rationality in the aetiology of crime. As we have seen in Chapter One, these theories (eg deterrence theory) have failed to account for the undermining impact of extraneous factors, such as impulsivity and limited awareness of the costs of behaviour, including criminal behaviour. These may also affect criminal behaviour. Some advocates of the view that crime is the product of rational choice have settled for a more flexible conceptualisation of rationality, namely, 'bounded rationality' (Von Hirsch et al, 1999: 6). This conceptualisation permits contextualised analysis of the considerations that precede criminal behaviour. For example, the notion of bounded rationality recognises that individuals differ in the extent to which they are willing to accept risks, or in the way they assess risks.

Nevertheless, with the support of the Conservative government of the time (the 1980s), the neo-conservatives provided the intellectual basis from which offence-focused crime prevention strategies emerged, including the popular strategy known as situational crime prevention (Clarke, 1980). The perspectives had a profound impact on the government's crime prevention policies. Consequently, the perspectives were described by some of the radical criminologists at the time (such as Jock Young) as 'administrative criminology' (Young, 1988: 176). This descriptor is a rather pejorative label. It refers to criminological perspectives and theories that, according to critics, validate the state's policy agenda. The perspectives are accused of overlooking entrenched structural problems that are more difficult to address. Rather, they trace the causes of crime to the immediate situation or contexts in which crime occurs. They recommend crime prevention measures that can be implemented easily. Their crime prevention strategies are often phrased in catchy sound bites, of which an example is 'target hardening'.[6] The latter refers to using devices like extra locks in cars and buildings to reduce access to people and objects that may, according to the neo-conservative criminologists, be targeted for victimisation (Clarke, 1992). As we shall see later on when we encounter 'right realism', another neo-conservative strategy is 'zero-tolerance policing', which involves increasing the levels of policing (typically in deprived areas) to address so-called 'incivilities' (Wilson and Kelling, 1982). This approach has been described as 'aggressive enforcement of minor offences' (Bowling, 1999: 531). Some neo-conservative writers also propose sentences that can be used for incapacitation such as imprisonment (Murray, 2001).

The crime prevention strategies that these writers propose are easier to implement than the structural inequalities that some critical criminologists identify as causal factors. Thus, it has been argued that the neo-conservative criminologists propose crime prevention measures that are 'easy to administer' (Vold, 1958, quoted in Taylor et al, 1973: 64). Although the measures that these theories propose are not necessarily evidence-based, the ease with which they may be implemented has meant that the theories have tended to have a significant impact on crime prevention policies. However, administrative criminology has generally been accused of 'analytical individualism' because it ignores societal structures and focuses on individual characteristics and how these may be transformed to prevent crime (Taylor et al, 1973: 14; van Swaaningen, 1997).

Neo-conservative criminology: right realism

Added to the influence of administrative criminology, another factor that provided the impetus for the decline in the popularity of Marxist criminology and positivism in the 1970s and 1980s is the emergence in the US of additional criminological perspectives on the Right of criminology. Jock Young described these perspectives as 'establishment criminology'. The latter had much in common with the 'administrative criminology' that was gaining ascendancy in the UK at the time. Young (1994: 80, 97) also described the perspectives as 'right realism' because, in his view, although the perspectives were located on the Right of criminology, they emphasised the reality of crime and the need for practical crime control strategies. They did not dismiss crime as a social construction. Rather, they described crime as a real problem, particularly in deprived communities (Young, 1994).

According to Young (1994), right realism emerged in response to the aetiological crisis in criminology. The right realists went on to influence the policies of the Conservative government of the 1980s because, in the midst of the aetiological crisis and the failure of Left criminologists to offer practical suggestions about how to best reduce crime and the fear of crime, right realism, like its neo-conservative counterparts cited earlier, presented ideas that policymakers could easily translate into crime prevention and control policies (Young, 1994). Examples include the zero-tolerance approach to policing mentioned earlier. Additional examples will be provided later on in this chapter.

The right realists advocated what they considered to be realistic crime prevention and control strategies. They claimed to have modest goals because they did not have much confidence in approaches that make bold claims about their ability to identify and address the fundamental causes of crime (Wilson, 1975). They also emphasised the importance of devising efficient crime control strategies that would be targeted selectively and effectively to save costs. An example is effective policing strategies. It follows that in line with other neo-conservative perspectives, such as rational choice theory and routine activities theory, right realists put forward ideas about crime and crime control that appeared to be consistent with neo-liberal concerns to rationalise penal policy and practice in order to promote efficiency and cost-effectiveness. The right realists argued that individuals who are classed as offenders are rational beings who make the rational choice to commit crime. Therefore, the right realists advocated crime control measures that would take this into account.

They acknowledged the role of adverse social conditions, such as poverty and unemployment, in crime causation. However, they did not trace these to structural factors like power and wealth inequalities, as the Marxist criminologists did. Rather, they claimed that defects within the individual give rise to adverse social conditions and to criminality. Therefore, although the *right* realists depicted the individuals that are classed as offenders as rational actors, they also (rather confusingly) espoused essentialist views about these individuals. They traced the origins of crime to biological causes and social maladjustment, but not to structural causes. Unlike the Marxist criminologists, who directed attention to unfair structural conditions and state complicity in the criminalisation of the less powerful, right realists harked back to biological positivism *and* classicist ideas about rational choice, and they located the cause/s of crime within the individual. It is worth noting that right realists overlooked the crimes that are committed by those who enjoy power and wealth in society. They focused instead on conventional crimes such as the predatory street crimes that are committed in deprived communities by the members of these communities against other members of their communities. The right realists justified their focus on convectional crime partly on the basis that these are the crimes that cause the public the greatest fear and anxiety. As we shall see in Chapter Eight, some critical criminologists have adduced evidence to show that although the crimes of the powerful may be less visible than conventional crimes, they cause extensive and serious harm.

James Q. Wilson, who was a policy adviser to the Ronald Reagan administration, and Charles Murray, a contributor to a right-wing think-tank, are prime examples of writers whose work reflects the key ideas associated with right realism and neo-conservative criminology. These ideas are summarised as follows:

- Essentialism – people who commit crime possess biological defects that predispose them to criminality.
- Rational choice – people who commit crime are rational beings who require rational penal responses.

- Predatory crimes such as street crime and burglary are prevalent in deprived communities, and they fuel public fear and anxiety.
- 'Realistic' crime prevention strategies should be introduced and targeted effectively to reduce crime and restore order.

Essentialism: biological accounts of crime causation

The right realists focused on street crimes and other crimes that are typically committed by socioeconomically marginalised people in deprived areas, and they put forward essentialist ideas about the people who commit these crimes. The latter, they argued, possess characteristics that make them different from others. Their immoral behaviour can be traced, in part to genetic factors and also to lack of adequate socialisation. According to the right realists, additional causal factors include what they described as the permissive liberal attitudes of the 1950s and the 1960s. These attitudes, according to the right realists, contributed to a decline in traditional moral values from the 1970s onwards.

It follows that, quite unlike the foundational critical criminological theories that had identified defects in society such as class conflict, structural inequality and so forth as key causal factors, right realists espoused ideas that complemented biological positivism. They argued that crime is the product of defects within the individual. In their view, these defects may be inherited or may stem from inadequate socialisation.

In the text *The Bell Curve*, Richard Hernstein and his colleague Charles Murray (1994) who is now recognised as a key right realist sought to reinforce these views. They argued that certain populations possess specific defects that predispose them to criminality. They claimed that some minority ethnic groups, particularly black people and Latin Americans are genetically disposed to low levels of intelligence. They based their conclusions on the Intelligence Quotient (IQ) test, which is now considered to be a much-contested measure of intelligence that is unable to account for several variables, including cultural difference. According to Delgado and Stefancic (2012: 117): 'Progressive scientists have challenged the premises of *The Bell Curve* and similar neo-eugenicist tracts, showing how they rest on discredited science. Critical race theorists have launched a thoroughgoing attack on the idea of conventional merit and standardised testing'.

Nevertheless, Hernstein and Murray went on to conclude that there are links between lower IQ test results and the propensity to commit crime. As Burke (2009) rightly observes, such 'scientific' evidence, though based on spurious and largely questionable premises, do seem attractive to regimes bent on differentiating target populations in order to stigmatise, criminalise and possibly annihilate them. Examples of these regimes abound in history, from the US in the slavery years to Nazi Germany and the former USSR.

Hernstein and Murray were certainly not the only right realists to offer questionable biological and social explanations of crime. Other writers who may also be described as right realists had previously demonstrated a similar tendency to trace the causes of crime to the biological constitution and the social experiences (the purported under-socialisation) of the offender. In *Crime and Human Nature*, Wilson and Hernstein (1985) traced the origins of crime to: the biological make-up of the individual; the environment that the individual was socialised in (including the influence of poor parenting skills); and the degree to which an individual internalises law-abiding values. Wilson and Hernstein also highlighted the influence of rational choice based on self-interest. Their views reflect the essentialist belief that there are biological and social pathological differences between offenders and non-offenders. Indeed, they stated that 'crime cannot be understood without taking into account individual predispositions and their biological roots' (Wilson and Hernstein 1985: 103). In short, they identified human nature as a key factor in crime causation.

In the 1970s and the 1980s, amid the aetiological crisis, the 'nothing works' ideology provided fertile ground for the growth of neo-conservative perspectives. These perspectives advocated practical crime control strategies and presented ideologically conservative views about the nature of the offender and the effective means of controlling crime. The right realists also embraced conservative ideas about social issues. For example, they advocated a return to traditional values and the reinvigoration of traditional institutions of control, for example, the family, educational institutions and correctional institutions, such as the police, to restore order. Clearly, unlike Marxist criminologists, they did not view the prevailing order or status quo as unequal in any way. Indeed, they overlooked structural factors that, according to Marxist criminologists, give rise to differential experiences and opportunities in society. Similarly, unlike positivist theories, which emphasise broad socio-economic and psychological causes, as already noted, the neo-conservatives espoused ideas that are rooted in biological positivism and classicism, and they traced the cause/s of crime to the individual.

The focus on predatory crime

Another key feature of right realism is the focus on predatory crime in deprived communities. As we have seen earlier, right realists maintained that a criminal type determined by biological features exists. They overlooked the crimes that are committed by higher-status groups and appeared to suggest that the groups that possess the attributes of the criminal type typically reside in, or gravitate towards, urban areas, particularly deprived urban areas, where they commit predatory crimes, such as street crime and burglary. Two key theses written by right realists highlight these ideas quite vividly. The two theses are the 'broken windows' thesis and Charles Murray's (1999; 2001) 'underclass' thesis. The first to be considered here is the 'broken windows' thesis.

The 'broken windows' thesis

In addition to his claim that crime can be traced to biological causes and rational choice, James Q. Wilson (with his colleagues George Kelling and Catherine Coles) went on to propose what is now described as the 'broken windows' thesis (see, generally, Wilson and Kelling, 1982; Kelling and Coles, 1996). The 'broken windows' thesis focuses on how to respond to predatory crime in deprived urban areas. It states that, left unaddressed, signs of disorder,[7] such as broken windows in properties, abandoned cars and graffiti on walls in an urban area, can lead to more serious crime. This is because the signs of disorder attract criminals who assume that the residents do not care about the area. Over time, respectable families move away and urban decay ensues as the area becomes crime-ridden. According to Wilson and Kelling (1982: 32):

> A piece of property is abandoned, weeds grow up, and a window is smashed. Adults stop scolding rowdy children, the children, emboldened, become more rowdy. Families move out, unmarried adults move in … teenagers gather in front of the corner store. The merchant asks them to move they refuse. Fights occur. Litter accumulates. People start drinking in front of the grocery store, in time; an inebriate drunkard slumps to the sidewalk and is allowed to sleep it off.

Apart from 'unmarried adults', teenagers in front of a store, litter, people drinking in front of a store and so forth, the authors of this thesis provide us with additional examples of people or activities that create images of disorder and also create fear of crime in a community: 'disreputable or obstreperous or unpredictable people: panhandlers, drunks, addicts, rowdy teenagers, prostitutes, loiterers, the mentally disturbed' (Kelling and Wilson, 1982: 2).

Reflecting their commitment to practical short-term crime prevention policies, Wilson and Kelling (1982) advocated greater police intervention to stamp out acts of disorder or what they term 'incivilities'. They aver that if left unabated, incivilities evolve into crime. Put simply: 'The "broken window" is a powerful metaphor for the absence of order and control' (Crawford and Evans, 2012: 786). Thus, the thesis emphasises that 'order maintenance' strategies should be put in place to address signs of disorder or decline that if left unaddressed, would evolve into more serious crimes and disorder (Kelling and Coles, 1996; Crawford and Evans, 2012: 786). Unlike critical criminologists, right realists, such as Wilson, believe that order maintenance should assume priority over striving for justice, including social justice. As Young (1994: 97) put it: 'Wilson's right realism prioritises order over justice'.

The 'broken windows' thesis was published at a time when there were ongoing debates in criminology about how best to deploy police resources for crime control, and official statistics appeared to reveal rising rates of crime and fear of crime. Views about early police intervention to address disorder chimed with the conservative sentiments about the importance of increasing police powers, particularly in deprived areas. Thus, the ideas of the right realists might have contributed to the emergence of 'zero-tolerance' policing policies on both sides of the Atlantic, and antisocial behaviour policies in the UK. Bowling (1999) points out that following the publication of Wilson and Kelling's 'broken windows' thesis, it became generally accepted that a progressive link exists between signs of disorder and serious crime. As noted earlier, the thesis suggests that aggressive policing is required to stamp out signs of disorder. However, Bowling (1999) also cites evidence which indicates that these ideas were widely held by the police before the thesis was published. It would appear, therefore, that Wilson and Kelling 'simply repackaged existing police wisdom' (Bowling, 1999: 544). In addition, the critics point out that there is limited evidence to support the 'broken windows' thesis and its central premise that signs of disorder in a community can attract criminal types who migrate to an area to and cause crime rates to rise within that area. There is also limited evidence to support the view that incivilities and acts of disorder can, if left unaddressed, evolve into criminality (see, eg, Pratt et al, 2011). Crawford and Evans (2012: 786) point out that 'Wilson and Kelling offer little empirical support for their claims regarding a causal relationship between disorder, fear, and increased crime' (see also Harcourt and Ludwig, 2006). In addition, some writers persuasively argue that structural or sociological factors, such as poverty, may be more closely linked to crime and disorder in deprived areas than signs of disorder (Sampson and Raudenbusch, 1999, cited in Crawford and Evans, 2012). Others have pointed out that the 'broken windows' thesis focuses unduly on the role of the police in crime reduction and overlooks the role of communities and other agencies can also play (Bowling, 1999). For Bowling, therefore, it would appear that Wilson and Kelling employed the phrase 'fixing broken windows' as a euphemism for 'fixing disreputable people' by exposing them to aggressive policing. According to Bowling (1999: 548):

> Their main policy recommendation to the police is to 'kick a★★★'. However, aggressive enforcement does not hold out the possibility for repair of communities ravaged by poverty.... Rather, it represents a superficial palliative to a set of fundamental social problems which are, at best, affected by police strategies and, at worst, exacerbated by them.

Indeed, Crawford and Evans (2012) refer to what appears to be a subsequent retraction by James Q. Wilson of his earlier suggestion that there are links between signs of disorder and crime. He reportedly made the following statement: 'I still to this day do not know if improving order will or will not reduce crime.... People have not understood that this was a speculation' (Hurley, 2004, cited in Crawford and Evans, 2012: 786). Nevertheless, in general, Wilson's ideas about crime and the punitive responses he suggested gained currency with neo-conservative governments on both sides of the Atlantic in the 1980s. Rigakos (1996: 83, emphasis in original) notes that:

As Reaganism gained its momentum, so did the politics of crime control advocated by Wilson.... The Conservative party of the early 1980s under Margaret Thatcher was, in part, empowered by a tough crime-control agenda borrowed from Wilson. Taylor (1981: 5) notes that '[i]n 1977 ... Wilson ... proceeded (on flimsy evidence) to reproduce for Britain the kind of analysis of crime developed by the radical right in the U.S.A.'.

The underclass thesis

As mentioned earlier, Charles Murray is another key contributor to right realism. He espoused ideas about crime and crime control that reflect neo-conservative ideals. Thus, he harbours an essentialist view of crime. He also overlooks the role of structural inequality and other root causes in crime causation. Charles Murray's work on the causes of crime focused on the notion that an 'underclass' exists in society. The idea that a social class that is located below the working class exists is a long-standing idea. Indeed, early writers like Karl Marx described this class as the lumpenproletariat (see Chapter Four). They have also been described as the socially excluded. But Murray's contribution to the study of the so-called underclass ignored the structural disadvantage that might help explain the experiences of this group. He focused exclusively on behavioural explanations that identified the culture of those he described as the underclass (primarily poor ethnic minority communities) as the key factor that explains their behaviour. According to Murray, the members of the underclass are responsible for most violent crimes in the US and UK. It is important to note two key points about Murray's underclass thesis. Like the broken windows thesis, his underclass thesis focused exclusively on predatory street crimes. The thesis also identified the perpetrators and victims of these crimes as people who live in socially deprived areas. Therefore, Murray overlooked the crimes that are perpetrated by rich and powerful groups who reside in affluent areas. Rather, Murray wrote his thesis in the 1980s about deprived populations, including populations of disenfranchised and marginalised young black men in the US, and later in the UK. He traced the origins of crime to the cultural environment those he describes as the underclass inhabit. He ascribed to them a culture of worklessness and dependency.

The thesis emerged in a period that witnessed a rise in the number of single mothers, an increase in the number of individuals who were reliant on social security benefits and a rise in crime and disorder rates. The thesis appeared to conflate these social issues. It went on to claim that the typical member of the underclass: is a young male; is work-shy; relies on social security benefits; is raised by a single mother who is unable to provide the positive influence that young men need; is poorly educated; is heavily involved in drug misuse; and is feckless and promiscuous. Indeed, Murray's thesis claims that criminality and the lack of a work ethic are culturally transmitted within this group. Members of the underclass inherit values and practices that discourage employment and encourage them to depend on social security benefits. According to Murray, crime (particularly violent crime) is also endemic in this class and is culturally transmitted through generations. For Murray, crime control is best achieved through reduced welfare provision to target the work-shy, and through incapacitative sanctions, particularly imprisonment, to address violent crime. Below, Murray (1999: 2–3) defines what he means by the 'underclass':

> Since 1989, I have been using three indicators as a concise way of tracking the underclass: criminality, dropout from the labour force among low-income young males, and illegitimacy, among low-income young women…. The habitual criminal is the classic member of an underclass.

Murray (2001) also went on to claim that there is an emerging underclass in Britain. Much of Murray's claims have been repudiated by researchers and other academics, who demonstrate convincingly that the thesis lacks empirical foundation and is limited by, among other factors, its failure to account for structural conditions (see, generally, Macdonald, 1997). For example, although Charles Murray (1999: 2) acknowledges that 'Most members of the underclass have low incomes', he does not indicate that this may be linked to the criminality that he ascribes to them. Rather, he goes on to state that the main characteristics of the underclass:

> are not poverty and unmet physical needs. The Underclass is marked by social disorganisation; a poverty of social networks and valued roles, and a Hobbesian kind of individualism in which trust and cooperation are hard to come by and isolation is common (1999: 2).

Thus, unlike many critical criminologists, Murray and other neo-conservative criminologists locate the causes of crime in the individual and do not recognise wider structural causal factors. Robert Macdonald (2008), an avid critic of the underclass thesis, posits that an important limitation of the thesis is: 'its over emphasis of individual choice and under emphasis of social constraint' (Macdonald, 2008: 243). Like other neo-conservative perspectives, it fails to acknowledge the socio-economic disadvantage that can constrain individual choice. Indeed, neo-conservative writers emphasise punitive responses *not* social responses to crime (Wilson and Hernstein, 1985).

The notion of the underclass has had a profound influence on social welfare and penal policies. Charles Murray traced crime to welfare dependency and advocated reduced welfare provision. His views became popular with the Conservative government of the 1980s because the government was committed to reducing welfare provision (Macdonald, 1997). They traced the rising crime rates of that period to the so-called 'generous' social welfare provision of their predecessor – the Labour government – and to the purportedly 'soft' penal welfare agenda of that government. They also traced the rising rates of crime and disorder in the

1970s and 1980s to what they described as the permissiveness of the Cultural Revolution that occurred in the 1950s and the 1960s. This revolution, in their view, encouraged the substitution of traditional values for more liberal values Therefore, unsurprisingly, the notion of an underclass, with all the negative connotations Murray ascribed to those he identified as the members of that class, resonated with the views of the Conservative government of the time about the role of the state in social welfare provision (Macdonald, 1997). His neo-conservative sentiments complemented the ideals of the Conservative government and went on to inform debates about how to deploy social welfare resources.

It has been argued that writers and commentators on the Right, such as the right-wing press and right-wing politicians, have co-opted the concept of the underclass and have transformed it into a descriptor of deprived groups or the long-term benefit-dependent unemployed (Downes and Rock, 2011). More recent debates about the 'underclass' are becoming increasingly race-neutral. Discussions about a supposed breakdown of moral values and social institutions, such as marriage and religion, are now increasingly directed towards the activities of disenfranchised and marginalised white groups. Indeed, Murray (2012: 12) himself has stated that 'America is coming apart at the seams – not the seams of race or ethnicity, but of class'. In the UK, there are now a myriad of fictional programmes that perpetuate the stereotype of the so-called underclass. These programmes focus on poor white unemployed and welfare-dependent groups. Just as Murray did, the programmes conflate single motherhood and welfare dependency, and identify these as the causes of crime. The drama serial *Shameless* represents an example. The programme is shown on Channel 4 and was first aired in 2004. According to a major UK newspaper it depicts 'the underclass in all its feckless, drunken, irresponsible, irrepressible, resourceful, violent and promiscuous splendour ... dole scams, housing benefit fraud, disability swindles' (Anthony, 2011).

Rational choice and 'realistic' crime prevention

Right realists argue that an individual who commits a crime should be viewed as a rational actor who has exercised free will and rational choice. Wilson and colleagues' 'broken windows' thesis and Murray's 'underclass' thesis presume that the offender is a rational being who chooses to engage in criminal behaviour and who is, as such, capable of responding to deterrent crime prevention and control strategies. Thus, there is a presumption that repairing broken windows, for example, should deter the potential criminal because he or she would make the rational choice not to engage in crime in an area that appears to be orderly. Equally, proponents of the 'broken windows' thesis believe that antisocial behaviour policies or policing activities that target what they describe as incivilities should deter those who engage in such behaviour, and others, from going ahead to commit crimes. Although Murray claims that the members of the groups he described as the 'underclass' lack adequate socialisation and therefore commit crime on impulse rather than through rational choice, his underclass thesis suggests otherwise. The thesis presumes that reducing social security benefits would curb welfare dependency. It should encourage those whose welfare dependency has robbed them of a work ethic to make the rational choice to engage in meaningful work, which, in Murray's view, would reduce their criminality.[8]

It follows that, similar to other neo-conservative criminologists, right realists resurrected the classicists' view of human beings as rational beings who are capable of calculating the costs and benefits of action before choosing the more beneficial line of action. By suggesting that the groups they focused their analyses on (the poor and marginalised) are capable of exercising rational choice, but are also constrained by predisposing biological defects, the right realists offer contradictory and potentially irreconcilable accounts (see also Tierney, 2009). They trace the causes of behaviour (including crime) rather deterministically to human nature, on the one hand, and then to rational choice, on the other hand. Several commentators have observed this rather puzzling state of affairs. For instance, Rigakos (1996: 82, emphasis added) describes it as a:

> a central inharmonious new-right axiom that, although criminals commit their acts because they possess a brain that is unable to learn otherwise, they must nonetheless be punished so that they may *learn* not to do it again.... From the perspective of the new right, whether one is genetically programmed or acts out of one's own volition, retribution is the rudimentary response to crime.

Surely, if 'criminals' cannot learn to refrain from crime because they are constrained by their nature (by their brain structure), then punishment, restricted social welfare provision or any other sanctions cannot possibly make them learn to refrain from crime. They cannot possibly exercise their rational choice to engage in or refrain from crime. This glaring inconsistency in the position of the neo-conservatives suggests that their views about crime and how best to respond to it are more ideologically driven than well-considered or evidence-based.

Criticisms

Criminologists have criticised neo-conservative explanations on several grounds. A key criticism is that neo-conservative theories overlook social responses to crime that may help address socio-economic disadvantages, which some believe are also linked to crime (Downes and Rock, 2011). More specifically, critics point out that situational crime prevention strategies can trigger 'displacement', in which potential offenders confronted with limited opportunities for crime in one area relocate their activities to other areas that provide greater opportunities for crime (Bottoms, 2012). In addition, as noted earlier, limited empirical support for the broken windows thesis exists. Murray's underclass thesis has attracted similar criticism. For instance, Macdonald (1997: 181; see also 2008) points out that 'the underclass theory is rhetorical, ideological and, in the main, untainted by empirical facts'. He goes on to state that 'Murray's account of the British underclass has the sparest of evidence' (Macdonald, 2008: 241). Downes and Rock (2011: 352) also note that 'the empirical evidence for the "welfare causes underclass" thesis is comparatively weak'. A criticism of the broken windows thesis and the underclass thesis is that both theses focus on crimes that are committed by marginalised groups in deprived areas. Therefore, the theses cannot explain white-collar crime and other crimes that are typically committed by the more powerful and affluent groups.

There is also the argument that far from the idea that signs of disorder can lead to increased crime rates in an area, socio-economic factors such as poverty and unemployment, are more closely linked to crime in deprived areas (Sampson and Raudenbusch, 1999, cited in Crawford and Evans, 2012). Equally, others maintain that social exclusion and disadvantage, not individual attributes, explain the experiences of the excluded groups Murray described as the underclass (Mann, 1992). In addition, several studies have challenged Charles Murray's position about the link between long-term unemployment, welfare dependency, a poor work ethic and crime (see, generally, Shildrick et al, 2012). These studies do not support Murray's views that values that are averse to work are being transmitted across generations or that the population in question have unconventional aspirations that make them averse to securing legitimate employment. According to the studies, lack of opportunity creates long-term dependency on social security benefits, not idleness or lack of a work ethic, as the thesis presupposes.

Shildrick and colleagues (2012), for example, explored the experiences of people in deprived areas in Glasgow and Middlesborough who had been out of work for protracted periods. They examined the factors that explain 'long-term detachment from the labour market' and whether this detachment could be traced to a culture of worklessness. They found that across the three generations they studied – the older, middle and younger generations – there was limited evidence to support the culture of worklessness thesis. Most of the respondents stated that they value paid work over a life of welfare dependency. They pointed out that surviving on benefits is extremely difficult. There was also very limited evidence to support the claim that this group prefer to engage in the informal economy while claiming social welfare benefits – an activity that is colloquially known as 'scrounging'. Only few of the interviewees had been involved in the informal economy. Of the remainder, most were engaged in forms of work that are not paid, but are nevertheless productive; these include the childcare duties performed by mothers and voluntary work. Most of the respondents were poor and lacked the skills and training required to secure profitable employment.

Socio-economic disadvantage, such as educational underachievement, social exclusion and poverty, were linked to long-term unemployment, not a so-called culture of worklessness. These socioeconomic factors appeared to fuel other problems that contributed more to worklessness than the presumed culture of worklessness. These additional problems were identified as: substance misuse;

family violence and instability; and physical and mental illness. Those affected did not have sufficient access to relevant welfare agencies.

Conclusion

In sum, although realism ideas attracted significant criticism and appeared to lack useful empirical support, by presenting what appeared to be realistic and practical crime prevention strategies, right realists were able to influence the policies of the neo-conservative governments on both sides of the Atlantic in the 1970s and 1980s. It has been argued that they achieved this because they presented a series of untested ideas that nonetheless resonated with 'populist beliefs and sound-bite criminology' (Downes and Rock, 2011). Right realists also influenced criminal justice policy because in the midst of the aetiological crisis and the failure of Left criminology to offer practical suggestions about how to best reduce crime and the fear of crime, these criminologists on the Right of criminology presented ideas that policymakers could readily translate into practical policies (Young, 1988, 1994). They proposed punitive and coercive strategies such as:

• the increased use of imprisonment;
• more severe punishment, particularly for incapacitation and deterrent purposes;
• targeting more people for penal regulation;
• tougher responses to political and industrial disorder;
• undermining advancements in liberal attitudes towards social issues, including women's rights;
• promoting instead, a moralistic conservative social agenda;
• an inordinate focus on street crimes; and
• the use of moral panics to fuel public fear and hostility towards marginalised groups, particularly ethnic minority groups (Cohen, 1983, cited in Rigakos, 1996).

Several commentators have since pointed out that the punitive and moralistic ideals espoused by the right realists had no observable impact on crime rates. As official statistics suggest, crime rates continued to rise unabated throughout the 1980s alongside a significant increase in the number of young people experiencing social exclusion (Craine, 1997). Ultimately, an important consequence of the rise of neo-conservative perspectives in the 1970s and 1980s was to reduce the popularity of Marxist criminology (and, to a lesser degree, positivism), and to orchestrate a shift towards the punitive crime control and social welfare policies that were proposed by those on the Right of criminology and politics.

SUMMARY

- The rise of perspectives on the Right of criminology in the 1970s contributed to the decline of Marxist criminology.
- The perspectives on the Right that emerged in the 1970s have been variously described as the 'new administrative criminology', 'neo-conservative perspectives', 'neo-liberal criminology' and 'establishment criminology'.
- These perspectives impacted on the policies of Conservative governments, primarily because the perspectives promoted ideas about crime and its control that are consistent with the ideology of the political Right. They also propose practical crime prevention measures that could be easily implemented.
- Rational choice theory, routine activities theory and right realism are perspectives on the Right of criminology that emerged in the 1970s and 1980s.
- Rooted as they are in classical criminology's notion of the rational offender, rational choice theory and routine activities theory have attracted criticisms that are quite similar to those levelled against other classical theories that emphasise the primacy of rationality in the aetiology of crime.
- Right realism is an additional neo-conservative perspective that emerged in the 1970s and 1980s. Right realists state that they do not concern themselves unduly with questions of aetiology. Nevertheless, they do go on to essentialise by tracing its origins to predisposing biological factors. But, rather contradictorily, they also identify rational choice as a key causal factor. They focus on predatory crimes and propose what they consider to be practical crime control and prevention strategies.
- In general, perspectives on the Right of criminology have been criticised on several grounds. Fundamentally, they have been accused of 'analytical individualism' (Taylor, Walton and Young, 1973: 14) because they offer explanations of crime and its control that overlook societal structures and focus on individual characteristics.

SAMPLE QUESTIONS

1. Do you agree that a criminal underclass is responsible for most crimes in society?
2. To what extent do the main features of critical criminology compare with the key ideas that right realists emphasise?

Notes

[1] There is a discussion of neo-liberalism in Chapter Twelve.

[2] The aetiology of an event refers to the explanation that can be offered for that event. It is the explanation given for the cause/s of a particular event. According to Young (1986), the aetiological crisis of the 1970s stemmed from the failure of the economic models of crime causation offered by positivists and radical criminologists. This is because while economic conditions improved and levels of unemployment and poverty fell in the 1960s in the wake of considerable government investment in social welfare provision, statistics

indicated that crime rates continued to rise in several Western jurisdictions (Young, 1986; 1997).

[3] According to Cavadino (2010: 468), 'penality' is 'a useful if slightly annoying word which is used to encompass both concrete penal practices and also ideas which people have about punishment'.

[4] 'Penal modernism' is a term that has been used to describe the approach to penality that, according to some commentators, reached its epoch during the post-war era, and suffered a decline (at least at the level of penal policy) in the late 1970s (Garland, 1996: 447; 2001). The approach prioritised the welfare of the offender. It was underpinned by the belief that rehabilitation should form the basis of penal intervention. This was to be achieved through the application of scientific methods of diagnosis and treatment, which should benefit not only the reformed individual, but also wider society (Garland, 2001; Cavadino, 2010).

[5] Rational choice theory also shares ideas in common with control theories in criminology. Control theories comprise diverse explanatory themes. Like the rational choice theories, control theories assert that most people would commit crime if they have the opportunity, and if the benefits outweigh the risks (Hirschi, 1969). To varying degrees, control theorists identify weakened or broken social bonds (with others in society) (Hirschi, 1969), and/ or lack of self-control (Gottfredson and Hirschi, 1990), as the factors that cause crime.

[6] Rational choice theorists proposed crime prevention strategies that are underpinned by the idea that human beings are rational beings who will choose to commit crime if the opportunity is available, and if the benefits outweigh the risks.

[7] Critical criminologists might argue that what the right realists described as 'signs of disorder' are signs of adverse social conditions or structural disadvantage.

[8] Charles Murray proposed the use of primarily incapacitative punishments for those he describes as the underclass. He argued that this is because they lack the socialisation required to make rational choices and they mainly commit violent crime. Therefore, according to Murray (2001: 9), deterrent measures, rooted as they are in the belief that the interactive or independent effect of the certainty, severity and celerity of punishment should deter people from making the choice to commit crime, are likely to be ineffective: 'Modest increases in the risk of imprisonment are irrelevant. The value of imprisonment for violent people is incapacitation, not deterrence. Prison gets them off the street'. Of course, it is easy to see that a major difficulty with Murray's proposal that people should be incapacitated in prison is that people who are held in prison will eventually be released. Even if we assume that imprisonment is an effective crime reduction mechanism we must confront the fact that many people who go to prison will eventually be released. In addition, statistics in the UK and the US reveal that many prisoners are reconvicted

within a few years of release (see, generally, Ministry of Justice, 2013). According to the Prison Reform Trust (2013: 1), in the UK:

> Prison has a poor record for reducing reoffending – 47% of adults are reconvicted within one year of release. For those serving sentences of less than 12 months this increases to 58%. Nearly three quarters (73%) of under 18 year olds are reconvicted within a year of release.

In the US, statistics published by the Bureau of Justice have revealed that three out of four prisoners in 30 US states are arrested within five years of release (see Cooper et al, 2014). We can therefore reasonably assume that, contrary to Murray's ideas, imprisonment can, at best, serve only as a temporary measure that, as the existing evidence suggests, is quite counterproductive.

SIX

Left realism: criticisms from within?

Introduction

This chapter analyses the criticisms that the foundational perspectives (particularly Marxist criminology) received in the 1980s from scholars in the UK who developed an ideological stance that has been described as 'radical realism' (Young, 1988: 178) or, more commonly, as 'left realism' (Lea and Young, 1984; Young, 1994). Some of the initial proponents of left realism had, indeed, contributed to the development of Marxist criminology in the 1970s in the UK.

Several criminology texts describe left realism, in its varying forms, as a perspective in critical criminology. Perhaps it is accurate to view left realism as a perspective that emerged from within the critical criminological tradition to challenge its fundamental ideas. This chapter explores the origins of left realism. It also examines left realist perspectives on crime causation and prevention.

Origins of left realism

Several developments in the 1970s and the 1980s can explain the emergence of left realism in the mid 1980s.[1] With the rise of neo-conservative criminological perspectives sympathetic to the political Right, positivism and Marxist criminology suffered a decline. Left realism emerged to counter the dominance of the neo-conservative perspectives. In the text titled *What Is To Be Done About Law and Order*, John Lea and Jock Young (1984, 1993) outlined what they described as a pragmatic agenda for explaining crime and for delivering effective crime control policy. They named their approach 'left realism' and they mounted a formidable critique of Marxist criminology. Incidentally, key proponents of left realism, such as Jock Young, had contributed extensively to the development of Marxist criminology in Britain. However, by the 1980s, for a range of reasons that we shall explore later, the left realists abandoned fundamental ideas associated with Marxists criminology and began to argue that crime is a real problem that requires practical or 'realistic' prevention policy strategies. Although they were located on the eft of criminology and they explained the causes of crime somewhat differently from the right realists, the left realists introduced ideas about crime causation and crime prevention that were quite similar to the ideas of the right realists. They also dismissed the transformative agenda of the Marxist criminologists as idealistic and utopian, and they proposed what they believed to be more practical crime prevention and control policy strategies.

The left realists described their position as 'Left' because, like other criminologists on the Left, they include in their description of crime causation an analysis of structural causal factors, from class inequality to gender inequality (Rock, 2012). According to Jock Young, whose contribution was pivotal to the emergence of left realism: 'Left realist criminology, as the name implies is radical in its criminology ... radical in that crime is seen as an endemic product of the class and partriarchal nature of advanced industrial society' (Young, 1997: 473). At the same time, the left realists described themselves as 'realists' to indicate that they are cognisant of what they consider to be the '*reality* of crime' (Young 1986: 21). The initial proponents of left realism accused their former colleagues within Marxist criminology (whom they disparagingly described as left idealists[2]) of overlooking this dimension of crime (the reality of crime) and the need to devise realistic responses to crime. As Jock Young put it: 'the central tenet of left realism is to reflect the reality of crime, that is in its origins, its nature and impact' (Young, 1986: 21). The left realists criticised Marxist criminologists for claiming that crime is a social construct or an 'ideological trick'. Rejecting this view, the early left realists sought to highlight the seriousness of crime for the victims, or as they put it, to: 'take crime seriously'. They emphasised what they described as the disproportionate victimisation of the most vulnerable in society: 'the poor, minority ethnic people and women' (Rock, 2012: 61; see also Lea and Young, 1984, 1993; Young, 1994). The early left realists went on to accuse their former colleagues in the Marxist criminological tradition of romanticising the criminal and ignoring the 'real' victims of crime (Lea and Young, 1984: 102). According to the left realists, Marxist criminologists portrayed the offender as the victim of crime. Matthews and Young (1986: Introduction) remarked that:

> The tide is turning for radical criminology. For over two decades it has neglected the effect of crime upon the victim and concentrated on the impact of the state – through the process of labelling – on the criminal ... it became an advocate for the indefensible: the criminal became the victim, the state the solitary focus of attention, while the real victim remained off-stage.

Key arguments in left realism

Young (1997: 473) described left realism as: 'realistic in its appraisal of crime and its causes ... it is realistic in that it attempts to be faithful to the reality of crime'. Thus, the left realists emphasise that crime is a real problem. They argue that crime is not the socially constructed product of inter–class warfare in capitalist societies, as Marxist criminologists suggest. Although the initial proponents of left realism ascribed criminogenic qualities to capitalist societies, they rejected the view put forward by some Marxist criminologists that crime is an act of resistance by the working class and it expresses their dissatisfaction with exploitative class relations. The left realists maintained that crime is intra–class. They also argued that the fear of crime is real, and it afflicts many working-class communities. Therefore, the left realists accused the Marxist criminologists of creating the inaccurate impression that the fear of crime is irrational and victimisation surveys are primarily tools that politicians and others use to mobilise support for harsh crime control policies. Indeed, the left realists emphasised that national victimisation surveys, underestimate the extent of crime. As Jock Young (1986: 14) put it:

> The chance of being criminally injured, however slightly, the British Crime Survey tells us, is once in a hundred years (Hough and Mayhew, 1983) and such a Home Office view is readily echoed by left idealists who inform us that crime is, by and large, a minor problem and indeed the fear of crime is more of a problem than crime itself. Thus, they would argue, undue fear of crime provides popular support for conservative law and order campaigns and allows the build-up of further police powers whose repressive aim is political dissent rather than crime.

According to left realists, to dismiss street crime as the socially constructed myths that fuel moral panics, is to overlook the harmful impact of street crime on the victims. In their view, this was one of several similarly unrealistic claims (made by radical criminologists) that created fertile ground for the emergence and growth of law and order perspectives on the political Right. Young (1975; 2012: 89, emphasis in original) remarked that:

> It is unrealistic to suggest that the problem of crimes like mugging is merely the problem of miscategorization and concomitant moral panics. If we choose to embrace this liberal position, we leave the political arena open to conservative campaigns for law and order – for, however exaggerated and distorted the arguments conservatives may marshal, the reality of crime in the streets *can* be the reality of human suffering and personal disaster.

The initial proponents of left realism also accused critical criminologists, particularly their former colleagues within Marxist criminology, of idealising or romanticising working-class offenders and portraying them as Hobsbawmian primitive class rebels or 'latter day Robin Hoods' (Lea and Young, 1984: 262). For the left realists, romanticising the criminal by transforming the criminal into a political rebel who is motivated by the gallant quest to redistribute societal resources equitably, or who is engaged in political resistance, overlooks the crimes that are committed for other reasons. The left realists also criticised mainstream theories. They accused positivist perspectives of ascribing the causes of crime to the pathology of the individual. They also accused classicist perspectives of focusing their analysis solely on the offence committed, or the individual involved. For the left realists, the more important aim should be to explore how best to create realistic responses to crime.

In the following extract, Young (1986: 21; emphasis in original) sets out the tenets of left realism:

> The central tenet of left realism is to reflect the reality of crime, that is in its origins, its nature and its impact. This involves a rejection of tendencies to romanticize crime or to pathologize it, to analyze solely from the point of view of the administration of crime or the criminal actor, to underestimate crime or to exaggerate it. And our understanding of methodology, our interpretation of the statistics, our notions of aetiology follow from this. Most importantly, it is realism, which informs our notion of practice: in answering what can be done about the problems of crime and social control.... Crime is not an activity of latter day Robin Hoods – the vast majority of working-class crime is directed within the working-class. It is intra-class *not* inter-class in its nature.

Although their criticism of Marxist criminology and other theories on the Left of criminology was somewhat scathing, the left realists stated that they did not totally reject Marxist criminologists' views about the harmful impact of crimes of the powerful or the criminogenic properties of capitalism. For Young (1986: 23–4), to insist that 'crime is not an activity of latter day Robin Hoods' and that crime is intra-class and also intra-racial, is not to:

> deny the impact of crimes of the powerful or indeed of the social problems created by capitalism which are perfectly legal. Rather, left realism notes that the working class is a victim of crime from all directions. It notes that the more vulnerable a person is economically and socially the more likely it is that both working-class and white-collar crime will occur against them; that one sort of crime tends to compound another, as does one social problem another. Furthermore, it notes that crime is a potent symbol of the antisocial nature of capitalism and is the most immediate way in which people experience other problems, such as unemployment, or competitive individualism. (See also Lea and Young, 1984.)

Thus, as the foregoing indicates, the original proponents of left realism believed that it is unwise to focus unduly on crimes of the powerful and on the criminogenic qualities of capitalism. According to them, such an approach overlooks the degree and impact of crime and victimisation in deprived communities.

In addition, the left realists rejected the contention of Marxist criminologists that crime control can be achieved through societal transformation to create wealth equality. The left realists dismissed this as an idealistic view that lacked practical merit and veered into the realms of utopianism (Lea and Young, 1984). They criticised Marxist criminologists for idealistically proposing that 'nothing much can be done short of fundamental transformations' (Young, 1997: 493). According to the left realists, this view rendered Marxist criminology unable to contribute meaningfully to law and order debates, or to proffer practical crime control strategies. As Young (1997: 493) put it: the left were unable to participate in 'the debate about law and order and to suggest immediate policies which will ameliorate the impact of crime and disorder upon wide sections of the population'. More recently, the left realist Elliott Currie (2010: 118) has reiterated this by pointing out that the so-called left idealists overlook the seriousness of crime and focus instead on highlighting the pervasiveness of unjust polices. As such, they do not countenance the importance of devising strategies that can humanise the criminal justice system. According to Currie (2010: 118): 'The left idealist position tends to avoid thinking about a criminal justice strategy at all beyond simple non-intervention.'

The original proponents of left realism argued that an unfortunate upshot of Marxist criminology's idealism was that neo-conservative criminology established itself as the arbiter of practical law and order policies and went ahead to monopolise political debates about crime control.

Like the right realists, the early left realists focused on predatory crime, such as street crime and burglary, in these communities. They conducted local victimisation surveys to explore the extent of crime in deprived areas (Jones et al, 1986; Crawford et al, 1990; Mooney, 2000). In addition, like the right realists, they identified rational choice as a casual factor. That said, unlike right realists, the left realists did acknowledge that crimes of the powerful are harmful and affect deprived groups the most. Another key point of departure from right realism is that the left realists described capitalism as criminogenic. They also emphasised the importance of addressing not only crime itself, but also its socio-economic causes. According to the left realists, the wider social factors that contribute to crime may be categorised as relative deprivation, marginalisation and subcultures. In addition, left realists argued that two dominant values in latemodern capitalist societies exacerbate the factors that cause crime. The values are consumerism and individualism (see also Young 1997; Tierney, 2009). The left realists described consumerism as the belief that social status is somehow determined by the amount of material possessions that one can accumulate. The left realists posited that consumerism can encourage people to become preoccupied with acquiring material possessions that they do not need. Indeed, people may go to extreme lengths to acquire these material things. They may resort to criminal activities. To a degree, this echoes Bonger's (1916) views about the consumerist values he believed that capitalism creates.

Left realists identified individualism as yet another dominant value in society. Young (1997) described individualism as the product of the free market economy that displaced Fordist industrial capitalism. The latter emphasised mass production and mass consumption. It was an economic system that was characterised by greater stability in the labour market, unlike the precarious employment arrangements that characterise the labour market institutions of latemodern societies. In these societies, leisure pursuits are directed towards asserting individual will and self-fulfilment over community-oriented endeavours. There is an emphasis on seeking instant gratification. Self-interestedness and hedonism are hallmarks of the latemodern market society, and they are also features of individualism. According to Young (1997), there are additional factors that exacerbate individualism. For example, as people progress up the social ladder and move out of their local communities, they lose the informal control mechanisms that used to regulate their behaviour. Another factor is the relocation of capital investment in deprived communities to other locations that are perceived to be more productive, and the destruction of families. Young argued that the latter has been precipitated by the decline in formal and informal sources of social welfare provision.

As mentioned earlier, the left realists identified consumerism and individualism as values that exacerbate the problematic factors that contribute to crime, namely, relative deprivation, marginalisation and subcultures (Young, 1997; Tierney, 2009).

Relative deprivation

For Lea and Young (1984), relative deprivation is a condition that affects people who believe that they have been deprived of the resources and possessions that others have, and which they believe they are entitled to. As such, they may feel that they have been denied the opportunity to acquire (through legitimate means, such as employment) the material things that other people possess.

According to Lea and Young, the values of consumerism and individualism make relative deprivation worse. They argued that consumerism, for example, fuels the belief that social status is somehow linked to the amount of material things an individual can acquire. Therefore, those who harbour consumerist values and feel deprived compared with others are more likely to feel that they have been deprived of access to the material things that they need to improve their status. In addition, the left realists maintained that individualism worsens relative deprivation because, in their view, relative deprivation can lead to crime in conditions where people who feel relatively deprived resort to selfish measures such as criminal activity to redress their condition. Young (1997: 488) noted that relative deprivation breeds discontent and crime where those who: 'experience a level of unfairness in their allocation of resources [relative deprivation] … utilise individualistic means to attempt to right this condition' (Young, 1997: 488). 'Individualistic means' might result in crime and other acts of deviance. According to Young, these acts amount to 'an unjust reaction to the experience of injustice' (p 488). Young believed that such a reaction can occur in any section of society, not only in the poorer sections. Indeed, left realists like Young insist that the individualistic impulse that triggers an 'unjust reaction' to perceived injustice has become a pervasive human trait in the UK and the US, and it contributes to crime in both jurisdictions (p 488).

The concept of relative deprivation was developed within the discipline of social psychology. However, left realists subsequently identified it as a criminogenic condition. One of its earliest proponents is W.G. Runciman, who defined relative deprivation as a perception or subjective assessment that one is the victim of injustice:

> We can roughly say that [a person] is relatively deprived of X when (i) he does not have X, (ii) he sees some other person or persons, which may include himself at some previous or expected time, as having X, (iii) he wants X, and (iv) he sees it as feasible that he should have X. (Runciman, 1966: 10)

If one does not feel more deprived than others, the experience of deprivation may be accepted. However, the perception that others possess what we have had and lost, or what we believe we could have (no matter how unrealistic it is that we could have it), creates a sense of injustice. Therefore, relative deprivation breeds discontent. Lea and Young maintained that there is no linear relationship between poverty and crime, unemployment and crime, or inequality and crime (see Lea and Young, 1984, 1993; Young, 1986, 1997). Rather, crime is the product of resentment about unfulfilled material expectations in late modern societies. According to Young, in these societies, added to the shift away from mass consumption as mentioned above, the dynamics of production have also been transformed. The advent of a market economy in the latemodern era and the precarious employment dynamics of its labour market institutions underpin this transformation. The fall of Keynesian expansionism (and the accompanying promise of full and stable employment) has led to the exclusion of large swathes of people who have been abandoned in wastelands of widespread unemployment and poverty. Trapped in these wastelands, they observe as others reap the rewards of full citizenship, and they become quite discontented. Thus, relative deprivation breeds discontent, and discontent without access to political means of rectifying the situation is criminogenic. According to Lea and Young (1984: 88): 'Poverty experienced as unfair ... creates discontent; and discontent where there is no political solution leads to crime. The equation is simple: relative deprivation equals discontent: discontent plus lack of political solution equals crime'.

Lea and Young (1993: 81, emphasis in original; see also 1984) went on to state that:

> Discontent occurs when comparisons between comparable groups are made which suggest that unnecessary injustices are occurring. If the distribution of wealth is seen as natural and just – however disparate it is – it will be accepted. An objective history of exploitation, or even a history of increased exploitation, does not explain disturbances. Exploitative cultures have existed for generations without friction: it is the perception of injustice – *relative deprivation* – which counts.

The left realists' supposition that relative deprivation can help explain crime, because it motivates the marginalised and disenfranchised to seek culturally defined goals through illegitimate means, echoes the views of Thomas Merton (1938), who introduced strain theory. As noted in Chapter One, the latter is also described as anomie theory. In line with one of the dimensions of Mertonian anomie theory, the left realists averred that the fractured relationship between cultural goals/expectations and social opportunities in capitalist societies (which are societies that are invariably characterised by inequality) creates crime. These societies hold out material accumulation as evidence of success, which is achievable by all. However, in reality, some are denied access to legitimate routes to acquiring the emblems of success. The marginalised may then resort to crime to attain cultural goals.

Thus, left realists insisted that it is not accurate to claim (as the mainstream theories do) that individuals who are classed as criminals lack normative values and are, as such, flawed. For the left realists, crime occurs because of flaws in the socio-economic structure of society, and not because of flaws within the individual. Indeed, the initial proponents of left realism argued that those who are classed as criminals possess superior consciousness. They are able to compare their situation with the situation of others, and to make the assessment that they have been unjustly denied the opportunities and the material wealth that others have access to. This perceived injustice fuels relative deprivation and crime. According to the left realists, as society has evolved, relative deprivation has grown with the proliferation of media sources, and with the expansion of social welfarism. Greater access to education, for example, has created higher expectations, with no corresponding rise in access to opportunity.

It is ironic that left realists vociferously rejected positivistic determinism but went ahead to adopt an approach that appears to anchor itself to the positivistic views espoused by Thomas Merton. It is also quite surprising that left realists embarked upon what might be considered to be a spectacular *volte-face* by engaging in activities that they had criticised those they labelled 'administrative criminologists' for. In the 1980s, left realists worked collaboratively with the state (specifically with Labour-run local councils) (Kinsey et al, 1986). As Rock (2012: 61) notes:

> Left Realism was to follow the earlier radical criminologists' injunction to act, but action was now much in the service of more effective and practical policing and crime reduction strategies.... Left Realists joined the formerly disparaged 'administrative criminologists' working in and for the (usually local) state to work on situationally-based projects to prevent crime and the fear of crime.

This apparent shift by left realists away from their previous ideological stance on the nature of crime and how best to address it must have been a surprising development at the time. What is less surprising is that, perhaps for obvious reasons, given that they had deprecated what they described as 'administrative criminology' in the 1970s, left realists such as a Jock Young did not declare their apparent affiliation with key ideas associated with 'administrative criminology'. In addition, they did not acknowledge the influence of Merton's strain theory and Runciman's work on relative deprivation. However, their elaboration of the concept of relative deprivation echoed aspects of the work of both theorists. According to Rock (2012: 47, emphasis added): 'An incarnation of anomie theory is thus to be found *muted* in "Left Realism"'.

Nevertheless it appears that there is empirical support for the view that relative deprivation may lead to crime. In his analysis of the links between economic conditions and crime rates, Box (1983) also analysed 17 studies and found that 12 of the studies appeared to suggest that income inequality (which could trigger perceived relative deprivation) is linked to levels of crime (mainly property crime) (see also Reiner, 2012b). Although the econometric studies that Box analysed have several methodological limitations and do not establish causality, they do lend some support to the view that there is a relationship between relative deprivation and property crime (Reiner, 2012b), or even homicide involving deprived young men (as perpetrators and victims) (Wilkinson and Pickett, 2009). Other studies reinforce this finding (Hale, 2005, cited in Reiner 2012b)).

Marginalisation

Left realists also identified the concept of marginalisation as a factor that is linked to crime. For the left realists, marginalisation operates interactively with relative deprivation to create crime (Young, 2002). They believe that relative deprivation (which can breed discontent) can also lead to crime 'where individuals feel marginalised socially and politically'. Young (1997: 488–9) commented that these individuals use 'individualistic means' to try to remedy the injustice they encounter. They may resort to riots and violent acts to get their voices heard. Left realists identify the population of young people (particularly young black men) who reside in social housing in inner-city areas as the population that experiences greater deprivation than those who reside in wealthier locations. Their ability to access mainstream resources, such as education and employment, is limited. They are socially excluded; they exist on the margins of society in conditions of deprivation and powerlessness (Young, 1994; 1997).

Subcultures

As noted earlier, the left realists identified subculture as another factor that contributes to crime. In their description of the nexus between subculture and crime, the left realists drew on Marxist criminology and subcultural theory. However, far from the Marxists' view that subcultural styles and behaviour are symbols of class resistance, the early left realists presented ideas that echoed Albert Cohen's (1955) subcultural theory. This theory posits that young people commit crimes because they are frustrated by their marginalisation and inability to access the resources they need to attain conventional and culturally set goals.

Their reaction or solution is to join or form delinquent subcultures or gangs. For the left realists, those who experience relative deprivation are more likely to gravitate to subcultures that encourage their members to adopt values that foster criminality. Consumerism and individualism represent prime examples of these criminogenic values. According to the left realists, consumerism and individualism are values that encourage the members of subcultures to commit crimes, especially acquisitive crimes like stealing, to acquire the material things and the status that they feel they have been deprived of in mainstream society.

They may even engage in non-utilitarian crimes, such as criminal damage, in order to acquire the respect of peers and elevate their status. Other factors, such as age, gender, class and ethnicity, also help explain the formation of subcultures. People who are denied access to the resources with which they can attain culturally defined goals because of their age, gender, class or ethnicity might resort to subcultures. According to Young (1994: 111, emphasis in original):

> Subcultures are problem-solving devices, which constantly arise as people in specific groups attempt to solve the structural problems, which face them. The problems are evaluated in terms of the existing subculture and the subculture changes over time in order to *attempt* a solution to those perceived problems. Crime is one form of subcultural adaption, which occurs where material circumstances block cultural aspirations and where non-criminal alternatives are absent or less attractive.

Crime prevention strategies: the square of crime and balanced interventions

The original proponents of left realism stated that their aim was to address what they considered to be the reluctance of theories on the Left of criminology (such as Marxist criminology) to acknowledge working-class crime and victimisation, and proffer translatable crime control solutions. The early left realists also challenged the law and order punitiveness of perspectives on the Right of criminology. Therefore, the left realists proposed what they considered to be practical crime prevention policy strategies to counter the Right's dominance over law and order. Unlike the right realists, who overlooked socio-economic causes, the left realists emphasised that social inclusion strategies can help control crime. They argued that crime control is best achieved if crime and its causes are targeted using a 'balanced intervention' strategy that addresses not only crime, but also its socio-economic causes. It follows that the left realists propose crime control strategies or 'interventions' that take into account *inter alia* the 'social causes' of crime. In their view, 'social causation is given the highest priority' (Young, 1997: 492). According to the left realists, crime control interventions should aim to address relative deprivation. They should also contribute to 'demarginalisation' or social inclusion. The interventions that seek to address social causes should be given greater priority, but they should coexist with community-level informal control strategies, and interventions by formal agents of social control including the police (p 492). Therefore, additional examples of the strategies the left realists propose include community-based sentences and restorative justice schemes. In their view, imprisonment should be avoided because it severs the prisoner's 'moral bond with the community'. Law and order policies, such as the punitive strategies proposed by the right realists, are also to be avoided in general because they exacerbate the disadvantage that deprived groups experience. The policies should be reserved only for serious cases. These ideas greatly influenced the New Labour government that was elected in Britain in 1997. The ideas were encapsulated in the government's promise to be 'tough on crime and tough on the causes of crime'.[3]

To explain the dynamics of crime and effective crime control, left realists designed a theoretical device they described as the 'square of crime' (see Figure 6.1). Initially, the square of crime comprised three interactive dimensions, namely: agents of social control (this includes state agencies and informal control agents); the offender; and the victim (Young, 1986). The left realists later expanded the square of crime to include the wider society or the public (Young, 1997).

Figure 6.1: The square of crime

Police/multi - agencies Social control agents	The offender
The victim	The public

Left realists maintain that interactions or 'social relationships' between the four elements of the square help explain crime and how best to control it (Young, 1997: 485). For example, the interaction between the offender and the victim 'determine the impact of crime' (Young, 1997: 485). In addition, interactions between state agencies and the offender affect crime rates. If state agencies deal with the offenders effectively, crime rates will decline. Thus, effective interventions by formal agents of social control are required to reduce reoffending, and crime in general. In addition, interactions between state agents, such as the police, and the public affect the effectiveness of state agencies in reducing crime. For example, good effective policing relies on good police–public relations that foster cooperation. Therefore, policing policies should be enacted through democratic processes within local communities. Left realists proposed minimal policing in most areas, but a greater concentration of policing in areas that seek greater police presence (see also DeKeseredy and Schwartz, 2012). The left realists emphasised that democratised control of the police within local communities would enhance police–public relations and improve crime prevention and control. Indeed, left realists propose the overall democratisation of crime prevention and control. In their view, this can be achieved through the devolution of crime policies to local councils. They maintain that it is important to decentralise decisions about policing, in particular, by transferring such decisions to local communities.

In sum, the left realists maintained that effective crime control involves improving the interactions between the four elements of the square of crime. Perhaps for this reason, they advocated the use of multi-agency strategies to control crime. These strategies should address each of the four factors that make up the square of crime. Such a multifaceted approach to crime control should also incorporate strategies that combine effective policing with social welfare provision. Young (1997: 492) described the balanced intervention that the left realists proposed as follows:

> For realism, then, the control of crime involves interventions on all levels: on the social causes of crime, on social control exercised by the community and the formal agencies, and on the situation of the victim. Furthermore, that social causation is given the highest priority, whereas formal agencies, such as the police, have a vital role, yet one which has in the conventional literature been greatly exaggerated. It is not the 'Thin Blue Line', but the social bricks and mortar of civil society which are the major bulwark against crime. Good jobs with a discernible future, housing estates that tenants can be proud of, community facilities which enhance a sense of cohesion and belonging, a reduction in unfair income inequalities, all create a society which is more cohesive and less criminogenic.

Comparing right and left realism

Ironically, although scholars on the Left of criminology developed left realism, there are several ideological similarities between left realism and right realism. Like the right realists, the left realists adopt an unproblematic conceptualisation of crime because they accept the state's definition of crime without question. Muncie (2000) aptly notes that: 'realist and administrative criminologies are trapped within a legal definition of "crime"'. Furthermore, like the right realists, left realists appear to focus on predatory crimes committed by deprived groups in deprived communities. They also appear to share the right realists' view that people who offend make the selfish choice to commit crime. This presumption reflects ideas that are congruent with the rational choice model. In addition, although left realists criticise neo-conservative criminologists, including right realists, for overlooking structural causes, some argue that identifying relative deprivation as a causal factor does not amount to a robust acknowledgement of the political economy of crime (Walklate, 2011).

A key difference that separates right realism and left realism is that they propose ideologically different crime control measures. Right realists advocate strategies that overlook socio-economic conditions and focus on the individual offender or the setting of the crime. Left realists propose strategies that target crime *and* its socio-economic contexts.

Right realists and left realists also espouse different views about effective policing. While right realists propose police empowerment from the centre, left realists advocate a more democratic and decentralised approach to policing. Although these are clearly different ideas about policing policy, some maintain that by advocating effective policing, the left realists adopted ideas associated with the administrative criminologists that they had previously disparaged quite scathingly (Rock, 2012). It is also argued that, ironically, left realists went ahead to work with the so-called 'administrative criminologists' on behalf of the state to devise crime preventions strategies! As Rock (2012: 61–2) observes quite perceptively: 'Were it not for their theoretical preambles, it was at times difficult to distinguish between the programmes of the Home Office or other state criminal justice ministries, on the one hand, and of Left realism, on the other'. That said, left realists generally distance themselves from right realism. As Friedrichs and Rothe (2012: 247) put it:

> left realists vehemently deny that their work leads in the same direction as right realists, because they differ from them in other important respects, namely they prioritise social justice over order, reject biogenetic, individualistic explanations of criminality and emphasise structural factors; are not positivistic insofar as they are concerned with the social meaning of crime as well as criminal behaviour, and connect links between law-making and law breaking and are acutely aware of coercive intervention, and are more likely to stress informal control.

Although there are important ideological differences between right realism and left realism, it would appear that the scholars who introduced left realism in the 1980s made quite a remarkable ideological U-turn, in the process, abandoning previous anti-essentialist and anti-establishment ideals in favour of some of the ideas and principles that they had strongly rejected in the not-so-distant past.

Criticisms

Left realism has sustained several criticisms. Gibbons (1994, cited in DeKeseredy, 2010), writing from the Right, argues that it focuses rather narrowly on the argument that it is important to take crime seriously. As such, it fails to develop a theoretical understanding of crime and crime control. Akers and Sellers (2009) reiterate this, pointing out that left realism lacks a sufficient empirical and theoretical basis. They do not offer testable theoretical insights, but, rather, simply set out a series of 'philosophical and political statements' about social issues (Akers and Sellers, 2009: 260).

Writing from the Left, Henry (1999, cited in DeKeseredy, 2010) comments that left realists do not provide original insights into the causes of crime (see also Coleman et al, 2009: 7). They are accused of simply attempting to 'synthesise diverse theories into just such a super "master narrative", with "left realism" combining key elements from strain, labelling, control and radical theories into one'. It attempts to integrate these theories into an overreaching 'master narrative' even when it has not managed to overcome the theoretical problems encountered by the theories that it has synthesised and borrowed from (Downes and Rock, 2007). Downes and Rock (2011) argue that left realism's key causal factor, namely, 'relative deprivation', over-predicts crime and exaggerates levels of criminality even in current times, particularly among women. Relatedly, it is argued that by combining potentially competing causal explanations, left realists encounter a 'multiplier effect', which amplifies its tendency to over-predict crime (Downes and Rock, 2007). Furthermore, the idea that relative deprivation helps explain crime is problematic and poses two difficulties. First, the early proponents of left realism focused on the crimes committed by the socioeconomically marginalised in working class areas. But, discontent is not exclusive to a specific class or group, it traverses all social classes. Left realists acknowledge this but point out that it is likely to be more potent among those who suffer social exclusion (Young, 2002). Thus they imply that discontent is more likely to trigger criminality among the socially excluded. Whether or not this is the case is perhaps open to question. Another analytical difficulty that afflicts the 'relative deprivation leads to crime' thesis is that it is perhaps unwise to trace all forms of crime to material deprivation. Indeed, it could be said that each one of us at some point or other in time feels materially deprived in comparison to some other person or group, but not everyone who feels relatively deprived resorts to crime as a solution.

Marxist criminologists criticise left realism for not paying sufficient attention to power dynamics and the role of the state in shaping crime and criminal justice (Sim et al, 1987). There is also the criticism that the earlier left realists emphasised the significance of black crime but overlooked the crimes that are committed by young white middle-class men. Indeed, some went as far as to accuse the authors of the text *What Is To Be Done About Law and Order* (Lea and Young, 1984, 1993) of racism for their alleged portrayal of young black men residing in inner-city areas as central figures in working-class crime (Lowman and Maclean, cited in Downes and Rock, 2011). Furthermore, although it addresses gendered violence and the victimisation of women, left realism has been criticised for overlooking feminist issues and the social inequalities that adversely affect women in patriarchal capitalist societies (Currie, 1991). Acknowledging this, more recent left realists comment that 'Perhaps the place where the left realists may be weakest is in response to a feminist critique' (Schwartz and DeKeseredy, 1991: 51). For some critics, left realists do not succeed in their attempt to balance their apparent commitment to mainstream criminological thinking with the somewhat radical rhetoric they also espouse (Menzies, 1992: 148). In addition, a criticism that can be levelled at both strands of realism is that they focus primarily on predatory crime, such as street crime and burglary. Right realists justify their focus on street crime with the argument that street crimes produce direct victimisation, are more visible, create greater fear of crime and undermine the quality of life (Wilson, 1975). We shall see that criminologists who study the crimes of the powerful have adduced evidence that suggests otherwise. According to these criminologists and others, the evidence indicates that crimes of the powerful produce more severe, and wider-ranging, victimisation than street crimes (see, eg, Hillyard and Tombs, 2005, 2007; Spalek, 2007). Meanwhile, in a recent review of the field, two writers who identify themselves as left realists drew attention to a possible reason why there appeared to be a focus on street crimes in the early history of left realism. In their view, much of the existing criminological theories on the Left in the 1980s tended to ignore street crimes, and this created a vacuum in knowledge about these crimes (DeKeseredy and Schwartz, 2012). They point to recent work done by left realists who have focused on the crimes of the powerful (DeKeseredy and Schwartz, 2012), although they do acknowledge that more work is required in this area.

Right realism, in particular, has been criticised for failing to acknowledge the impact of socio-economic and political disadvantage on offending behaviour. It has been argued that the key theses that underpin right realism, namely, the broken windows thesis and Murray's underclass thesis, lack sufficient empirical bases. In addition, critics point out that the punitive law and order policies proposed by the right realists were largely ineffective. Official statistics indicate that crime rates soared throughout the 1980s.

In response to some of the criticisms left realism received, Jock Young did go on to state that left realism did not (at least in its original formulation) understand crime to be an unproblematic concept, nor did it accept without question popular understandings of crime or definitions of crime by the criminal law (Young, 1991). He also asserts that left realism did not discount corporate crime as irrelevant. Rather, when it emerged in the 1980s, it sought to highlight the extent of intra-class victimisation in deprived communities. Its aim at the time was to proffer ameliorative policy strategies that would counter the prevailing law and order punitiveness of perspectives on the Right of criminology.

Conclusions

Left realists in Britain, such as Jock Young, turned their attention towards more structuralist accounts of crime in the 1990s (Young, 1999), and subsequently to culturalist accounts (Young, 2011; Hayward and Young, 2012).[4] In the US, writers such as Elliot Currie, Walter DeKeseredy and others have continued to develop left realism. Currie (2010) describes his version of left realism as 'plain left realism'. For Currie, plain left realism, just like the original version, is 'realist' because it emphasises that crime should be taken seriously as it is a reality for the individuals and communities affected by it. He endorses several arguments about crime put forward by the Left. Therefore, he recognises that crime is socially constructed and some acts that are harmful are not defined as crime. He also acknowledges that some people are more vulnerable to criminal justice interventions than others.

However, he believes that crime is much broader in its nature and impact. Therefore, it is reductionist to define it solely as a socially constructed phenomenon, created by the state and right-wing politicians, and exaggerated by media reports that fuel public fear and racist sentiments. In his view, such a definition attempts to replace distorted messages about crime with a rather unhelpful reductionist definition that minimises it. Currie ascribes the reductionist definition to *left idealism*, which he reconceptualises as *liberal minimalism*. Echoing the arguments of the original proponents of left realism, Currie (2010) goes on to state that a reductionist definition of crime is 'empirically misleading and ... politically disastrous' because it ignores public concerns and cedes control of law and order issues to the Right. His brand of left realism echoes most of the arguments of the earlier versions of left realism. That said, plain left realism has attempted to address some of the problems that the critics of left realism identified, such as its excessive focus on young black males in deprived inner-city areas. In his study of the aetiology of crime among white middle-class young people, Elliott Currie (2005) emphasised the impact of social Darwinism in neoliberal societies such as the US. In his view, the form of social Darwinism that exists in these societies can be criminogenic. It manifests itself as a culture of competiveness. Some argue that the latter can create feelings of real or perceived failure, which can in turn undermine self-worth and trigger lack of empathy for self and for others. Social Darwinism it is argued, gives rise to individualism, which as we have seen above has been linked to criminality. In the case of the middle-class young people Currie studied, individualism appeared to be a reaction to the problems posed by the culture of competiveness they have to contend with, and the inadequate support provided by formal and informal institutions.

Left realism has also re-emerged in the UK through the work of Roger Matthews (2009; 2014), who was one of its original proponents, and more recently, as mentioned earlier, in the US through the work of DeKeseredy and Schwartz (2010). In the UK, Roger Matthews (2009; 2014) reignited left realist debates, which were published in a special issue of the peer-reviewed journal *Theoretical Criminology*. Similarly, the journal *Crime Law and Social Change* also published a special issue on left realism in 2010 (DeKeseredy and Schwartz, 2011).

SUMMARY

- Left realism emerged to counter the dominance of the Right over crime control debates, and to contribute to debates about 'law and order'.
- Left realists are so described because some of the ideas they espouse are associated with perspectives on the Left of criminology, and also because they describe their position on the aetiology of crime as 'realist'. They assert that this is because they acknowledge that crime is a real social problem. They do not dismiss crime as a social construct.
- The original proponents of left realism:
  - described Marxist criminologists as 'left idealists' and criticised them for romanticising working-class offenders by portraying them as victims of exploitation and rebels on a quest to redistribute societal wealth more equitably, and for dismissing crime as a social construction, thereby failing to take crime seriously;
  - focused mainly on crime in working-class communities, and argued that, contrary to the view of Marxist criminologists that crime is primarily inter-class, crime is intra-class and working-class people commit crimes against other working-class people;
  - traced crime in capitalist societies to relative deprivation, marginalisation and subcultures, and identified consumerism and individualism as dominant values that contribute to these factors;
  - designed the square of crime which comprises the agents of social control, the offender, the victim and the public – to explain the dynamics of crime and effective crime control, arguing that interactions between the four elements of the square help explain crime and how best to control it; and
  - introduced ideas about crime that were quite similar to the ideas of the right realists, for example, they focused on predatory crime in deprived communities and identified rational choice as a causal factor like the right realists did.
- In general, an important difference between both strands of criminological realism is that unlike the right realists, the left realists include in their description of crime causation an analysis of structural causal factors, such as class inequality and gender inequality. The left realists also advocate that crime control and prevention strategies should focus not only on crime, but also on the causes of crime.

SAMPLE QUESTIONS

1. Left realism and right realism are ideologically different perspectives in criminology. Discuss.
2. In what ways do left realism and right realism contribute to our understanding of crime and how best to control crime?

Notes

[1] According to Jock Young (1991: 15), who is a key writer in this field, left realism emerged 'the post-1985 period'.

[2] It has been argued (and it certainly seems to be the case) that the left realists used the term 'left idealism' to describe the position of not only their former colleagues within Marxist criminology, but also the work of interactionists, abolitionists and other approaches that explore how the state exercises its power (Carrabine et al, 2009).

[3] This phrase was included in the New Labour government's election manifesto in 1997. In the manifesto, the Labour Party stated that:

> On crime, we believe in personal responsibility and in punishing crime, but also tackling its underlying causes – so, tough on crime, tough on the causes of crime, different from the Labour approach of the past and the Tory policy of today.

[4] Chapter Ten focuses on cultural criminology. It examines the work of criminologists who have offered culturalist accounts of crime.

SEVEN

Feminist critiques

Introduction

This chapter explores feminist perspectives in criminology. It is probably impossible to define feminist criminology. This is because it comprises numerous strands. As DeKeseredy (2010: 29) observes: 'there are at least 12 variants of feminist criminological theory'. Daly and Chesney-Lind (1988: 502) offer a broad definition that appears to capture its key themes. They define feminist criminology as 'a set of theories about women's oppression and a set of strategies for change'. Chesney-Lind and Morash (2013: 288) go further to state that at the core of feminist thought in criminology is the theoretical and empirical examination of the gender dimension of crime and crime control.

As the foregoing suggests, there are several feminist criminological perspectives. It has been argued that the perspectives share some explanatory themes in common with other critical criminological perspectives. Daly (2010: 229) observes that 'there is a good deal of affinity and cross over between feminist perspectives in criminology and those termed critical, anti-racist, multi-ethnic or cultural criminology'. For example, like other critical criminological perspectives, some feminist perspectives emphasise that power defines the dynamics of social interactions in society (see Daly, 2010). Another feature some feminist criminologists share in common with critical criminological perspectives is the view that crime is a social construction,[1] and power dynamics shape its construction. Tombs (2013: 236) notes that:

> Whilst there are clear differences between the labelling perspective, Marxism and feminism, they share the theoretical commitment to move beyond the narrowest confines of criminology, to deconstruct dominant categories of crime and to view these constructions, and the criminal justice systems based upon them, as an effect of, but also a means of reproducing power.

There are, of course, as Tombs points out, differences in the empirical and theoretical focus of different strands of critical criminology. In addition, although feminists collectively believe that gender inequality exists and should be addressed, they differ in their views about the source of such inequality, or the appropriate strategies for addressing it (Flavin, 2001). Moreover, for some feminist writers, to describe feminist criminology as a critical criminological perspective is an inaccurate depiction because feminist criminology is quite unique. For example, feminist criminology places gender at the core of its analysis of crime. Indeed, feminist criminologists accuse not only mainstream or orthodox criminology, but also most critical criminological perspectives, of 'gender-blindness' for overlooking female offending and female victimisation (Gelsthorpe and Morris, 1988: 98). Feminist criminologists also maintain that the existing social order is androcentric (or male-centred) (see also Daly and Chesney-Lind, 1988).

Origins of feminist criminology

Feminist criminology traces its roots to the second wave of feminism that emerged in the US and flourished in the UK in the late 1960s (Heidensohn, 2012). It provided the impetus for the advent of feminist criminology in the 1970s. The key text that launched feminist criminology in Britain is *Women, Crime and Criminology*, which was written by Carol Smart and published in 1976[2] (see Box 7.1).

Box 7.1: The origins of feminist criminology

A radical criminologist in her own right, Carol Smart[3] was a student of one of the original proponents of radical criminology in Britain, Ian Taylor. In an important text on feminist criminology titled *Women, Crime and Criminology*, Smart (1976) criticised orthodox criminology, radical criminology and interactionist studies of deviance for overlooking female criminality and victimisation. Smart also criticised these theories and perspectives for excluding women from discussions about the oppression and victimisation of less-powerful groups in capitalist societies. In addition, Smart criticised positivism for describing female offenders according to stereotypes that portrayed women in general as psychologically or biologically determined and inferior. An extract from the text is reproduced below.

> This book began as a postgraduate dissertation, which I wrote for a Master's degree in criminology. It was during this time as a postgraduate that I became aware of the overwhelming lack of interest in female criminality displayed by established criminologists and deviancy theorists.... I began searching for sources ... I realised that the one thing most of the papers and books had in common was an entirely uncritical attitude towards sexual stereotypes of women and girls. From Lombroso and Ferrero (1895) to ... G. Konopka (1966) the same attitudes and presuppositions reappeared, confining the biologically determined inferior status of women not only in conventional society but also in the 'world' of crime and delinquency. The material that I uncovered presented mainly cultural stereotypes and anti-feminist ideology.... The lack of interest in female criminality which is displayed by orthodox criminology has also had the effect of rendering it insignificant to more contemporary schools of thought within the discipline. There appears to have been no need to counter the conservative tradition with a more liberal perspective, nor indeed to replace the liberal tradition with a radical or critical analysis largely because of the insignificance of female criminality in the 'old' criminology ... in the case of studies of male criminality a certain progression may be traced from the

classical school of Beccaria, to the emergence of positivism which upholds a belief in biological or psychological determinism, to the subcultural and interactionist theorists and finally to those works displaying a Marxist influence. With the study of female criminality this development has largely been arrested at the positivist stage with the result that our present understanding of female deviance is based predominantly upon biological or psychological drives and urges which are deemed to be peculiar to the female constitution or psyche. (Smart, 1976: 4)

Key arguments in feminist criminology

A fundamental feature that unites the diverse feminist perspectives is that they are critical of traditional criminological theories. They are also *critical* of critical criminological theories. Downes and Rock (2011: 278) note that 'the rise of feminism in the 1970s generated a critical attack on critical criminology'. Broadly, feminist criminologists accuse other criminological theories of the following:

- gender-blindness, which may be described as the undue focus on a male-centred view of the world, and the pursuit of 'malestream' male-centred criminology (Gelsthorpe and Morris, 1988: 96);
- a failure to address the glaring gender gap in offending that exists because men commit significantly more crime than women (Heidensohn and Silvestri, 2012); and
- a failure to account for the experiences of women in the criminal justice system as offenders and victims (Eaton, 1986) or as officials (Heidensohn, 1992).

Early writers in the field of feminist criminology, such as Carol Smart, explored a broad range of issues, including gender and crime (see also Naffine, 1997). Subsequent work in the field has examined additional issues, such as the experiences of women in the criminal justice system as defendants or offenders (Gelsthorpe, 2006), and the experiences of women as victims of crime (Dobash and Dobash, 1998). Some have also explored the gender distribution of criminal justice employees (Heidensohn and Silvestri, 2012).

Gender and crime

Before the advent of feminist criminology, criminology as a discipline paid little attention to how gender (female and male) affects crime. The experiences of women as offenders or victims of crime were largely ignored. DeKeseredy (2010: 27) points out that 'even Taylor, Walton and Young's (1973) *The New Criminology*, perhaps the most important work of its generation, ignores women and gender'. Feminist criminologists decry this, and point out that, historically (since the mid-20th century), criminology has focused on theorising the aetiology of crimes committed by men, and has relied mainly on positivist theories and research methods (Chesney-Lind and Morash, 2013). Indeed, according to Chesney-Lind and Morash (2013: 287), 'the founders of criminology almost completely overlooked women's crime, and they ignored, minimized, and trivialized female victimization'. There was a focus on positivistic explanations of male offending. Even well-known qualitative researchers in the field of criminology who contributed significantly to the development of key criminological theories proceeded on the basis of their male-centred view of the world and focused on the deviant activities of boys and young men. Chesney-Lind and Morash (2013) cite the examples of Thrasher's (1927) and Cohen's (1955) work on deviant behaviour.

It is argued that in their limited incursions into this area, mainstream criminological theories focused on stereotypical ideas about female offending. These ideas were deterministic and had their bases in biological and psychological positivism. Biological positivists, including Lombroso, believed that women posssess certain biological attributes that make them unlikely to commit crime. It was presumed that these attributes determine aspects of their personality and behaviour, such as their 'temperament, intelligence, ability and aggression' (Smart, 1995: 18). Women who did go on to commit crime were therefore considered to be either naturally criminal or afflicted with mental instability. It was believed that their behaviour contravened the biologically programmed (law-abiding) quality women were deemed to possess. It was also believed that women who offend possess masculine attributes. Indeed, Smart (1995) notes that much of female offending was explained with reference to biological factors such as hormonal problems. According to Smart (1995: 18), this amounts to 'biological determinism'. Structural factors, like class and power, were not given due consideration (Smart, 1995). Ideas about female criminality were also based on the sexist[4] views of criminologists who had minimal understanding of women's social worlds (Daly and Chesney-Lind, 1988). There was therefore a tendency to conflate sexual deviance with criminal deviance. Descriptions of female criminality were infused with culturally determined notions of female sexuality. In general, because women who offend were considered to be anomalous, limited effort was made to study female offending and female victimisation.

The advent of feminist criminology helped reverse this trend. Feminist criminologists now study gender and crime. As we shall see later, the diverse feminist perspectives that now exist, offer explanations for female offending. Feminists also draw attention to the gender gap in offending. It is widely accepted that a gender gap in offending exists because men commit far more crimes than women: 'That men and boys are responsible for the majority of offending behaviour remains an uncontested feature within criminology and debates about gender and crime' (Heidensohn and Silvestri, 2012: 348). That said, there has been limited effort in criminology to theorise the gender gap (Chesney-Lind and Morash, 2013). In the following statement, Heidensohn and Silvestri (2012: 336) suggests that the gender gap is now being theorised mainly because feminist criminology emerged and drew considerable attention to the phenomena:

Men commit crime at higher rates than women, are involved in more serious and violent offending, and are more prone to recidivism. [This] was unconsidered ... for much of the subject's history. That it is now a central and much debated matter is due largely to the advent of feminist criminology, which took the 'gender gap' in recorded crime as one of its key themes.

Some feminists, such as liberal feminists, suggest that the gender gap may be a feature of the different socialisation processes that men and women undergo, which render men more likely to engage in aggressive behaviour, including criminality. Scholars who study masculinities and crime also explore the factors that help explain the gender gap. These issues are addressed later on in this chapter.

Women in the criminal justice system

Feminist criminologists argue that criminology does not pay sufficient attention to the experiences of women within the criminal justice system as offenders and victims. Two schools of thought have emerged from the work of feminists who study the experiences of women as offenders in the criminal justice system. These are mutually reinforcing theses and they may be classified as the chivalry thesis and the double deviance thesis. Both theses suggest that the treatment female offenders receive may depend on stereotypical ideas about what constitutes 'normal' female behaviour. Women who offend or who have been accused of crime may receive chivalrous treatment if their circumstances, demeanour and the offences that they have committed do not contravene stereotypical ideas about what constitutes conventional femininity. On the other hand, women may receive a more punitive response than their male counterparts if they are deemed to have violated socially accepted definitions of the role and behaviour of women. They may be punished twice: for violating social norms; and for violating the criminal law (Carlen, 1983).

Studies support both theses and suggest that sentencing practices involving women offenders are often inconsistent (Eaton, 1986). This inconsistency depicts the tension between stereotypical portrayals of women as either weak and deserving of chivalrous responses, or as 'doubly deviant' individuals who have violated not only the law, but also socially constructed ideas about femininity, and are, as such, vulnerable to harsh formal and informal sanctions. Studies also indicate that defendants who conform to traditional ideals about gender roles are more likely to receive lenient treatment compared with those who do not, such as homosexuals, single mothers or others who contravene accepted beliefs about gender roles, for example, those branded 'bad' mothers (Eaton, 1986; Heidensohn and Silvestri, 2012: 351). Other studies reveal that young women may be punished more severely for sexual misconduct compared with men accused of similar conduct (Gelsthorpe and Sharpe, 2006). In addition, Heidensohn and Silvestri (2012) point to the possibility that the gender gap in offending may place the few women who do offend at greater risk of harsh punishment. This is because they are more likely to be deemed guilty of anomalous behaviour. Consequently, added to penal sanctions, they may also suffer social stigmatisation and informal sanctions, such as partner violence (Carlen, 1983). Although some studies suggest that the experiences of women in the system as offenders may be more related to stereotypical assumptions about their gender than to the offence that they have been prosecuted for or convicted of, it is worth noting that other studies have found limited differences in the sentencing of men and women who were convicted of similar crimes (Daly, 1994).

In terms of the experience of female prisoners, studies in England suggest that although there are few female prisoners, the prison establishment (including actual prisons) are designed for men and are, as such, inadequate for women (Corston Report, 2007). It is also argued that: there are not enough prison places for women (there is no female prison in Wales); the Mother and Baby Units available are insufficient; and the plight of the children of imprisoned mothers deserves critical attention because women tend to be the primary carers of their children. In addition, studies suggest that probation services are not sufficiently geared towards the needs of women (Martin et al, 2009).

As mentioned earlier, feminist criminologists also study the experiences of women as the victims of crime. Radical feminist criminologists, for example, have conducted studies to explore the violent victimisation and re-victimisation of women by men, and the insufficient protection afforded to women by the criminal justice system (Dobash and Dobash, 1998). Through their work on the victimisation of women, particularly women in deprived communities who suffer repeat victimisation, feminists have uncovered hidden female victimisation in contexts such as the home, where the perpetrator and the victim are known to each other. For example, the study by Painter (1991), which explored rape in relationships, found that, contrary to common assumptions, rape committed by men against women that they are in intimate relationships with was more common than rape committed against women by strangers. Consequently, feminists have challenged the long-standing view (often bolstered by official crime statistics) that violent crime is: typically random; often perpetrated by strangers; and the victims are usually young men who are likely to be out on the streets. Feminists and, indeed, other criminologists have since challenged the idea often promoted by the media that the home (rather than the street or other sites of interaction, such as the workplace) is a safe place for women. As Ferrell (2005: 150) rightly states, news media representations highlight 'the criminal victimization of strangers rather than the dangerous intimacies of domestic or family conflict'. Feminists and others assert that the perpetrators of violent crimes against women are typically people who are known to the victims. Indeed, studies and statistics support this contention. A report by Hester (2013), which presented the findings of research into the criminal justice system's response to sexual offences and sentencing in the North East Region of England, found that the victims knew almost all of the perpetrators. However, criminal justice agents and the media tend to focus on random street crimes by, and against, men.

Feminist criminologists have contributed to the development of the field of study known as radical victimology. They have worked strenuously to counter the concept of 'victim precipitation' in certain crimes, such as rape. In their view, victim precipitation echoes positivistic ideas of victim culpability and amounts to 'victim blaming' (Mawby and Walklate, 1994). Some feminists argue that when applied in rape cases, the concept of victim precipitation also perpetuates stereotypes about 'femininity' and 'appropriate female behaviour'. In doing so, the concept reinforces patriarchal ideals about the inferior role and nature of women. Those whose actions deviate from these stereotypes are more likely to be accused of victim culpability or victim precipitation. Some feminists also maintain that women are more vulnerable to specific forms of victimisation, such as rape and domestic violence, in patriarchal societies where men occupy positions of power in all contexts of social interaction, from the workplace to the home (Dobash and Dobash, 2004).

In recent years, radical feminists[5] have contributed to the transformation of criminal justice policies that affect women. They have drawn policy attention to so-called 'hidden crimes', which, they argue, tend to victimise women and children disproportionately. These crimes include domestic violence and sexual abuse (Dobash and Dobash, 2004). Radical feminists have also campaigned to protect the victims of sexual abuse from court proceedings that might stigmatise them, re-victimise, or both. The victims are now able to give their evidence in private. Furthermore, feminists have campaigned (with some level of success) for criminal justice reforms to improve police efficiency in recording and also in responding to these crimes (Matczak and Lindsay, 2011). Police intervention in these cases has traditionally been far from robust. Unfortunately, recent studies and reports suggest that policing is still not as robust as it should be. A recent inspection of police responses to domestic abuse cases found that only eight out of the 43 police forces in England and Wales responded effectively to such incidents (Her Majesty's Inspectorate of Constabulary, 2014). Other feminists in this field have extended the study of female victimisation to accommodate wider ethnic, cultural and structural concerns. They have explored the experiences of the victims of other hidden crimes, such as honour killings, and patterns of abuse in black and minority ethnic families.

Feminist criminology: the diverse perspectives

What I have presented so far is a review of the origins of feminist criminology and some of the key issues it concerns itself with. What follows is a description of the diverse strands of feminist criminology. Perspectives in feminist criminology converge around the strands of mainstream feminist thought, which may be broadly classified as: liberal feminist theory; radical feminist theory; Marxist feminism; socialist feminism; and postmodern feminism (Burgess-Proctor, 2006; Chesney-Lind and Morash, 2013). These schools of feminist thought have been described as the 'best known of the early theoretical influences on criminology'

(Chesney-Lind and Morash, 2013: 290). According to Carol Smart (1999), these categories of feminist thought held sway in the 1970s and 1980s. Added to the strands of feminist thought, there are epistemological orientations that influence how feminist criminologists conduct empirical research and construct knowledge. These epistemological orientations are feminist empiricism, standpoint feminism and postmodern feminism (see Harding, 1986; Comack, 1999; Smart, 1999). Gelsthorpe (2002) and others have described the epistemological positions as empiricism, standpointism and deconstruction[6] (see also Naffine, 1997; Daly, 2010: 230). These are not exclusive categories; some feminists incorporate aspects of more than one in their empirical work (Smart, 1999). The following description of feminist perspectives begins with an examination of the schools of feminist thought and then proceeds to a discussion of the three epistemological positions.

Liberal feminist theory

Feminist criminologists who advocate equal rights for both genders are described as liberal feminists. In the study of women and crime or women and criminal justice, some of the early feminists were liberal feminists, who proposed that male and female offenders should receive equal treatment. In general, liberal feminists view gender as a social construct. They posit that men and women are essentially the same. Therefore, they advocate equal rights and equality of opportunity for men and women. They trace the oppression of women to the way in which gender roles are defined during socialisation (Burgess-Proctor, 2006). Similarly, feminist criminologists who subscribe to liberal feminism trace the treatment of women in the criminal justice system, and also the way women are portrayed by mainstream criminologists, to the differential definition and allocation of gender roles during socialisation.

Liberal feminists believe that the way in which society defines gender roles and gender differences creates attitudes and stereotypes that disadvantage women. Men are given higher-status social roles that place them in positions of power (Burgess-Proctor, 2006). It is socially acceptable for men to be 'competitive and aggressive' (Burgess-Proctor, 2006: 29). These are accepted 'male' or masculine attributes. Women, on the other hand, are expected to be 'nurturing and passive' (Burgess-Proctor, 2006: 29). The latter are considered to be 'female' or feminine attributes. Consequently, women who commit crime may be punished more severely for violating social norms and social expectations about acceptable female behaviour. It could be argued that the chivalry thesis and the double deviance thesis described earlier, reinforce the position of the liberal feminists. As we have seen, both theses point to the differential treatment that women receive in criminal justice contexts. The theses trace this to the influence of social norms and beliefs about appropriate gender roles. Unfortunately, women who do not conform to the socially constructed gender roles may be vulnerable to more punitive responses within the criminal justice system.

Liberal feminists point out that men and women learn about socially constructed gender roles during socialisation. Indeed, liberal feminists also try to explain the gender gap in offending by referring to the dissimilar socialisation processes that men and women undergo. Thus, liberal feminists believe that the gender gap in offending exists because the way in which women are socialised gives them fewer opportunities to engage in crime. Women are subject to stronger controls than men (Heidensohn, 1996). Mainstream criminological theories emphasised this view. For example, Cohen (1955: 14), who developed the subculture theory of crime, put it that 'the delinquent is a rogue male'. Thrasher, a sociologist who contributed to the development of the first Chicago School, conducted an ethnography of youth gangs and remarked that:

> First, the social patterns for the behaviour of girls, powerfully backed by the great weight of tradition and custom, are contrary to the gang and its activities; secondly, girls, even in urban disorganised areas are much more closely supervised and guarded than boys and usually well incorporated into the family groups or other social structures. (Thrasher, 1947: 228)

Liberal feminists argue that given the historical advantage that men have had over women in many aspects of social life, there is a need to modify existing structures to achieve a balanced society in which men and women enjoy equal rights. There should also be an effort to reshape the socialisation of both genders to avoid the internalisation of unequal gender roles that are socially constructed and which ultimately disadvantage women socially, economically and politically. Feminist criminologists who subscribe to liberal feminist thought echo this view. They believe that changing the way in which boys and girls are socialised, and removing gender bias from sentencing, which disadvantages women, should help to reduce and redress the problems that women encounter because of their gender (Chesney-Lind and Morash, 2013).

For some commentators, an upshot of liberal feminism and the women's movement it spawned has been to alter traditional sex roles, engender greater gender equality and provide greater opportunities for women, including occupational opportunities. The latter has led to a significant increase in the representation of women in the workforce (Adler, 1975; Akers and Sellers, 2009). It is argued that these factors have enabled women to undertake roles previously reserved for men, and to acquire masculine traits that are linked to criminality. They are now increasingly involved in activities previously considered to be male–dominated, including criminal activities. These ideas have been described as the 'masculinity hypothesis' (Akers and Sellers, 2009: 274). There is a belief that improved conditions for women account for the greater participation of women in crime (Adler, 1975). However, although it is generally acknowledged that rates of female offending (young offenders and adult offenders) have increased, it has been argued that the reasons for this increase are perhaps not as clear-cut as the masculinity hypothesis presupposes. As Heidensohn and Gelsthorpe (2007: 392) put it: 'the female share of crime does seem to be increasing, if slightly ... part of the change can be attributed to drugs crimes, and partly to increasing violence among women, although there are many myths about this'.

Others also reject the claim that improved conditions for women have triggered an increase in rates of female offending on the basis that the claim lacks empirical support. They argue that the increase in female crime is linked to the inclination of some women to commit specific types of crime, namely, property crimes. The increase may also be attributable to criminal justice policies that have targeted specific ethnicities, particularly black people, in jurisdictions such as the US in the guise of equal treatment (Renzetti, 2012). Some also attribute the increasing presence of women in official crime statistics to the phenomenon of net-widening, which occurs when the system takes proactive steps to incarcerate more women in order to assuage public fear and anxiety about the activities of the so-called 'violent girls' that are often portrayed in the media. Worrall (2004: 56–7) points out that:

> No one would deny that young women are capable of acts of violence but the category 'violent girls' is a social construction.... It is a way of managing the anxiety, fear, and suspicion that troubled and troublesome women provoke in respectable citizens. It is a form of insurance against the perceived threats of ever-increasing numbers of Myra Hindleys, Rose Wests, and Josie O'Dwyers. Yet nothing is more certain to ensure the enlargement of the next generation of such women than locking up increasing numbers of our teenage daughters.

Feminist perspectives that propose gender equality have been criticised for failing to acknowledge that gender is a socially constructed concept and for not sufficiently problematising androcentric notions of normality that disadvantage women. Consequently, they have been accused of accepting the view that men represent the norm, or the standard against which issues of equality should be measured (Smart, 1995). According to Smart (1995: 42): 'Basically the equality paradigm always affirms the centrality of men. Men continue to constitute the norm, the unproblematic, the natural social actor. Women are thus always seen as interlopers into a world already organised by others'.

Thus, some emphasise that advocating gender equality without problematising existing male dominance and privilege is tantamount to accepting that men, and the provisions available to them, represent the norm or archetype. According to the critics, this is quite problematic because it can expose women to treatment that is more suitable for men. Indeed, it has been argued that in criminal justice settings, the sanctions available are primarily androcentric. For example, as mentioned earlier, in England, it has been noted that most prison establishments are designed for men. Baroness Corston's wide-ranging review of the experiences of female prisoners in England recommended that custodial arrangements should be designed specifically to meet the unique needs of women because the existing arrangements had been designed for men (Corston Report, 2007). The review found that existing provisions in prison disadvantage women quite significantly. Equally, probation services have been traditionally geared towards the needs of men (Martin et al, 2009). Perhaps this illustrates the danger of advocating equality: it may 'yield equality with a vengeance' (Daly and Chesney-Lind, 1988: 525).

Liberal feminists have also been criticised for overlooking structural conditions that disadvantage women, particularly racial difference, social class and gender relations, and other factors that render the experiences of men and women in society qualitatively different (Burgess-Proctor, 2006; MacKinnon, 1991). They are accused of presuming that the law is gender-blind or objective and immune to the dynamics of gender relations that disadvantage women. Critics argue that gender relations do, indeed, affect the law and its operation (Burgess-Proctor, 2006). Smart (1995: 43) comments that 'Law does not stand outside gender relations and adjudicate upon them. Law is a part of these relations, and is always already gendered in its principles and practices.'

Radical feminist theory

Radical feminist theory has also influenced some feminist criminologists, particularly those who have gone on to draw attention to the crimes of violence men perpetrate against women in order to dominate and control them. Radical feminists generally identify patriarchy (male dominance) as a key factor that explains the experience of women in society (Burgess-Proctor, 2006; Chesney-Lind and Morash, 2013). A patriarchy exists where the structure of a society and gender relations in that society are characterised by male domination. In such societies, men occupy positions of power and privilege, and they oppress women. Hartmann (1981: 175) defines patriarchy as the 'set of social relations between men, which have a material base, and which, though hierarchical, establish or create interdependence and solidarity among them that enable them to dominate women'. Radical feminists argue that patriarchy is woven into the fabric of society. Patriarchy transcends all other factors that may affect women's experiences, such as race and social class. It shapes gender relations and social interactions (Burgess-Proctor, 2006).

Radical feminists believe that patriarchy pervades not only social structures, but also intimate gender relations. Some posit that patriarchal gender relations enable men to control the sexuality of women, including their 'reproductive capacity', through acts of violence and abuse, which may take the form of rape and other forms of domestic violence (Chesney-Lind and Morash, 2013: 290). As mentioned earlier, radical feminists pay particular attention to crimes of violence committed by men against women (Dobash and Dobash, 1998; 2004; Burgess-Proctor, 2006; Maidment, 2006; Tierney, 2009). They cite domestic violence, rape and other violent crimes perpetrated by men against women as expressions of patriarchy in intimate relationships. They also aver that female offending is usually the product of violent victimisation by men (Burgess-Proctor, 2006). According to radical feminists, men generally assume a sense of superiority over women and believe that they are entitled to exercise power over women in all sites of interaction, including heterosexual relationships and criminal justice contexts. As already noted, some studies that have explored responses to the crimes of violence that men commit against women (usually against the women they share an intimate relationship with) reveal that despite attempts in recent years to encourage the police and other criminal justice professionals to take these crimes seriously, there still remains a general reluctance to pursue these cases vigorously.

In patriarchal societies where partriachial gender relations dominate both social and familial contexts, men define women's roles and feminist attributes, using definitions that oppress women and further the interests of men (Dobash, 1979). Radical feminists also argue that in capitalist societies, women are disenfranchised because they are denied access to work and are instead constrained within a labour force of unpaid workers who cater for the male labour force. While Marxist criminologists identify the working-class proletariat as the exploited class in capitalist societies, radical feminists identify women as the exploited and oppressed in such societies.

In sum, radical feminists believe that existing social structures and institutions oppress women. Radical feminists criticise liberal feminists for not proposing more far-reaching changes that can create better circumstances for women. The radical feminists believe that existing social structures are in place to 'preserve male power and ensure female subordination' (Renzzetti, 2012: 134). Thus, they propose that all patriarchal institutions should be dismantled in order to eradicate male power and domination (Chesney-Lind and Morash, 2013; Tierney, 2009).

Critics argue that radical feminist criminologists overlook significant reforms to the criminal law in recent years to protect female victims of rape and other forms of violence, particularly domestic violence (Renzzetti, 2012). While it must be acknowledged that significant improvements have been made,[7] recent studies and official inspections suggest that much still has to be done to police and prosecute such crimes effectively. Critics also point out that radical feminists unfairly present a deterministic account of men as being essentially inclined to oppress and victimise women. It is argued that while they portray men in such a negative light, they portray women quite positively, and overlook female perpetrators of violent crimes (Tierney, 2009). Radical feminism is also accused of failing to countenance additional demographic attributes that can intersect with gender to produce adverse outcomes for women. Examples of these attributes are race and class (Burgess-Proctor, 2006).

Marxist feminist theory

Marxist feminists focus their analysis not on patriarchy or gender relations, as the radical feminists do, but on class relations in capitalist societies (Daly and Chesney-Lind, 1988). They believe that capitalist production mechanisms disadvantage women because women occupy low-status roles. These roles tend to be performed largely on a part-time, low paid basis. Furthermore, the roles generally reflect dominant views about the primary role of women. For example, women are expected to engage in domestic duties, unlike the high-powered roles that men occupy in the production process. Thus, women suffer socio-economic disadvantage. They experience the disadvantage that exploited classes in capitalist societies are exposed to. According to Marxist feminists, the socio-economic marginalisation of women in capitalist societies, places them in lower-class status, and may explain why women commit crime: they might commit crime in response to economic disadvantage (Carlen, 1988; Burgess-Proctor, 2006).

Critics of this perspective reject the notion that such a linear relationship exists between socio-economic disadvantage and crime in general. They criticise Marxist feminists for focusing unduly on class difference and for excluding women who are not involved in capitalist production, such as unemployed women. Marxist feminist criminologists have also been criticised for not paying attention to forms of inequality (apart from economic class) that also explain the experiences of women (Maidment, 2006). For example, they are accused of overlooking racial inequality and how it may be linked to gendered differences in rates of victimisation, and also the experiences of women within the criminal justice system.

Socialist feminist theory

Like Marxist feminists, socialist feminists trace women's experiences to class relations in capitalist societies. However, like the radical criminologists, they also identify patriarchy (male domination) as a key factor that affects the experiences of women (Burgess-Proctor, 2006; Hartmann, 1981). It follows that class and gender are key dimensions of social feminists' analyses (Chesney-Lind and Morash, 2013).

Echoing the arguments of Marxist feminists, socialist feminists aver that in capitalist societies, economic relations are characterised by class difference. Men occupy the powerful ruling class and women are over-represented among the working class who sell their labour for often inadequate wages. According to socialist feminists, inequality and exploitative conditions in capitalist societies disadvantage women. Like Marxist feminists, they trace the origins of female criminality to the adverse economic circumstances created by capitalism. They posit that the disadvantaged working class (including women) are more vulnerable to criminalisation by the state. The latter prioritises capitalist interests over social welfare provision for the disadvantaged (Maidment, 2006). This is quite similar to the arguments of Marxist feminists. However, it is argued that, unlike Marxist feminists, socialist feminists merge women's welfare needs with wider working-class interests. They do not describe women's needs as less important than 'working class struggles' (Maidment, 2006: 50). As noted above, socialist feminists focus not only on class relations, but also on gender relations, in capitalist societies (Tierney, 2009). They argue that gender inequality (underpinned by patriarchy) shapes the nature of female offending (Messerschmidt, 1986; Chesney-Lind and

Morash, 2013). Indeed, like radical feminists, socialist feminists pay particular attention to gender relations. They believe that capitalism bolsters patriarchy (male domination) and the economic marginalisation of women. In terms of the latter, capitalism deprives women of the opportunity to participate fully in production and consumption in capitalist societies. This disadvantages women because in patriarchal capitalist societies, the powerful are those who are able to freely participate in the production and consumption of goods and services. These invariably tend to be men. Thus, socialist feminists propose that there should be reforms to dismantle patriarchy and create more equitable gender relations. There should also be economic reform. A move towards socialism, for example, should help alleviate the economic marginalisation that places women in lower-class positions, and increases their vulnerability to oppression (Chesney-Lind and Morash, 2013).

Socialist feminists have been criticised for failing to pay sufficient attention to the impact of race relations in capitalist societies, and how racial inequality intersects with class and gender to disadvantage women (Maidment, 2006). They are also accused of providing a deterministic account that traces the experiences of women to adverse structural factors, such as class difference and patriarchy.

We have seen that feminist criminologists draw on several substantively different feminist traditions. As mentioned earlier, feminist criminologists are also influenced by different epistemological orientations, namely, feminist empiricism, standpoint feminism and postmodern feminism. These epistemological positions are described below.

Feminist empiricism

Feminist empiricism is an epistemological stance that Identifies scientific methods of inquiry (if purged of sexist prejudice) as effective means of generating 'objective' non-gendered accounts of crime (Naffine, 1997, quoted in Tierney, 2009: 80). According to Comack (1999: 288, emphasis in original): 'feminist empiricists, by and large, left the scientific enterprise intact and called for more studies "on" women in order to fill the historical gap which had been created by the exclusion of women as research subjects'.

Liberal feminists, particularly the early writers in the field, have been described as feminist empiricists (Smart, 1999; Tierney, 2009). They believe that scientific methods of inquiry utilised by mainstream criminologists can be used to generate 'objective' knowledge about female crime. However, feminist empiricists have been criticised by postmodernists for not problematising the presumption that scientific methods of enquiry can be employed to discover objective 'facts' (Smart, 1995: 4). It has been argued in defence of feminist empiricism that although its epistemological position is considered to be questionable to its critics, it is nevertheless important not to overlook the objectives of the early feminists who subscribed to feminist empiricism sought to achieve. They had a 'political agenda', which was to alter the status quo in some way to benefit women (Smart, 1995: 4).

Their objective was to generate empirical knowledge that would ultimately impact on state policies and enhance the feminist agenda. According to Carrington (2008: 83), the early feminists who embraced mainstream 'scientific' methods of inquiry sought to produce potentially emancipatory and transformational knowledge that could lead to social change. It was only when standpoint feminism (which is discussed in more detail later) emerged that questions about epistemological approaches and their impact on the processes and outcomes of feminist research surfaced. These questions centred on whether knowledge production by feminist researchers is, or should be, *on* women or *for* women (Smart, 1995). It appeared to the critics that in the search for 'objective' knowledge, the feminist empiricists adopted methods that marginalised the viewpoints of women and treated them as the objects, rather than the subjects, of research. The critics believe that, in doing so, feminist empiricists conducted research *on* women but not *for* women.

Standpoint feminism

Early standpoint feminism emphasised the importance of generating knowledge *for* women (Harding, 1986; Cain, 1990; Comack, 1999). There was an implicit suggestion that feminist empiricism was geared towards generating knowledge *on* women and not necessarily *for* women. Unlike feminist empiricism, which, as we saw earlier, was criticised for its proposition that objective social-scientific methods of research can produce non-gendered 'truth' about criminality, standpoint feminists adopted an epistemological position that prioritises the knowledge provided by women about their experiences. According to Smart (1999: 43), 'the epistemological basis of this form of feminist knowledge is experience'. Underpinning standpoint feminism is the presumption that women are marginalised in society. It is also believed that the accounts offered by the marginalised about their experiences are more likely to be accurate depictions of reality (Flavin, 2001). This is because, compared with the dominant group (according to standpoint feminists, men are the dominant group), the marginalised may not have as much interest in masking the conditions that disadvantage them. The dominant group may be more motivated to offer distorted views in order to mask the conditions that place them in positions of advantage (Harding, 1991, cited in Flavin, 2001). Moreover, the experience of women as the marginalised in society is characterised by struggle and oppression. It is, as such, presumed to be more accurate than the perspectives of the dominant group because the latter benefits from the unfair status quo (Smart, 1995). Standpoint feminists also believe that the intellectual and political action that women engage in, response to oppression, shapes their experiences. Knowledge of their experiences can therefore serve useful purposes. For example, it could inform state policies, including criminal justice policies, in ways that work to the advantage of women (see also Harding, 1993, cited in Smart, 1995). According to Smart (1995: 43; emphasis in original):

The epistemological basis of this form of feminist knowledge is experience. However, not just any experience is deemed to be equally valuable or valid. *Feminist* experience is achieved through a struggle against oppression; it is therefore, argued to be more complete and less distorted than the perspective of the ruling group or men. A feminist standpoint is therefore not just the experience of women, but of women *reflexively* engaged in struggle (intellectual and political).

Early standpointism was also underpinned by the idea that traditional methods of 'scientific' inquiry and the knowledge generated using these methods are male-centred. Thus, unlike feminist empiricists' scientific search for objective 'truth', standpointism prioritises methods of empirical inquiry that enable the researcher to generate knowledge from the standpoint of women in order to promote the interests of women (Harding, 1986; Cain, 1990). This sums up their political position: to engage in action that ultimately helps advance women's interests (Smart, 1999). Standpoint feminists believe that the knowledge generated from women is 'epistemologically privileged' provided that methods of inquiry that conform to certain rules are employed to generate such knowledge (Cain, 1990: 126).

More recent renditions of standpoint feminism have revised some of its original tenets. For example, some standpoint feminists have since underplayed the earlier claim that women's accounts of their experiences reflect the only reality or truth about the social world (Harding, 1991). They appear to acknowledge (like the postmodernists do) that 'multiple realities' exist that are relative to context (Smart, 1999: 204). That said, standpoint feminists continue to claim that specific perspectives about the social world are more objective, or 'less partial', and superior to conventional or elitist and androcentric accounts (Smart, 1999: 205). In other words, although some acknowledge that there can be several truths about the social world, standpoint feminists appear to still prioritise the perspectives of women as the more objective truth (Smart, 1999). For this reason, Smart (1999: 205) asserts that standpoint feminism 'can, it would seem, both have its cake and eat it'.

Standpoint feminism has contributed to the growth of new forms of knowledge about violence against women in intimate relationships, particularly sexual offences and domestic violence (Smart, 1995). Several studies of female victimisation have been conducted by radical feminists who adopted standpoint feminism as their epistemological position. Nevertheless, standpoint feminism has been criticised for ascribing greater significance to the knowledge produced by academics. According to Smart (1999: 11), standpointism portrays the academic researcher involved in standpoint feminist inquiry as the authoritative 'interpreter and disseminator' of women's perspectives. It is accused of splitting knowledge into hierarchies in order to prioritise certain forms of knowledge (primarily knowledge generated from women and interpreted by academics), and it justifies this on the basis of its emancipatory political agenda. Early standpoint feminism was also criticised for harbouring an essentialist view of women, which asserts that women share identifiable attributes in common. Critics point out that standpoint feminists presumed that women are a homogeneous group that they can speak for as one (Smart, 1999). As Carrington (2008: 84) states:

> they presumed that commonalities shared among the female sex made it possible to analyse women as a singular unitary subject of history … despite their astonishing historical, cultural, socio-economic, ethnic and racial diversity. The diversity of women's experiences of criminalisation and victimisation could not be adequately represented by merely adopting a singular feminist standpoint.

Perhaps in response to these criticisms, subsequent standpoint feminists began to acknowledge that women's experiences, perspectives and identities are diverse, and should be reflected in the knowledge production process (Harding, 1991; Cain, 1990; Comack, 1999). It was also acknowledged that the feminist researchers' accounts of women's experiences might not necessarily reflect such experiences accurately.

Postmodern feminism

Like feminist empiricism and standpointism, postmodern feminism also focuses mainly on questions of epistemology. It is concerned with epistemological questions to do with how knowledge is produced and the power relations that underpin its production (Carrington, 2008). Feminist criminologists influenced by postmodernism emphasise the social construction of knowledge, including knowledge about social categories, such as gender, crime and deviance. They explore how socially constructed knowledge about crime and deviance intersect with constructions of gender, and how the intersection impacts on women. They reject any suggestion by standpoint feminism or others that 'one reality' exists (Smart, 1995: 45). Indeed, given its roots in postmodernism, postmodern feminism is anti-foundationalist. According to Smart (1995: 8), 'It makes us rethink and reconsider the foundations of what we think we know'.

Postmodern feminists also reject the idea that women's accounts of their experiences represent superior knowledge or the only 'truth that has "political force"' (Smart, 1995: 10). Rather, they emphasise the existence of multiple realities (see also Flavin, 2001). In addition, postmodern feminists do not subscribe to the view that scientific methods can be used to discover universal 'truth' about any aspect of reality, including gender. Rooted as it is in postmodernism, the epistemological position of postmodern feminists leads them to assert that truth is relative to the condition or context from which it emerges.

Postmodern feminists have accused liberal feminist criminologists of 'feminist empiricism' for presuming that scientific methods of inquiry can be used to generate gender-neutral 'truth' or objective knowledge (Smart, 1995). Postmodern feminists describe truth claims made about the social world, including the truth claims made about crime for example, as nothing more than the constructions of the powerful. There is no universal 'truth' about crime, criminal behaviour or, indeed, gender that is true for everyone, everywhere, all the time (see also Flavin, 2001). Therefore, postmodern feminists do not essentialise gender or sexual difference (Smart, 1999): they do not believe that there are pre-given, biologically determined or natural differences between men and women. According to postmodern feminists, dominant knowledge about gender differences and, indeed, about gender in general are socially constructed or 'constituted' (Smart, 1995: 10). Knowledge is linked to power. Thus, the theoretical and empirical agenda of postmodern feminists is to deconstruct dominant knowledge. Their aim is to unravel discourses that are crafted about female criminality by the powerful (mainly men). They believe that the discourses disadvantage women (Smart, 1995). Postmodern feminists also seek to bring to the fore the discourses constructed by women themselves (see also, Maidment, 2006; Heidensohn and Silvestri, 2012; Chesney-Lind and Morash, 2013). Far from feminist empiricism's search for scientifically derived 'truth', or standpoint feminists' concern to generate 'truth' from the viewpoint of women, postmodern feminism focuses on deconstructing the language and other means of communication that are used to construct accepted 'truth' about women. According to Smart (1995: 44–5):

> It would be a mistake to depict feminist postmodernism as the third
> stage or synthesis of feminist empiricism and standpoint feminism.…
> The core element of feminist postmodernism is the rejection of the
> one reality which arises from 'the falsely universalizing perspective of
> the master' (Harding 1987: 188). But unlike standpoint feminism it
> does not seek to impose a different unitary reality. Rather it refers to
> subjugated knowledges, which tell different stories and have different
> specificities. So the aim of feminism ceases to be the establishment of
> the feminist truth and becomes the aim of deconstructing Truth and
> analysing the power effects that claims to truth entail.

As postmodernists, they emphasise that language and other forms of communication are used to construct so-called 'truth' about women in ways that disadvantage them (Smart, 1995). They argue that the dominant forms of knowledge with which we make sense of the world are not neutral or objective: 'some accounts become dominant, not because they are "truthful", but because they reflect hierarchies of power' (Tierney, 2009: 86). Therefore, as already noted, postmodern feminists believe that knowledge is inextricably linked to power. However, they maintain that power does not reside in any one group, context of interaction or gender. Rather, it is 'ubiquitous' and can, as such, exist in many different groups and contexts (Smart, 1999: 46).

The postmodern approach has been accused of relativism. It is argued that the latter can foreclose rational explorations of women's experiences. If postmodern feminists dismiss every explanation or knowledge of the experiences of women as social constructions, or if they do not privilege any account, or any form, of knowledge over the others, how do those interested in studying these experiences overcome the relativism that such an ontological position engenders? Furthermore, critics claim that by dismissing dominant explanations as social constructions, postmodern feminists may overlook the need to continue to study and problematise dominant discourses in order to challenge them, and provide alternative accounts that best depict the experiences of women (see, generally, Cain, 1990).

In addition, some feminists believe that postmodern feminists do not identify tangible or practical strategies that may be used to alter the social structures and policies that disadvantage women (Gelsthorpe, 1997). Smart (1995: 206) observes that some standpoint feminists, for example, describe postmodern feminism as 'apolitical or (worse) reactionary'. For some critics, postmodern feminism appears to suggest that there is no need to strive for justice and equitable treatment for women because these are outcomes that are likely to mean different things to different people in different contexts, and there is no standard measure by which they can be defined.

Notwithstanding these criticisms, some suggest that postmodern feminists may be commended for highlighting the importance of acknowledging the diversity among women (Flavin, 2001). Postmodern feminists recognise that there are diverse attributes that make one woman's reality different from another woman's reality. Race and social class represent prime examples of these attributes.

Masculinities

Masculinities as a field of study in criminology emerged in the early 1990s from the work of criminologists who explored links between masculinities (the features associated with the male gender) and crime (Messerschmidt and Tomsen, 2012). It is a relatively recent field of study. It has been noted that its origins can be traced to: 'feminist work on gender, and from men's involvement in feminism; as well as the growing field of gay and lesbian studies' (Heidensohn and Silvestri, 2012: 348). It focuses on the different ways that men define and exhibit their masculinity, and how these are linked to crime. It has been argued that for too long, criminology focused on men but overlooked gender. The discipline did not theorise the relationship/s between gender (female gender and male gender) and crime (Flavin, 2001). The work that feminists have done on the impact of gender (being female) on women's experiences of crime and criminal justice has paved the way for studies that now explore possible links between masculinities (the male gender) and crime (Flavin, 2001). Scholars in this field, study the nexus between gender identity and crime. There is a perception that this nexus is often taken for granted. Masculinities theorists also examine how the links between masculinities and crime help us understand the gender gap in offending (Chesney-Lind and Morash, 2013).

It follows that masculinities theorists acknowledge that such a gap exists. As Messerschmidt and Tomsen (2012: 190) put it: 'Male offenders commit the great majority of crimes ... and men have a virtual monopoly on the commission of syndicated, corporate and political crime'.

Indeed, masculinities theories in criminology emerged from the work of feminists and others who theorised the reasons for the gender gap in offending (Heidensohn and Silvestri, 2012). Masculinities theorists examine the reason for the gender gap. The question they explore is this: 'what is about men as men not as working class not as migrants not as underprivileged individuals but as men that induces them to "commit crime"?' (Grosz, 1987, cited in Heidensohn and Silvestri, 2012: 348). According to Messerschmidt and Tomsen (2012: 190), traditional criminological theories have tended to focus on exploring the criminal justice system's response to 'dangerous' expressions of masculinity. The focus is typically the offending behaviour of young working-class males (Messerschmidt and Tomsen 2012). These theories overlook the possibility that the quest to attain 'masculine status and power' may be linked to male criminality (Messerschmidt and Tomsen, 2012: 151). For masculinities theorists, the quest or, indeed, the pressure on men to exhibit socially defined features of masculinity might explain the gender gap, and male criminality in general (Chesney-Lind and Morash, 2013).

This is not to stay that masculinity is the exclusive preserve of men, or to claim that women are not able to exhibit masculine traits, or even to deny that there are different types of masculinities (Connell, 1995, 2000; Heidensohn and Silvestri, 2012). Masculinities writers do, indeed, acknowledge that although men commit most crimes, men do not have a specific unique attribute (including criminality) that can explain all male behaviour (Messerschmidt, 1993). Indeed, they believe that the concept of masculinity itself has no fixed essence. Messerschmidt explains that:

> Because masculinity is a behavioural response to the particular conditions and situations in which men participate, different types of masculinities exist in the school, the youth groups, the street, the family, and the workplace. In other words, men do masculinity according to the social situation in which they find themselves. (1993: 83–4)

Thus, masculinities theorists emphasise that masculinity is socially and culturally constructed. For example, although aggression is associated with masculinity, theorists in this field insist that it is not a biologically determined male attribute. Rather, they argue that it is learned behaviour. It is a culturally determined feature of masculinity. Indeed, masculinities studies illuminate the impact of culturally accepted definitions of 'maleness' or masculinity on male aggression, and how constructions of masculinity might explain the dominance of men in crime statistics compared with women (Messerschmidt, 1993). Thus, masculinities theorists argue that if we wish to understand the gender gap in offending, the study of how men try to define and demonstrate their masculinity might be a good place to start.

Masculinities theorists have been influenced by the work of Connell (1995), and particularly by Connell's taxonomy of 'hegemonic masculinity' (see also Messerschmidt and Tomsen, 2012: 174). Hegemonic masculinity is a sociological concept that describes the features of culturally determined male identity. It is a form of masculinity that exists in many societies, and it promotes patriarchy and male dominance. Some masculinities theorists assert that the behaviour of some men, including their involvement in criminal activity, may, in part, be attributable to the quest to attain hegemonic masculinity. The features of hegemonic masculinity include 'heterosexuality, toughness, power, authority and competition' (Heidensohn and Silvestri, 2012: 348). These may manifest behaviourally as active homophobia, aggressiveness, competitiveness, striving for achievement and status, and so forth (DeKeseredy, 2010). Some masculinities theorists assert that men are socialised into internalising these values at the risk of suffering repercussions if they fail to do so (DeKeseredy, 2010). Alternative masculinities may also evolve from hegemonic masculinity. For example, according to Heidensohn and Silvestri (2012: 348), hegemonic masculinities may be differentiated from the 'subordinated masculinities' associated with homosexual men. Nevertheless, masculinities writers maintain that the effort to attain hegemonic masculinity may explain some male crimes. For example, socially excluded young men who lack access to, or are not amenable to (or in some cases, attuned to) legitimate means of expressing hegemonic masculinity, such as academic achievement or legitimate recreational activities, may resort instead to illegitimate routes, including crime (Messerschmidt, 1993). Excluded young men may find that crime is an avenue for 'doing masculinity' or asserting their masculinity (see also Heidensohn and Silvestri, 2012: 349). This is akin to the arguments of the subcultural theorists, who argued that socially excluded young men may suffer 'status frustration' and drift into subcultures of likeminded and similarly socially excluded peers, where they strive to achieve the status that eludes them in mainstream society (Cohen, 1955). In these subcultures, they express their masculinity through crime. Their exclusion from good education, employment and other mainstream avenues for achieving success, as defined by the 'dominant' culture, leaves them disenfranchised and unable to achieve masculine status through legitimate means. The dominant culture in this context was defined as the 'White Anglo-Saxon Protestant culture ... the ascetic, achievement-orientated, highly competitive, middle-class way of life' (Downes and Rock, 2011: 133).

Masculinities theorists also cite 'corporate–executive masculinity' as a feature of the corporate world (Messerschmidt, 1993: 136). Unlike the violent expression of masculinity that may occur in other sites such as the factory and the streets, corporate–executive masculinity expresses itself through the actions of men who believe that success and other positive benefits in the corporate world reflect masculinity. These men become competitive in their quest to attain the positive benefits they identify as evidence of masculinity (Messerschmidt, 1993). Some might even resort to corporate crime in order to achieve success and maintain corporate masculinity (Messerschmidt, 1993).

It is also argued that there are men who express their masculinity through other criminal behaviour, such as hate crimes, which may be in the form of 'racist and homophobic violence' (Perry, 2003, cited in DeKeseredy, 2010: 65). Several writers believe that these crimes stem from the actions of white men who are motivated by perceived superiority (in the case of racist violence) and by the perceived need to assert their masculinity (in the case of homophobic violence) (Perry, 2003, cited in DeKeseredy, 2010). These men justify their actions on the basis that their actions do not violate cultural norms, but rather affirm the hegemonic masculinity enshrined in cultural norms. The features of this hegemonic masculinity are 'aggression, domination and heterosexuality' (Perry, 2003, quoted in DeKeseredy, 2010: 36) and it is used to validate not only racist and homophobic violence, but also other violent acts perpetrated by men in other contexts (DeKeseredy, 2010).

Masculinities theories have been criticised for focusing narrowly on the link between masculinity as a socially constructed concept and male criminality. However, in their defence, it is useful to acknowledge that masculinities theorists do recognise that masculinity represents one of a broad spectrum of factors that can help explain male crime and the gender gap in offending (Messerschmidt, 1993). They also recognise that crime is not the only medium through which men can express their masculinity. Criminologists on the Left have argued that the concept of hegemonic masculinity is not sufficiently cognisant of the impact of social structure on behaviour. Further, they assert that the concept contradicts the professed anti-essentialism of masculinities theories because it suggests that working-class men possess traits that make them *essentially* 'violent and destructive' (Hall, 2002, cited in Messerschmidt and Tomsen, 2012: 174).

Criticisms

In general, feminist criminology has been criticised for several reasons. For example, feminists have been accused of 'dogma preservation', politicising domestic violence, offering a one-dimensional explanation of crime that focuses on patriarchy and supporting their arguments with manufactured data (Dutton, 2006 cited in DeKeseredy, 2010: 30). In defence of feminism, some point out that all social science theories and other approaches to understanding the social world are far from objective or 'value-free' (Harding, 1997 cited in DeKeseredy, 2010: 30). Moreover, the criticism erroneously overlooks the multidimensionality of feminism: as a field of study, it comprises several strands (DeKeseredy, 2010).

Although critics might argue that feminists focus on the victimisation of women by men, and overlook the ability of women to exercise a degree of agency, feminist studies do explore female offending (Gelsthorpe, 2004). In addition, they present the accounts of women offenders themselves (see, generally, Carlen, 1985; Gelsthorpe 2004). There is also the argument that feminist criminology has tended to focus on gender without a corresponding interest in other demographic attributes that also place women at greater risk of oppression. As mentioned earlier, examples of these attributes include race and class (Daly and Stephens, 1995). When feminism initially emerged, there appeared to be an internal consensus about its key concerns. Carol Smart (1995: 45) uses the term 'sisterhood' to describe the sense of unity within feminism at the time. It appeared that there was a joint struggle against androcentrism, and also a joint effort to unravel constructions of knowledge or 'truth' that disadvantage women. In the 1980s, this 'sisterhood' somewhat imploded when it became apparent that early feminist ideas about 'womanhood' and the experiences of women could not be generalised to all women. These ideas were perhaps more relevant to women who are 'white, middle class, and of Anglo-Saxon protestant extract' (p 45). This meant that the ideas were not representative of the experiences of ethnic minority women, for instance, and other women who do not belong to this category (Smart, 1999: 45). Some feminists began to emphasise that the early feminists did not recognise that class, race, ethnicity and other attributes are factors that intersect (operate interactively) to render the experiences of women qualitatively different. Describing this development, Comack (1999: 288) notes that:

> For feminists in both criminology and elsewhere, the task of producing feminist knowledge initially appeared to be straightforward one. There was a broad consensus, which emanated from the point that we knew what we were rejecting: the androcentricism of the traditional research enterprise. However, as feminists began to respond to this common problematic, cracks in the consensus began to appear.

This decline of the sense of unity that pervaded early feminism was accompanied by disagreements over how best to generate 'authoritative' knowledge about the experiences of women (Daly, 2008: 10). As we have seen earlier, feminist criminologists now subscribe to diverse epistemological positions. Several feminist traditions have also emerged. Postmodern feminism, for example, recognises that women are not a homogeneous group. Therefore, they assert that any study of the experiences of women should take into account factors (such as race and class), that can expose women to different realities. Indeed, a field of study now known as 'black feminist criminology' has emerged. In her seminal text titled *Ain't I a Woman*, the African-American bell hooks (1981) drew attention to intersectionality[8] (the combined impact of factors that define an individual's status and experience, such as gender, class, ethnicity and so forth). Her work and the work of others indicated that the experiences of some women (for example, black women) do not conform to the generalised descriptions of 'womanhood' and women's experiences that prevailed in feminism at the time. Her text successfully refuted the long-held view by white feminists that women in general were not given access to politics because of the stereotypical frailty and delicacy of women (Chesney-Lind and Morash, 2013), and pointed out that this stereotype does not apply to black American women because of their unfortunate exposure to violent acts of abuse in the days of slavery. The text directed attention to the relevance of intersectionality and the possibility that inequality may stem from any, or a combination, of factors of which gender represents but one example (see, generally, Burgess-Proctor, 2006: 28; Chesney-Lind and Morash, 2013). According to Chesney-Lind and Morash (2013: 293), 'African American scholar and activist bell hooks' book, *Ain't I a woman* (1981), highlighted and forever invalidated the sole focus on gender'.

As mentioned earlier, a 'black feminist criminology' has since emerged and it continues to break new ground in the field of criminological theory and research. This dimension of feminist criminology brings to the fore the issue of race as an added structural dimension that explains the experiences of minority ethnic women as offenders and victims. Black feminist criminologists have begun to highlight the 'lived experiences of black women' and the adverse experiences they contend with because of their race and gender (Potter, 2006; Renzzetti, 2013: 136)..

Conclusion

Although they may be underpinned by sometimes-disparate theoretical and epistemological traditions, together, feminist perspectives in criminology share several features in common. They accuse criminology as a discipline of an androcentrism that overlooks women as offenders and victims and/or portrays them in stereotypes that disadvantage them. Criminology is criticised for: being gender-blind; failing to theorise the gender gap that exists because men commit more crime than women; and failing to theorise female offending and victimisation.

The feminist perspectives have been criticised on several grounds. Nevertheless, they have made important contributions to our understanding of crime and to criminal justice policy on both sides of the Atlantic. Indeed, it has been noted that the perspectives have helped to reverse the androcentrism that tended to dominate not only criminology, but also many fields of study. Daly and Chesney-Lind (1988: 498) rightly state that 'Theories and concepts rooted in men's experience formerly monopolized intellectual inquiry, but today disciplinary debates in some fields reflect the impact of feminist thought, albeit uneven, across the disciplines'.

Feminist criminologists have provided theoretical and empirical insights into the nature of female offending and female victimisation, and how best to respond to both issues. In particular, they have successfully drawn attention to the violent crimes that men commit against women, including the so-called hidden crimes that occur in intimate relationships. Feminists have been able to direct policy attention to these typically under-reported and under-recorded crimes. Policies have been introduced to encourage the police to respond to these crimes more effectively. That said, the degree to which these policies have achieved their objectives remains open to question. For example, recent studies have found significant shortcomings in the way in which the police respond to incidents of domestic violence in England and Wales.

SUMMARY

- Feminist criminology traces its roots to the second wave of feminism that emerged in the US and flourished in the UK in the late 1960s (Heidensohn, 2012).
- Feminist criminology falls within the ambit of critical criminology because it shares several concerns in common with critical criminological perspectives. Fundamentally, it recognises that power defines the dynamics of social interactions in society (see Daly, 2008).
- It is probably impossible to define feminist criminology. Its definition is as diverse as its numerous strands.
- A fundamental feature of the diverse feminist perspectives is that they are critical of mainstream or orthodox criminological theories. They are also critical of most critical criminological theories.
- They accuse criminology of: gender-blindness; overlooking the gender gap in offending (men commit more crimes); and overlooking women's experiences in the criminal justice system as offenders, victims and officials. In addition, feminist criminology accuses the existing social order of androcentrism.
- Feminist criminologists have strived to redress the neglect of women in criminological theorising. For example, radical feminist criminologists have helped uncover hidden crimes against women, and have drawn policy attention to these crimes.
- Feminist criminology has also helped to uncover and alleviate, to a degree, the adverse experiences of women in the criminal justice system.

SAMPLE QUESTIONS

1. What are the similarities and differences between the strands of feminist criminology?
2. To what extent are feminist perspectives in criminology useful for understanding the experiences of women as victims or as offenders?

Notes

[1] It is worth noting that some feminists also accuse the critical criminological perspectives that view crime as a social construction of minimising the impact of crimes such as rape, sexual assault and domestic violence, which produce many female victims (Smart, 1976).

[2] Carrington (2008) points out that others, such as Heidensohn (1968, cited in Carrington, 2008), were also writing about criminology's failure to incorporate feminist issues around the time Smart's (1976) seminal text was published. According to Daly and Chesney-Lind (1988: 507–8), as far back as the 1960s, female criminologists Marie Bertrand), Frances Heidensohn), and the criminologist Walter Reckless, pointed to the marginalisation of women from criminological theorising. However, Smart's (1976) text is recognised as the definitive text that provided an overview of the existing work on female offending.

[3] Smart later became a postmodern feminist (see, eg, Smart, 1999).

[4] Smart (1999) argues that the explanations were sexist mainly because they ascribed to one sex (women) negative characteristics and presented these characteristics as the intrinsic characteristics of women.

[5] Radical feminism is examined in more detail later in the chapter.

[6] Deconstruction or deconstructionist approaches fall within the ambit of postmodern feminism. There is a concern to deconstruct and uncover the power dynamics that underpin knowledge that is accepted as truth (Carrington, 2008).

[7] Indeed, as mentioned earlier, radical feminist criminologists contributed significantly (through their research and sustained campaigns) to the introduction of reforms that aim to protect female victims of rape and other forms of violent abuse, particularly domestic violence. Flavin (2001: 276) notes that 'Radical feminist approaches ... arguably have had more impact on woman abuse research than any other theoretical perspective'.

[8] Burgess-Proctor (2006: 31) points out that, 'Intersectionality recognizes that systems of power such as race, class, and gender do not act alone to shape our experiences but rather, are multiplicative, inextricably linked, and simultaneously experienced'.

Part Three
Contemporary critical criminology

EIGHT

Critical perspectives on crimes of the powerful

Introduction

In the 1970s and 1980s, when the foundational critical criminological perspectives were making their mark in the field of criminology, additional critical criminological traditions emerged. An important tradition that emerged in that period is the tradition that focuses on studying the crimes of the powerful.[1] Criminologists study crimes of the powerful from a range of different perspectives. However, the criminologists who study crimes of the powerful from a critical perspective argue that the powerful (those who possess power and wealth) influence the creation and operation of the law. The law protects their interests and they enjoy considerable impunity when they violate the law.

Indeed, it has been argued that theoretical and empirical studies of crimes of the powerful fall within the ambit of critical criminology rather than mainstream criminology. Lynch (2011: 22) observes that an important difference between critical criminology and mainstream criminology 'involves the extent to which each addresses the crimes of the powerful. The emphasis on exploring the crimes of the powerful is one of the significant contributions of critical criminology'.

Alvesalo and Tombs echo this view. They point out that research studies that explore crimes of the powerful (such as corporate or business crimes), instead of the conventional crimes associated with the less powerful, are generally perceived to be orientated towards the critical criminological tradition:

> From the point of view of critical criminology, almost any form of research into economic crime is critical per se. Such research immediately and inevitably indicates the extent to which criminal justice systems work in a biased fashion, prioritizing some forms of offending – traditional or conventional crimes associated with lower-class offenders – as opposed to the illegalities produced by businesses and business-people. (Alvesalo and Tombs, 2002: 21)

Notwithstanding the foregoing, accounts of the origins of this field of study vary. Downes and Rock (2011) note that the Marxist criminological perspectives of the 1960s and 1970s laid the foundations for much of the work that has been done on crimes of the powerful. Friedrichs and Rothe (2012) trace the early history of studies of crimes of the powerful to Edwin Sutherland's (1949) work. They also trace its early history to the work of others who responded to Sutherland's call to explore white-collar crime, such as his former student Donald Cressey, and also to the work of Richard Quinney, who (perhaps rather tellingly) went on to become a Marxist criminologist. Although it can be acknowledged that not all criminologists who study crimes of the powerful can be described as critical criminologists, it is clear that several criminologists who contribute to this field of study still identify with the arguments of Marxist criminologists, who emphasised that crime is constructed and responded to in ways that reflect capitalist interests (Slapper and Tombs, 1999). In their view, responses to the crimes and misconduct of powerful corporations, for instance, are bound up with, and cannot be divorced from, the political economy of capitalist societies. These criminologists maintain that in the unequal political and socio-economic structure of capitalist societies, the powerful (wealthy capitalists) enjoy impunity when they violate the law. That said, some other criminologists who trace crimes of the powerful to structural causes do not necessarily focus on capitalism as the key explanatory framework (Box, 1983).

Key arguments

Criminologists who study crimes of the powerful from a critical perspective re-emphasise the arguments of the foundational critical criminologists, who persuasively argued that power is a crucial variable that shapes the nature of crime and responses to crime. Indeed, as noted above, some of the criminologists who began to study crimes of the powerful in the 1980s were influenced to a degree by Marxist criminologists, who drew attention to what they considered to be the ability of the ruling class to influence the creation of laws and avoid law enforcement (see Downes and Rock, 2011). Marxist criminologists argued that crime is not peculiar to any social class or group. The difference between crimes of the powerful and crimes of the less powerful resides in the operation of the law: 'upper class' or higher-status criminals (including corporate criminals) are less visible.[2] Even when they are visible, they are under-prosecuted, and the relatively few prosecutions attract relatively lenient and mainly financial sanctions (Tombs, 2013: 228). It is argued that there is a tendency to focus on crimes committed by the lower classes,[3] and to present such crimes as the most serious crimes. By contrast, crimes of the powerful are overlooked or underplayed within orthodox criminology, official statistics, policymaking, media reports and political pronouncements. Steven Box (1983: 14) explains this phenomenon thus:

> not only does the state with the help and reinforcement of its control agents, criminologists and the media conceptualise a particular and partial ideological version of serious crime and who commits it, but it does so by concealing and hence mystifying its own propensity for violence and serious crimes on a much larger scale.

The previous quotation is taken from the text by Steven Box (1983) titled *Power, Crime, and Mystification* (see also Box 8.1). In the text, Box provided a detailed account of the structural dynamics that contribute to the magnification of crimes committed by the less powerful and the minimisation of crimes of the powerful. Criminologists who study crimes of the powerful believe (like other critical criminologists do) that power is a key concept that shapes crime and criminal justice.[4] They argue that, unlike the powerful, those who are less powerful in society are more likely to have their actions defined as crime. They are more likely to be arrested, prosecuted and convicted if their actions violate the criminal law.

Box 8.1: Crimes of the powerful

The text by Steven Box (1983) titled *Power, Crime, and Mystification* described the extent of crimes of the powerful, the relative impunity the powerful enjoy and the structural factors that explain this impunity. In the text, Box presented persuasive arguments. He also cited studies and statistics which demonstrate that crimes of the powerful, such as corporate crimes (crimes committed by those who run large corporations for the benefit of the corporation), produce far greater victimisation than crimes of the less powerful, which dominate orthodox criminology, official crime statistics, media reports and political rhetoric. He argued that information about crime obtained from these sources fuels public fear, fractures communities, incites punitive sentiments and legitimises harsh law and order policies that have proven to be counterproductive. Such information diverts attention away from the crimes that do cause the greatest harm. These crimes tend to be crimes of the powerful. In what follows, I have reproduced an extract from the text.

> Murder! Rape! Robbery! Assault! Wounding! Theft! Burglary! Arson! Vandalism! These form the substance of the annual official criminal statistics on indictable offences.... Aggregated, they constitute a major part of 'our' crime problem. Or at least, we are told so daily by our politicians, police, judges and journalists who speak to us through the media of newspapers and television ... the typical people criminally victimising and forcing us to fear each other and fracture our sense of community are young uneducated males, who are often unemployed, live in a working-class impoverished neighbourhood, and frequently belong to an ethnic minority....

> it might be prudent to consider whether murder, rape, robbery, assault and other crimes focused on by state officials, politicians and the media, and the criminal justice system do constitute the major part of our real crime problems. Maybe they are only a crime problem and not the crime problem. Maybe what is stuffed into our consciousness, as the crime problem is in fact an illusion, a trick to deflect our attention away from other, even more serious crimes and victimising behaviours, which objectively cause the vast bulk of avoidable death, injury, and deprivation. At the same time, it might be prudent to compare persons who commit other serious but under-emphasised crimes and victimising behaviours with those who are officially portrayed as 'our' criminal enemies. For if the former, compared to

the latter, are indeed quite different types of people, then maybe we should stop looking to our political authorities and criminal justice system for protection from those beneath us in impoverished urban neighbourhoods. Instead maybe we should look up accusingly at our political and judicial 'superiors' for being or protecting the 'real' culprits. (Box, 1983: 1–3)

Conceptualising 'crimes of the powerful'

There is considerable confusion in criminology over how best to define and categorise crimes of the powerful. A review of key criminology texts reveals a threefold categorisation of these crimes: white-collar crime, corporate crime and state crime. Criminologists who study crimes of the powerful suggest that these crimes attract similar responses. They tend to be minimised or even overlooked by the media, politicians, the general public and even within criminology and the criminal justice system. Much more tends to be made of the conventional crimes associated with the less powerful (see also Box 8.1).

White-collar crime and corporate crime: untangling key definitional issues

As mentioned earlier, there is considerable disagreement over the appropriate classification of crimes of the powerful. A source of confusion relates to how criminologists define 'white-collar crimes'. Although some criminologists understand the latter to be primarily crimes that are committed by individuals of high socio-economic status in positions of trust, other criminologists use the term 'white-collar crime' to describe the crimes that are committed by people of high socio-economic status *and* large organisations (Sutherland, 1949; Croall, 2001; Friedrichs and Rothe, 2012).[5]

Edwin Sutherland (1949: 9) coined the term 'white-collar crime' in a speech he delivered in Philadelphia to the American Sociological Society in 1939, and in his text titled *White-Collar Crime* (Sutherland, 1949). He stated that white-collar crime might 'approximately' be defined as crime committed by 'a person of high respectability and high status in the course of his occupation'.[6] This definition focuses on the offender and suggests that it is the character and socio-economic status of the offender that makes the crime a white-collar crime. Yet, Sutherland focused much of his analysis of white-collar crimes on crimes committed not by individuals, but by corporations for their financial benefit. As Friedrichs (2002: 242) put it: 'Sutherland's (1949) own major work on white collar crime focused on the crimes of corporations'. It has also been noted that, 'having defined the field in terms of people, he proceeded to study corporations' (Cressey, cited in Tombs, 2013: 228). It follows that Sutherland's definition of white-collar crime also includes corporate crimes, which are crimes committed by powerful people who run large corporations to benefit their corporations.

Like Sutherland did, other criminologists have used the term 'white-collar crime' to describe not only crimes committed by high-status individuals, but also crimes committed by corporations to further their interests (corporate crime). Croall (2001), for example, describes white-collar crime as crimes committed by employees against organisations (occupational crime) or crimes committed by organisations against their employees and others (typically conceptualised as corporate crime, as noted earlier) (see also Walklate, 2011; Friedrichs and Rothe, 2012). This appears to be consistent with Sutherland's (1949) definition of 'white-collar crimes' as crimes of higher-status individuals and organisations/corporations. Croall (1989: 157) points out that 'White-collar crime is traditionally associated with high status and respectable offenders: the "crimes of the powerful" and corporate crime'. Croall (1989: 158) goes on to state that 'Offenders are often assumed to be large corporations making huge profits at the expense of the consumer by placing profit above health and safety considerations or by "conning" consumers through misleading marketing and advertising strategies'.

Similarly, Friedrichs (2002) argues that 'corporate crime and occupational crime are the two principal, or "pure", forms of white collar crime' (see also Friedrichs and Rothe, 2012). Thus defined, white-collar crimes may comprise not only crimes committed by an employee to further his or her own interests (occupational crime), but also corporate crime.

However, for some commentators, the crimes that are committed by corporations for their benefit are best described as corporate crimes[7] not white-collar crimes (Tombs, 2013). For these criminologists, white-collar crimes are crimes that are committed by individuals in violation of their organisation's policies purely to benefit themselves (Tombs, 2013). These crimes are also described as occupational crimes. Defined this way, the key difference between corporate crime and white-collar crime is the objective of the crime. Corporate crimes are committed to further an organisation's goals and interests. By contrast, white-collar crimes are committed in violation of an organisation's goals and interests, for the individual offender's benefit.

Power and status: the sine qua non or fundamental dimension of crimes of the powerful

It is important to emphasise that white-collar crime and corporate crime become crimes of the powerful when they are committed by people, institutions, or organisations that possess high socio-economic and political status. The status of the perpetrator is crucial because it transforms these crimes into crimes of the *powerful*. Not all white-collar crimes and corporate crimes can be described as crimes of the powerful. According to Croall (2001), businesses that are much smaller in size than the large corporations that some criminologists focus on in their analyses of crimes of the powerful also commit acts of misconduct and crime. Small businesses commit offences that range from 'false description of goods' and selling contaminated food to contravening 'food hygiene regulations' (Croall,

1989: 159, 161). These small businesses include bakeries, restaurants, garages and street market traders (Croall, 1989). However, because they occupy a lower socio-economic status compared with large corporations, the crimes that small businesses commit cannot be properly described as 'crimes of the powerful'. Equally, some low-status individuals who cannot be described as powerful (mainly because they do not possess power and wealth) also commit white-collar crimes. Therefore, not all white-collar crimes may be described as crimes of the powerful. Indeed, some writers recognise this. They have offered definitions of white-collar crime that focus not on the status or other attributes of the offender, but on the nature of the offence. Power is not perceived to be a key variable; rather, it is the nature of the crime that makes it a 'white-collar crime'. Brightman (2009: 3), for example, defines the concept as a 'non-violent act committed for financial gain, regardless of one's status'. Writers Weisburd and colleagues (2008) restrict their definition of white-collar crime to non-violent offences committed by employees for financial gain in the course of employment to benefit themselves (occupational crime[8]). These definitions suggest that low-status individuals may also commit white-collar crime, and it is the nature of the offence (financial crime) and the setting of the offence (inside an occupational setting) that makes it a white-collar crime. In this sense, white-collar crimes are not solely crimes of the powerful. As Croall (1989: 157) points out, it is misleading to presume that only people who occupy high-status positions perpetrate white-collar crimes: 'The definition of white-collar crime has always been problematic, particularly its inclusion of "high status" offenders. Some white-collar offences are committed by offenders clearly not of "high status and respectability", such as motor repair fraud'.

In light of the foregoing, it is clear that there is considerable confusion over how best to classify the crimes that constitute 'crimes of the powerful'. However, it would appear that both white-collar crime and corporate crime are typically theorised and studied as 'crimes of the powerful'. In terms of white-collar crime in particular, there is a tendency to portray those who are classed as white-collar criminals as individuals who possess relatively higher social status compared with the individuals who are associated with the conventional crimes that dominate official crime statistics. White-collar criminals are said to occupy positions of trust in their employment. According to Slapper and Tombs (1999: 14), white-collar crime is best described as crimes that are committed by the 'individually rich or powerful which are committed in the furtherance of their own interests often against corporations or organisations for or within which they are working'. This highlights the general assumption that higher-status individuals commit white-collar crimes.

Similarly, in terms of corporate crimes, it is generally believed that large corporations in particular can influence legal authorities. Indeed, Sutherland argued that those who run large business and those who exercise legal authority in society belong to the same social group, which is located at the higher end of the social strata (see also Tombs, 2013). Sutherland also maintained that because they share similar ideological experiences and perspectives, legal authorities define and implement the law in favour of businesses (Tombs, 2013). Echoing these views, Tombs (2013) points out that corporate crimes are typically regarded as crimes of the powerful because they are crimes that may be committed by those who occupy the most senior positions within large organisations. These are individuals who typically possess wealth and political power/influence.[9]

The foregoing suggests that one way out of the definitional quagmire that surrounds this field of study is to presume (as many criminologists who study crimes of the powerful appear to do) that white-collar crimes, corporate crimes and state crimes are crimes that are typically committed by individuals of high socioeconomic status, large corporations, institutions and nation states.

State crime

State crimes or state-organised crimes may also be classed as crimes of the powerful. These are crimes that are committed in pursuit of the aims or interests of the state (Chambliss, 1989; Green and Ward, 2004). They include acts and omissions that violate the criminal law and international law (Lynch, 2011). Examples of state crimes are: human rights abuses; and religious persecution (see, generally, Barak, 1991). Cohen (1993) analysed the mechanisms that explain how and why individuals, institutions and states commit atrocities, cause human suffering and then try to deny involvement or culpability. Cohen (1995) also explored the strategies that can be employed to revisit and address state crimes that were committed in the past (see also Rothe and Friedrichs, 2006; Rothe et al, 2009). 'State-corporate crime', which is crime committed by the state in collusion with a corporation, or crimes that occur because the state does not prevent a corporation from causing harm, are also described as crimes of the powerful (Kramer and Michalowski et al, 2002).

Differential responses to crimes of the powerful

Radical perspectives on crimes of the powerful trace these crimes to structural inequalities that create power differentials between the social classes. The radical perspectives insist that perpetrators of these crimes occupy a high socio-economic status. Some may even possess the ability to influence the creation of laws and to escape law enforcement. Indeed, they are said to enjoy relative impunity or leniency when they violate the law compared with the perpetrators of conventional crimes (Tombs, 2013).[10]

In terms of corporate crimes, for example, studies that have examined responses to these crimes suggest that in many jurisdictions, 'non-enforcement' of the law is the norm within regulatory regimes (Tombs, 2010: 238). Enforcement is typically reserved for the least-powerful individuals and organisations, and the sanctions imposed are usually lenient and are also typically financial penalties (Snider, 1993; Tombs, 2013; Tombs and Whyte, 2013). The general view is that these crimes are typically reported, recorded or prosecuted at a much lower rate than conventional crimes, and crimes of the powerful are generally subject to lenient law enforcement policy and practice (Tombs, 2013). They are said to be relatively unregulated and under-enforced, or 'relatively decriminalized' (Tombs, 2013: 233). In the UK, they are not included in official crime statistics, and unlike conventional crimes, the statistics make no mention of hidden corporate crimes, which are estimated by some to be quite extensive (Tombs, 2013).

Writers from the radical perspective decry the relative impunity that large corporations enjoy. They advocate more punitive regulation and enforcement as preferable alternatives to extant policies that prioritise self-regulation (Tombs and Whyte, 2013). That said, Almond and Colover (2012), and others, note that dichotomous views exist about how best to respond to corporate crime. While some scholars prefer punitive deterrent enforcement (see, eg, Pearce and Tombs, 1998; Tombs, 2013), others, including scholars in the field of regulatory studies, prefer a compliance-oriented approach that encourages self-regulation as the alternative to punitive law enforcement, except in serious cases (Hawkins, 1984; Ayres and Braithwaite, 1992; Hutter, 2001). Almond and Colover (2012) describe the latter approach as the 'regulatory orthodoxy', which proposes that tough enforcement, such as prosecution, should be the 'last resort' (Almond and Colover, 2012: 1010; Tombs and Whyte, 2013: 747).

It has been suggested that the fundamental difference between those who advocate compliance-oriented strategies and those who propose more punitive regulation rests on their different ideas about the nature of corporations. Some believe that corporations can be trusted to reconcile profitability concerns with the need to conduct their business in a moral and socially responsible manner that will also shield them from reputational damage (Tombs, 2013). On the other hand, others assume that to trust that corporations would act morally and responsibly is to overlook the pressures on those who run corporations to maximise profitability while operating within sometimes-constraining business contexts (Tombs, 2013).

One of several explanations that have been proffered for the apparent disparity in responses to corporate crime compared with conventional crime is social status (Tombs, 2013: 233). Tombs points out that so-called 'conventional criminals' are perceived to contribute less to society than corporations. Therefore, corporate crimes are minimised and dismissed as one-off incidents and technical violations of the law, not 'real crimes'. Tombs (2013: 233) maintains that the media reinforces this spurious distinction between corporate crime and 'real' crime and criminals by devoting greater attention to its coverage of conventional crimes and by using more positive terms such as 'mis-selling, scandals, disasters and accidents' to underplay the immorality and seriousness of corporate crimes.

It has also been argued that another factor that may explain the differential response to corporate crimes is that the impact of such crimes is not direct or personal. Culpability is typically attributed to the corporation involved in corporate crime rather than to the individual perpetrators. Thus, the latter do not attract moral indignation compared with the perpetrators of conventional crimes. The latter tend to be identifiable individuals who cause direct and visible harm to their victims (Croall, 2001).[11] Equally, the harmful activities of the powerful (which, according to some criminologists who study crimes of the powerful, should be described as criminal activities) are typically defined and responded to as breaches of civil law or other regulations (Tombs, 2013). Examples include violations of health and safety regulations, which are enforced by the Health and Safety Executive (HSE) rather than criminal justice services, such as the police or the criminal courts. For this reason, scholars who are sometimes described as Zemiologists argue that the term 'crime' should be replaced with 'social harm' (Hillyard and Tombs, 2007). According to the Zemiologists, 'social harm' is a more comprehensive term that can cover the harmful activities of the powerful that are not currently described, or prosecuted, as crimes.

Lack of resources may also explain the apparent failure to prosecute crimes of the powerful, such as corporate crimes, as stridently as other crimes. According to Almond (2013: 21), the cost of prosecution is one of several reasons why it appears that there is a 'law as last resort' mentality in relation to these crimes. Nelken (2012: 624) notes that in the UK, factories are inspected for compliance with health and safety laws and regulations approximately on a four-yearly basis,, and prosecution is very much viewed as the least-favourable option. Indeed, in the UK, although the HSE, which oversees corporate conduct and enforces health and safety regulations, may work with the police to investigate serious incidents, such as work-related deaths, the HSE assumes the lead role in such cases.[12] Yet, the HSE, along with the other regulatory agencies responsible for enforcing compliance and prosecuting corporate crime, operates from outside the main criminal justice institutions – the Ministry of Justice and the Home Office (Tombs, 2013). This, again, sets corporate crimes apart from conventional crimes. The latter is, of course, always the subject of investigation and prosecution under the criminal law. Relatedly, while 'zero tolerance' law and order, and promoting victims' rights are typically the subject of political pronouncements about conventional crimes, hardly any effort is ever made to relate these themes to crimes of the powerful (Tombs, 2013).

The difficulty of ascribing culpability accurately in cases involving large corporations has been identified as yet another factor that explains the under-prosecution of corporate crimes. For example, in the event of an occupational hazard in a large corporation, who should be held responsible for the harm caused by the hazard (eg for injury and death)? As Walklate (2005; 120; see also 2011) puts it: 'the diffusion of responsibility that exists within many organisations makes it difficult to identify who is both legally and criminally responsible for an event'. Indeed, an important reason why serious crimes of the powerful, such as corporate manslaughter, appear to be relatively overlooked by the criminal justice system is the difficulty of establishing culpability. This difficulty presents itself because many large corporations have complex hierarchical structures and diffuse chains of responsibility.

In the UK, the Corporate Manslaughter and Corporate Homicide Act (CMCHA) 2007 came into force in 2008. Before the Act came into effect, prosecutions for deaths in the workplace caused by the failure of an organisation to comply with health and safety laws were governed by the common law and it was generally believed that the common law made it difficult for companies to be prosecuted for deaths in the workplace. This is because under the common law, the prosecutor had to establish that a duty of care existed between the employer and the employee and there has been a breach of the duty of care. It was therefore quite difficult to identify the individual who had breached the duty of care, or that the breach caused the employee's death.

No organisation was prosecuted for this offence until the commencement of the CMCHA in 2008. The Act covers deaths in the workplace caused by gross breach of the duty of care. It appears to be broader in scope but only very few organisations have been convicted under the Act. Some argue that the Act is still not broad enough because it identifies a corporate body as the defendant, not an individual director or manager. It does not apply to individuals. It also requires the prosecutor to prove that the harm caused death. Therefore, it excludes other forms of serious harm that may cause significant injury even if they do not necessarily lead to death (Almond, 2013).

It is, of course, important to recognise that several commentators contend quite persuasively that the under-prosecution of corporate crimes stems mainly from an evident reluctance to prosecute such cases (Tombs, 2013). While it can be acknowledged that it is perhaps onerous to establish liability in large organisations with complicated hierarchical and management arrangements, it still remains the case that the harmful activities of large corporations are typically not the subject of criminal justice enforcement. As noted earlier, regulatory bodies such as the HSE, which cannot impose criminal liability and criminal convictions, typically regulate the activities of corporations. It is also argued that even where such crimes are prosecuted within the criminal justice system, the courts tend to impose lenient sanctions, such as fines. For example, an organisation that is found guilty of the serious offence of corporate manslaughter is liable to an unlimited fine. While this may cause the corporation considerable hardship, which may even be filtered down to consumers and others (Tombs, 2013), none of its directors or executives receives a prison sentence. The latter is arguably the most severe sentence on the sentencing tariff, particularly if it is a long-term prison sentence that reflects the seriousness of a crime like corporate manslaughter. The Act does provide that the courts may impose a publicity order, requiring the organisation to publicise details of its conviction and fine. The Act envisages that the publicity order, which could potentially damage the corporation's reputation, will punish large corporations, particularly where a hefty fine is unlikely to have any significant impact. The courts may also impose a remedial order, which requires the organisation to address the problems that caused the death. Nevertheless, despite the existence of the Act and other pieces of legislation that criminalise some corporate crimes, some criminologists argue that the state is complicit in the under-prosecution of crimes of the powerful, particularly corporate crimes. These criminologists assert that the state protects the interests of industry. For example, it may protect corporations that overlook health and safety laws in order to reduce the overall expenses incurred during production (Nelken, 2012).

Crimes of the powerful are diverse in their nature and impact but a unifying feature is the wider public's attitudes towards such crimes. The public do not readily identify the harmful activities of the powerful as criminal behaviour mainly because of the following reasons:

- Official statistics and media accounts suggest that the 'typical' offender is the socioeconomically deprived individual who is likely to commit 'conventional crimes' such as street crimes and burglary. The perpetrators of crimes of the powerful do not fit this image. Studies indicate that the media portrays these crimes differently and more positively: 'The reporting of white-collar crime tends to be concentrated in "quality" newspapers and is often restricted to specialist financial pages, sections, or newspapers … framed in ways that mark it off from "real" crime' (Greer and Reiner, 2012: 249). In addition, positive terms are frequently employed to underplay the immoral quality and the seriousness of the crimes committed by higher-status individuals and powerful corporations (Tombs, 2013). For example, stealing from an employer might be classed as embezzlement instead of theft, defrauding the taxpayer by making fraudulent expenses claims becomes an 'expenses scandal' and incidents in which people lose their lives because a corporation has failed to comply with health and safety regulations become 'accidents'.
- Equally, corporations do not have the physical characteristics that human beings have. Thus, they do not fit the stereotypical image of the criminal (Tombs, 2013). Furthermore, the perpetrators of crimes of the powerful tend to occupy respectable positions in society.
- Crimes of the powerful, such as corporate crimes and misconduct, are typically the subject of regulation, not criminal justice enforcement. Corporations that commit crimes 'are not treated as real criminals by criminal justice systems or political elites' (Tombs, 2013: 241). This also helps explain why they are viewed as different from conventional crimes. In England and Wales, regulatory agencies, which include the HSE and the Food Standards Agency, enforce compliance with relevant legislation. It is argued that these agencies are often ill-resourced and ill-equipped to deal with non-compliance (Tombs and Whyte, 2010) and this may, in part, explain the low rates at which violations are detected, prosecuted and punished (Walklate, 2011). Moreover, as noted earlier, it is clear that even where such cases are successfully prosecuted, the sentences imposed tend to be more lenient – fines being typically imposed (Croall, 2001; Tombs, 2013).
- Crimes of the powerful are less visible. They are crimes that do not dominate public consciousness and create fear. In addition, higher-status offenders are less visible than lower-status offenders, such as young black men, who may have a greater presence in the streets and are, as such, more likely to encounter the

police. They are also more likely to be the victims of discriminatory policing practices (Croall, 1989).

• Victims and other members of the public cannot readily perceive the impact of crimes of the powerful because such crimes tend to be less direct than the harms caused by conventional crimes.

To expand on the latter point, the victim of a violent crime is more likely to experience direct consequences, such as physical and mental harm. Burglary victims may experience physical harm (if they are assaulted by the burglar). They may also experience emotional harm that may arise from feeling violated. In addition, they experience financial harm where, for example, there is loss of property. By contrast, the victims of crimes of the powerful are often unaware that they have been victimised. For instance, the victims of tax avoidance by large companies or the victims of irresponsible banking practices that spark a global fiancial crisis may find it difficult to appreciate the significant victimisation that such crimes can cause, not least because it can affect their financial well-being for a protracted period of time. Indeed, it is argued that victims of white-collar crimes may not even realise that they have been victimised: 'The majority of those suffering from corporate crime remain unaware of their victimisation – either not knowing it has happened to them or viewing their "misfortune" as an accident or "no one's fault"' (Box, 1983: 17).

The victims of occupational hazards that are caused by violations of relevant health and safety or other workplace regulations may not realise that the perpetrator is the company official who is responsible for ensuring compliance with the regulations. People are usually unaware that they have been overcharged for goods or that foods are not accurately labelled. Even when they are aware, they might not be able to locate the culprit or they may lack the resources and the support (from enforcement agencies and bodies) required to pursue prosecutions against such culprits as large and powerful organisations (Tombs, 2013).

Not only is it difficult to unravel the intricate threads that connect crimes of the powerful to their victims, but it is also generally believed that the absence of immediate and direct harm means that these crimes do not create as much fear and concern as conventional crimes create, even where they produce more significant victimisation. Notwithstanding this, studies now show that crimes of the powerful produce extensive victimisation (Tombs and Whyte, 2007; 2010), and they can produce effects that are similar to the impact of conventional crimes (Spalek, 2007).

The impact of crimes of the powerful

Mainstream criminologists, including neo-conservative criminologists, and also left realists, have been criticised for focusing mainly on street crimes. Although there are important ideological differences between criminologists who belong to both camps, they invariably defend their position by arguing that street crime produces the greatest impact because it causes direct victimisation and is more visible. However, the evidence suggests that crimes of the powerful produce far greater costs than conventional crime. There are direct physical costs, such as the deaths and injuries that are caused by occupational health and safety crimes. There are also economic costs to taxpayers and others affected by the frauds committed by large corporations (Tombs, 2013) and by white-collar criminals, particularly white-collar criminals in positions that grant them access to considerable sums of money, such as taxpayers' money, pension funds and other people's savings.

Accurate information about the exact extent of crimes of the powerful, such as the financial and other crimes committed by large corporations, is not available. However, criminologists provide useful estimates of the extent of these crimes. Slapper and Tombs (1999) estimate that annually in England, the Serious Fraud Office deals with cases that involve up to £5 billion. This far exceeds burglary cases, which amount to £1 billion (see also Minkes, 2010). The International Labour Organisation (ILO) asserts that more than 2.3 million work-related fatalities occur annually worldwide. The organisation states that:

> Workplaces claim more than 2.3 million deaths per year, out of which 350,000 are fatal accidents and close to 2 million are work-related diseases. In addition, 313 million accidents occur on the job annually; many of these resulting in extended absences from work. The human cost of this daily adversity is vast and the economic burden of poor occupational safety and health practices is estimated at 4 per cent of global Gross Domestic Product each year. (International Labour Organisation n.d.)

In the UK, the work-related deaths recorded by the HSE are quite minimal and are by no means a comprehensive record because they exclude several industries, including the fishing and gas industries. According to Tombs and Whyte (2013), health and safety is an under-regulated area; consequently, the statistics on work-related deaths, injuries and illnesses produced by the HSE underestimate the scale of these unfortunate incidents by up to six times. However, other studies suggest that deaths caused by work-related illness in the UK amount to approximately 50,000 each year, which is more than four times the number estimated by the HSE (Palmer, cited in Tombs and Whyte, 2013).

The text *The Rich get Richer and the Poor get Prison* by Reiman (1979)[13] presents comprehensive statistics which indicate that crimes of the powerful produce far greater victimisation than the conventional crimes that dominate official statistics. The text successfully challenges popular ideas about crime and its perpetrators. To illustrate that murder, for example, can occur in wider contexts than what is depicted in official statistics, Reiman (1979) drew on statistics to show that of the 168,600 people 'murdered' in the US in 1974, a significant proportion was caused by occupational hazard in medical establishments. The text *Power, Crime, and Mystification* (Box, 1983) also presented statistics to show that police-recorded homicides between 1973 and 1979 were significantly lower than deaths caused by occupational hazards (see also Slapper and Tombs, 1999). Barak (2012, cited in Nelken, 2012) estimates that approximately 30 to 40 million people have been affected by the risky activities of financial institutions. In the text titled *Corporate Manslaughter and Regulatory Reform*, Paul Almond (2013) cites statistics published by Eurostat, which produces statistics for the European Union (EU). The statistics suggest that there were 5,785 deaths at work in the 27 EU member states in 2007 (Eurostat, 2010, cited in Almond, 2013). In the US, official data suggests that there were 5,214 work–related deaths in 2008 (Occupational Safety and Health Administration, cited in Almond, 2013).

A study that provides useful empirical evidence of the direct impact of corporate crime and misconduct on victims is the study by Spalek (2007). The study explored the impact of the fraudulent activities of the late multimillionaire businessman Robert Maxwell, who was a former owner of *The Mirror* newspaper. The study also examined the impact of the financial crimes committed by the directors of the Bank of Credit and Commerce International (BCCI) (see Spalek, 2007). In the study, Spalek found that the victims of these crimes reported experiences that are similar to the experiences of the victims of conventional crimes. They revealed substantial 'emotional, psychological, behavioural, physical and financial' suffering (p 2). They also reported psychological difficulties that include: 'anger, anxiety, fear stress, fear and depression' (p 2). Some of the former employees of these companies reported experiences that are also similar to the social problems associated with labelling. They felt stigmatised and even found it difficult to secure alternative employment because of the stigma attached to their previous employers. The study highlighted the extensive victimisation that corporate crimes and misconduct can cause. The Robert Maxwell case alone produced over 30,000 victims who had invested their pensions in Maxwell's companies.

Zemiology

Some criminologists argue that the parameters of criminology should be expanded to incorporate the study of not only acts that are defined as 'crime', but also acts that cause social harm. The work of these criminologists has been described as Zemiology. In the text *Beyond Criminology: Taking Crime Seriously*, which was edited by Paddy Hillyard, Christina Pantazis, Steve Tombs and Dave Gordon (2004), several criminologists set out arguments in favour of expanding the remit of criminology and the criminal law to cover a wider range of social harms, from harmful state activities like human rights abuses, to environmental pollution, poverty, and health and safety violations (see also Tombs, 2007; Tombs and Whyte, 2007). These writers were not the first to propose that definitions of crime should be expanded to include harmful actions. In several publications in the 1970s, Schwendinger and Schwendinger (1970, 1972, 1977) argued that the crime' is not an unproblematic or unbiased concept. In their view, the definitions of crime reflects class relations and race relations. It reflects the nature of wealth distribution in society. Consequently, the criminal law focuses attention on areas that suit the interests of those who create the law. Schwendinger and Schwendinger pointed out that to address this, the legal definition of crime should expand to include other areas, including human rights violations.

Zemiologists argue that criminology should abandon the concept of 'crime' and replace it with a social harm perspective (Hillyard and Tombs, 2007). They criticise mainstream criminology for its uncritical acceptance of 'crime' as an unproblematic concept. Hillyard and Tombs (2005: 7) maintain that criminology's focus on crime overlooks the harmful activities of the powerful: 'there is little doubt that the undue attention given to events which are defined as crimes distracts attention from more serious harm [and] positively excludes them'. Zemiologists also point out that criminology has turned away from previous debates about what constitutes valid social science knowledge and about the impact of structural factors on crime, and has embraced, instead, an empiricist agenda. The decline of criminological theorising fuels this agenda. The quest to secure research funding from government departments has contributed to a myopic focus on devising criminological perspectives that are designed to fulfil short-term state-defined objectives.

Zemiologists adopt an anti-essentialist stance. They argue that crime is a social construct: 'Crimes – and criminals – are fictive events and characters in the sense that they have to be constructed before they can exist. Crime is thus a "myth" of everyday life' (Hillyard and Tombs, 2007: 10).

According to the Zemiologists, although crime is nothing more than a 'myth' because it has no intrinsic quality, criminologists help perpetuate the concept of crime. Criminologists perpetuate the myth of crime when they refer to crime in articles, textbooks and journals without questioning the concept itself. In their debates about crime causation and control, criminologists portray crime as an unproblematic and uncontested concept with identifiable intrinsic qualities: 'The issue of what crime is, is rarely stated, simply assumed' (Hillyard and Tombs, 2007: 11).

Zemiologists assert that although the public believes that 'crime' is a serious problem, when compared with the significant impact of other acts that are harmful but are not considered to be 'crimes', many of the acts that are accepted as 'crimes' and recorded in police statistics produce a relatively minor impact on the victims. Yet, Zemiologists point out that these minor crimes dominate police statistics and public perceptions of serious crimes, not only because the criminal law defines them as crime, but because of selective criminal justice processing.

Zemiologists believe that criminal justice officials, from the police to the sentencers, use their discretion to decide which crimes to ascribe a specific level of seriousness to. By prosecuting and imposing punishment on the minor crimes that dominate official crime statistics, criminal justice officials reinforce public views about the seriousness of these crimes. Therefore, criminal law definitions of crimes and criminal justice practices do not tell us much about the nature and extent of serious crimes. The sentences imposed on those who are typically labelled as criminals do not protect society from the most dangerous people or from the most dangerous acts and events that produce the greatest harm. According to Zemiologists, most of these acts and events are not defined as 'crime', and even if they are defined as such, they are not processed through the criminal justice system. They cite the example of corporate crime and state crime, which, in their view, create substantial and widespread victimisation but are nevertheless largely overlooked across the ambit of law enforcement and criminological theorising. In the focus on acts that are defined as crime, harmful acts and events that not defined as crime become marginalised or even totally excluded from dominant discourses about crime causation and control.

The key themes that Zemiologists emphasise include the following:

- 'Crime has no ontological reality' (Hillyard and Tombs, 2007, p 10).
- Criminologists perpetuate the 'myth of crime' as a real phenomenon by failing to clearly acknowledge that it is a contested and problematic concept (Hillyard and Tombs, 2007, p 19). There has been a decline in criminological theorising and a rise in an 'empiricist' agenda that satisfies the short-term pragmatic interests of recent governments (Hillyard and Tombs, 2007, p 9).
- Acts and events that are defined as 'crime' are relatively minor compared with the acts and events that cause the greatest harm but are not defined as crime, and are overlooked by criminal justice officials.
- The criminal law uses faulty measures to assess whether a crime has been committed. This is because crime lacks any intrinsic qualities.
- The criminalisation process leads to, or is the outcome of the process of, defining an event as a 'crime'. This process inflicts greater harm on the offender than the original offence caused to the victim because the offender has to run the gamut of labelling and punishment, which may, in turn, create social problems such as stigmatisation, job loss, reduced employment prospects, loss of accommodation, loss of family life and many other losses. These are difficulties that tend to affect the more vulnerable in society.
- The criminal justice system is ineffective despite considerable investment in the system. The system does not achieve its stated aims of rehabilitation, deterrence and other principles. In addition, despite its stated aims, it is clear that the prison, for example, serves to fulfil other purposes; for example, it serves as a means of controlling target populations in neo-liberal capitalist societies.
- The existence of 'crime', legitimises the growth of the crime control machinery. Hillyard and Tombs (2007: 15) describe the latter as 'the crime control industry'. Modern societies are confronted by the dual problem of unequal employment opportunities and wealth inequality (Hillyard and Tombs, 2007). The industry provides employment and serves as a means of controlling those who are unable to gain access to paid work or who suffer other forms socioeconomic marginalisation.
- '"Crime" helps to maintain power relations in society' (Hillyard and Tombs, 2007, p 15). Its existence facilitates the labelling and control of the less powerful.

For Zemiologists, a social harm approach within criminology and within criminal justice policy should ensure that the physical harms perpetrated by the powerful come under criminal law enforcement policy and practice. These harms include harms that are perpetrated by state officials, those in violation of environmental laws and those who violate workplace health and safety regulations. A social harm perspective in criminology and criminal justice should also ensure that financial/economic harms that produce extensive victimisation would also come within the ambit of criminal justice policy. These include poverty, misappropriation of funds by government officials, and taxation policies that oppress the poor and enrich the wealthy. In sum, Zemiologists suggest that if there is genuine concern to address the problems that are associated with crime, then every effort will be made to address those activities that produce the most harm:

> if our concern with crime is driven by fears for social stability, personal safety and social justice, then we may be well advised to look beyond 'crime' to discover where the most dangerous threats and risks to our person and property lie. Poverty, malnutrition, pollution, medical negligence, breaches of workplace health and safety laws, corporate corruption, state violence, genocide, human rights violations and so on all carry with them more widespread and damaging consequences than most of the behaviors and incidents that currently make up the 'problem of crime'. (Muncie, 2000)

Criticisms

Some of the criminologists who study crimes of the powerful, and who have been influenced by the Marxist critique of capitalism, attribute the crimes of large corporations to the quest to secure capitalist interests, and some also hint at state complicity (see, eg, Friedrichs and Rothe, 2012). These criminologists focus on corporate crime (committed by large corporations) in their study of crimes of the powerful (see, eg, Tombs, 2013).[14] They insist that capitalist societies breed crimes of the powerful. A criticism of this perspective is that it suggests that crimes of the powerful are only inherent in capitalist societies. Socialist societies, for example, are deemed to be free of such crimes. Those who reject this proposition argue that crimes of the powerful also occur in socialist societies (Minkes, 2010). In addition, critics assert that criminologists who focus on rational choice as a primary explanatory theme portray the powerful as 'amoral calculators' who make calculated decisions to embark on criminal activities and misconduct in order to maximise the corporation's profit (Nelken, 2012: 637). These criminologists believe that deterrent strategies are appropriate preventive measures. Unsurprisingly, criminologists who adopt the 'rational choice' perspective when they explain crimes of the powerful have confronted some of the criticisms that the rational choice theorists encounter. A key criticism is that the idea that rational choice precedes behaviour overlooks the possibility of impulsive decision-making and other factors that are said to override the ability of potential offenders to make rational decisions about the certainty, celerity or severity of punishment before they commit crime (Doobs and Webster, 2003). Moreover, it is argued that decision-making processes in large corporations, for instance, are too complex and cannot be reduced to the rational choice of individual actors (Minkes, 2010). Rejecting this view, others point out that large corporations tend to calculate the potential consequences of their actions, and deterrent strategies are most effective where those targeted for such strategies are 'future-oriented' in this way (Tomb and Whyte 2013: 750). It is argued that senior-level individuals in corporations possess the motivation and the 'information gathering' resources needed to make long-term strategic plans in order to maximise profitability (Tombs and Whyte, 2013: 750–1). Tombs (2013: 234) notes that:

> One of the defining characteristics of a corporation is the potential for rational action, based upon strategic calculation, including the ability to anticipate and to predict external responses to its actions – in order to maximise its long run profits, the corporate raison d'être.

Explanations of corporate crime that are based on Merton's anomie theory have been accused of over-predicting crime. These explanations are rooted in the idea that corporations may resort to illegitimate means of securing profit if legitimate means are blocked to them (Box, 1983; Slapper and Tombs, 1999; Nelken, 2012). Thus, it is argued that the quest for profit and other successful outcomes motivates illegal business activities, particularly where legal means of maintaining profitability are blocked (Box, 1983). According to some commentators, this presumption overlooks the stable trade that occurs between different nations, including numerous transactions in contexts where opportunities for crime abound and risks of detection are minimal (Nelken, 2012).

Some commentators also point to improvements that have been made to-counter crimes of the powerful. These commentators argue that the improvements are perhaps not fully taken into account by those who argue that the powerful enjoy considerable impunity when they violate the law. Almond (2013: 4), for instance, states that 'We are safer now than we have ever been (at least within the Western world), and this is a point which even the most strident critics of safety regulation must concede'. It is, indeed, the case that Western governments, such as the UK and the US, have introduced criminal and legislation to complement existing civil enforcement laws and address the under-prosecution of serious corporate crimes. The CMCHA 2007 represents one example of such legislation in the UK. Almond (2013) points out that the Act represents an example of the effort to shift from a regulatory framework to a criminal law framework for responding to corporate crime and misconduct. Nelken (2012) also states that much has been done to improve the safety and quality of goods produced by capitalists.

However, pieces of legislation that criminalise certain serious corporate misconduct, such as the CMCHA 2007, exist alongside a more dominant regulatory framework that operates outside the criminal law. Almond (2013: 22) notes that prosecutions are still rare under the Act, and are predominantly pursued outside the realm of the criminal law:

> Prosecution is not a core component of the regulatory process, and convictions when they do occur, result in sanctions that are less harsh than found elsewhere in the criminal law. Health and safety violations, even those causing death, are rarely treated as matters of criminal law *per se*.

Therefore, criminologists who study crimes of the powerful from a critical perspective believe that more work remains to be done to address the relatively lenient prosecution and enforcement of crimes committed by the powerful, and to counter the tendency to portray such crimes as somewhat less criminal than conventional crimes, and not 'real crimes'. Tombs (2013: 241) asserts that 'there still remains significant political and social distance between corporate entities and their crimes, and those of "real" criminals'. Studies and official statistics in the US (Pontell et al, 2014) and UK (Almond, 2013) continue to indicate that although crimes of the powerful, such as the financial and health and safety crimes committed by large corporations, are quite extensive in scale and impact,[15] they are under-prosecuted under the criminal law,[16] and even under administrative laws and the civil law. When they are prosecuted, the fines imposed are typically quite small. Indeed, the trend seems to be moving quite rapidly towards even greater non-intervention. In the UK, there has been a move to radically reduce the rate at which workplaces are inspected for compliance with health and safety regulations (Tombs and Whyte, 2013). Indeed, what is occurring is the 'retreat of proactive inspections and enforcement' (Tombs and Whyte, 2013: 758). Corporations, therefore, are set to enjoy even greater impunity than they had in the past. As Tombs and Whyte (2013: 758) observe: 'the removal of surveillance sends a message to employers that they might endanger workers' lives and livelihoods with greater impunity'. Moreover, many businesses are now exempt from inspections (Department for Business, Innovation and Skills, 2012, cited in Tombs and Whyte, 2013). In addition, crimes of the powerful continue to be marginal to criminological theorising.

Conclusion

Criminologists and others who study the crimes and other harmful activities of the powerful, and the responses to these activities, may not all be influenced by the arguments of the early Marxist criminologists. Nevertheless, by drawing attention to crimes of the powerful, these criminologists and others in this field of study have developed critical perspectives on crimes of the powerful. They have expanded on the arguments of the early Marxist criminologists, who insisted that criminal behaviour is not unique to the members of any class or group in society. However, those on the lower end of the social strata are more likely to have their activities defined as crimes. Their activities tend to dominate official crime statistics and to feature heavily in dominant discourses about the typical criminal.

In addition, criminologists who study crimes of the powerful from a radical perspective provide useful insights into the links between power, crime and responses to crime. They identify power as the common denominator that shapes legal definitions of crime, conventional views about crime and responses to crime. They contend that powerful groups are able to influence the creation of laws, and they prioritise laws that protect their values and interests.

SUMMARY

- Since the 1980s, studies of crimes of the powerful have proliferated in criminology. There are now several often-differing categorisations of crimes of the powerful. White-collar crime, state crime and corporate crime are the commonly cited categories of crimes of the powerful.
- Overall, it is generally agreed that crimes of the powerful are crimes that are committed by relatively higher-status individuals and powerful organisations, such as large corporations and nation states. These groups can be said to possess socio-economic advantage. Some also possess political power. They are different from the stereotypical offender of lower socio-economic status who is typically associated with conventional crime. Unlike crimes of the powerful, conventional crimes dominate mainstream criminological theories of crime, official statistics, media reports and public consciousness.
- Criminologists who study crimes of the powerful argue that compared with conventional crime, the crimes and misconduct of the powerful create more victims and produce greater harm. However, crimes of the powerful tend to be overlooked or minimised compared with so-called conventional crimes.
- Zemiologists also focus on crimes of the powerful. They maintain that replacing the term 'crime' with 'social harm' will broaden the scope of criminology and criminal justice to encompass the many harmful activities of the powerful.

SAMPLE QUESTIONS

1. Do you agree that the criminal justice system does not respond to crimes of the powerful and conventional crimes in the same way?
2. Describe the factors that influence public perceptions of the crimes and harms of the powerful.

Notes

[1] The phrase 'crimes of the powerful' is borrowed from Frank Pearce's (1976) text titled *Crimes of the Powerful* (see also Friedrichs and Rothe, 2012).

[2] Tombs (2013) notes that corporate crime has become more visible in recent years in the aftermath of the economic crisis and the backlash against bankers and other companies

implicated in forms of corporate misconduct. In the UK, for example, the growth of the private sector following the neo-liberal agenda to privatise large segments of the public sector has also heralded the proliferation of private sector businesses that now interact more closely with the public. The activities of these businesses are therefore more likely to come under public scrutiny. Greater publicity through social media networks has also enhanced the visibility of these crimes, as have investigative journalism and campaigns run on behalf of victims and others affected by corporate crimes. However, despite these developments, factors such as lenient law enforcement help underplay the visibility of these crimes, at least in mainstream definitions of crime and in law enforcement.

[3] The lower-class or lower-status groups referred to here include the less educated, the socio-economically marginalised, minority ethnic groups and also poor unemployed people (Box, 1983).

[4].Some feminists also contribute to knowledge in this field. Radical feminists, for instance, argue that, rather than socio-economic status or class, in patriarchal societies, gender is the key feature that explains the impunity that the powerful (men) enjoy when they commit crime or other harmful acts (against women). Added to feminist criminology, green criminology is another field of study within critical criminology that also contributes to insights into crimes of the powerful. Green criminologists explore the harms that powerful groups, including large corporations, cause to the environment, and the relative impunity that they believe the corporations enjoy. Chapter Ten explores key themes in green criminology.

[5] Criminologists who study the crimes of large corporations reject this. They argue that white-collar crime is quite different from the crimes committed by corporations, which are best described as 'corporate crimes' (Tombs, 2013).

[6] Sutherland's definition of white-collar crime was broad enough to encompass misconduct that is not defined as crime by the criminal law (see also Tombs, 2013).

[7] Corporate crimes may include financial crimes (such as pension fraud), crimes committed against consumers (such as selling contaminated goods) and employment-related offences, including racial discrimination and occupational health and safety crimes (Tombs, 2013).

[8] There is no general agreement over what constitutes occupational crime. There are several definitions but Friedrichs (2002: 243) offers a useful definition, and defines occupational crime as: 'illegal and unethical activities committed for individual financial gain – or to avoid financial loss – in the context of a legitimate occupation'. Thus, occupational crimes may range from stealing from an employer and fiddling expenses to cheating customers. Friedrichs (2002) differentiates occupational crime from occupational deviance, which, according to him, includes drinking on the job and sexual harassment. Friedrichs also differentiates occupational crime from workplace crime, which he argues incudes rape and assault.

[9] Some writers argue that corporate crime is crime committed within *legitimate* organisations (Friedrichs and Rothe, 2012). Sutherland's (1949) definition of 'white-collar crime' also appeared to focus on the activities of respectable people engaged in legitimate occupations. Croall (2001) argues that the term 'legitimate' is problematic in this context because it is often difficult to establish the legality of businesses. Some businesses may appear to be legitimate but, in fact, are primarily engaged in illegitimate activities (Croall, 2001).

[10] It is worth noting that not all white-collar criminals wield the degree of power or possess the amount of wealth that can shield them from law enforcement. Friedrichs (2002: 248) notes that 'many legal occupations are essentially devoid of real wealth and political power', with such levels of wealth and power tending to reside in the 'elite or at least upper middle class realm'. Indeed, the same can be said of corporate criminals. Small businesses that commit corporate crime can hardly be described as 'powerful', and they are unlikely to enjoy the levels of impunity that large multinational corporations are said to enjoy (Croall, 1989).

[11] However, see Almond (2013), who cites the Corporate Manslaughter and Corporate Homicide Act (CMCHA) 2007 (UK) as an example of recent efforts to respond to serious corporate crimes with the criminal law, which can perhaps communicate the normative dimension of such crimes more effectively than prevailing civil law regulations.

[12] Almond (2013) argues that enforcement is one of the many roles that the HSE undertakes, and the HSE tends to view the role as a minor role. The low prosecution rates reflect this.

[13] The text is now in its 10th edition (Reiman et al, 2013).

[14]. Not all criminologists who study corporate crime are influenced by Marxism.

[15] It is difficult to ascertain the scale of white-collar crime because it is under-reported and under-recorded in official crime statistics. As Nelken (2012: 623) puts it: 'most white collar crimes are not included in the official statistics'.

[16] Commentators observe that even in jurisdictions as the UK and US, where the possibility of prosecution under the criminal law exists, such prosecutions remain a minor element of the regulatory framework, which is primarily governed by the civil law (Almond, 2013). What has emerged is a 'two-track model of corporate liability', which comprises offences that are subject to either regulatory law or criminal law enforcement depending on how serious, harmful and socio-politically impactful the offences are (Almond, 2013: 22).

NINE

Green criminology

Introduction

This chapter introduces green criminology, which focuses on the impact of the harms and crimes that are committed against the environment and its species. It has been described as 'an emergent' critical criminological perspective[1] (Ruggiero and South, 2013a: 359), but not an established theory (South, 1998; White, 2010a). It is a field of study within the critical criminological tradition (Ruggiero and South, 2013a: 361) mainly because it locates its study of crime and responses to it within the wider context of social, economic and political arrangements in society.

Origins

Green criminology emerged from the work of writers who, in the 1990s, began to write about the impact of crimes and other harms[2] on or through the environment (see, generally, Lynch, 1990; 2011; 2013; Lynch et al, 2010; South and Beirne, 2006; South et al, 2013). Arguably, these writers built on the work that criminologists had done in the past on environmental dangers and crimes. However, some of the key writers in this field state that they have proceeded to create 'a new and original profile' for the subject matter (Lynch, 1990; Ruggiero and South, 2013a: 359).

Several definitions have been offered for green criminology. Thus, it lacks precise definition. Michael Lynch coined the term 'green criminology' but the term has been contested by those who prefer alternative terms, such as 'conservation criminology' (Gibbs et al, 2010) or 'environmental criminology' (Rugierro and South, 2013a). 'Eco-global criminology' and 'eco-crime' are additional concepts that have been proposed as alternatives to the term 'green criminology' (Ruggiero and South, 2013a). This apparent disagreement over what should constitute the appropriate terminology is widely acknowledged in the field. Brisman and South (2013: 2), for example, recognise that although there is disagreement over what should be the appropriate label, criminologists mainly use the term 'green criminology' to describe studies of the causes of, and responses to, activities that harm the environment.

Given the vast array of issues it addresses, it is argued that green criminology is best viewed as 'an interdisciplinary and multidisciplinary rendezvous' (Ruggiero and South, 2013a: 361). It shares common areas of interest with diverse disciplines, from psychology to conservation and environmental sciences (Ruggiero and South, 2013a: 361). That said, a key area of interest within green criminology is the concern to ameliorate environment degradation and its consequences for humanity and also for non-human species.

As mentioned earlier, various definitions have been offered for green criminology. According to Gibbs and colleagues (2010) each definition provided is shaped by the author's philosophical position on how human beings should interact with nature, what the causes of green crime are and how best to respond to these crimes. Those who advance a human-centred mode of interaction would prioritise definitions that focus on the harms that are caused to human beings. By contrast, those who prioritise a nature-centred mode of interaction would focus on the harms caused to the environment. There are also some whose views incorporate elements of both positions. They emphasise the harms caused to both humans and the environment (see, generally, Gibbs et al, 2010). For example, Ruggiero and South (2013a: 360) state that:

> Green Criminology can be defined as a framework of intellectual, empirical and political orientations toward primary and secondary harms, offences and crimes that impact in a damaging way on the natural environment, diverse species (human and non-human) and the planet. Introducing such a green or environmentally sensitive framework into criminology does not set out any one particular theory but rather introduces a perspective (South [1998]), which can inform theoretical and empirical work…. [It is] a perspective which, while transcending the conventional ambit of criminology, addresses the large array of legitimate or illegitimate conducts harming the environment and the species inhabiting it.

The foregoing suggests that green criminology addresses not only harmful acts to the environment and to humans, but also harmful acts perpetrated against non-human organisms. Green criminology also involves the study of corporate crimes and activities that harm the environment. Green criminologists argue that mainstream criminology overlooks these activities (Lynch et al, 2013). It follows that green criminology covers a broad range of diverse issues to do with the physical environment. According to Ruggiero and South (2013b: 14), 'it is not intended to be a unitary enterprise – diversity is one of its key strengths'. Writers in the field summarise the topics that green criminologists study to include environmental harms and crime, and also environmental justice. Green criminologists who focus on environmental justice draw attention to the adverse impact of environmentally harmful activities (including corporate activities) on human populations. These include health and safety violations, the pollution of natural resources, and wars (Ruggiero and South, 2013a, 2013b; Lynch et al, 2013; White, 2010a, 2010b). In addition, green criminologists study ecological justice, which refers more specifically to the role of human beings in environmental degradation (White, 2010a).

Environmental harms and crimes

Some green criminologists study environmental harms and crimes (Ruggiero and South, 2013a: 360). They prefer the broader concept of 'harm' to 'crime' because 'harm' includes but transcends legal definitions of crime. The bulk of the analyses done in this field consist of using case studies to illustrate the nature, frequency and impact of environmental misconduct. Lynch and colleagues (2013) note that this approach dominates the field of green criminology. There is an emphasis on the harmful activities of large corporations, such as multinational oil companies, situated in developing countries (Ruggiero and South, 2013a, 2013b). For example, commenting on the situation in Nigeria, which is an oil-producing country, Brisman and South (2013: 6) put it that 'Nigeria ... has suffered spills equivalent to that of Exxon Valdez in every year since 1969 and ... in 2009 it had 2,000 active spills'. They insist that these companies enjoy relative impunity, although some of their activities (such as oil spillage) can cause substantial pollution and destruction. The green criminologists argue that these incidents occur because of the failure of the companies to comply with regulations (albeit typically lax regulations). Green criminologists have commented extensively on the catastrophic impact of oil spills linked to oil extraction in several oil-producing countries. It is argued that the efforts of corporations to conceal the often-devastating impact of their activities exacerbate matters, and may also explain, in part, the impunity that they enjoy when they cause harm to the environment (Rugierro and South, 2013b).

Rugierro and South (2013b) point out that in the specific context of the global oil industry, for example, the state allows large oil companies to formulate the measures for estimating the degree of oil spills and damage. According to Ruggiero and South (2013b), studies reveal that the estimates provided often underplay the true degree of spill and damage. In addition, in their view, the estimates do not cover unreported spill and damage. Rugierro and South (2013b) describe the latter as incidents that occur frequently all over the world.

Environmental justice: the anthropocentric approach

Green criminologists who explore 'environmental justice' or 'green issues of justice', argue that these issues are still very much overlooked within criminology (White, 2010a: 411; Lynch et al, 2013: 998). Within the environmental justice perspective, there is a focus on the impact of environmental harms on humans, particularly on vulnerable populations within a specific region. According to White (2010a: 411), the field of environmental justice addresses green issues to do with the ability of populations in a specific area to access natural resources,, and the practices that harm the populations that reside in these areas and impede such access. There is a focus on human populations and the dynamics of 'production and consumption' that affect the welfare of these populations and impede their access to natural resources (White, 2010a: 411). Some green criminologists identify the most vulnerable or least powerful as the typical victims of these crimes (White, 2010a: 412). Minority ethnic groups and indigenous populations in societies where large corporations perpetuate environmental harms are said to be the worst affected by the pollution and environmental degradation caused by the activities of these corporations (see also Gibbs et al, 2010; Rugierro and South, 2010). White (2010a) cites less-powerful indigenes of Canada, Australia and the US as examples of the populations affected.

As mentioned earlier, green criminologists study the dynamics of production and consumption that affect the welfare of these populations, and impede their access to natural resources (White, 2010a). For example, some green criminologists point out that the areas in Nigeria where a significant proportion of Nigerian oil reserves are located have suffered the adverse impact of oil extraction by multinational oil companies, but have not benefited from the accompanying wealth (Ruggiero and South, 2013b). Indeed, according to Ruggiero and South (2013b: 16):

> In general terms, the multibillion-dollar oil industry of Nigeria has not produced an increase in per capita annual income in the country: in fact, income has fallen, with the number of Nigerians living on less than one dollar a day increasing from 36 per cent in 1970 to more than 70 per cent in 2000. Moreover, foreign companies operating in the country have set up their own paramilitary forces to protect their business and funded local groups of mercenaries to respond to attacks by violent political organisations (Watts 2008). In this way, corrupt practices, impoverishment of local people and military action have mingled and fed on each other in many oil-producing countries (Amnesty International 2001; Everest 2003; Klare 2004; Parra 2004).

Green criminologists also study the adverse impact of other types of environmentally harmful industrial activity, such as the inefficient waste management that occurs in what they describe as the 'hyper-consumer' societies of the West (Ruggiero and South, 2010: 251). They point out that in contemporary Western societies, the exponential growth in rates of consumption has been accompanied by a corresponding rise in the rate at which waste is produced. This, in their view, has given rise to waste management problems that are currently being ignored for a range of reasons. One reason given for this is that it is problematic to seek solutions to the large-scale consumerism that generates significant waste production. Another reason is that waste disposal is lucrative business (Rugierro and South, 2010). It has been suggested that, just like most of the victims of environmental harms caused by large corporations, the harmful activities of the waste industry impact mainly on the least-powerful people in the world. Again, the poorest people in society are said to be the worst affected who tend to live in areas where industries that process waste, and other industries that engage in similarly hazardous activities or produce toxic products, are located (Simon, 2000, cited in Rugierro and South, 2010; Stretesky and Lynch, 2002; Lynch and Stretesky, 2007). It is also argued that the powerless indigenous victims of environmental harm and crimes are often unaware of the cause of their predicament, perhaps because they lack awareness or because they may trace the problem to spiritual or other causes (White, 2010a). The victims are also often unable to avoid victimisation because there are 'socio-economic' considerations that almost compel them to overlook or adapt to these problems (White, 2010a: 412). Proponents of the environmental justice perspective define environmental crime as 'environmental racism or classism' (Gibbs et al, 2010: 126). This is because in their view, environmental harms tend to be perpetrated to a greater degree in areas that are inhabited by deprived and minority ethnic groups.

Ecological justice: biocentric and ecocentric approaches

Green criminologists also study ecological justice, which pertains to the impact of human activities on the planet and its non-human inhabitants, (plant and animal species) (White, 2010a). The study of ecological justice comprises bio centric approaches and eco centric approaches.

Unlike environmental justice approaches, biocentric approaches do not emphasise the welfare of human beings. Rather, they are more concerned about the fate of the environment and its natural resources. According to Gibbs and colleagues (2010: 127), '[Biocentric] perspectives prioritise the intrinsic value of ecosystems over human interests. Accordingly, human beings are the cause of environmental harm and need to be controlled.' Controversially, within this perspective, there are some who believe that conditions such as 'AIDS or famine', which are destructive to humans, may be deemed natural population control mechanisms that are beneficial to the environment (White, 2010a). This approach has been described as a 'fundamentally misanthropic perspective', which attributes the problem of environmental harms to human beings, and proposes sometimes excessively harmful measures such as eradication as effective solutions (White, 2010a: 413).

By contrast, although eco-centric perspectives focus on the impact of environmental degradation on the natural environment, and the role of human beings in such degradation, the perspectives are concerned with the impact of environmental harms crimes, not only on non-human species, but also on human populations. In addition, eco-centric perspectives focus to a greater degree on the links between political economy and environmentally harmful activities (White, 2010a). The latter are said to be closely linked to the process of production, which is under the control of the powerful, who own large corporations[3] and occupy upper-class positions in society (Simon, 2000, cited in White, 2010a; Lynch et al, 2010; 2013; Rugierro, 2013; White, 2013). Indeed, some green criminologists identify 'members of the capital class' as 'the most criminogenic agents of environmental harm within a global capitalist political economy' (White, 2013, cited in Ruggiero and South, 2013b). Green criminologists who adopt this stance aver that environmental harm and social injustice are the products of similar causal factors (see also Gibbs et al, 2010). Those who argue from a Marxist perspective assert that these causal factors can be traced to the production dynamics of the capitalist economic system, which, in their view, operates to further the interests of the wealthy capitalists – the owners of the means of production – but exploits and disadvantages other humans and the environment.

It follows that some green criminologists infuse their analyses of green crimes and responses to those crimes with considerations of political economy. They believe that links exist between the structural constitution of capitalist societies and green crime. They trace the origins of some green crimes to the production dynamics of capitalism (see, generally, Lynch et al, 2013; Rugierro and South, 2013a; 2013b; White, 2013). These production dynamics might involve activities that are beneficial to the expansion and profitability of capitalism but they also cause considerable damage to the natural environment in some way. For example, the activities might involve using chemicals to aid production. This, according to Lynch and colleagues, has led to a marked increase in levels of toxic waste and other hazardous pollutants in the environment. Furthermore, Lynch and colleagues point out that capitalist activities might involve the excessive consumption and waste of natural resources, which ultimately inhibit the conservation process that supports nature's growth. Oil extraction represents a key example. The extraction process is said to involve altering and often damaging the environment to facilitate extraction (see also Lynch et al, 2013; Rugierro and South, 2013b). These capitalist production activities are considered to be environmentally destructive. They are also believed to cause environmental problems, such as climate change. Proponents of the eco centric perspective believe that these activities should be defined as crimes. According to Lynch and colleagues (2013: 10):

> Capitalism's unending desire to accumulate and its ecologically destructive forces are serious crimes. Capitalism is based on the exploitation of nature and human labour, and the unequal distribution of the results of exploitation. It does not seek justice; rather it is simply in search of more.

Responses to green harms and crimes

Formulating adequate responses to activities that harm the environment represents yet another area of concern for green criminology (Ruggiero and South, 2013a). Green criminologists generally offer diverse views about how best to respond to green harms and crimes. White (2010a) provides a useful classification of the perspectives that explore how best to respond to green harms and crimes. He identifies three main approaches: the socio-legal approach; the regulatory approach and the social action approach. The socio-legal approach focuses on definitions of green crimes enshrined in the criminal law. Thus, proponents of the approach describe green crimes as activities that violate the criminal law. They believe that criminal sanctions are appropriate responses to these crimes (see also Gibbs et al, 2010). Some proponents of the socio-legal approach propose that the criminal law should be reformed to enhance its effectiveness (White, 2010a). According to White (2010a: 420), 'The main emphasis in the socio–legal approaches is how to best utilise existing legal and enforcement mechanisms to protect environments and creatures within specific environments (e.g. illegal fishing)'. A criticism of socio–legal approaches is that they focus on activities that fall within the narrow ambit of the criminal law and exclude a wider range of activities that also cause considerable harm. There is also the argument that socio–legal approaches overlook the anthropocentricism (human-centeredness) of the regulatory framework (Gibbs et al, 2010).

Some green criminologists prioritise a regulatory approach to reducing environmental harms. This approach may operate through informal social control mechanisms and 'self-regulation' to reform production and consumption systems (White, 2010: 419). It has been suggested that the effectiveness of the regulatory approach is subject to the degree to which such approaches may be supplanted by other state priorities, including neo–liberal imperatives (White, 2010a).

Unlike the green criminologists who restrict their analysis to crimes defined by the law as green crimes, some green criminologists, particularly those who study green crimes through the lens of political economy, define green crime as a social construct. They state that 'the legal definition of crime is not an objective, scientifically derived definition. Legally, crime is simply a behaviour that the law labels as such' (Lynch et al, 2013: 1005). Besides, there are debates over which behaviours ought to be labelled as environmental crimes. The various definitions of green crime in contained diverse pieces of legislation illustrate this disagreement over what the appropriate definition should be (Lynch et al, 2013). There is also the argument that the law does not label many of the environmental activities that cause considerable harm and produce many victims as crime. Just as the criminologists who study crimes of the powerful from a radical perspective do, the green criminologists who adopt a critical perspective that focuses on the political economy of green crime, assert that the green crimes committed by the powerful (typically large corporations) produce significant victimisation but attract relative impunity. They aver that the activities that harm the environment, and green crimes in general, produce far more victims than the conventional crimes that dominate official crime statistics. As Lynch and colleagues (2013: 998) put it: 'green harm and crime are more widespread, have more victims and produce more damage than crimes that "occur on the streets"'. Lynch and colleagues (2013: 999) also surmise that 'A single green crime may produce hundreds, thousands or even millions of human victims'. It is argued that green harms and crimes, such as releasing toxic material that pollutes the environment, have rendered some affected areas uninhabitable (Lynch et al, 2013). Yet, these crimes attract relative impunity. Some believe that this is mainly because the powerful groups who cause large-scale environmental harms possess the political and social influence with which they can ensure that environmental laws are constructed in their favour (Ruggiero and South, 2010; Lynch and Stretesky, 2003). Lynch et al (2013) point out that 'Environmental law allows many harmful behaviors to escape regulation because political and social interest groups strongly influence environmental law decision-making practices'. Thus, these green criminologists believe that states and corporations seeking to protect their mutual interests might overlook the environmental harms caused by production processes (Ruggiero and South, 2013b). It is argued that this perhaps explains, in part, why the response of some states and corporations to green issues has been somewhat ambivalent.

Green criminologists who explore the political economy of green harms and crimes argue that corporations are not usually compelled to address the environmental harms and crimes caused by capitalist production (Rugierro and South, 2013a, 2013b). Governments typically assume responsibility for repairing and containing the damage caused. Some insist that a possible reason for this is that governments have to reconcile the competing demands of capitalism, protecting the environment and safeguarding the welfare of and its citizens (Lynch et al, 2013). For example, governments have to consider the economic impact of passing on the costs of environmental damage to the responsible corporations. A possible implication of taking this course of action is that the affected corporations may move production to other jurisdictions that have less onerous environmental policies (Lynch et al, 2013). For this reason, Lynch and colleagues (2013) propose treaties or other regulatory policies that are agreed by governments and can serve as unified responses to the harms caused by capitalist production. In general, for green criminologists who subscribe to the eco-centric perspective, the best response to green crime is to transform the unequal capitalist system and shift towards an economic system that will foster social and environmental justice (Gibbs et al, 2010).

The social action approach to dealing with environmental crime advocates social action and transformation. It encourages citizen action and other radical activities to dismantle the dominance of nation-states and large corporations in defining the debates and policies that define environmental issues (see, generally, White, 2010a). A limitation here is that such activities may breach the boundaries of legality and will encounter significant challenge from the 'powerful interests' that fuel most of the activities that cause environmental harm (White, 2010a: 421). It follows that radical action to effect social change is likely to create conflict in society.

It has been argued from a 'green victimological perspective' that the alternative to green crime, which may be described as 'green compliance', can also victimise the vulnerable populations that are often the victims of green crimes. Green compliance involves complying with relevant green laws and generally avoiding activities that harm the environment (Davies, 2014). But, green compliance can curtail the production activities of large corporations with adverse consequences for vulnerable populations. This is because these populations often rely on these large corporations for the employment opportunities they offer (Davies, 2014: 1), and also for the goods and services they produce. Green compliance could, as such, impact negatively on these populations. The possibility that green compliance may victimise vulnerable populations seems rather ironic given that green compliance is precisely what green criminologists propose. Therefore, green criminologists may face ethical difficulties in situations where it becomes incumbent on them to balance considerations of environmental justice against social justice issues, such as the right to earn a livelihood. In such cases, 'The social right to livelihood is pitted against the environment and imperatives to sustain environments' (Davies, 2014: 13).

Criticisms

Some reject the term 'green' because they believe that it suggests a kind of affiliation with politically motivated movements or even Green political parties, and may, as such, undermine the scientific objectivity of social researchers who work in the field of green criminology (Ruggiero and South, 2013a). Some green perspectives in criminology have also been criticised by those who point out that in the focus on the activities of powerful capitalist corporations and nation-states, there has been a tendency to overlook the need to explore the experiences of the victims of environmental harm, particularly those in developing countries who have to contend with polluted drinking water, degraded soils and other consequences of environmental harm (Spencer and Fitzgerald, 2013). Others have formed the view that the term 'green' does not sufficiently accommodate the range of activities that harm the environment (Halsley, 2004).

Gibbs and colleagues (2010) have also identified several limitations that, in their view, are associated with green criminology as a field of study. For example, they point out that environmental justice approaches to the study of green harms and crimes have been accused of anthropocentrism. This is because they emphasise the impact of environmental harms on human beings, and appear to overlook the impact on the environment or the 'ecosystems' (2010: 127). In addition, Gibbs and colleagues argue that green criminological perspectives tend to focus on a narrow set of issues. According to Gibbs and colleagues, there is also a tendency to overlook the possibility that compliance with green laws can impede production and cause considerable hardship to vulnerable populations who rely on production for wages, goods and services. Equally, some green criminologists are criticised for focusing on corporate activity and its link to green harms or crimes while overlooking the harms and crimes that individuals cause to the environment. Gibbs and colleagues (2010: 128) cite examples of pollution caused by the cars that individuals use and the 'consumption choices' that individuals make. While it has been stated that 'global corporate interests' shape human consumption patterns, Gibbs and colleagues (2010: 128) maintain that individuals exercise a degree of autonomy, and the choices they make affect the environment. Another criticism is that green criminological perspectives propose responses to green harms and crimes without due consideration of the possibility that, in some contexts, the responses proposed might be inappropriate. For example, the perspectives that advocate social justice are said to overlook the ameliorative impact of responses such as 'regulation, enforcement, education' and so forth (2010: 128). Gibbs and colleagues (2010) also assert that the explanations of green crime offered by green criminologists, and the responses they propose, are based mainly on anecdotal evidence. In addition, green criminologists are accused of espousing rigid views because they tend to promote the interests of either human beings, or non-human species or nature. Some are also criticised for defining all activities that harm animals as bad. Critics posit that such a rigid approach to the study of green harms and crime does not permit contextualised analysis of the key issues. It is also argued that green criminology does not sufficiently engage with other allied disciplines. Critics imply that an interdisciplinary focus is required to broaden the field of study (see, generally, Gibbs et al, 2010).

Conclusion

Green criminologists provide very useful insights into the nature and consequences of destructive activities, including the activities of large corporations, which cause significant harm to the environment and impact on many victims globally. Minority ethnic groups and indigenous populations of societies where large corporations are located are said to be particularly vulnerable to the harmful impact of the environmentally destructive activities of these corporations. A key concern for green criminologists is to ameliorate environment degradation and the adverse implications for the human and non-human species that inhabit the environment. Criminal prosecution, regulation, global treaties and social action are some of the strategies that green criminologists have proposed as possible responses to environmental harms and crimes.

SUMMARY

- It is generally agreed that green criminology focuses on the study of activities that cause harm to the environment and to human and non-human species. Green criminologists also study responses to environmental harms.
- Some critical criminologists argue that powerful organisations are largely responsible for most green harms and crimes.
- Green criminologists identify the poorest and minority ethnic or indigenous communities as the typical victims of environmental crimes.

SAMPLE QUESTIONS

1. How should green criminologists address the challenges posed by the tension between green crime and green compliance?
2. Assess the view that the political economy of green crime is crucial for our understanding of green crimes, and the responses to these crimes.

Notes

[1] Ruggiero and South (2013a) point out that although green criminology originates from the critical criminological tradition, it has the capacity to accommodate the work of others outside this tradition who share a similar interest in addressing environmental harms.

[2] According to Lynch and colleagues (2013), green criminology has predominantly focused on the study of green 'harms', eschewing the notion of green 'crime' in order to also draw attention to harmful activities that may not be defined as crimes. Lynch and colleagues (2013) trace this tendency to focus on the concept of 'harm' to the influence of the social harm perspective proposed by Hillyard and Tombs (2005; 2007). Others, such as Ruggiero and South (2013b), believe that the focus on harms stems from Sutherland's (1949) call for those who study the crimes of the powerful to broaden their remit beyond the narrow confines of the acts and omissions defined as crime by the criminal law.

[3] Large corporations owned by wealthy capitalists have been identified as the key perpetrators of green crimes. However, green criminologists do acknowledge that green harm is not the exclusive preserve of privately owned corporations. In terms of oil extraction by large corporations, for example, Rugierro and South (2013b) cite several pieces of evidence to support their view that even where states assume responsibility for the oil industry, they may not do much to limit the risks associated with the industry. That said, White (2013, cited in Rugierro and South, 2013: 20) acknowledges that 'not everything that TNCs [transnational corporations] do is bad or wrong, and not every TNC necessarily engages in things that harm the environment.... This complicates analysis of perpetrators'. As Rugierro and South (2013b) point out, those who consume the goods generated through environmentally harmful mechanisms contribute to pollution. They also push for the production of these goods. Gibbs and colleagues (2010: 124) note that environmental harms are caused by 'individual, collective, corporate and government actions'.

TEN

Cultural criminology

Introduction

This chapter introduces readers to cultural criminology, which has been described as 'one of the newest directions in critical criminology' (DeKeseredy and Dragiewicz, 2012: 11). It emerged in the mid-1990s and its key proponents include Jack Katz (1988), Jeff Ferrell (1999; 2005), Mike Presdee (2000; 2004) and Keith Hayward and Jock Young (2012). As a field of study, it lacks precise definition. According to Jeff Ferrell (2013), he, and other cultural criminologists, have been reluctant to define cultural criminology, preferring instead a fluid 'anarchist' approach that emphasises how culture intersects with crime. Nevertheless, Ferrell provides a description of the field in the following comments:

> As I've reflected on cultural criminology's maturation, the critiques of it, and the larger history and nature of critical criminological itself, I've found myself more willing to define cultural criminology—at least along the lines of one particular intellectual and political focus. This is its focus on the human construction of meaning. Put differently, cultural criminology increasingly strikes me as an orientation designed especially for critical engagement with the politics of meaning surrounding crime and crime control, and for critical intervention into those politics. (2013: 258)

Similarly, Hayward and Young (2004: 259) describe cultural criminology as:

> the placing of crime and its control in the context of culture; that is, viewing both crime and the agencies of control as cultural products – as creative constructs. As such, they must be read in terms of the meanings they carry.

In other words, in its effort to understand crime, cultural criminology looks to the culture or the ideas, values, beliefs and other collectively shared characteristics that infuse crime and crime control activities with meaning, and illuminate the nature of both phenomena. In this chapter, there is an examination of the intellectual foundations of cultural criminology. The chapter also describes the tension between culturalist and structuralist perspectives within cultural criminology. The culturalist approach highlights the values, styles, symbols, conventions and foreground factors such as the emotions that make crime and deviance meaningful to the perpetrators. By contrast, structuralist approaches emphasise the 'background' factors (such as the structural inequalities) that are said to shape the culture of crime.

This chapter also describes a key dimension of cultural criminology which is the study of the meanings that shape crime and crime control. As the definitions provided above indicate, in their study of crime, cultural criminologists draw attention to the meanings that control agents, and other high profile groups such as the mass media, legal authorities, politicians and corporations, attach to crime. Cultural criminologists believe that these meanings contribute to constructions of crime, and shape responses to crime. Indeed, of particular importance to cultural criminologists is the study of subcultures and their representation in, for example, media outlets and political rhetoric, and the construction of their aesthetic attributes and their activities as crime and deviance. Thus, some highlight the criminalisation of the groups they describe as illicit subcultures (for example street gangs).[1] In addition, there is an examination of the tendency to criminalise 'culture products' (such as rap music), and to portray such products as criminogenic (Ferrell, 1999: 404). Furthermore, some cultural criminologists allude to what they describe as the commercialisation of products that are linked to illicit subcultural styles, symbols and activities.

Cultural criminologists also explore the meanings the targets of social control attach to their own activities. For example, they study the shared codes, symbols, styles and other forms of cultural expression that underpin the activities of illicit subcultures. They explore the emotions that arise from and sustain crime and deviance. In addition, Cultural criminologists examine how criminal and deviant subcultures interpret the responses of control agents and others. Cultural criminologists argue that these interpretations shape subcultural activities. For example, illicit subcultures might engage in further acts of deviance in response to, and as acts of resistance to, images or representations of them in the media. Some illicit subcultures might also engage in risky thrill-seeking acts of crime and deviance not only for the excitement the activities provide but also as a form of resistance to structural inequalities that place them in positions of socioeconomic disadvantage.

These themes are explored in detail in this chapter.

Cultural criminology's intellectual heritage

Cultural criminology is an eclectic subfield of criminology and it draws on diverse criminological traditions. In terms of their theoretical heritage, cultural criminologists are influenced by the foundational critical criminological perspectives, postmodern theory, radical perspectives on the culture of deviant subcultures, and the early work of US subcultural theorists, such as Albert Cohen (1955) and Sykes and Matza (1957).

Some cultural criminologists define crime as a social construct. This is not surprising given their roots in the foundational critical criminological perspectives

– Marxism and interactionism. These cultural criminologists examine the cultural contexts in which acts are defined as crime. As Mike Presdee (2000: 16) pointed out:

> We need to continually remind ourselves of one single simple statement, that a criminal act has to be defined through social and cultural processes that are in themselves played out separate from the essence of the act itself. For example, the act of taking a life does not become 'murder' until defined as such through the discourses of the powerful. It is these cultural discourses that both designate and define any particular act as criminal…. The political processes of the powerful have been the ability to make criminals of us one day and heroes the next.

As already mentioned, some cultural criminologists are also influenced by postmodern theory (see, eg, Ferrell, 1999), which rejects universal explanations or 'truths' about social phenomena, such as crime. There is a view that conventional explanations of crime are, in essence, myths that are created by the powerful. Cultural criminologists point out that in order to understand human behaviour like crime, it is necessary to explore the language that the powerful employ to construct crime. Crime is perceived to be a social construction that is used by the powerful in society to control the activities of others. Thus, cultural criminologists deconstruct texts, such as newspapers, to demonstrate how dominant discourses about the activities of target populations are constructed. It is argued that these discourses help maintain structures of power and oppression and subsequently assume the status of objective 'truth' or conventional wisdom (Ferrell, 1999).

The influence of perspectives on criminal and deviant subcultures

As we shall see below in the discussion about the criminalisation of culture, some cultural criminologists study crime and crime control by examining the activities of the members of subcultures. Some study the meanings that the members of illicit subcultures apply to their activities and aesthetic attributes or styles, and how others, such as legal authorities and the media, interpret these activities and attributes as crime (see, generally, Ferrell, 1999). As Ferrell (1990: 403) puts it: '… cultural criminologists have investigated style as defining both the internal characteristics of deviant and criminal subcultures and external constructions of them'.

In their study of subcultures and constructions of crime, cultural criminologists are heavily influenced by the work of British scholars who were based in the CCCS at Birmingham University, or the 'Birmingham School', in the 1970s and 1980s (see Chapter Four). The CCCS at Birmingham produced significant work that explored youth cultures from the mid-1970s to the 1980s (Clarke et al, 1976). Researchers in the CCCS drew on Marxist and feminist perspectives, and they explored how socio-structural disadvantage and youth culture interact to inform youth identity and behaviour. They laid the foundations of what later came to be known as youth subcultural studies.

Some cultural criminologists who study criminal and deviant subcultures are influenced by the work of writers in the CCCS such as Tony Jefferson (1975: 82), whose study of Teddy Boys revealed the importance of image and styles (mode of dressing, personal appearance). These aesthetic attributes were imbued with meaning in that they represented forms of resistance to the exclusionary capitalist order. In addition, they were said to represent the one aspect of their lives the boys felt they had control of. Acts of disorder were typically geared towards defending their ability to control this aspect of their lives (Jefferson, 1975).

Cultural criminologists also subscribe to the view that socio-economically marginalised groups who have been denied access to the resources they need to attain culturally defined goals may feel excluded from mainstream society, and may join deviant subcultures that comprise people who share similar experiences of deprivation. Thus their views about criminal subcultures also echo Becker's (1963) description of the nature and role of deviant subcultures. In addition, they are, as already mentioned, influenced by the earlier subcultural theories of sociologists like Albert Cohen.

The culture–structure debate

The relevant literature suggests that cultural criminologists typically embrace one of two broad approaches to the study of culture and crime: the culturalist approach and the structuralist approach. Webber (2007: 140) notes that 'There is a conundrum at the heart of this enterprise. Some cultural criminologists are more culturalist and agency oriented.' Others are more structuralist. The culturalist approach focuses on 'culture' as the key explanatory theme, while the structuralist approach focuses on social structure as the key explanatory theme. Some argue that Ferrell (a key proponent of cultural criminology) adopts a culturalist approach to the study of culture and crime. This approach is quite different from the structuralist approach of other writers in the tradition, such as Mike Presdee, Keith Hayward and Jock Young (Presdee, 2000; Webber, 2007).

The culturalist approach

As noted earlier, some cultural criminologists adopt a culturalist approach that does not emphasise the impact of structural factors, such as class and ethnicity, on crime. The culturalist approach traces crime to the culture of those who engage in crime and deviance (or transgressions).[2] A key question that then arises is this: what do cultural criminologists mean by 'culture'? Despite Ferrell's attempt to offer a unifying explanation of the theoretical contours of cultural criminology, it would appear that writers in the tradition do not necessarily subscribe to a consensually agreed definition of the term 'culture'. Ferrell (1999) describes culture as the shared way of life, or the values and beliefs, of a particular social group; the culture of a group explains everything the members of the social group do – the way they dress, the way they behave and the way they interact with each other.

According to Ferrell and colleagues (2008: 2–3), 'Cultural criminology understands "culture" to be the stuff of collective meaning and collective identity'. This definition suggests that some cultural criminologists view culture as the shared identity and shared understanding that exists within any group, and there are various cultures in society, from the mainstream culture to the subcultures that exist outside the mainstream.

The structuralist approach

Presdee (2000), who is another original proponent of cultural criminology, is associated with the structural Marxist approach to the study of culture and crime that was adopted by scholars who were based in the Centre for Contemporary Cultural Studies (CCCS) at Birmingham University in the 1970s and 1980s. Cultural criminologists who subscribe to the structuralist approach assert that structural inequalities produce forms of behaviour, (including crime) which manifest as the 'culture of everyday life' (Presdee, 2004; Webber, 2007: 142). Presdee (2004: 180) observes that cultural criminology is 'a specific form of criminology … that attempts to unravel and make sense of the processes whereby cultural forms and cultural expressions themselves become criminalised'. Presdee (2004: 275–6) also describes cultural criminology as part of an 'on-going tradition [that] acknowledges that what is important is the analysis of the way in which humankind makes sense of and, at times resists, existing and developing social structures'.

The eclectic approach

Cultural criminologists do not fit neatly into the two broad categories mentioned earlier. Some of the writers in this field who have embraced the culturalist approach at some point have also embraced the structuralist approach at another point in time. For example, although it is argued that Ferrell subscribes to the culturalist approach, he also recognises that structural factors can shape human culture:

> For us, human culture – the symbolic environment occupied by individuals and groups – is not simply a product of social class, ethnicity, or occupation; it cannot be reduced to a residue of social structure. Yet culture doesn't take shape without these structures, either; For all the parties to crime and criminal justice – perpetrators, police officers, victims, parole violators, news reporters – the negotiation of cultural meaning intertwines with the immediacy of criminal experience (Ferrell, 2008: 2–3).

This suggests that to argue that culture is the product of structural factors, such as class, ethnicity or occupation, is rather simplistic, but that these structures do shape mainstream culture and subcultures. Indeed, Ferrell has also provided a definition of crime causation that combines structuralist elements (background factors) with the agency of the transgressor (foreground factors). Ferrell (1992: 118–19) describes a criminal event as:

> the acts and actions of the criminal, the unfurling interactional dynamics of the crime, and the patterns of inequality and injustice embedded in the thoughts, words, and actions of those involved. In a criminal event, as in other moments of everyday life, structures of social class or ethnicity intertwine with situational decisions, personal style, and symbolic references. Thus, while we cannot make sense of crime without analyzing structures of inequality, we cannot make sense of crime by only analyzing these structures, either. The esthetics of criminal events interlocks with the political economic of criminality.

This definition clearly acknowledges the role of structural factors in crime causation, although Ferrell does make the point that structural factors are not the sole causal factors.

Similarly, Keith Hayward (2004) presents both a culturalist and a structuralist perspective when he avers that crime is the product of a specific mode of consumption that has emerged in advanced capitalist societies. This mode of consumption is consumerism, which, as we saw Chapter Seven, has been described as a culture that encourages material aspiration and the acquisition of material possessions and services. People acquire these goods and services not because they need them, but because of a *culture* that fuels greed and insatiability. Cultural criminologists who focus on consumerism in their description of the aetiology of crime also espouse a structuralist explanation because they trace the culture of consumerism to the structural conditions created by capitalism. They argue that there is cultural inclusion in capitalist societies – all are invited through advertisements and other media productions to participate in a consumer culture. Nevertheless, according to the cultural criminologists, cultural inclusion accompanied by the structural problem of material exclusion marginalises the impoverished and, in doing so, may compel the marginalised to resort to illegitimate routes to material success. Thus, 'cultural inclusion [which] is accompanied by structural exclusion' can explain crime (Young, 1999: 45).

It follows that cultural criminologists such as Keith Hayward (2004) and others, including Jock Young, have embraced culturalist explanations of crime that include the foreground and other factors that are said to infuse crime with meaning. But, they have gone on to reject what they describe as the tendency of some cultural criminologists to overlook the social contexts in which crime occurs (such as socio-economic inequality). For example, Hayward and Young (2012) reject Katz's (1988) view that explanations of crime that focus on socio-economic factors are 'irretrievably positivistic' (Hayward and Young, 2012: 123). It follows that cultural criminologists differ in the degree of importance that they attach to the impact of social structures on human behaviour. The next section explores the foreground/background debate, which also underlines the culturalist/structuralist tension in cultural criminology.

The foreground/background debate

In their study of crime and deviance, some cultural criminologists emphasise the foreground factors that, in their view, explain deviant activity. They argue that their task is to highlight the 'foreground experiences of the actor' (Katz, 1988; Ferrell et al, 2008: 70). Foreground factors include emotions such as: 'hatred, anger, frustration, excitement and love' (see Presdee 2000: 4, see also Box 10.1 below). Thus foreground factors are different from 'background factors'. The latter are structural factors like 'social class or education' (Ferrell et al, 2008: 70).

For cultural criminologists who embrace structuralist and culturalist approaches to the study of crime, crime is considered to be as much the product of the foreground factors (the emotions, thrills and other sentiments that are said to sustain it), as it is the product of background or structural factors. These cultural criminologists study the structural dimensions of crime or the 'social context in which crime comes into being and is played out' (Presdee, 2000: 16). But, they accuse positivist criminology of focusing narrowly on 'background structural factors' and overlooking cultural dimensions of crime, such as the foreground factors that provide insights into the meaning of crime. Indeed some suggest that the study of foreground factors is central to cultural criminology. As Hayward and Young (2004: 266) put it: 'Important here is the stress placed by cultural criminology on the foreground of experience and the existential psychodynamics of the actor, rather than on the background factors of traditional positivism (e.g. unemployment, poverty, poor neighbourhoods, lack of education, etc.)'. The criminological perspectives that emphasise structural causal factors are accused of determinism and a failure to grasp the complex nature of crime. The perspectives are also accused of overlooking the meanings, emotions, seductions and other foreground dimensions that make crime meaningful to its perpetrators (Hayward and Young, 2012; Reiner, 2012).

In an account of crime causation that combines both a structuralist dimension (which refers to the role of 'background' factors), and a culturalist dimension (which highlights the relevance of foreground factors), Presdee (2000) argued that those who are economically marginalised might resort to crime (and the emotions it generates) as an important outlet for their frustrations. He maintained that the belief that one is challenging established authority and exclusionary social structures also contributes to the excitement that some seek when they commit crime. As Presdee (2000: 7) put it: 'The quest for excitement is directly related to the breaking of boundaries, of confronting parameters and playing at the margins of social life in the challenging of controllers and their control mechanisms'. Presdee's claim that marginalisation can contribute to crime highlights the structuralist element of his account, while his suggestion that crime might provide emotional relief for the perpetrator or serve as a form of expression, reveals the culturalist dimension of his account. Presdee (2004: 276) also commented that:

> The antecedents of cultural criminology lie within the longstanding recognition of the importance of cultural ethnographies and artifacts in understanding human social behaviour. This ongoing tradition acknowledges that what is important is the analysis of the way in which humankind makes sense of and, at times resists, existing and developing social structures.

Box 10.1: Foreground factors that infuse crime with meaning

In *Cultural Criminology and the Carnival of Crime*, Mike Presdee (2000) challenged conventional criminology's tendency to overlook the foreground dimension of crime. Extracts from his text are reproduced in the following.

> The way we enjoy violence, crime, humiliation and hurt is part of the equation and needs to be examined and thought through. Even the enjoyment of doing wrong, which many of us have felt at some time in our lives, becomes important as it puts us all in some sense 'in touch' with crime, connecting us to it in an emotional way so that we become acquainted with emotions of criminal life through our own transgressions. Indeed, crime is as much about emotions – hatred, anger, frustration, excitement and love – as it is about poverty, possessing and wealth. In a society such as ours where emotion stands against the rational and material world, those without wealth are left only with the world of emotions to express their hurts, their injustices and their identity. Their transgressions, arising as they do from this world of emotions, are as a consequence steeped in emotive elements. Rage, anger and hatred are commonplace characteristics in the performance of crime. The feeling of 'getting away with it' that comes as part of doing wrong, the buzz and excitement of the act of doing wrong itself, of living on the 'edge' of law and order, are all emotions that many seek out in the daily performance of their lives....
>
> This book ... is an argument for the necessity for both a cultural criminology and a passionate criminology, that can truly attempt to understand the richness of responses to the economic structures that surround us, that we all act out during what we have come simply to call 'life'. (Presdee, 2000: 4–5)

Cultural criminologists criticise not only traditional or mainstream theories, but also the entire criminological project, for overlooking the foreground factors mentioned earlier, which, in their view, infuse crime with meaning. Foreground factors are said to sustain criminality to a greater degree than the other concerns that criminology focuses on, such as material deprivation or the costs and benefits of crime. Thus, for instance, some cultural criminologists explore the emotions and other sentiments that sustain deviant activity. These include the excitement of crime, the adrenaline rush, the risks, the sense of danger and the thrills that make crime seductive and addictive.

Cultural criminologists who focus on this area of study have developed what they describe as 'edgework'. This is a field of study that explores 'acts of extreme voluntary risk-taking' by people who are equipped with 'highly honed subcultural skills' (Ferrell et al, 2008: 72; see also Ferrell, 2012: 260). Cultural criminologists map the emotions and thrills that those involved in these activities (the edgeworkers) experience.

The criminalisation of culture

According to Ferrell (1999; 403) '... much of what we label criminal behaviour is at the same time subcultural behaviour' (Ferrell, 1999: 403). Therefore, the study of illicit subcultures is a key aspect of cultural criminology. Cultural criminologists describe subculture as counterculture because it is different from mainstream culture. Subcultures are said to be 'Collectivities of alternative meaning' (Ferrell, 2013: 260). Indeed Ferrell (1990: 401) identifies 'police associations and political interest groups' as 'subcultures concerned with crime and crime control'. But, in their study of subcultural activity, cultural criminologists have tended to focus on the activities of illicit subcultures such as street gang members and graffiti writers. Subcultures are typically structured around specific aims and activities. Examples of these activities include illicit risk-taking activities that provide excitement or serve as acts of resistance to structural disadvantage (Ferrell, 2013). In addition, subcultures tend to have their own styles and forms of cultural expression. They may also provide members with a range of resources (eg members can gain identity, status and excitement) that they do not have access to in mainstream society (Ferrell, 1999).

Some cultural criminologists study the various means through which the styles and activities of illicit subcultures are constructed as crime. They examine the meanings that social actors, including members of these subcultures, apply to their deviant activities and aesthetic attributes of styles, and how others, such as legal authorities and the media, interpret these activities and attributes (see, generally, Ferrell, 1999).

According to Ferrell (1990; 2013), the media and legal authorities respond to illicit subcultures and their styles and activities, by interpreting these as crime. This contributes to the demonisation and criminalisation of the members of subcultures.

Cultural criminologists provide several examples of how social control agents construct stigmatising discourses about subcultural styles and activities. For example, media images have been used to create stereotypes of gang members. These images suggest that the demographic is typically the young (often black) male, inner-city resident. Their style is the hoodie, their attitude is defiant and anti-authoritarian, and their main activity is violent street crime.[3]

Cultural criminologists argue that media images like these create myths, not reality. Subcultural styles (as depicted in media images), such as their mode of dressing and the symbols they use to communicate with each other, are not necessarily always crime-related. They may simply be the means by which members of subcultures communicate shared meanings to each other. These styles and symbols might be incomprehensible to outsiders, but they tend to form part of the group's identity. As Ferrell (1999: 403) puts it: 'subcultural behaviour [is] collectively organized around networks of symbol, ritual, and shared meaning'.

Nevertheless, media-generated myths about the links between subculture styles and behaviour can trigger the practice of profiling in criminal justice and could render target groups, particularly ethnic minority groups, vulnerable to criminalisation. In the US, for example, styles of dressing associated with gang members have informed racial profiling (Ferrell, 1999). Young black men, in particular, have been targeted for surveillance and criminalisation (Ferrell, 1999). In the UK, a shopping centre recently banned people wearing hoodies because they are now seen as the style of illicit subcultures. For the cultural criminologists, because marginalised groups are more likely to experience marginalisation and to resort to subcultures, associating the styles of subcultures with criminality is one of several means by which marginalised groups find themselves vulnerable to criminalisation, surveillance and control.

It is worth noting that cultural criminologists do acknowledge that the composition of subcultures is not primarily determined by racial, class or other social categories. As mentioned earlier, Ferrell (2013) points out that subcultures are usually structured around specific activities. For example, subcultures may comprise graffiti writers, street hustlers, pimps, computer hackers, drug runners, email fraudsters and other groups perceived to be 'outlaws' (Ferrell, 2010: 161). The proliferation of social media networks like Facebook and Twitter means that deviant subcultures no longer have to be located within a specific geographical area (Ferrell, 1999). For instance, the members of a deviant subculture that is made up of computer hackers do not have to be located in a particular place or region. They can connect with each other all over the virtual world through social media and related sites. Subcultures that comprise members who are located all over the world still have shared symbols and styles. However, the way they communicate with each other is now different from traditional means of communication. They are now able to communicate on a global scale using internet communication facilities (Ferrell, 1999).

Like the interactionists, some cultural criminologists believe that the crimes committed by illicit subcultures reflect, in part, societal expectations of them. These crimes can be described as the reactions of subcultures to the way in which the media and control agents portray them. The crimes may be acts of resistance to established authority. Thus, subcultures might engage in activities that may reinforce media-constructed ideas. Stereotypical media depictions may, then, become a self-fulfilling prophecy. In their study of subcultural activity, cultural criminologists promote the use of ethnographic methods that can capture the lived realities of criminal and deviant subcultures and the culture that make their criminal and deviant activities meaningful. For example, according to Ferrell (1999: 400) criminological *verstehen* is an 'extreme version' of the ethnographic methodology cultural criminologists employ. Ferrell (1999: 400) remarks that:

> the concept of criminological verstehen denotes a field researcher's subjective appreciation and empathic understanding of crime's situated meanings, symbolism, and emotions, in part through the sorts of directly participatory research that can foster a methodology of attentiveness.

Thus, criminological *verstehen* is an appreciative approach to the study of the subculture activity and other forms of human activity (Ferrell, 1999). For Ferrell, the unique styles and activities of subcultures should be studied appreciatively to understand the meanings and other factors that shape the activities of subcultures, including the acts of crime and deviance they might engage in. There should be: 'appreciation and empathic understanding of crime's situated meanings, symbolism and emotions' (Muzzatti, 2012: 142).

The criminalisation of culture products

Cultural criminologists also trace the origins of crime to the activities of those who label 'culture products' as crime (Ferrell, 1999: 404). Culture products include artistic products like photographs, and may also include television programmes, movies and music (Ferrell, 1999). Cultural criminologists argue that control agents sometimes justify their decision to criminalise culture products on the basis that the products promote criminality (Ferrell, 1999). There have been campaigns and even protests by groups asking that the cultural products they view as inappropriate or criminogenic should be banned. Examples of cultural products that have been described as criminogenic include 'gangsta rap' material. It has been argued that such material reflects and promotes youth criminality (see, generally, Ferrell, 1999: 405). Indeed, there have been campaigns to ban some 'gangsta rap' songs, posters and other related products. In 2005, *The Guardian* (2005) published a story that described how posters promoting a gangster rap–related movie were banned in the US. Control agents in the US launched a successful campaign to ban posters promoting the film 'get rich quick ...', which was based on the life of the rapper '50 Cent'. Here, in the UK, politicians and other interest groups have also occasionally called for the prohibition of rap music. In 2003, the BBC ran the following headline: 'Minister attacks rap lyrics'. The story went on to say: 'Culture Minister Kim Howells has launched another attack on rap music claiming it "glamorises" gun culture. Dr Howells, who is MP for Pontypridd, blamed the music industry for promoting material, which glorifies guns as fashion accessories' (BBC News, 2003).

Some rap artists do comment about drug use, gun violence and other crimes in their songs. However, arguing that the products of culture (such as the 50 Cent poster) are criminogenic is tantamount to assuming that young people will go out and buy guns to shoot other people with simply because they have seen an image of 50 Cent holding a gun. Such a contention presupposes that individuals cannot exercise a degree of moral agency. It implies that human beings respond unthinkingly to images. Some have suggested that by criminalising culture products, or by depicting them as criminogenic, the control agents attach meaning to cultural products in order to stigmatise the products and their creators (Ferrell, 2010). Their actions help to create cultural 'outsiders'.

The commercialisation of the culture/crime nexus

Added to their study of how legal authorities and the media respond to illicit subcultures and culture products, cultural criminologists also study how corporations (with the help of the media) respond to culture products, particularly the culture products that appear to glamorise illicit subcultures and activities. They describe the response of corporations as the 'commodification of crime' (Hayward and Young, 2012: 124). This involves trying to generate profit by marketing products that glamorise crime, in order to attract the patronage of young people. The media play a key role; they help advertise these products. Hayward and Young (2012: 126) observe that: 'crime is being packaged and marketed to young people as a romantic, exciting, cool, and fashionable cultural symbol'. It is also marketed as 'entertainment and amusement' (p 126). Large corporations convert the illicit styles of subcultures into products that they can sell to make a profit. Hayward and Young (2012) argue that the culture of consumption that has emerged in late-modern societies provides fertile ground for the marketing of illicit products to flourish. Advertisements serve as the means of conflating wants and needs, and promoting the idea that status is commensurate with spending power (see also Ferrell, 2010). For Hayward and Young (2012) glamorising crime in the way described above is not necessarily a direct cause of crime, rather it contributes to the contemporary tendency to portray crime or illicit activities as exciting activities that are also linked to enhanced self-worth and material success.

Examples of this trend include the creation and sale of *Ghettopoly* and *Chavopoly*, which are board games that parody the popular board game Monopoly. Unlike Monopoly, which takes players through mainstream locations and activities printed on the board, Hayward and Young (2012) describe *Ghettopoly* and *Chavopoly* as board games that depict what can be generally described as illicit lifestyles. As Hayward and Young (2012: 125) state: '*Ghettopoly* for example, is: a *Monopoly*-style game in which "playas" move around from "Tyrone's gun shop" to "Ling Ling's Massage Parlour", building crack houses, "pimping" and selling guns as they go'. These are some examples of products that are marketed as part of the 'commodification of crime'.

Criticisms

Cultural criminology has attracted several criticisms. Some critics point out that it fails to provide a precise definition or theorisation of the concept of culture, which forms the core of the tradition (Webber, 2007). It is argued that cultural criminologists do not agree on whether culture is the product of structural factors or whether it exists independently of structural factors (O'Brien, 2005; Webber, 2007). They are accused of applying both meanings of the concept. There is also the criticism that cultural criminologists attach greater importance to the culture of the targets of social control; the deviants, or those they refer to as transgressors. O'Brien (2005) is of the view that although cultural criminologists claim to focus their empirical lenses on the culture that shapes transgression and social control, it appears that they attach greater sentimentality to their analysis of the culture of transgression, such as graffiti-writing, than the culture of control agents, such as anti-graffiti campaign groups.

Critics of the perspective also highlight its theoretical eclecticism as a limitation. For example, Spencer (2011: 198) describes cultural criminology as a 'theoretical soup' rather than a coherent theory. Webber (2007: 146) remarks that 'Cultural criminology posits a manifesto, but not a unified theory; it is a perspective rather than a school ... a series of criminologies interested in culture, rather than a cultural criminology'. Others question whether it really provides a new direction in criminology. Some critics believe that cultural criminologists provide no new insights, but simply repeat ideas that have been covered extensively by other criminological perspectives. O'Brien (2005: 600) comments that 'whether cultural criminology really does represent a new intellectual endeavor rather than a logical elaboration of previous work on deviant subcultures is itself debatable'. In addition, for Webber (2007), by emphasising the importance of foreground factors to the study of crime, cultural criminologists risk overlooking background structural factors, such as unjust structural arrangements. Indeed, another criticism is that cultural criminologists ignore structural, 'background' or macro-level explanations of crime, such as capitalist exploitation and the unfair criminalisation of the exploited, and focus rather narrowly on the foreground dimensions of crime (Hall and Winlow, 2007). Thus, some believe that in their study of deviant subcultures, cultural criminologists occasionally strip culture of its structural components, and present it as the core element of the foreground factors that, in their view, explain crime. Webber (2007: 146) observes that:

> Although Ferrell includes politics in the remit of cultural criminology, it is not as prominent as it could, or maybe should be ... [cultural criminology] under-politicizes culture, turning it into a study of foreground factors that leads to a blurring of the background structural issues that help shape, and are shaped by, such behaviour.

Nevertheless, we have seen earlier that not all cultural criminologists focus solely on foreground factors. Key proponents of cultural criminology, including Jeff Ferrell, trace their intellectual heritage to the labelling tradition, which emphasises that crime is a social construction. At the same time, cultural criminologists such as Jock Young subscribe to a realist ontology – which we encountered earlier in our discussion about left realism. Thus, cultural criminologists draw on traditions that are ideologically irreconcilable in certain important respects (Spencer, 2011).

The appropriateness of the methodology – *criminological verstehen* – that some cultural criminologists employ may be problematic in certain contexts. For example, applying the methodology to study the excitement, thrills and euphoria that accompany serious crimes, such as assault and other violent crimes, is likely to give rise to ethical issues. There is nothing to suggest that cultural criminologists advocate that the method may, or should, be used to study such crimes. However, the call for appreciative inquiry opens up the possibility that such an approach can be applied to the study of serious crimes. Besides, ethical problems are likely to arise whenever researchers immerse themselves in the activities of those who engage in deviant behaviour. Cultural criminologists perhaps recognise these tensions. They have tended to use the method to study relatively minor crimes, but then they have been criticised for focusing mainly on minor crimes!

Cultural criminologists are also accused of sometimes romanticising crime by portraying the criminal as the victim of socio-economic disadvantage who is also adventurous and thrill-seeking. A related criticism is that cultural criminologists glorify harmful activities and empathise more with the offenders. As Webber (2007: 143) puts it: cultural criminologists 'glorify the resistance itself – This leads to an almost in-built affinity with the resisters'. However, some aver that cultural criminologists are not consistent because their empirical activities occasionally evince greater empathy for the agents of social control (Webber, 2007). This, in their view, is a position that runs contrary to Becker's (1967) injunction that sociologists should, in the course of social research, empathise with the targets of social control who can best be described as the underdogs and the victims of structural inequality. Webber (2007) cites Ferrell's (2004) study, which overlooked the plight of those involved in illegal drugs as possible victims of unfair structural arrangements.

There is also the argument that cultural criminology is nothing more than a criminology of 'thrills and risks', but Hayward and Young (2012: 123–12) contest this. They emphasise that cultural criminologists do not focus solely on sensational illicit activity such as graffiti writing, they also study less exciting activities that include 'DVD piracy'. Nevertheless, the critics insist that cultural criminology focuses on the emotive and sensational dimensions of crime at the expense of more mundane dimensions, which nevertheless cause harmful victimisation (Webber, 2007). Indeed, Webber suggests that cultural criminology ignores the impact of criminalisation in general; it is accused of overlooking the impact of crime not only on the victims (eg the impact of victimisation), but also on offenders (eg the impact of criminalisation). Webber (2007: 141) goes on to state that the tradition would benefit from also exploring 'the outcome of the criminalisation process'.

Cultural criminology has also been criticised for portraying mainstream culture as negative and unable to offer the emotional thrills provided by risk-taking subcultures. Critics point out that, in doing so, cultural criminologists overlook crimes that are committed by members of the mainstream culture, such as white-collar criminals. The latter are often considered to be part of mainstream culture but they also engage in illicit risk-taking activities, such as excessive drinking and drug taking, gambling and more serious crimes like domestic violence and child abuse (Tierney, 2009).

In their defence, it could be argued that cultural criminologists appear to eschew the condemnatory approach to the study of crime and deviance that is associated with mainstream criminological theories. Rather, cultural criminologists promote the tradition of appreciative and empathetic enquiry, which explores the meaning of deviance for the key actors. The latter are the deviants, and their views tend to be marginalised (Young, 2009). In addition, it is quite possible that some of the criticisms cultural criminology have encountered may be attributable to the reactionary attitudes of commentators who reject cultural criminology's appreciative approach to the study of illicit activities, and seek instead to promote mainstream criminological explanations.

Conclusion

Despite the criticisms it has received, cultural criminology has made several contributions to criminology. It attempts to revive previously discarded criminological theories. Indeed, its proponents assert that it reinserts theory into criminology at a time when administrative criminology, and a specific empirical approach that emphasises government research agendas and quantitative methods, is dominating criminology. It appears that the importance of ethnographic methods is increasingly being de-emphasised (Young, 2010). Some cultural criminologists believe that this is regrettable because ethnographic methods seek to highlight the typically ignored viewpoints of the less powerful groups in society, who tend to be disproportionately vulnerable to criminal justice intervention. Official statistics compellingly indicate that these groups are predominantly the most vulnerable and marginalised in society (Hayward and Young, 2004; 2012). Cultural criminology also draws our attention to a previously ignored dimension of crime: the emotions of crime. Traditional criminological theories overlooked the possibility that emotions like excitement make up for the blocked opportunities or other disadvantages that may contribute to crime (Tierney, 2009; Hayward and Young, 2012). Cultural criminologists insist that in order to understand crime, it is important to study these emotions. Cultural criminologists also provide insights into the processes through which target populations, particularly marginalised groups, become vulnerable to constructions of crime and crime control by control agents and sections of the media. Cultural criminologists point out that, principally, the tendency to stigmatise and criminalise the activities, styles and other attributes of these populations is a key factor that renders them vulnerable to criminalisation.

SUMMARY

- Cultural criminology is a relatively recent development in critical criminology. It comprises several perspectives. Together, the perspectives examine the culture of crime and crime control.

- Some cultural criminologists provide an account of crime and crime control that emphasises the culture or shared identities and meanings that shape a social group's ways of life or activities. Thus, there is also an analysis of the foreground factors that in their view, infuse crime with meaning. Examples of these factors include the emotions and thrills that are said to sustain criminality. Others incorporate in their account of the culture/crime nexus, an analysis of the structural factors (the social, political and other arrangements in society) that in their view, inform the culture of crime and crime control. Cultural criminologists sometimes offer accounts that focus on both the culture of crime and crime control, and the structure of society.

- An important aspect of cultural criminology is the study of illicit subcultures. Cultural criminologists study how the media, legal authorities and other groups in society such as corporations respond to subcultures. Cultural criminologists also study how the subcultures respond to the images constructed of them by outsiders, such as the media. Cultural criminologists suggest that the subcultures may engage in further acts of deviance in response to, and as acts of resistance to, the images that the media and legal authorities construct of them and their activities.

SAMPLE QUESTIONS

1. Should cultural criminologists focus on structuralist explanations of crime instead of culturalist explanations?
2. To what extent do foreground factors help us understand crime?

Notes

[1] Illicit subcultures are subcultures that engage in unlawful or deviant activities.

[2] Some cultural criminologists refer to the deviant as a 'transgressor', and they use the term 'transgression', which appears to be a broader term that encompasses a wider range of behaviour than the term 'crime' (see, eg, Hayward and Young, 2012).

[3] For a critique of popular media and general images of 'gang' members, see Alexander (2008).

[4] This method involves immersing oneself in the world of the group under study. The German word *Verstehen* has no direct translation in English but it has been closely linked to the word *understanding*. It has its basis in the work of the German philosopher Max Weber,

who advocated an interpretive approach to social research, which enables the researcher to appreciate the meanings that social actors use to define their social world and their behaviour (Ferrell, 1999).

ELEVEN

Critical Race Theory

Introduction

Critical Race Theory (CRT)[1] is an interdisciplinary movement that brings together the work of legal scholars and activists who explore how race, class and gender shape the dynamics of societal institutions, including the criminal justice system (Schneider, 2003; Ross, 2010). Critical race theory draws on several theoretical traditions, from radical feminism to Marxism (Matsuda et al, 1993; Schneider, 2003). It is also influenced by liberalism and the idea that individuals should be freed from the straitjackets of the established social order. Furthermore, critical race theorists are influenced by the work of scholars who have contributed quite significantly to understandings of how the social structures that disadvantage the less powerful in society. Key influences include: the Marxist Antonio Gramsci; the French philosopher and deconstructionist Jacques Derrida; radical African-American scholars, such as Frederick Douglas, Martin Luther King Junior and the sociologist W.E.B. Du Bois; the black and Chicano civil rights movements of the 1960s; and also as noted above, radical feminism (Delgado and Stefancic, 2012).

Early writers in the field set out to develop theories and conduct studies to address insidious forms of racism. These writers include Derrick Bell, who has been described as 'the movement's intellectual father figure' (Delgado and Stefancic, 2012: 5), and one of the CRT movement's 'founding fathers', alongside Mari Matsuda and Richard Delgado. Another prominent early writer is Alan Freeman.

There are several definitions of CRT but Delgado and Stefancic (2012: 3) offer a useful definition. They describe CRT as follows:

> The critical race theory (CRT) movement is a collection of activists and scholars interested in studying and transforming the relationship among race, racism, and power. The movement considers many of the same issues that conventional civil rights and ethnic studies discourses take up, but places them in a broader perspective that includes economics, history, context, group- and self-interest, and even feelings and the unconscious.

The perspective emerged in the mid-1970s within the discipline of law, specifically from the intellectual movement that is known as critical legal studies (Delgado and Stefancic, 2012). Other disciplines, from education[2] to political science, began to develop the theory as it evolved (Schneider, 2003; Delgado and Stefancic, 2012).

CRT's early history has also been traced to the black activism of the 1930s and 1940s in the US, while its more recent origins can be traced to the 'leftist legal movement' of the 1970s (Ladson Billings, 1998: 10), and the expansion in the 1970s of the civil rights movement that began in the 1960s. The influence of the civil rights movement is evident in CRT's concern, *inter alia*, to remedy past injustices, and to engage in activism that leads to the transformation of unequal societal structures (Delgado and Stefancic, 2012).

It has been described as a discipline that has a unique attribute: it is an intellectual movement that is committed not only to propounding theories of race and crime, but also to an activism that seeks to change or transform the hierarchical structures in society that are defined by race (Delgado and Stefancic, 2012). Critical race theorists believe that the established legal and social order creates conditions that disadvantage black people and many others who fit into the 'non-white' category. A key priority of contributors to this field of study is to expose racial domination, and to transform the societal structures that reinforce it. Thus, like Marxist criminology, CRT has a transformative agenda. It seeks to eliminate oppression of all kinds, including racial oppression (Schneider, 2003). CRT focuses on examining what its proponents describe as institutionalised racial oppression and the dominance of white ideology and discourses (Crenshaw et al, 1995; Ross, 2010; Milovanovic, 2011b: 137). As mentioned above, critical race theorists study, among other topics, how racial dynamics shape societal structures and institutions, including the criminal justice system. Key concepts covered include race, crime and justice (Schneider, 2003; Ross, 2010; Delgado and Stefancic, 2012).

In general, critical race theorists believe that racism is a normal feature of social relations. It is not an aberration. Rather, it is prevalent but insidious, and only the most obvious forms of racism are responsive to race equality laws. Indeed, critical race theorists argue that racism is enshrined in the US constitution. They reject claims that in the US, there has been a shift towards a more colour-blind, egalitarian and meritocratic society. They point out that intentional discrimination exists and undermines the veracity of such claims (Ross, 2010). They also assert that racism underpins the activities of key societal institutions and industries, from financial and healthcare institutions, to educational and criminal justice institutions (Ross, 2010). Its continuing pervasiveness, in their view, has forced black people and many others who fit into the 'non-white' category, into positions of considerable disadvantage. Therefore, critical race theorists believe that, despite claims to the contrary, US governmental institutions are not 'race-neutral' (Crenshaw et al, 1995; Matsuda et al, 1993). Indeed they insist that the institutions benefit from racial inequality. For critical race theorists, the dominance of the white group over other racial groups persists because it protects the 'material' interests of the white elites, and the 'psychic' interests of the white working class (Delgado and Stefancic, 2012: 8). According to critical race theorists, the 'interest convergence' principle explains this phenomenon (Delgado and Stefancic, 2012: 8). The principle is explored in more detail further below. For now, it will suffice to state that interest convergence refers to the tendency of the white dominant group to manipulate race issues in ways that protect their self-interests. Critical race theorists also believe that categories like race, gender and so forth are socially constructed. Indeed, critical race theorists reject all truth claims (including truth claims about race) as social constructions. They state that 'in social science and politics ... truth is a social construct created to suit the purposes of the dominant group' (Delgado and Stefancic, 2012: 104). According to critical race theorists, people of the same origins might share certain physical attributes including skin colour, but it has been scientifically proven that physical attributes are quite different from, and have no impact on, the core attributes or qualities that define human beings, examples of which include 'personality, intelligence, and moral behaviour' (Delgado and Stefancic, 2012: 9).

Critical race theorists study how society constructs race and ascribes supposedly immanent traits to groups according to constructed ideas about racial difference. They also study how groups become racialised in different societies to suit specific social conditions, including labour market demands. Also central to the work of critical race theorists are the concepts of intersectionality and anti-essentialism. This aspect of their work is based on the belief that no one has a unique identity. Rather, each individual has a conglomeration of identities. To illustrate this, Delgado and Stefancic (2012: 10) point out that 'A Latino may be a Democrat, a Republican, or even a black – perhaps because that person's family hails from the Caribbean'. Critical race theorists study how these features intersect to impact on the experiences of minority ethnic groups. Another central idea within CRT is the 'voice-of-colour thesis'. Perhaps rather contradictorily, given their anti-essentialist position on the nature of human identity, critical race theorists believe that people of colour possess a unique voice regarding racial issues. They are deemed to be in the best position to communicate these issues given their historical experience of racial disadvantage.

As the foregoing implies, in their study of race issues in criminal justice, critical race theorists explore a wide range of issues. They define race, gender and other social categories as social constructs. They also argue that the key phenomena that explain black people's experience of criminal justice include differential racialisation and interest convergence. They highlight the relevance of what they describe as legal indeterminacy, which is the idea that any legal case has more than one correct outcome. In addition, they reject what they have identified as triumphalist history and deficit thinking. These concepts are examined in the following sections.

The construction of social categories

Although critical race theorists explore diverse issues to do with the nature and impact of racial dynamics on social structures and societal institutions, it can be argued that, generally, critical race theorists reject dominant definitions of such social categories. Examples of the latter include, as mentioned earlier, race, gender and crime. They maintain that they are products of white male ideology and they bolster white male dominance. Thus, in their view, 'race' is a socially constructed concept that lacks biological or other empirical justification but that is nonetheless falsely held out to be an adequate descriptor of minority ethnic groups, to whom specific biological traits are fallaciously attributed. It is a term that is used to justify social injustice and the domination of the target population. Their anti-essentialist stance manifests itself in their belief that individuals do not possess unique traits that make it possible to separate one individual from another. They argue, for example, that because any one individual may possess several attributes, from religious orientation to sexuality and race, in responding to racially motivated crimes, one cannot easily isolate the victims' race as the attribute that exposed them to victimisation (Ross, 2010). This is because the diverse attributes may intersect to produce outcomes.

Differential racialisation

CRT scholars apply the concept of differential racialisation, to their study of racial issues. The concept refers to the argument that racial groups have unique origins and unique experiences in society (Delgado and Stefancic, 2012). Historically, Asians[3] and black people, for example, have had different experiences of racism, which have evolved in different ways, making their experiences in society qualitatively different. Critical race theorists point out that the critics who claim that CRT focuses unduly on the disfranchisement of black people and overlooks the successes that ethnic minority groups such as Jewish people have achieved within an unequal social order (see, eg, Farber and Sherry, 1997) do not fully countenance CRT's notion of differential racialisation.

According to critical race theorists, one of several factors that can shape the experiences of ethnic minority groups is the way they are depicted in popular media. Critical race theorists argue that the ways they are portrayed vary over time. Significant events, such as the recent activities of people of Arab origin and some Muslims, have led to the perception that these groups pose greater danger than others and deserve increased state surveillance (Ross, 2010). In other words, these events have led to the increased racialisation of the target population. Also central to the differential racialisation thesis is the idea that market forces dictate how the dominant groups define the status of minority ethnic groups in a society. For example, illegal immigrants who provide cheaper labour than the indigenous population may be valued at one point in time and denigrated at another point in time. They might be: 'highly sought-after ... valued and accepted', and categorised as 'migrant workers' irrespective of their immigration status (Ross, 2010: 401). But, according to critical race theorists, when political rhetoric and media representations create connections between these workers and other social and even economic problems, public perceptions change and they become 'illegal immigrants'. Thus, the experiences of minority ethnic groups can sometimes be very much tied up with the demands of the labour market. Delgado and Stefancic (2012: 9) provide additional examples of how this phenomenon occurs:

Critical writers in law, as well as social science, have drawn attention to the ways the dominant society racialises different minority groups at different times, in response to shifting needs such as the labour market. At one period, for example, society may have had little use for blacks, but much need for Mexican or Japanese agricultural workers.... Popular images and stereotypes of various minority groups shift over time, as well. In one era, a group of colour may be depicted as happy-go-lucky, simpleminded, and content to serve white folks. A little later, when conditions change, the very same group may appear in cartoons, movies, and other cultural scripts as menacing, brutish, and out of control, requiring close monitoring and repression.

Interest convergence

According to Ross (2010: 397), 'interest convergence (or material determinism)' is another key concept critical race theorists employ in their study of racial dynamics in society. The interest convergence principle emphasises that white groups manipulate racial issues to protect their material and other interests. As Bell points out:

> Given their history of racial subordination, how have black people gained any protection against the multifaceted forms of discrimination that threaten their well-being and undermine their rights? The answer can be stated simply: Black rights are recognised and protected when and only so long as policymakers perceive that such advances will further interests that are their primary concern. (2004: 49)

Racism may thrive in periods when it benefits the white group materially or in other ways. However, interest convergence occurs when, for example, the dominant white group, through its institutions, such as the courts, make decisions that favour black people, and such decisions are made not for altruistic reasons to do with promoting justice, but because the decisions also protect the interests of the dominant white group (Bell, 2004). It has been argued that significant successes in the quest for civil rights for black people in the US (of which the decision in the 1954 case of *Brown v. Board of Education of Topeka Kansas*, which outlawed school segregation, represents a prime example) can be attributed not only to humane considerations, but to the attempt to concede to the pressures posed by the racially charged climate at the time (Bell, 2004; Ross, 2010; Delgado and Stefancic, 2012). This climate was deemed to be inimical to national security and to the international image of the US (Bell, 2004; Ross, 2010; Delgado and Stefancic, 2012). According to Delgado and Stefancic (2012), the court reached the decision in that case because 'the interest of whites and blacks, for a moment, converged'.

Critical race theorists also apply the concept of interest convergence to practices in the criminal justice system. As an example, Ross (2010) cites the case of *Powell v. Alabama*, which is colloquially known as the 'Scottsboro case'. In that case, nine black men were accused of raping two white women. According to Ross (2010), the Scottsboro case represents an example of how interest convergence in the criminal justice system can operate to override institutionalised injustice, even where such institutionalised injustice is underpinned by deeply entrenched racial prejudice and repression. In the Scottsboro case, eight of the nine men accused of raping two white women were convicted on the basis 'of shallow evidence' and sentenced to death. The Supreme Court reversed the convictions because the state of Alabama did not provide adequate legal assistance to the accused, as was required by the US constitution. While this case and others have been cited as evidence of progressive judicial reforms, particularly in respect of protecting due process rights in the US, critical race theorists believe that there is ample evidence to show that the impact of the case has not been as far-reaching as they could have been (American Civil Liberties Union, 2003). They argue that in several subsequent cases, including capital cases, many black defendants charged with capital offences have found themselves lumbered with incompetent state-appointed attorneys and this has placed them at greater risk of receiving, or even suffering, the death penalty (American Civil Liberties Union, 2003).

As Supreme Court Justice Ruth Barber put it:

> I have yet to see a death case among the dozens coming to the Supreme Court on eve-of-execution stay applications in which the defendant was well represented at trial? People who are well represented at trial do not get the death penalty. (American Civil Liberties Union 2003: 1)

Ross (2010) maintains that events since the decisions in the cases discussed earlier, and other similar cases, appear to lend credence to the interest convergence thesis, which also suggests that the gains made in the aftermath of cases like these where interest convergence produces favourable outcomes for black people are often transitory. Positive outcomes, such as enhanced civil rights, are typically short-lived (Ross, 2010). Ross (2010) points out that racial discrimination across most sectors, including the education system, in the US continues to plague African-Americans, albeit in ways that are often more subtle than those that obtained in the 1950s when efforts were made to abolish school segregation. As Ross (2010: 398) put it: 'Today, students of colour are more segregated than ever before in the educational system ... instead of providing for better educational opportunities, school desegregation has meant increased white flight along with a loss of Africa-American and administrative positions'.

Legal indeterminacy

Another concept that critical race theorists employ to unravel the intricate patterns of racial discrimination that, according to them, pervade US institutions is the concept of legal indeterminacy. 'Legal indeterminacy' refers to the idea that a legal case may have more than one correct outcome (Tushnet, 2005; Ross, 2010). In most legal cases, there is usually an opposing rule, authority, argument or doctrine that, if applied, could create a different outcome. Therefore, for some critical legal theorists, the court has the power to determine the outcome of a case any way it pleases. It could simply select a specific legal argument or doctrine that suits its decision. This leaves considerable room for discretionary and potentially discriminatory decision-making on racial or other grounds.

Rejection of triumphalist history

Critical race theorists also reject what they describe as 'triumphalist history'. The latter is a version of history that casts the historical decisions made by the dominant white group in a positive light. For example, a triumphalist account of historical developments in the experiences of black people in the United States would emphasise that the white dominant group have made advances towards racial equality. The decision in *Brown v. Board of Education of Topeka Kansas* might be cited as an example. But, critical race theorists reject triumphalist accounts. They point out that historically; positive legal outcomes and other development that appear to favour black people have tended to lose their potency over time (Bell, 2004; Ross, 2010; Delgado and Stefancic, 2012). As such, the critical race theorists embrace revisionist accounts of history. These accounts challenge the view that advances have been made in the quest for racial equality. The accounts provide insights into the disenfranchisement and marginalisation that black and other minority ethnic groups continue to contend with.

Challenging 'deficit thinking'

Critical race theorists explore how 'deficit thinking' in societal institutions, such as criminal justice systems, can disadvantage minority ethnic groups. Deficit thinking involves constructing negative narratives which suggest that a specific group possesses inherent defects, or deficits, that can be traced directly to their pathology or biological constitution. Yosso (2005: 82) notes that critical race theories emphasise the importance of replacing these deficit narratives, which have been targeted at 'people of color', with alternative narratives that highlight the strengths of this group. Yosso states that:

> ... CRT research begins with the perspective that Communities of Color are places with multiple strengths. In contrast, deficit scholars bemoan a lack of cultural capital or what Hirsch (1988, 1996) terms

'cultural literacy' in low income Communities of Color. Such research utilizes a deficit analytical lens and places value judgments on communities that often do not have access to White, middle or upper class resources. In contrast, CRT shifts the research lens away from a deficit view of Communities of Color as places full of cultural poverty or disadvantages, and instead focuses on and learns from these communities' cultural assets and wealth. (2005: 82)

For critical race theorists, in criminal justice settings, the deficit narratives of 'deficit scholars' can create and perpetuate the myth that minority groups including black people are less amenable to rehabilitative intervention and are more likely to display psychopathic tendencies (Ross, 2010). Critical race theorists draw on radical criminology and trace the criminalisation of black people and other minority ethnic groups, in part, to the negative stereotypes that have been constructed about these groups. In their view, these constructions and myths about minority ethnic groups perpetuate the phenomenon of 'racial profiling', in which policing activity is shaped by myths about the purported propensity of these groups to commit crime. Indeed, critical race theorists also trace the disproportionate exposure of black people and minority ethnic groups to policing activity, and even to the very construction of the concept of crime itself. They argue that the activities that minority ethnic groups typically engage in, such as grouping together in public places and graffiti-writing, are more likely to be defined as crime (Ross, 2010). These activities are said to be typically subject to greater police intervention, unlike the harmful activities of the powerful, which may include 'marketing defective automobiles, alcohol and pharmaceuticals' (Ross, 2010: 404). This echoes the arguments of the radical theorists who, as we have seen in previous chapters, have decried the relative impunity the powerful enjoy when they cause dangerous harm to others.

An examination of criminal justice statistics in the US indicates that black people are, indeed, over-represented in penal statistics. Sherman (2010: 382) notes that:

> While the process of punishing black people today is far more legalistic than it was a century ago, the result appears far more punitive. The institutions of reaction to crime now mete out more punishment per person to black people than at any time in US history. In mid-2008, almost 1 in 20 black American males (4,777 per 1000,000) were incarcerated in prison or local jails (Bureau of Justice Statistics 2009a). This compared to 727 per 1000,000 for white males. Whatever the reasons that can be given to support the legality of this result, the appearance of bias – on top of 300 years of more open discrimination – may deeply affect the moral sentiments of both blacks and whites about crime, law and punishment.

What I have outlined in the preceding discussion are some of the key concepts that underline Critical Race Theory. Not all critical race theorists subscribe to all the ideas previously discussed. It is also worth mentioning that critical race theorists employ additional concepts in their exploration of how race intersects with other factors to shape the experiences of black people in society. One such concept is 'microaggression'. According to Delgado and Stefancic (2012: 2), microaggression refers to the many relatively minor but nonetheless hurtful acts of unkindness that black people encounter because of their race. These acts tend to be surprising, spontaneous and hurtful. They could be acts of conscious or unconscious racism and they stem from widely held constructed ideas about racial difference. These ideas are embedded in all private and social institutions, from schools and churches, to private sites of human interaction.

Critical Race Theory's empirical agenda

Critical race theorists argue that 'people of colour' should conduct empirical and theoretical work on race matters because they are best placed to offer counter-narratives that highlight the real experiences of 'race' and challenge the claims about race neutrality by the white dominant class. In particular, they seek to present stories told by black people themselves. The critical race theorists hope that, in doing so, they can help narrow the gulf between the worlds of black people and others. Therefore, the methodological approach that the critical race theorists employ includes eliciting narratives from people of colour about their lived experiences. Critical race theorists use methods such as 'storytelling, family histories, biographies, scenarios, … chronicles and parables' and so forth (Ross, 2010; Yosso, 2005: 74). According to Delgado and Stefancic (2012: 10), 'the legal storytelling movement' is central to CRT. It is a movement that encourages writers of colour to also contribute insights on their own experiences of racism and of the legal system. It encourages them to draw on their own perspectives to evaluative the 'master narratives' propounded by the law (Delgado and Stefancic, 2012: 10). They acknowledge that a particular problem in this context is the difficulty of trying to develop counter-narratives that can challenge dominant but harmful stereotypes, constructs and myths about race that fossilise in white people's narratives, such as the myth of black criminality that is promoted by sections of the media and the legal system.

Criticisms

Writers in the field, such as Delgado and Stefancic (2012), Levit (1999), Ross (2010) and others, have provided useful accounts of the criticisms that CRT has sustained. Critics have accused critical race theorists of, *inter alia*: 'playing the race card' (Delgado and Stefancic, 2012: 52); playing the 'victim' without demonstrating why they deserve better treatment; propounding irrational ideas; sacrificing objective theoretical analysis for subjective storytelling; implying that all black people think alike; and focusing narrowly on perceived white male dominance (Faber and Sherry, 1997). In addition, critics reject CRT's social constructionist position and its critique of the law. CRT is criticised for arguing that objective truth claims that are made about the social world are constructs of the white dominant group. Consequently, critics insist that CRT challenges the Enlightenment foundations upon which the legal academy is built (Faber and Sherry, 1997; Judge Richard Posner, cited in Levit, 1999). Some critics have gone as far as to state that, alongside postmodernism, CRT represents the 'lunatic core' of 'radical legal egalitarianism' (Judge Richard Posner, cited in Levit, 1999: 795). In addition, critical race theorists have been described as 'radical multiculturalists' and 'extremists' (Judge Richard Posner, cited in Levit, 1999: 795). Reflecting on the emotive language that some critics have employed, Levit (1999: 795) points out that the tone of the criticisms 'suggest a breakdown in the civility of academic discourse and an extraordinary tolerance of intolerance'.

Some critics also argue that the empirical methods that critical race theorists employ to present what they consider to be the lived experiences of black people (such as legal storytelling) do not conform to the standards of scientific research (Faber and Sherry, 1997). It is therefore argued that the narratives presented may be distorted and unrepresentative. As Schneider (2003) observes, some insist that critical race theorists use their storytelling techniques to construct narratives that manipulate emotions and exploit racial issues to their advantage (Faber and Sherry, 1997). However, critical race theorists point out that storytelling unites minority ethnic groups by their shared experiences and enables researchers to bring to the fore the previously ignored narratives by black people about the reality of their experiences (Yosso, 2005). Delgado and Stefancic (2012: 103) state that 'critical race theorists deploy stories and narratives as a means of building cohesion within minority groups and shattering the mind-set created by the stories of the dominant group'.

Critics have also questioned whether minority ethnic scholars are necessarily experts in the study of race relations simply because of their ethnicity (Delgado and Stefancic, 2012). Furthermore, CRT is criticised for arguing that the scholarly work of minority ethnic groups have been marginalised by the mainstream. According to Delgado and Stefancic (2012), the critics believe that merit not discrimination determines the level of attention that scholarly work receives: good articles attract requisite attention (Faber and Sherry, 1997). There is also the question of whether CRT is pessimistic when it describes racism as 'normal and embedded in society' (Delgado and Stefancic, 2012: 15). Relatedly, the critics maintain that it is pessimistic of critical race theorists to suggest that members of the white dominant group who try to address racism are motivated by their selfish interests (Delgado and Stefancic, 2012).

Delgado and Stefancic (2012) acknowledge that the CRT movement has also encountered internal criticisms. Some of its members have questioned whether it possesses any practical utility. There is a suggestion that it seems to offer no alternatives to the social arrangements it criticises. Some have questioned why it prioritises theoretical work over activism, and why it challenges civil rights laws. Additional issues raised by its members include the possibility of expanding the remit of the movement to embrace white membership and also to address additional forms of discrimination, such as religious discrimination and so forth. There is also the contention that critical race theorists abandon their traditional focus on materialist issues that affect disenfranchised minority ethnic groups, and focus instead on matters that appeal more to middle-class members, such as microaggression (Delgado and Stefancic, 2012). Furthermore, critics claim that CRT focuses unduly on issues to do with anti-essentialism and identity. Another criticism is that they have not theorised the 'colour-blind racism' that now occurs in the contemporary US, which is a jurisdiction that claims to be post-racial (Delgado and Stefancic, 2012: 108). In response to some of the internal criticisms, critical race theorists emphasise the importance of combining theory and practice. They also point out that they are striving to develop alternatives to existing social arrangements that disadvantage black people. They insist that progress that has been made through the work that Derrick Bell and others have done to improve the experiences of black people in the legal system.

Exploring the racial dynamics of crime and criminal justice in other jurisdictions

CRT (to the extent that it addresses issues within criminology and criminal justice) is based mainly on experiences in the US. Its creators write that it has expanded to encompass Asian-American groupings. It has expanded its range beyond legal studies to other disciplines, from education to LatCrit and queer-crit studies (Delgado and Stefancic, 2012). It is now taught in several law schools, and lawyers employ its ideas in their advocacy work with clients and to challenge discrimination in the legal system (Delgado and Stefancic, 2012). Much of this work has been carried out in US settings.

How, then, can we explore the impact of race (if any) on criminology and criminal justice in other Western jurisdictions? To answer this question, there are criminologists who, although they may not necessarily describe their work as 'critical race theory', have incorporated the issue of race in their analyses of crime and criminal justice. It is to their work that we may now turn for further insights into the intersections between race, criminology and criminal justice.

Indeed, interest in this subject dates back to the origins of criminology as a discipline. Lombroso, the early biological positivist, conducted a series of experiments in which he sought to establish that individuals who posses specific physical characteristics are more likely to exhibit criminal tendencies than others. Attempts by Lombroso and other criminologists to establish that links exist between race and criminality may be considered futile, not least because their efforts have failed to withstand empirical and theoretical scrutiny (see also Carrabine et al, 2009).

Bowling and Phillips (2012) provide a useful overview of historical attempts to perpetuate the myth that there is a relationship between ethnicity and crime. According to this myth, some ethnic minority groups exhibit a higher degree of criminality. Bowling and Phillips (2012) trace the origins of this myth to 'pseudoscientific' ideas that emerged during the European Enlightenment era. There was an attempt to construct a racial hierarchy and to situate white people in Northern Europe at the top this hierarchy. Other ethnic groups were considered to be inferior across several variables, from morality to intellectual ability.

Bowling and Phillips (2012) cite the work of the biological positivist Lombroso, which appeared to suggest that there is a relationship between race and crime. To support this claim (which, as mentioned above, has since been discredited), Lombroso tried to demonstrate that those who have multiple convictions also have specific physical characteristics that savages and the 'coloured races' possess (Bowling and Phillips, 2012: 371). Other white groups including Irish and Jewish people who were classed as 'racially "other" whites' were also deemed to possess these physical characteristics (Bowling and Phillips, 2012: 317). These ideas were used to legitimise acts of exploitation and oppression of target populations, from slavery, imperialism and colonisation, to the anti-Semitism that heralded the Holocaust (Bowling and Phillips, 2012). There have been attempts to remove racial ideas from the study of the physical and social world by improving awareness of the fallacy of racial superiority, and by directing attention to the nature of 'race' as a social construct and not a biologically determined human quality.

Although there is no reliable evidence to support the contention that ethnicity is in any way linked to criminality, the composition of prison populations in many Western countries would tend to suggest otherwise. People who are 'darker-skinned' tend to be over-represented in prisons within these countries (Bowling and Phillips, 2012: 370). In addition, although criminologists, such as the right realists and others, who deny the causal impact of socio-economic marginalisation may disagree, it has been argued that socioeconomic marginalisation and the discriminatory practices of criminal justice agents may help explain why black people and other marginalised groups dominate official crime statistics. For example, Bowling and Phillips (2012: 373–5) observe that:

> Collectively, minority ethnic communities remain geographically concentrated in urban neighbourhoods where unemployment and social deprivation are greatest.... It would be surprising if people concentrated in urban areas, often in the worst parts of those areas, experiencing social and economic exclusion, poor housing, and schools were never involved in crime.

Minority ethnic groups also express greater fear of crime and they are more vulnerable to victimisation (Ministry of Justice, 2013a). The British Crime Survey suggests that socio-economic deprivation and being a resident of an inner-city area explains this vulnerability to victimisation more than ethnicity. That said,

Bowling and Philips (2012: 378) suggest that the socio-economic deprivation they suffer and the tendency to reside in deprived areas may, indeed, stem from 'discrimination in housing and employment'.

Bowling and Phillips (2012) state that myths or stereotypes that associate specific ethnic groups with criminality may also help explain the racial discrimination that they encounter in the criminal justice system. In Britain, discourses about crime often have a 'racial undertone', which subtly attributes crime to 'racial degeneration' (Pearson, 1983, quoted in Bowling and Phillips, 2012: 374). There is a tendency to highlight issues of 'ethnicity and culture' in crimes involving black people and Asians (p 374).

Myths about black criminality are likely to fuel problems that include racial profiling. This, in turn, may place black people at greater risk of criminal justice intervention than other groups. For example, in the UK, official statistics and other studies consistently show that the police are more likely to use 'stop and search' powers to stop, question and arrest black people quite disproportionately (Ministry of Justice, 2013a). There is ample evidence of the disproportionate use of 'stop and search' powers in cases involving minority ethnic groups (especially black people, Asians and mixed ethnic groups) under the Police and Criminal Evidence Act 1984 and under section 60 of the Criminal Justice and Public Order Act. These Acts authorise stops and searches without suspicion where the suspect is carrying a weapon, drugs or stolen property or where serious violence is likely or has occurred within the vicinity. 'Stop and search' powers are also enshrined in the Terrorism Act 2000, which removes the need for any kind of suspicion before a stop and search is conducted (Parmar, 2011). In a periodic statistical publication on race issues, the Ministry of Justice noted that:

> In 2011/12, a person aged ten or older, who self-identified as belonging to the Black ethnic group was six times more likely than a White person to be stopped and searched under section 1 (s1) of the Police and Criminal Evidence Act 1984 and other legislation in England and Wales; persons from the Asian or Mixed ethnic group were just over two times more likely to be stopped and searched than a White person. (2013a: 11–12)

Some might argue that the demographic composition of black groups[4] and their tendency to reside in deprived areas (which typically attract greater policing activity) may help explain their over-representation in stop and search statistics. However, as Bowling and Phillips (2012: 383) observe: 'Whatever the explanation, the disproportionate use of stop and search is clearly a problem: it seems inherently unfair, contributes to the criminalisation of minority ethnic communities, and undermines public support for the police'.

Indeed, the disproportionate use of 'stop and search' powers in inner-city areas in London is a long-standing practice that has undermined relations between the police and black people. It sparked the Brixton riots of 1981, which, in turn, led to the inquiry led by Lord Scarman. The inquiry produced a report that revealed the discontent and resentment among black communities in inner-city areas concerning the discriminatory and heavy use of stop and search powers on black people (Scarman Report, 1981). The Scarman Report recommended that there should be changes to police training and strategies and there should also be more black and minority ethnic (BME) people recruited into the police force.

Have these changes materialised? Well, almost 20 years after the Scarman Report was published, the Macpherson inquiry, which examined how the Metropolitan Police investigated the murder of the teenager Stephen Lawrence by racist men in 1993, found evidence that black communities were dissatisfied with the actions (or inaction) of the Metropolitan Police in investigating the case. Importantly, the inquiry found evidence that 'institutional racism' was entrenched in the culture of the Metropolitan Police (Macpherson, 1999: 46.1). Institutional racism may be described as a form of racism that could occur not only intentionally, but also at a subconscious level of reasoning and action. It is:

> The collective failure of an organisation to provide an appropriate and professional service to people because of their colour, culture, or ethnic origin. It can be seen or detected in processes, attitudes and behaviour which amount to discrimination through unwitting prejudice, ignorance, thoughtlessness and racist stereotyping which disadvantage minority ethnic people. (Macpherson, 1999: 34)

Since the publication of the Macpherson Report, further evidence has emerged to suggest that racial discrimination, while not as overtly acknowledged as it used to be in the 1980s (Smith, 1995), still persists. The often-cited BBC documentary *The Secret Policeman* revealed a catalogue of racist attitudes among police recruits towards BME people. Some of the recruits openly boasted that they specifically target BME people for 'stop and search' activities.

The evidence also suggests that black people do not fare any better in the court system. As Bowling and Phillips (2012: 370) point out, if criminologists wish to uncover the factors that help explain the over-representation of black people in official crime statistics, 'the criminological problem is not "race" but racism and the task is to explain how racial prejudice and discrimination cause the over-representation of certain groups in prison'. A key factor that determines the proportion of black people in prison is sentencing practice. Moxon's (1988) study of disparities in the sentencing imposed on diverse ethnic groups did suggest that sentencing outcomes though higher in cases involving black and Asian defendants, could be attributed to offence type and previous antecedents. However, there is stronger evidence that the reason BME people receive more severe sentences compared to other groups is not because of the nature of the offences that BME people commit or because of their previous record.

Barbara Hudson's (1989) large-scale study found that the higher rates of custody for black defendants could not be explained solely by offence type and previous antecedents. Even where the nature of the offences committed by black people and the number of previous convictions were taken into account, the differences in the sentencing of black people compared with other groups could not be explained in any other way apart from the possibility of bias.

We cannot necessarily conclude that black people receive more severe sentences in court solely because of racial bias. This is because it is difficult to take into account all the possible factors that can affect sentencing decisions. However, Roger Hood's (1992) study of sentences imposed in 3,317 cases in five crown courts in the West Midlands area of England found what has since been described as 'definitive evidence of discrimination in sentencing' (Bowling and Phillips, 2012: 385). The study found higher rates of custodial sentencing for black people (in particular) and Asian people compared with white people, particularly in cases where judicial discretion was permissible. Some outcomes were not explainable by the approximately 100 variables that were taken into consideration. The outcomes could, as such, be attributed to bias. In youth justice contexts, Feilzer and Hood (2004) analysed over 31,000 records kept by Youth Offending Teams, and found evidence of discrimination against black, Asian and mixed race young people throughout the youth justice process.

There is also evidence which suggests that BME people are further disadvantaged within the penal system – in prison and on probation. Studies have found evidence of racial discrimination from prison staff and other prisoners (Edgar and Martin, 2004; Cheliotis and Liebling, 2006). The study by Genders and Player (1989) examined the experiences of this group in prisons and found evidence of negative stereotyping by prison officers, which had an impact on the quality of treatment the black prisoners received. In the youth justice sector, the murder of a young Asian prisoner, Zahid Mubarek, by a mentally ill racist prisoner who he was sharing a prison cell with illuminated the problem of institutional racism, which manifested itself in the failure of officers to recognise the dangers posed by the prisoner who had previously espoused racist sentiments.

In England and Wales, one of several possible ways in which the actions of probation officers may influence sentencing outcomes is the production of pre-sentence reports (PSRs). Using PSRs, probation officers can make proposals that may inform sentencing decisions. Studies also suggest that some probation officers prepare poorer-quality risk assessments for BME people compared with their white counterparts. A recent study of pre-sentence reports and risk assessments involving Asian offenders in one probation area found evidence of stereotyping, 'distancing' comments, superficial comments and exaggerated risks (Hudson and Bramhall, 2005: 727). This is an unfortunate finding given that poor-quality PSRs may disadvantage an offender, particularly if it influences the decision of the court. In the light of these findings, it is difficult to know what to make of additional findings which suggest that black and Asian offenders tend to have lower levels of assessed risks compared with other groups (see Raynor and Lewis, 2011). All convicted offenders supervised in prison or in the community are assessed so that they can be allocated a score that shows the level of risk they pose to society. They are also allocated a score that shows how high or low their needs are. A study by Raynor and Lewis (2011) found that BME offenders have lower risk–need scores than other groups and the differences are, in most cases, significant. Raynor and Lewis (2011: 10) noted that:

> Studies in England and Wales that have compared offenders who were similarly placed in the criminal justice system and that included analysis of risk–need scores by ethnicity have typically shown that average risk–need scores for minority ethnic offenders are lower than for comparably placed or comparably sentenced white British offenders. Differences are … in most cases, significant and the direction of the differences is strikingly consistent.

Raynor and Lewis (2011: 10–11) also remarked that: 'official studies of reconviction rates following different sentences consistently show that minority ethnic offenders are less likely than white offenders to be reconvicted'. Raynor and Lewis believe that this points to the possibility that at the time of sentencing, BMEs typically pose a lower risk of reoffending than other groups.

While it could be argued that the lower-risk status of black and Asian offenders should prove advantageous and could warrant less severe sentences, a question that arises is this: do poor-quality PSRs tip the scales of justice in a different direction? This is an empirical question but it alerts us to the possibility that the actions of some probation officers may expose black and Asian offenders to more severe punishment.

In terms of their experiences on probation, there is hardly any evidence available on the experiences of black offenders on probation to reach firm conclusions. In particular, there has been hardly any criminological research on the experiences of black and other ethnic minority women on probation or in the criminal justice system, and, it has been noted that: 'The gendered experiences and needs of minority female offenders, however, remains rather neglected in both the policy and academic arena' (Gelsthorpe, 2005, cited in Bowling and Phillips, 2012: 388).

Conclusion

In the US (and, more recently, in some other North American jurisdictions), critical race theorists have theorised the range of factors that, in their view, demonstrate that black people and some other ethnic minority groups are exposed to discriminatory policies and practices in criminal justice contexts, and in the wider legal system. CRT offers a different set of lenses through which we may view the operations of the criminal justice system (Ross, 2010). The range of concepts that CRT employs in its analyses of black issues alert us to the factors that can potentially explain the experiences of black people within the criminal justice system and wider society. As Ross (2010: 407) persuasively argues:

Race continues to play a significant role in explaining inequality, discrimination, and disparities in American justice systems. One way to understand and appreciate the dynamic intersection between issues of race, crime, and justice is through an examination and appreciation of critical race theory.

In England and Wales (as in the US), official statistics consistently indicate that black people are over-represented in the prison population compared with their overall representation in the wider population. Studies in the UK also reveal that black people do not commit more crimes than other ethnic groups, and along with Asians (from the Indian subcontinent), they tend to have lower levels of assessed risk of harm and risk of reoffending compared with other groups (Cavadino and Dignan, 2007; Raynor and Lewis, 2011). What, then, explains their over-representation in prison statistics, and, indeed, in police statistics, compared with their overall representation in wider society? The preceding discussion about the experiences of black people in the criminal justice system in the US and in England and Wales provides useful insights. It may also contribute to our understanding of the possible reasons why black people are over-represented in criminal justice statistics. Of course, it is unrealistic to ascribe the over-representation of black people and their experiences in the criminal justice system entirely to discrimination. However, it is equally difficult to overlook the possibility that such practices expose black people to more punitive criminal justice intervention.

SUMMARY

- CRT has been described as an intellectual movement that draws on diverse intellectual traditions and has dual aims: it seeks to develop theories about race and crime; and is committed to activism geared towards transforming wider society to dismantle racial inequality and racism.

- A key aim is to study institutionalised racial oppression and what is considered to be the dominance of white ideology and discourses. In the context of crime and justice, critical race theorists study the racial dynamics that shape understandings of both phenomena.

- Critical race theorists who have studied intersections between race, crime and justice have based their studies mainly in the US. In other Western jurisdictions, such as the UK, criminologists have studied the experiences of BME groups in the criminal justice system. Studies and statistics in this field of study reveal that although BME people (particularly black people and Asian people from the Indian subcontinent) do not commit more crimes than other groups, they tend to be arrested, prosecuted and imprisoned at a higher rate than other groups. They also receive longer prison sentences. Reasons offered for this unfortunate state of affairs range from policing activity and their experiences in court, to the likelihood of racial discrimination.

> **SAMPLE QUESTIONS**
> 1. To what extent does CRT help us understand the experiences of black people in the US during their interactions with societal institutions, including the criminal justice system?
> 2. What factors can explain the over-representation of black people in criminal justice statistics in the UK?

Notes

[1] Much of the work that critical race theorists have done on race and crime has been based on conditions in the US.

[2].Delgado and Stefancic (2012) point out that in the UK, CRT has been used by scholars in the field of education to explore inequality in educational matters.

[3] In official documents and statistics, the term 'Asian' typically refers to people from the countries that make up the Indian subcontinent – India, Bangladeshi and Pakistan. 'Black', 'Asian' and 'Mixed race' categories represent the greater proportion of minority ethnic groups within the criminal justice system.

[4] UK census statistics indicate that there is a large proportion of young people in that group.

Part Four
Critical perspectives on punishment

TWELVE

Punishment and control

Introduction

This chapter will examine the work of penal theorists, who have explored trends in punishment from a critical perspective. Some of the penal theorists have examined the political economy of punishment in several Western capitalist societies. They argue that in these societies, punishment serves as a means of controlling the labour force that sustains capitalist production. Others who have not focused on materialist explanations have nevertheless argued that in contemporary societies, punishment serves as an instrument that is used to pursue a given agenda. One such agenda might be to control target populations. The critical perspectives on punishment discussed in this chapter are perspectives: on the political economy of punishment; Foucauldian analysis of punishment; the dispersal of discipline thesis; late-modern penality and neo-liberal penality; the 'new penology'; abolitionism; and convict criminology.

The political economy of punishment

Key writers who have examined the political economy of punishment include Georg Rusche and Otto Kirchheimer (1939). Indeed, as Lynch (2011) felicitously puts it: 'One of the most influential works [in the political economy of punishment] is *Punishment and Social Structure* (Rusche and Kircheimer 1939)'. According to Lynch (2011), the text 'informs most critical criminological analyses of punishment'. Reiner (2012b: 312) describes Rusche and Kircheimer as 'Two of the Frankfurt School refugees from Nazism'. They settled in the US in the 1930s and published their seminal text in 1939. However, the book became popular in 1968, when it was republished amid the emerging popularity of critical criminology (Reiner, 2012b). Other scholars who have also explored the political economy of punishment in Western capitalist societies include the Italian criminologists Dario Melossi and Massimo Pavarini (1981) and the Norwegian abolitionist Thomas Mathiesen (1990) (see, generally, van Swaaningen, 1999).

Scholars who study the political economy of punishment identify the economic structure or the mode of production that prevails in any society as the key factor that shapes punishment in that society. Some have drawn on empirical data on punishment trends from as far back as the early medieval era to support their argument that the prevailing mode of production in a society, including the availability of and the demand for labour in a society at any given time, shapes punishment trends in that society. For these writers, formal punishment does not operate as an instrument of public protection. Rather, economic conditions in a society shape the nature of punishments imposed. Rusche and Kircheimer (1939) theorised these ideas (see Box 12.1).

They traced the emergence of the prison (which is now a main form of punishment in several Western capitalist societies) to capitalist imperatives. They described the prison as the primary source of a steady labour force. They argue that the prison serves as a means of instilling in prisoners (who tended to be invariably drawn from the lower classes) the skills, discipline and obedience required of productive workers (Rusche and Kirchheimer, 1939; Ignatieff, 1978; Melossi and Pavarini, 1981). They also described the prison as an instrument of control. In their view, the prison operated as a means of controlling the lower classes whose actions threatened the existing social and economic order, particularly those convicted of petty offences, such as vagrancy, drunkenness, and other activities associated with the lower classes. Rusche and Kircheimer (1939) argued that when labour is scarce and, as such, more valuable, the penal system becomes less brutal and more focused on enhancing the productive capability of the poor who find themselves within the system. It becomes necessary to ensure that the poor are able to engage in productive work or that they at least learn the skills required for productive activity within and outside the penal system. Thus, the penal system in capitalist societies exists to perform a social and economic function. Respectively, the penal system maintains the capitalist economic system by providing a steady stream of workers, and it maintains the class structure that capitalist production relations create. Reforms to the system are therefore, unlikely to be successful because of the important functions the system performs. In the exploitative productive relations that characterise the capitalist economic system, the penal system in capitalist societies ensures that the proletarian class (those who sell their labour for wages) are deterred from crime and are able to maintain their position in the production process (as workers) (Rusche and Kircheimer, 1939; De Giorgi, 2007).

Consequently, some Marx-inspired penologists such as Rusche and Kircheimer (1939) have been described as 'left functionalists' for espousing ideas that are quite similar to Durkheim's views about the role or function social institutions perform in maintaining the prevailing order (Cavadino, 2010: 448).

Box 12.1: Punishment and political economy

In the text *Punishment and Social Structure*, Rusche and Kirchheimer (1939) argued that in capitalist societies, in periods of labour scarcity, states become more concerned to enhance the ability of prisoners to provide cheap labour. Consequently punishments become less extreme. For example, rates of execution might fall to ensure that a steady stream of cheap labour can be maintained. However, in periods when labour becomes readily available, punishments become more severe. Imprisonment also becomes an important mechanism for reducing the pool of surplus labour in order to reduce labour costs. Thus, Rusche and Kirchheimer believed that in the shift from feudalism to capitalism, the prison became a main instrument of punishment because it served as a setting in which the labour force could be regulated and controlled. The following extract encapsulates Rusche and Kircheimer's ideas.

> In order to provide a more fruitful approach to the sociology of penal systems, it is necessary to strip from the social institution of punishment its ideological veils and juristic appearance and to describe it in its real relationships. The bond, transparent or not, that is supposed to exist between crime and punishment prevents any insight into the independent significance of the history of penal systems. It must be broken. Punishment is neither a simple consequence of crime, nor the reverse side of crime, nor a mere means which is determined by the end to be achieved. Punishment must be understood as a social phenomenon freed from both its juristic concept and its social ends. We do not deny that it can be understood from its ends alone.... Punishment as such does not exist; only concrete systems of punishment and specific criminal practices exist. The object of our investigation, therefore, is punishment in its specific manifestations, the causes of its changes and developments, the grounds for the choice or rejection of specific penal methods in specific historical periods. The transformation in penal systems cannot be explained only from changing needs of the war against crime, although this struggle does play a part. Every system of production tends to discover punishments which correspond to its productive relationships. It is thus necessary to investigate the origin and fate of penal systems, the use or avoidance of specific punishments, and the intensity of penal practices as they are determined by social forces, above all by economic and then fiscal forces. (Rusche and Kircheimer, 1939; 2009: 5)

Others, including Melossi and Pavarini (1981), have reinforced Rusche and Kircheimer's views about the role of the prison as an instrument that is used to regulate the labour force in capitalist societies. They described the prison as an instrument that was used to discipline workers in industrial capitalist societies in order to instil obedience and conformity.

More recent writers have also incorporated Marx-inspired principles of political economy in their account of the evolution of punishment in advanced capitalist jurisdictions from the 1970s onwards. Following in the tradition of the earlier Marxist sociologists, such as Rusche and Kircheimer, these Marx-inspired theorists trace prevailing modes of punishment to the economic imperatives of advanced capitalist societies. De Giorgi (2007), for example, argues that penal theorists, including Rusche and Kircheimer and others who developed a Marx-inspired political economy of punishment, and Foucault, whose work is discussed later in this chapter, located their critiques of punishment within the Fordist system of capitalist production, which had distinct social and economic conditions. De Giorgi (2007) insists that the critique of punishment that these theorists offered is no longer tenable in contemporary societies. This is because, in his view, there has been a shift from Fordism to post-Fordism, which has been accompanied by social and economic changes. De Giorgi points out that post-Fordism is a system of deregulated capitalist production. It is characterised by, *inter alia*, a service economy, unstable labour markets and flexible employment. It is quite different from Fordist industrial capitalism and its hallmarks of mass production, stable labour markets, stable employment and social welfarism. De Giorgi describes the penal system as part of an overall system of penal surveillance and control that complements the fragmented labour markets that exist in post-Fordist capitalist societies. Combined with a punitive immigration strategy, the penal system in these societies produces a vulnerable workforce that sustains the fragmented labour market (De Giorgi, 2010). Citing the example of global economic migration, particularly across Europe since the mid-1970s, De Giorgi maintains that non-Western migrants have been targeted for punitive immigration policies. They have also been targeted for criminalisation, which heightens their marginalisation and their vulnerability as a labour force. However, their vulnerable position is useful for post-Fordist labour markets because they can easily be exploited and transformed into a steady source of labour. Here, De Giorgi has applied Rusche and Kircheimer's critique of political economy to his study of the links between punishment and the social, economic and political conditions of what he describes as the post-Fordist era. He argues that penal systems within post-Fordist jurisdictions regulate and control immigrants in order to transform them into a productive labour force. His account echoes Rusche and Kircheimer's view that penal systems reinforce the production relations that sustain the capitalist order.

Foucauldian analysis of punishment

The French philosopher and historian Michel Foucault (1977) is another commonly cited scholar who offered critical perspectives on punishment in modern Western societies. Unlike Marx-inspired accounts of punishment, Foucault's account de-emphasises the link between economic imperatives and punishment. Rather, it emphasises power and discourse as the key variables that have shaped the nature and development of punishment or the penal system from as far back as the 18th century. Nevertheless, Foucault's work has Marxist undertones, particularly his views about the role of punishment as an instrument that operates to transform the body into a productive resource that can contribute to the progress of capitalism. According to Foucault (1977: 220–1):

> If the economic take-off of the West began with the techniques that made possible the accumulation of capital, it might perhaps be said that the methods for administering the accumulation of men made possible a political take-off in relation to the traditional, ritual, costly, violent forms of power, which soon fell into disuse and were superseded by a subtle, calculated technology of subjection. In fact, the two processes – the accumulation of men and the accumulation of capital – cannot be separated; it would not have been possible to solve the problem of the accumulation of men without the growth of an apparatus of production capable of both sustaining them and using them; conversely,

the techniques that made the cumulative multiplicity of men useful accelerated the accumulation of capital.

Foucault (1977: 138) identified those targeted for penal confinement and for transformation into 'a docile'[1] labour force as the poor who did not actively contribute to production. Those he identified as key members of this group include beggars, the poor, and the unemployed (Foucault, 1965 [1961]; 1977). Before the emergence and dominance of the modern prison, institutions such as poorhouses, houses of correction and workhouses served as the primary means of containing this group. (De Giorgi, 2010). The prison subsequently became the primary institution responsible for containing transforming these groups into a productive workforce.

Foucault's work on the history and development of punishment has influenced other scholars who have gone on to also proffer critical perspectives on punishment. Examples of these scholars include Loic Wacquant and David Garland.[2] Wacquant (2010: 204) acknowledges that 'Michel Foucault (1977) has put forth the single most influential analysis of the rise and role of the prison in capitalist modernity'. Perhaps ironically, although several criminologists have drawn on Foucault's work, his work on punishment clearly demonstrates that he was very much 'anti-criminologist' (Carrabine et al, 2009: 112). In the text *Discipline and Punish*, Foucault (1977) set out a perspective on punishment that has been described variously as post-Marxist, postmodernist and poststructuralist (Cavadino, 2010).[3] Foucault sought to present an account of the 'history of the present', which, in essence, means using historical accounts to review contemporary conditions (see also Garland, 2001; Braithwaite, 2003).

The role of power and discourse

In *Discipline and Punish*, Foucault (1977) argued that power[4] and discourse[5] have historically shaped the nature of punishment. In his view, both factors contributed to the rise of the prison as the main mode of punishment in modern society. Foucault charted the development of punishment from as far back as pre-modern times and continued his analyses to the period in the 19th century when the prison began to occupy a key role in punishment across Europe and the US. In *Discipline and Punish* Foucault maintained that specific social conditions and new power relations contributed to the rise of the prison. Before the 18th century, the prison served the primary purpose of detaining those awaiting punishment, execution or (later in the century) transportation. Punishment in that period primarily assumed the form of physical attacks on the body, in the form of executions and corporal punishments dispensed in public. An important objective of the public dramatisation of brutal punishment was to reinforce the prevailing order of the time (the aristocratic order).

The new social order that emerged in the shift towards industrial capitalism was accompanied by new power dynamics. According to Foucault, these new dynamics altered the nature of punishment in industrial capitalist societies. There was a gradual shift away from the dominant use of brutal and publicly inflicted punishments. The prison became the primary mode of punishment. Shortly after the rise of the prison, public executions were also abolished. Foucault maintained that the emergence of new forms of power is a key theme that explains these developments in punishment. The new forms of power shaped the discourses that came to dominate the operation of punishment. Thus, power and discourse are central to Foucault's critical analyses of punishment.

Unlike Marxist criminologists, who traced power to the ruling-class capitalists and the state, Foucault argued that the distribution of power is more diffuse. It finds expression in the ability to transform the mind to ensure compliance with formulated norms. As Godfrey (2012) notes, Foucault maintained that power is exercised through the formulation and preservation of norms.

In his description of the rise of the modern prison and its role as an instrument of discipline and control, Foucault argued that power resided in the human science disciplines including criminology,[6] psychology and psychiatry. He traced the power to inflict punishment (that was designed to regulate behaviour) to the discourses that were produced by the human science disciplines. The discourses established the 'norms' that everyone was expected to comply with. Foucault pointed out that the discourses subsequently came to represent accepted knowledge about individuals who were identified as criminals, and classed as abnormal because they had deviated from the established norms. As such, they were portrayed as offenders who deserved to be subjected to surveillance, discipline and control (Carrabine et al, 2009). In their interpretation of Foucault's work, Carrabine and colleagues (2009: 113) observed that the discipline – criminology – was deemed to be:

> the discourse that invents or produces its own set of ideas and languages about the criminal as an object to be studied, backed up by many institutions such as the prison and the courts. Power works its way distinctly though this discourse to help shape the whole society's view of crime.

Thus, the disciplines became the arbiters of normality. They exerted power through their ability to categorise individuals as normal or abnormal depending on assessments of the degree to which individuals could be said to conform with, or deviate from, the norm of behaviour set by the disciplines (Foucault, 1977; Carrabine et al, 2009). They used what Foucault considered to be spurious scientific credentials to validate their role in the regulation of normality. The role of the disciplines consisted of the observation, discipline and control of individuals they assessed as 'abnormal' because the individuals did not conform to the norms they themselves (the disciplines) had set. The judicial system provided the requisite legal basis for the role of the disciplines in regulating normality (Foucault, 1977). Ironically, through the constant observation of those assessed as abnormal and confined in penal institutions, such as the prison, the human science disciplines were able to generate further knowledge with which they developed their discourse: 'Training was accompanied by permanent observation; a body of knowledge was being constantly built up from the everyday behaviour of the inmates; it was organized as an instrument of perpetual assessment' (Foucault, 1977: 294).

As already noted, the discourse constructed by the disciplines shaped public perceptions of crime, and beliefs about those who were assessed and classified by the disciplines as criminals (or abnormal). Therefore, the knowledge that emerged from the disciplines served as a means of control. It served as a means of controlling not only the 'abnormal' in prison and in other institutions, but also the rest of the masses.[7] It provided the requisite justification for punishment and control:

> Psychiatric expertise, but also in a more general way criminal anthropology and the repetitive discourse of criminology, find one of their precise functions here: by solemnly inscribing offences in the field of objects susceptible of scientific knowledge, they provide the mechanisms of legal punishment with a justifiable hold not only on offences, but on individuals; not only on what they do, but also on what they are, will be, may be. (Foucault, 1977: 18–19)

Foucault employed the concept of genealogy[8] to explore the historical and social trajectories of discourses. His aim was to uncover how discourses change over time. He sought to demonstrate that discourses do not constitute objective truth. They are constructed forms of knowledge. They are not arrived at through any rational and linear progressive process. Therefore, Foucault rejected the commonly held notion that the changes to modes of punishment over time occurred because of insights gleaned from progressive Enlightenment ideals. He pointed out that the changes occurred because of a shift towards surveillance and discipline as means of control, and as strategies that could be used to target populations into conformist bodies and productive workers. Central to this shift was the exercise of power by the human science disciplines. As noted above, Foucault argued that the power of the disciplines manifested itself in their ability to construct discourses about what constitutes normality, and to categorise individuals as normal or abnormal depending on assessed levels of conformity with, or deviation from, the standards of normality set by the disciplines themselves.

In the text *Discipline and Punish*, Foucault's (1977) genealogical account of the historical development of the prison demonstrates how, alongside the prison, different institutions, from orphanages to asylums, subsequently came to serve as the means of transforming the people held in these institutions into docile norm-abiding bodies. The institutions became part of an overall system of discipline and control, even where the institutions were not originally designed to operate that way. Together, the institutions formed a crucial aspect of what Foucault conceived of as a 'carceral society', or the 'carceral archipelago', in which widespread surveillance through diverse means proliferated to ensure conformity to the established norm or set standard of behaviour (Foucault, 1977: 297; Downes and Rock, 2007). He maintained that the institutions he described as the 'carceral archipelago' (eg the prison and the asylum) served as sites in which the populations they catered for (eg prisoners and the mentally ill) could, through the rigours of discipline, surveillance and control, learn how to become normalised individuals who could conform to the norms that protect property and regulate production (Cohen, 1985). It was expected that those who were confined in these institutions would be transformed into docile norm-abiding bodies attuned to established standards of behaviour. Indeed, Foucault suggested that the carceral archipelago connects the prison to other institutions and systems of power and discipline that regulate normality in wider society. Thus, the prison is part of an extensive carceral system of discipline and control that is embedded in wider society. The prison does not achieve its aim of crime reduction, but continues to exist because it is an important part of a system of surveillance, regulation and discipline that has become legitimised and is now considered to be a normal feature of society (Carrabine et al, 2009).

Foucault argued that discipline within the carceral archipelago consists of consistent supervision, regulation and control. Panoptic[9] surveillance serves as a means of exerting disciplinary power and control, unlike previous penal arrangements in which the exercise of power was made clearly visible, and was even exaggerated:

> Traditionally, power was what was seen, what was shown and what was manifested.... Disciplinary power, on the other hand, is exercised through its invisibility; In discipline, it is the subjects who have to be seen. Their visibility assures the hold of the power that is exercised over them. It is the fact of being constantly seen, of being able always to be seen, that maintains the disciplined individual in his subjection. They did not receive directly the image of the sovereign power; they only felt its effects – in replica, as it were – on their bodies, which had become precisely legible and docile. (Foucault, 1977: 187–8)

It follows that the form of discipline described by Foucault involves surveillance, which may be real or imagined. Nevertheless, the overall aim is to discipline and reform the thoughts of the observed (eg prisoners) in order to transform them into 'docile' norm-abiding individuals and useful members of the capitalist production system. According to Foucault (1977: 136): 'A body is docile that may be subjected, used, transformed and improved.' Compared with brutal and publicly inflicted punishment, Foucault believed that discipline through surveillance and regulation is a more efficient means of transforming prisoners into docile conformists (see also Downes and Rock, 2007). Over time, the observed, never sure of whether or not the observation is constant, is likely to internalise the idea of being under constant observation. This should transform the observed into a docile subject who is capable of self-regulation, and automatic compliance with the norm (Liebling and Crewe, 2012). This means of exerting power and control in order to reform the prisoner was deemed to be highly efficient and cost-effective, not least because it involved a few observers observing masses of people at any one point in time (Downes and Rock, 2007). According to Welch (2011: 301), this was a system that allowed 'the few to see the many'. It combined architectural design (which provided the opportunity to observe prisoners) with economy (few officials observing many prisoners) (Welch, 2011). Violence or coercion was not required because the prisoners were isolated and they learnt to regulate themselves, making the use of violence or other cost- or energy-intensive forms of power highly unnecessary (Foucault, 1977; Downes and Rock, 2007).

Foucault's genealogical account of the growth of the prison is a revisionist account. It challenges the idea that the growth of the prison was a linear process that occurred as the product of the humanitarian concerns of penal reformers to move away from the use of corporal (physical or bodily) punishment in the 18th century. Indeed, penal reformers had hailed the rise of the prison and the abolition of public executions and corporal punishments as evidence of progress. They pointed out that the rise of the prison signalled a shift away from the use of barbaric punishments towards more humane and rational responses to crime. Foucault and others rejected these claims. Marx-inspired penologists, such as Rusche and Kircheimer, attributed the rise of the prison to its role as an instrument of control that complemented the rise of the capitalist mode of production. The notion of humanitarianism has been described as a 'Whig interpretation of history'. This is an approach to explaining political and constitutional developments (including penal developments) that focuses on notions of progress, reform and other humanitarian ideals that some trace to the advent of the Enlightenment (Emsley, 1997). Humanitarian achievements do exist, and an example is the laudable contributions of penal reformers such as Elizabeth Fry (1780–1845). However, Marx-inspired penologists and other writers, including Foucault, offer revisionist accounts of these developments. Foucault argued that, far from altruism, concerns about the impact of changing power dynamics in the shift towards industrial capitalism informed the reformers' agenda. There was a shift from aristocratic rule to more diffuse forms of power that were geared in large part towards normalising the population. As already noted, the human science disciplines played an important role in the use of power to normalise society. There was a commitment to the cost-effective but efficient use of power to secure conformity (among prisoners and the wider population) to the emerging capitalist order (see also Carrabine et al, 2009). Central to the diffuse forms of power was the prison, which came to serve as an instrument of discipline and control.

In the opening pages of *Discipline and Punish*, Foucault (1977) used the difference between a dramatic, brutal and public execution in 1757 and a regime of punishment for young offenders in a penitentiary in 1838 to highlight the shift away from punishment that is inflicted on the body in public, towards non-bodily punishment that is inflicted on the mind or the 'soul' in private. He pointed out that the new mode of punishment was based on established rules and the principles of reason and rational thought that accompanied the Enlightenment.

New techniques were introduced. Constant surveillance and discipline in the privacy of the prison replaced the brutal pain and torture inflicted in public. There was a quest for the 'interiorisation' of control (Gordon, 1971, cited in Reiner, 2012b) or to 'make the controlled control themselves' (Reiner, 2012b: 58). Ultimately, the aim was no longer to destroy the body, but to transform the soul and ensure conformity to the 'norm'.

The dispersal of discipline thesis

Some scholars expanded on Foucault's ideas about the role of punishment as an instrument of social control. Cohen (1985), for example, argued that state control mechanisms are increasingly expanding beyond the traditional confines of the criminal justice arena. He averred that the lines between the prison and the community, and between the public and the private, have become increasingly blurred. For example, using a fishing net metaphor, Cohen (1985) suggested that the reach of formal social control has extended beyond formal settings, such as the prison, into the community and the lives of ordinary citizens. Cohen refers to this as the 'dispersal of social control' (Cohen, 1979, 1985). In Cohen's view, the introduction of various sentences, including, for example, community-based alternatives to punishment, represents an example of a strategy that has contributed to this development. According to Cohen, an implication of introducing alternatives to custody, such as community-based orders, is that what he described as 'net-widening' occurs. The latter occurs when people who would not have received a custodial sentence receive an alternative to punishment, which, in effect, pulls them into the net of criminal justice. People are also drawn into this net when they violate the terms of alternative punishments. Thus, the effect of alternative punishments is to widen the net of criminal justice intervention.

Net-widening can lead to 'uptariffing', which can occur when people who have received one of the alternative sentences subsequently receive a higher tariff sentence (a more severe sentence) because they reoffended or violated the terms of the alternative sentence received. 'Thinning the mesh' is a metaphor that describes the impact of making the alternatives to punishment more severe so that they last longer and those caught up in the net of formal social control remain in the net for longer periods. 'Penetration' occurs when formal control mechanisms become intertwined with informal mechanisms. The cumulative effect of these processes is to widen the reach of social control by blurring the boundaries between interventions in custodial settings and interventions in the community. Thus, the processes described extend the reach of formal penal control beyond the prison walls, into wider society (see, generally, Cohen, 1979, 1985).

Punishment in late modernity

Others who explore trends in contemporary penality from a critical perspective have also examined the social and economic conditions that have shaped the development of punishment in the period they describe as a late-modern era[10] (Garland, 2001) and a post-Fordist era (Wacquant, 2009). In his book *The Culture of Control*, the criminologist Garland (2001) theorised the use of punishment as an instrument for securing specific objectives including political imperatives in late-modern societies. He focused on the UK and the US, but he appeared to suggest that his account has broad applicability because, in his view, the conditions in both societies generally reflect conditions in other late-modern societies. Wacquant (2010: 206–7) describes *The Culture of Control* as 'a sweeping and stimulative account of the nexus of crime and social order put forth since Foucault'. Reiner (2012b: 320) describes the text as 'A magisterial analysis of the epochal shift from the penal welfarism to more punitive and persuasive penal and preventative policies'. Although Garland does not necessarily offer a Marx-inspired critique of punishment, he provides a critical account of penal developments in contemporary Western societies, particularly the UK and the US. His critical account of punishment identifies links between punishment and the social, economic and cultural conditions of late-modern societies. Like the Marx-inspired theorists, Garland suggests that punishment performs several functions. Thus, his analysis of punishment emphasises the instrumental role of punishment in latemodern societies. He argues that, principally, penal policies serve as strategies governments use to reassert their sovereignty. They also serve as the prevailing mode of governance governments employ.

In *The Culture of Control*, Garland (2001) argued that late modernity is characterised by specific social, economic and cultural changes that make the era markedly different from the modern era. These changes have given rise to specific modes of responding to crime, and thinking about social welfare provision. Garland asserts that in the modern era, particularly in the period after the Second World War, social welfarism prevailed. There was a commitment to providing social security for all. Expansionary Keynesian policies were introduced. According to Garland, it was a period of employment stability bolstered by a thriving manufacturing industry, shared community spirit, and shared values, including the values of hard work and production (see also Young, 2009).[11] Penal welfarism, or what Garland (1996: 447; 2001: 53) refers to as 'penal modernism', was the ideal. It had as its primary aim the rehabilitation of offenders through scientific methods of diagnosis and treatment (Garland, 2001).

Garland points out that, by contrast, late-modern societies have witnessed the ascendency of a 'culture of control'. The culture of control is markedly different from modernist penal welfarism and its transformative ideals. There has also been an accompanying drive to reduce spending on social welfare provision. Central to this has been the tendency to demonise unemployed claimants by portraying them as work-shy individuals who subscribe to a culture of dependency. In his work on the development of penal policies in late-modern societies, Garland argues that there are links between socio-economic and cultural changes in late-modern societies from the 1960s onwards, and the introduction of penal policies that are infused with a culture of control. He points out that the changes that explain late-modern penality include the rise in socio-economic inequality, the decline of social collectivity and the rise of individualism. He also maintains that in that period, increased mobility weakened community and familial ties, socially and culturally fragmented societies emerged, and changes to the labour market destroyed economic stability. These problems were accompanied by increases in official rates of property and violent crime. Garland (2001) identifies these conditions as the precipitating factors that gave rise to prevalent fear of crime, exacerbated by media and political rhetoric. The conditions have also given rise to the normalisation of crime as one of several risks one has to contend with as part of daily life (Garland, 1996; 2001).

In response to these problems, governments on both sides of the Atlantic have adopted a two-dimensional approach to criminal justice. This comprises 'denial' strategies and 'adaptive' or 'adaptation' techniques (Garland 1996: 445; 2001: 105). Both strategies have been devised in response to what Garland (1996: 446; 2001) considers to be the 'predicament of crime control' that contemporary governments must now confront. This predicament consists of the realisation by governments that they, and their agencies, can no longer retain sole responsibility for crime control. They have to cede some of their crime control powers and functions. Garland suggests that this may in part, be explained by changes to the global economy, which have reduced the sovereignty of nation-states. However, governments also realise that devolving their crime control responsibilities will engender considerable political costs. As Garland (1996: 447; see also Garland, 2001) notes:

> The state's claims in respect of crime control have become more modest and more hesitant…. There is a new sense of failure of criminal justice agencies, and a more limited sense of the state's powers to regulate conduct and prohibit deviance. Attention is being shifted to dealing with the effects of crime – costs and victims and fearful citizens – rather than its causes. Above all there is an explicit acknowledgement of the need to rethink the problem of crime and the strategies for managing it.

The 'denial' strategies for responding to the problems that have accompanied late modernity manifest as the occasional use of expressive (harsh) punishments, such as long-term prison sentences. This approach amounts to 'hysterical denial' of the 'predicament of crime control' (Garland, 1996: 449; 2001: 130). The strategies represent attempts to reassert state authority and to mask the state's inability to respond effectively to social problems, including crime. Garland (1996: 460; see also Garland, 2001) notes that the strategies also serve a symbolic purpose. They represent: 'A show of punitive force against individuals … to repress any acknowledgement of the state's inability to control crime to acceptable levels'. They are also used to assuage public fears and anxiety. They create the impression that 'something is being done'. As such, they can be politically expedient. Central to the punitive approach governments adopt is penal populism, which, according to Garland, is a key dimension of penal policymaking. Penal populism involves formulating punitive penal policies on the basis of public opinion for political gain (see, eg, Bottoms, 1995; Garland, 2001; but for a dissenting perspective, see Matthews, 2005). It also involves mobilising public support for punitive policies by, inter alia, exaggerating the fear of crime, emphasising victims' rights and highlighting public protection and risk management as key policy objectives (Garland, 2001). Garland argues that penal populism is also central to the politicisation of crime by politicians who have placed crime at the top of the policymaking agenda, ahead of health, education and other policy areas.

Garland (1996: 461; 2001: 184) states that a brand of criminology he describes as the 'criminologies of the other or criminologies of the self' provides intellectual justification for the punitive penal approach that governments have adopted. This brand of criminology that fuels public fear and anxiety by portraying the offender as a 'dangerous' outsider, an 'alien other' who belongs to a different racial and social 'underclass' group. These sentiments are used to validate the incapacitation of the offender either through long-term imprisonment in the UK or execution in the US. Garland emphasises that the criminology that validates these sentiments and the policies that accompany them are not underpinned by evidence. He maintains that 'It is, moreover, a "criminology" which trades in images, archetypes and anxieties, rather than in careful analyses and research findings – more a politicized discourse of the unconscious than a detailed form of knowledge-for-power' (Garland, 1996: 461). It is a criminology that supports the demonisation of groups that have been affected the most by the social and economic changes of late modernity. These groups are the poor, those who rely on social security benefits, and ethnic minority groups. The criminologies of the other/criminologies of the self also validate the deployment of rhetoric that fuels public fear and anxieties. This brand of criminology also validates the mobilisation of support for punishment policies as part of the overall effort to secure political advantage.

As mentioned earlier, Garland identifies adaptation techniques as the second approach to criminal justice that governments adopt. Quite unlike the punitive approach, 'adaptive strategies' (Garland, 1996: 445; 2001) are used to confront the 'predicament of crime control' Garland alluded to. In Garland's words, the strategies represent: 'an attempt to face up to the problem and develop pragmatic new strategies that are adapted to it' (Garland, 1996: 449; see also Garland, 2001). The adaptation techniques constitute 'new modes of governing crime' (Garland, 1996: 450). Garland (1996: 461; 2001: 127) describes the criminologies that validate these new modes of responding to crime as 'the criminologies of everyday life'. Quite unlike the criminologies of the other, which cast the offender as a 'dangerous' outsider, the criminologies of everyday life portray the offender as a rational being who is no different from anyone else in society.

The criminologies of everyday life are the neo-conservative administrative criminologies, such as the rational choice and routine activities theories discussed in Chapter Six. These theories describe crime as a normal aspect of social life. They trace crime to availability of opportunity and the rational calculation of risks. Therefore, the theories validate the growing crime prevention and community safety machinery that focuses on reducing opportunities for crime and increasing the risks of apprehension. The machinery shifts the onus of crime prevention and control from the government and its agencies to the potential victims. The offender and his or her attributes are deemed marginal to crime control and prevention concerns. Reducing opportunity and access (not reforming the offender) is believed to be the key to effective crime prevention and control.

Garland (2001) describes yet another adaptation strategy that governments employ as a 'responsibilisation strategy'. In Garland's (2001: 124) view, 'The attempt to extend the reach of state agencies by linking them with the practices of actors in the "private sector" and the "community" may be described as the responsibilisation strategy'. To develop the concept of 'responsibilisation', Garland draws on Foucauldian governmentality, which represents, *inter alia*, a mode of governance that entails scaling down the government's role in crime control. Garland argues that contemporary governments have realised that they cannot retain responsibility for all aspects of social life, including crime control. Therefore, they engage in what Garland (2001: 127) describes as 'Governing at a distance' (see also Rose, 1999; 2000; Rose and Miller, 1992). The 'responsibilisation' of citizens serves as a useful strategy for governing at a distance. It involves devolving responsibility for crime control not only to local governments, but also to the private and the voluntary sector, and, the wider community. Indeed, there has been an expansion of privatised crime control (Garland, 1996; 2001). However, the devolution of responsibility for crime control enables the state and its agencies to govern indirectly through private agencies and organisations. The responsibilisation strategy 'does not entail the simple off-loading of state functions.... Rather it is a new form of governance-at-a-distance ... a new mode of exercising power. It is a new mode of governing crime' (Garland, 1996: 454; see also Garland, 2001).

Reducing the influx of people into the criminal justice system by diverting them away using sanctions, such as the caution, represents yet another adaptation strategy. This amounts to 'defining deviance down' (Garland, 1996: 456; see also Garland, 2001). The objective is to reduce the costs of criminal justice. State agencies have also sought to reduce public expectations and to define their role and objectives in narrower terms.

In sum, Garland's account of the development of punishment suggests that the changing social, economic and cultural changes of the 1960s onwards signalled 'the coming of late modernity'. These changes gave rise to feelings of insecurity and other social problems. Crime control measures have been used to respond to these problems. For example, the responsibilisation strategy enables governments with weakened ability to manage these problems effectively to allocate the role to other parties. Governments may then avoid direct involvement in crime prevention activities. Instead, they are able to 'govern from a distance'. Another strategy governments employ in their effort to address the social problems that have accompanied the advent of late modernity is is the expressive punitive approach that involves *inter alia* the penal containment of groups who have been portrayed as 'dangerous' and held responsible for the social and other problems of late modernity (Garland, 1996: 461). The groups targeted are racial groups and others who have been marginalised by the free-market policies of late-modern societies (Garland, 1996; 2001). Garland's account is a critical perspective on punishment because it emphasises the role of punishment as an instrument that governments use to respond to adverse social and economic problems in ways that control target populations and boost political capital.

Governing through crime

Jonathan Simon (2007) has developed these ideas in what has been described as the 'governing through crime' thesis. The thesis reinforces the view that suggests that contemporary governments respond to social problems with crime control measures. It also points to the social changes that have orchestrated the mass incarceration of young black men in the US. The thesis links social changes in the US, in particular, to the form of penalty that has emerged in that jurisdiction. The thesis holds that following the attacks on the Twin Towers of the World Trade Centre in New York on 11 September 2001, crime control has increasingly become a central organising feature of US social policy. A 'war on crime' has emerged and it infiltrates almost all aspects of social life, and key social institutions, from the family and the school to the workplace. In these institutions, individuals are treated as either criminals or victims. All aspects of social interaction in the family, the school and at work have become potential avenues for crime control activities in the form of police intervention, drug testing, criminal record checks, litigation and so forth. Citizens' rights are increasingly being undermined, while victims' status has become elevated. These developments have eroded faith in social institutions and in legal institutions, such as the judiciary. The ability of the judiciary to impose sufficiently harsh sentences is constantly questioned. The upshot of this has been an increase in the use of harsh penal sanctions. The latter are primarily standardised rather than individualised. In addition, the prison serves as an instrument for containing the socioeconomically marginalised (typically African-American men).

Neo-liberal penality

Another penal theorist who has provided a critical account of punishment is the French scholar Loic Wacquant (2009). He identifies neo-liberalism as the key factor that has shaped the development of penal policy in the US, and several European jurisdictions, since the late 20th century.[12] Wacquant defines neo-liberalism as a political agenda that has emerged across several Western societies. It comprises 'four institutional logics': 'economic deregulation'; 'welfare state devolution, retraction, and recomposition'; 'the cultural trope of individual responsibility';

and 'an expansive, intrusive, and proactive penal apparatus' (Wacquant, 2009: 207). The foregoing in Wacquant's view, is a sociological definition of neo-liberalism. He believes that the deregulation and disintegration of the labour market, and a two-pronged model of governance, are key features of neo-liberalism. The two-pronged model of governance comprises a social welfare agenda of reduced provision of health care, education, housing and so forth, and a penal agenda of enhanced criminal justice intervention. The latter manifests itself in the form of a punitive and hyperactive criminal justice apparatus that comprises the 'police, the courts, and the penitentiary' (Wacquant, 2010: 198).

Neoliberal control mechanisms: workfare and penal regulation

Wacquant argues that in neo-liberal societies, particularly the US, social welfare has been reconceptualised as workfare, which he also describes as 'disciplinary workfare'. The latter, in his view, has replaced Keynesian social welfarism and its underlying emphasis on the rights of citizens to adequate welfare provision (Wacquant, 2010: 198). According to Wacquant (2010: 198), workfare is characterised by '"illiberal social policies" that seek to direct citizens' conduct coercively' (Desmond King, 1996, quoted in Wacquant, 2010: 217). 'Deterrence, surveillance, stigma and graduated sanctions' are the key strategies that now underpin not only penal policies, but also social welfare policies (workfare). Wacquant believes that these strategies are employed to regulate the behaviour of the marginalised. Indeed, he argues that workfare and the prison have combined forces to form a single organisational unit that renders the target groups invisible by removing them from social welfare records and by containing them in prisons. Wacquant identifies the target groups as the 'The black subproletariat', who have incidentally been marginalised by neo-liberal policies (Wacquant, 2010: 198), and the 'roaming sex offender', who is also a prime target for penal regulation. According to Wacquant (2010: 199), these groups are designated as 'problem populations'. Furthermore, they are propelled into a burgeoning ancillary labour market that is deregulated, fragmented and exploitative.

Neo-liberal workfare and penal regulation as responses to social insecurity

For Wacquant, social insecurity in neo-liberal societies, such as the US, is ubiquitous and stems from the fragmentation of the labour market. It mainly afflicts those who are situated on the lower positions of the social strata. Economic deregulation has exacerbated social insecurity and led to increases in rates of civil disorder across urban areas. Wacquant identifies yet another factor that has contributed to social insecurity. He believes that in the US, the 'political elites' (Wacquant, 2010: 198) (whom he also describes as the 'state elites'; Wacquant, 2010: 218) have reacted against the social progress of the 1960s that heralded improved race and class relations. Consequently, the late 20th century has witnessed heightened racial division, and state elites have reconstructed black identity as a symbol of danger

(Wacquant, 2010).[13] According to Wacquant (2009), in response to growing social insecurity, state elites have introduced policies that have led to a phenomenal rise of the penal state in the US, which now has the highest prison population in the Western world. Wacquant (2010: 208) argues that the prison has become a political instrument for responding to 'social insecurity', not 'criminal insecurity'. He cites statistics to demonstrate that the unprecedented rise in US incarceration rates is not linked to any corresponding rise in crime rates. In Wacquant's view, what he describes as the 'penalisation of poverty' through reduced welfare provision (or workfare) and enhanced penal regulation, also serves as a means of addressing civil disorder. It is used to discipline the unemployed poor, whom Wacquant (2010: 198) describes as 'fractions of the post-industrial working class'. Wacquant also believes that an important outcome of the hallmarks of neo-liberalism, which include a deregulated labour market, reduced social welfare provision and enhanced penal regulation, has been to regulate economically marginalised populations (the poor) and to concentrate them in the lower end of the socio-economic strata, and also in the ghettos (deprived urban areas).

Reasserting state authority through neoliberal workfare and penal policies

According to Wacquant, a key role of the two-pronged mode of governance which, as described above, combines reduced welfare provision (or workfare) with enhanced penal regulation, is to facilitate the continued exercise of authority by the political elites in a climate of reduced public legitimacy. The reduced legitimacy of state authority stems from the perceived failure of state officials to sustain expansionary Keynesian social welfare policies. In response to the problem of reduced legitimacy, the prison has been stripped of its rehabilitative agenda. It has been transformed into an instrument for managing the adverse impact of neoliberal social and penal policies (Wacquant, 2009). It is also used to manage marginal groups. It helps remove the 'most disruptive' poor people from visibility (Wacquant, 2010: 204). In doing so, it reduces the demand for ever-declining social welfare provision, and it channels the target group into invisibility.

In sum, Wacquant's account of punishment echoes the accounts of other theorists who describe punishment as an instrument of control. Wacquant believes that neo-liberal penal policies overlook the structural marginalisation that has been engendered by the hallmarks of neoliberalism which include: deregulated labour markets; reduced social welfare provision; and enhanced penal regulation. Rather, the causes of crime are traced to the individual, particularly to those who have been marginalised by neo-liberal policies and are considered to be threats to the neo-liberal order. The prison serves as a means of containing these populations.

Box 12.2: Penal and social regulation as instruments of regulation and control

In the text titled *Punishing the Poor*, the French scholar Loic Wacquant (2009) argues that the factors that have contributed to the unprecedented rise of the 'hyperactive' penal machinery that operates in the US are the combined use of social welfare policies and penal polices to regulate and control the poor, and the failure to develop social policy. Restricted welfare provision corresponds with enhanced penal regulation. This is a key political agenda that is motivated by 'moral behaviourism', or the effort to use punitive social and penal measures to regulate the behaviour of the poor (2010: 198). Social and welfare policies have been merged into a singular mechanism for responding to those who have been portrayed as the main sources of social insecurity and anxiety. These are mainly the poor – welfare dependants and those convicted of street crime. They are presented to the public as morally deficient individuals whose actions threaten the social order. They are as such, targeted for penal regulation in prison. A racially charged discourse is used to create a perceived need to contain black people in order to address these problems. The following is an extract from the text.

> *Punishing the poor is intended as a contribution to the historical anthropology of the state and of the transnational transformations of the field of power in the age of ascending neoliberalism*, in that it purports to link the modifications of social policies to those of penal policies so as to decipher the *double regulation* to which the post-industrial proletariat is now subjected through the joint agency of the assistantial and penitential sectors of the state. And because the police, the courts, and the prisons are upon close examination, the sombre and stern face that the Leviathan turns everywhere toward the dispossessed and dishonoured categories trapped in the hollows of inferior regions of social and urban space by economic deregulation and the retrenchment of schemes of social protection. In sum, the present volume is a study not of crime and punishment, but of the remaking of the state in the era of hegemonic market ideology: penal expansion in the United States, and in the Western European and Latin American countries that have more or less slavishly followed its lead, is at the bottom a *political project*, a core component of the retooling of public authority suited to fostering the advance of neoliberalism. (Wacquant, 2009: xviii; emphasis in original)

Wacquant also asserts that his sociological understanding of neo-liberalism requires that we should view penal institutions such as the prison as:

> a core political institution, instead of a mere technical implement for enforcing the law and handing criminals, and, second that we recognise that 'workfare' and 'prisonfare' are two integral components of the neoliberal Leviathan, and not passing contradictions or accidental sideshows to the grand narrative of the alleged advent of 'small government'. (Wacquant, 2009: xviii)

According to Wacquant, a sociological understanding of neo-liberalism also:

> puts in the spotlight the distinctive *paradox of neoliberal penality*: the state stridently reasserts its responsibility, potency, and efficiency in the narrow register of crime management at the very moment when it proclaims and organises its own impotence on the economic front ... (Wacquant, 2009: xviii)

The impact of neo-liberalism

Apart from Wacquant, other penal theorists who offer critical perspectives on punishment also draw parallels between neo-liberalism and enhanced punitiveness. In their text *Penal Systems: A Comparative Approach*, Cavadino and Dignan (2006) compared 12 jurisdictions and examined how the political economy that operates in each jurisdiction affects penal policy and practice in that jurisdiction. The overall objective was to identify whether there are links between political economy[14] and penal strategies. They found that there is a relationship between the political economy of a jurisdiction and the levels of punitiveness in that jurisdiction. Neo-liberal countries, such as England, Wales and the US, appeared to be the most punitive. The study described neo-liberal countries as countries with limited welfare provision, large discrepancies in income and wealth, greater individualism than collectivism, growing social exclusion, and greater dominance of right-wing politics (see also Reiner, 2012b). There is also a higher incidence of 'law and order' politics and exclusionary penal sanctions in neo-liberal countries. Studies suggest that compared with social-democratic countries, neo-liberalism breeds inequality, unemployment and social exclusion, which, in turn, contribute to conditions that are linked to high rates of property and violent crimes (Hale, 2005; Reiner, 2012a; 2012b).

It is argued that populations that are marginalised in neo-liberal societies are also more vulnerable to the exclusionary penal sanctions that prevail in these countries. Some scholars in this field argue that the marginalised populations have been categorised as 'risks' to the dominant capitalist order. They have been targeted for penal surveillance and control. The populations targeted include: the long-term unemployed poor; welfare dependants; immigrants; and others who are typically engaged in work that falls short of accepted ideas about what constitutes mainstream gainful employment. The latter is now increasingly posited as the passport to social inclusion and full citizenship in neo-liberal jurisdictions, particularly the US and the UK (see, generally, Beckett, 1997; Cavadino and Dignan, 2006; Young, 2007; Wacquant, 2009).

The 'new penology'

Additional writers in the critical tradition who have theorised the nature of punishment in neoliberal societies also point to the rise of penal strategies that operate as instruments of control. Some contend that 'risk' management has become a key aim of punishment in contemporary Western societies, such as the

US and some European jurisdictions. Penal theorists who make this claim point to the rise of an actuarial mode of penality that, in their view, has signalled the 'end of ideology' (van Swaaningen, 1999: 13). This penal development focuses on assessing how to manage and control those assessed as 'risks' efficiently and cost-effectively. The penal development has been described as a 'new penology' that is based on actuarial justice principles rather than traditional legal principles of the rule of law (Feeley and Simon, 1992; van Swaaningen, 1999). It is a risk-focused penality because it prioritises the efficient management and control of populations assessed as 'risks' over humanistic ideals, such as rehabilitation. Malcolm Feeley and Jonathan Simon (1992) are widely cited as the pioneers of this field of study. Their work directed attention to the emergence of the 'new penology'. They argue that in contemporary penal arrangements, punishment is no longer underpinned by traditional penal objectives, such as deterrence, rehabilitation or retributivist ideals. Rather, its primary goal is the effective control and management of 'risky' populations. Some critical criminologists have taken issue with this development. For example, van Swaaningen (1999: 16) sums up the approach thus:

> A key element of actuarialism is that moral questions are scrubbed round and translated into technical questions of implementation. State action is mainly informed by statistical scenarios and risk assessments. The implicit vision of mankind has changed from accountable citizen to the irresponsible object of control. Breaches of law are no longer judged in terms of culpability but in terms of potential risks for the social order.

Origins of risk as a centralising penal discourse

The idea that 'risk' has become a centralising discourse in contemporary penal policy can also be traced to the work of other scholars. Key examples include Ulrich Beck and Anthony Giddens who have theorised what they describe as risk-aversive sentiments that have emerged in some Western societies, including many countries in Western Europe and North America (Giddens, 1991; Beck, 1992). As Giddens (1991: 4) remarks: 'The latemodern world – the world of what I term high modernity – is apocalyptic, not because it is inevitably heading towards calamity, but because it introduces risks which previous generations have not had to face'.

Equally, Beck (1992) states that we now live in a 'risk society'. In his view, this is because there has been a decline in traditional sources of security, such as extended family networks. This decline has intensified feelings of insecurity and has diminished 'positive ideals and solidarity' in society. It has generated instead 'a negative solidarity of shared fears' (van Swaaningen, 1999: 16). It has also been argued that feelings of insecurity have been intensified by global changes. Examples of these changes are increased cross-continental migration and climate change (see also Giddens, 1991; Feeley and Simon, 1992; Ericson and Haggerty,

1997; Hudson, 2003). It is worth noting that the idea that 'risk consciousness' has become a pervasive feature of contemporary Western societies has been contested. According to some commentators, there is insufficient empirical evidence to support the proposition that 'risk consciousness is as generalised or as novel as is claimed' (O'Malley, 2010: 12).

Managerialism

Some theorists who offer critical perspectives on punishment have also identified managerialism as yet another ascendant penal policy strategy that is also quite different from penal welfarism and its transformative ideals (van Swaaningen, 1999). It is described as an approach to criminal justice that also reflects the instrumental character of penality in contemporary Western societies, such as the US and the UK. Some point out that it complements the risk-focused penal agenda that is said to prevail in these jurisdictions (Feeley and Simon, 1992).

Broadly conceived, managerialism is a system-focused policy agenda. This means that it prioritises practices that aid the smooth running of the criminal justice system. The cost-effective management of people convicted of offences and promoting efficiency are key principles of managerialism (Senior et al, 2007). Thus, it prioritises the aesthetics of criminal justice[15] like measurable outputs over intangible concerns, such as rehabilitative practices and outcomes. Consequently, for some, managerialism is another penal development that has contributed to the 'end of ideology' in social control policies. Cohen (1994, quoted in van Swaaningen, 1999: 16) notes that 'The new round of "the end of ideology" game has left its mark on social control systems and ideologies. In the crime control business, we see an ascendancy of managerial, administrative and technocratic styles'.

Echoing these arguments, Feeley and Simon (1992: 452) point out that managerialism encourages a focus on the 'managerial rather than the reformative'. Other commentators observe that the impact of managerialism has been to remove moral and other sentiments from punishment (Fionda, 2000). There is an emphasis on a business-oriented approach to dealing with offenders. Van Swaaningen (2000) criticises managerialism and argues that it has displaced traditional penal concerns, such as rehabilitation. He points out that the rationales given for criminal justice intervention now seem meaningless: 'Nowadays, officials mainly speak about criminal justice in terms of business management' (2000: 91). According to the German criminologist Sebastian Scheerer (2000: 248–9), this is 'the phenomenon of managerialism, now a pervasive trend in criminal justice systems'. Reinforcing this, Garland (1996: 59) points out that under managerialist arrangements, ideas about the moral role of punishment have become marginal to the operation of punishment whilst punishment has become quite technocratic with an increasing focus on managing 'inputs and outputs, risks and resources'.

Abolitionism

Some writers in the critical criminological tradition have extended their critique of contemporary penality quite radically by calling for the abolition of formal penal arrangements in society (Sim, 1994). The work of these writers has been described as abolitionism (van Swaaningen, 1997). In their view, established crime control mechanisms are generally counterproductive but they continue to exist because they help maintain an unequal social order. Abolitionists insist that the prison, for example, serves as a means of incapacitating powerless groups. This view echoes the position of the theorists cited earlier who also describe punishment in instrumental terms.

Broadly defined, abolitionism is a critical criminological perspective that advocates the abolition of state or formal mechanisms of crime control, particularly imprisonment (Hulsman, 1986; Mathiesen, 1990; Christie, 1981; 2000; 2003). Abolitionists emphasise sometimes-divergent themes, but, collectively, they advocate 'full-scale abolition of prisons as opposed to reforming them' (Cavadino, 2010: 449). The perspective is regarded as a development that has emerged mainly from European countries, such as the Netherlands, where it has had a significant impact on penal policy (Downes and Rock, 2011). Van Swaaningen (1999: 11) identifies the Norwegian Nils Christie, and the Dutchmen Herman Bianchi and Louk Hulsman, as 'abolitionism's founding fathers'. Nils Christie (2004) traces the origin of the term 'abolitionism' to the activities of the abolitionists who struggled to abolish or limit slavery.

Abolitionists have been described as idealists. Indeed, the origins of penal abolitionism have been traced to a period in the 1960s when the prevailing political culture and ideal was one of optimism about the possibility of humanising the penal system of jurisdictions in Western Europe. Willem de Haan (1990; 1991; 2010), the Dutch abolitionist, identifies the strands of abolitionism as: 'a social movement' against imprisonment and, indeed, against the penal system; a theoretical approach that advocates that the criminal law should be replaced with approaches that prioritise conflict resolution; and a political stance that proposes the abolition of aspects of the penal system, such as imprisonment, without suggesting alternative penal responses (see, eg, Mathiesen, 1974).

The social movement strand has its roots in the campaign against the use of imprisonment that spread across Western Europe and North America in the 1960s and 1970s. The aim of the movement was to alleviate the adverse impact of imprisonment on prisoners, and to humanise the treatment of prisoners, with a view to replacing imprisonment with more humane crime control measures (De Haan, 1990; 2010). Over time, as academic contributions to the movement increased, the social movement evolved into a theoretical perspective in critical criminology, which critically assesses dominant penal discourses, including the discourses that revolve around such concepts as crime and punishment, penal practices, and so forth (De Haan, 1990; 2010). Indeed, abolitionists view crime as a social construction. According to De Haan (1991), abolitionists propose that existing definitions and dominant discourses about crime should be dismantled, along with the entire penal system. The dominant discourses, in their view, disadvantage the powerless and expose them to greater criminal justice intervention, particularly in the form of imprisonment. Abolitionists state that in order to deal with crime differently, it is necessary to revise the existing vocabulary (including the labels) that we use when we talk about crime (van Swaaningen, 1999).

It is also argued that abolitionists offer what some describe as a 'replacement discourse' (van Swaaningen, 1999). The latter consists of 'speech, words, grammar' and discourses that can replace potentially harmful but dominant discourses (Arrigo, 2001: 220). Abolitionists proffer a 'replacement discourse' because they present not only critical theoretical analyses of punishment, but also alternative ideas about how to transform the existing penal structure. They reconceptualise crime or criminal incidents as social problems or conflict. As alternatives to formal sanctions that are based on notions of guilt and punishment, they propose responses such as decentralised, community-level and participatory approaches to conflict resolution (De Haan, 2010). Peaceful conflict resolution represents an example of the community-level strategies the abolitionists propose. As the abolitionist Nils Christie (2004: 126) puts it: 'The abolitionists raise questions like: What logic, and ethic, makes it so certain that punishment has priority over peacemaking?' Equally, they argue that if existing punitive laws and strategies are exclusionary and do not achieve their aim of reduced reoffending, they should be replaced with reintegrative alternatives. It is therefore not surprising that in place of existing penal strategies, such as imprisonment, abolitionists advocate 'compensation rather than retaliation; reconciliation rather than blame allocation' (De Haan, 1991: 211).

Abolitionists believe that the prison maintains and reproduces structures of inequality and social division. They assert that the prison is typically populated by the socially, economically and politically marginalised – the less powerful (Ryan and Sim, 2007; Sim, 2009). Nils Christie (2004: 93) observes that 'Most prisoners from all countries, independently of political systems are poor and miserable'. Those who advocate abolition of the prison believe that the prison is used to control powerless groups, including the poor, and also minority ethnic groups (see also Box 12.3). Consequently, the prison reinforces dominant discourses about the nature of crime. These discourses portray crime as a key feature of the activities the powerless engage in (Mathiesen, 1974).

Box 12.3: Imprisonment as an instrument of control

In the text *A Suitable Amount of Crime*, Nils Christie (2004) explores penal trends in the US, which now has the highest prison population in the Western world. His views about penal policy and practice in the US illumine key abolitionist views about the structural role of the prison. These views are worth representing here, as follows.

To me, the US penal system is a system that negates the fundamental values they claim as their own ... what goes on in the US penal system for two million people, and for the additional more than four and a half million on probation and parole, has since long passed the level of what can be understood as reflecting their values. It is materially the wealthiest country in the world. Nonetheless, it is a country that uses prison instead of welfare. It is a country that continuously talks about freedom. Nonetheless, it has the largest prison population in the world. It is a country that fought a fierce civil war in which the abolition of slavery was at least some of the motivation. Nonetheless, it has an abnormal proportion of black people within its prison walls.... In sum, it is a country that uses exclusion instead of inclusion, and in addition executes a portion of the most unwanted.

As noted earlier, De Haan (1990: 2010) identifies a third strand of abolitionism, which is the political strand. From De Haan's (2010) point of view, the political strand developed out of the struggle of prison reform groups who advocated penal and social reform. This strand of abolitionism now concerns itself with proposing complete abolition of the existing penal system. Until quite recently, it did not offer any alternative replacement/s. It has since proposed decentralised or informal forms of justice as alternatives to the formal criminal justice system. Furthermore, the political strand of abolitionism recognises that in order to dismantle or significantly reform the existing penal system, a corresponding restructuring of existing power arrangements in society is also required. Therefore, it proposes that the prevailing capitalist order should also be dismantled alongside the criminal justice system (De Haan, 1990, 2010).

Penal abolitionists, such as Thomas Mathiesen (1974), whose work is associated with the political strand of abolitionism, criticise the reformist agenda of liberal writers and others who advocate penal reform. They argue that the reformers do not challenge the penal agenda of the state (see also Sim, 2009). Mathiesen (1974: 19, emphasis in original), for example, points out that the reformers 'use the language of the powerful ... defining the problems at hand as the powerful *usually do*'. Perhaps unwittingly, they do more harm than good because they reinforce the justifications and power dynamics that facilitate the continuing existence of the prison (Sim, 2009: 154; see also Ryan and Sim, 2007). In addition, despite critiques of the system and 'endless reforms' since the 18th century to improve its effectiveness, the prison still produces the same discouraging results, yet it continues to exist (Foucault, 1977; Sim, 2009). Some penal abolitionists also criticise reformers for overlooking boarder structural factors. The penal abolitionists insist that a structuralist perspective on the role of the prison would highlight the role of the prison as a state institution that exists to maintain an unequal social order that is characterised by divisions along several lines, including class, gender, race and sexuality (Sim, 2009).

Convict criminology

'Convict criminology' is a field of study that originated in the US. It comprises the work of academics (some of whom are in prison, or have been to prison),[15] who are critical of existing criminological literature and policies (Richards and Ross, 2001: 180; Richards, 2013). Thus it is a field of study that also offers critical perspectives on punishment. The proponents of convict criminology describe it as a 'school and social movement' (Richards and Ross, 2001; Richards, 2013: 177). They describe convict criminology as '"a new criminology" … led by ex-convicts who are now academic faculty' (Richards and Ross, 2001: 180). According to the convict criminologists, convicts are: 'the victims of the criminal justice machine' (Richards and Ross, 2001: 178).

Stephen Richards and Jeffery Ross named this field of study 'convict criminology' (Richards, 2013). Proponents of convict criminology state that it emerged in the 1990s, and its pioneers expected it to be an approach that would address the limitations of existing work in the field of criminology and criminal justice, particularly in the field of punishment (Newbold and Ross, 2013). A key limitation identified by the early convict criminologists was that hardly any of the existing theoretical and empirical insights on the prison system had been produced by those who had first-hand experience of the penal system as prisoners. It became apparent to the early proponents of the field of study that it was necessary to bring to the attention of policymakers and practitioners the nature and impact of imprisonment as narrated by prisoners and ex-prisoners. Indeed, convict criminologists maintain that much of the academic literature reflects the views of those who devise and implement prison policy (Richards, 2013: 377). It overlooks the perspectives of the convicts about what prison means to them or how they experience it. The literature presents a glossier image of prison life, which obscures the 'horrors' that prisoners have to contend with (Richards and Ross, 2001; Richards, 2013: 377). Even existing critical criminological perspectives that propose reforms to the system ignore the views of convicts. According to Richards and Ross (2001: 184), convict criminologists seek to 'provide the public with a more realistic understanding of crime, criminal justice and corrections, one based on experience and cutting edge research'.

Although mainstream criminology conceptualises prisons as mechanisms of rehabilitation, convict criminology views prisons as mechanisms of punishment, damage and torture (Richards and Ross, 2001; Richards, 2013). Like several other criminologists who offer critical perspectives on punishment, convict criminologists argue that the prison has failed to achieve its objective of crime reduction. They believe that the prison has failed because people are sent to prison not necessarily because they have committed a crime. Many people in prison are not violent or risky people. Many are incarcerated for unduly long periods. However, very little is done to help rehabilitate those in prison. The prison is, in effect, designed to contain people and punish them. This implies that convict criminologists also view punishment, particularly imprisonment, in instrumental terms.

Criminologists in this field of study reject what they describe as 'managerial criminology, criminal justice and corrections' (Richards and Ross, 2001: 183). They maintain that their agenda is to advance reforms that can help create a more humane criminal justice system. They make several recommendations on how to humanise the penal system, reduce reoffending and reduce prison numbers. They recommend that efforts should be made to: 'dramatically decrease the national prison population by reducing prison sentences for prisoners; reduce prison time for good behaviour; require that all prisoner have single cells or rooms; better food and clothing; vocational and family skills programmes; higher education opportunities; voting rights for all prisoners and felons; voluntary drug education therapy; an end to the use of prison snitches; and the termination of the drug war' (Richards and Ross, 2001: 185; see also Richards, 2013).

Criticisms

Marx-inspired theorists, such as Rusche and Kircheimer, who described the prison as an instrument that is used to control lower-class groups in order to transform them into a productive workforce in capitalist societies, have been accused of economic determinism. In other words, they have been accused of offering a reductionist account that identifies the economic imperatives of capitalism as the sole factor that explains the use of punishment in capitalist societies.

Moving on to Foucault's account of the role of punishment, critics argue that contrary to Foucault's position on the controlling effect of panoptic-style regulation, panoptic strategies create resistance rather than conformity, although it is acknowledged that Foucault himself recognised this (Welch, 2011). For Mathiesen (1997), an important error in Foucault's account of panoptic surveillance as a strategy that enables a few to observe many, is the failure to recognise that mass media outlets such as the television have made it possible for synoptic observation to emerge, in which the many are able to observe a few. The existence of panoptic and synoptic processes has created a 'viewer society' in which synoptic observation, not necessarily panoptic observation, serves as the means of creating self-regulating individuals who conform to the established norms of the capitalist order (Mathiesen, 1997: 215).

Other criticisms include the claim that Foucault's account is riddled with inaccuracies about historical and contemporary developments in punishments (Braithwaite, 2003: 6–8). In addition, revisionist accounts of punishment such as Foucault's, have been criticised *inter alia* for suggesting that domination pervades all social interactions and arrangements, for oversimplifying intricate developments, for overstating the instrumental role of punishment, for failing to acknowledge that there might be widespread approval for punishment (Garland, 1990, cited in Carrabine et al, 2009) and for overlooking the punishment of women (Carrabine et al, 2009). In addition, some critics reject what they perceive to be Foucault's somewhat impenetrable linguistic style. They have found it difficult to unravel his complex arguments or to relate them to real-life issues (see also Carrabine et al, 2009).

Although he drew on aspects of Foucault's work, Wacquant rejects some of his ideas. For example, Wacquant (2010) argues that, contrary to Foucault's supposition that the penitentiary (confinement institutions, including the prison) would recede in significance, the prison has resurfaced as the primary mode of punishment in the 20th century. Wacquant also takes issue with Foucault's key idea that disciplinary techniques are employed to transform those held in prison into norm-abiding bodies. Wacquant argues instead that the techniques are not applied in contemporary penal institutions for reasons that range from prison overcrowding and lack of resources to an overall lack of interest in, or hostility towards, rehabilitation. For Wacquant (2010: 205), 'the contemporary prison is geared toward brute neutralisation, rote retribution, and simple warehousing – by default if not by design'. He also maintains that, far from Foucault's predictions about the dispersal of carceral institutions and their disciplinary agenda across society, what has occurred has been the extension of the net of punishment (particularly the prison) to cover a specific segment of society – minority ethnic groups and those who are located on the lower levels of the social strata. Crimes of the powerful, such as the crimes committed by large corporations, have not been dragged into the net of punishment. Wacquant (2010: 205–6) observes that:

> At the dawn of the twenty-first century, America's urban (sub) proletariat lives in a 'punitive society,' but its middle and upper classes certainly do not. Similarly, efforts to import and adapt U.S.-style slogans and methods of law enforcement – such as zero tolerance policing, mandatory minimum sentencing, or boot camps for juveniles – in Europe have been trained on lower-class and immigrant offenders relegated in the defamed neighborhoods at the center of the panic over 'ghettoization' that has swept across the continent over the past decade.

Wacquant also rejects Foucault's claim that with the rise of the prison, punishment was removed from the public sphere. In Wacquant's view, the symbolic representation of law and order in mass media and other outlets has proliferated. For example, many television shows now depict the workings of the criminal justice system.

Furthermore, in his review of Garland's work, Wacquant (2009, 2010) identifies neo-liberalism, not late modernity, as the key factor that has sparked changes in contemporary social and penal policies. Wacquant also asserts that the phenomenal rise and expansion of the prison since the 20th century refutes Garland's contention that nation-states now increasingly acknowledge their weakened ability to address crime effectively. Wacquant (2009: 310) insists that the 'rapid turnings of the law-and-order-merry-go-round are an index of the reassertion of state sovereignty, not a sign of weakness'. He believes that the accounts of punishment presented by Foucault and Garland do not sufficiently explain the merger of penal and social policies into an instrument for regulating the poor in neo-liberal societies. He notes that this merger:

> is also not captured by Michel Foucault's vision of the 'disciplinary society' or by David Garland's notion of the 'culture of control', neither of which can account for the unforeseen timing, steep socioethnic selectivity, and peculiar organisational path of the abrupt turnaround in penal trends in the closing decades of the twentieth century. For the punitive containment of urban marginality through the simultaneous rolling back of the social safety net and the rolling out of the police-and-prison dragnet and their knitting together into a carceral–assitantial lattice is not the spawn of some broad societal trend – whether it be the ascent of 'biopower': or the advent of 'latemodernity' – but, at the bottom, an exercise in *state crafting*. (Wacquant, 2010: 210; emphasis in original)

Wacquant's work has also attracted criticisms. Primarily, critics argue that his account contains several generalisations (see, generally, Squires and Lea, 2012). For example, some argue that it is perhaps inaccurate of Wacquant to imply that social and penal policies in the US also apply in other jurisdictions, including Europe. Some critics cite statistics which indicate that such 'policy transfer' has not occurred in other neo-liberal jurisdictions, at least not to the degree that Wacquant suggests (Nelken, 2012). As we shall see below, this criticism has also been levelled at Garland's (1996; 2001) work. Others have pointed out that although Wacquant provides a very useful account, his account ignores feminist issues. Gelsthorpe (2010), for example, asserts that women represent a significant proportion of those affected by the advent of 'workfare' (Gelsthorpe, 2010; Heidensohn and Silvestri, 2012). It is also contended that Wacquant ignored the ability of the socio-economically marginalised targets of harsh penal and social policies to exercise their agency and resist the conditions that disadvantage them. Squires and Lea (2012: 13) point to what they describe as 'the relative lack, in Wacquant's work of a sustained focus on resistance. The precariat[17] remain largely as the objects of the penal state and its consequent victims'.

Just as some have criticised Wacquant for generalising his ideas, others point out that Garland's account of developments in the period he refers to as late modernity may not be relevant to many Western jurisdictions that have undergone the social and economic changes described by Garland. Some of these jurisdictions have not responded to the changes by opting for neo-liberalism, reduced welfarism and exclusionary penal punitiveness. They have also maintained much lower rates of crime and punishment (see also Tonry, 2004). Critics argue that although Garland generalises most of his ideas about the development of punishment to the UK and the US, these are quite different jurisdictions. Therefore, they are not always directly comparable. Similarly, De Giorgi's (2007; 2010) account of the political economy of punishment in advanced capitalist societies has been criticised because it implies that the changing dynamics of production and immigration, and the impact on punishment, have affected all jurisdictions equally (Lacey, 2008). In general, several accounts of punishment in Western societies have been criticised for not taking into account the specificities or exceptionalism of individual jurisdictions (Nelken, 2012). Field and Nelken (2010: 288) cite several comparative studies which demonstrate that 'the social construction of problems and solutions in relation to crime may be highly culturally specific, relating closely to the institutional relations and the social and political cultures of particular jurisdictions'.

Cohen's ideas about the dispersal of formal control have been criticised for focusing unduly on the role of alternatives to custody as forms of control/ discipline. Some argue that the most frequently imposed sanction – the fine – cannot be conceptualised as a mechanism that extends the disciplinary reaches of the state because the fine is not a disciplinary penalty (Bottoms, 1983). In addition, it has been suggested that the question of whether other alternatives, such as probation, are properly classified as 'disciplinary' sanctions is debatable. Such a classification overlooks the altruistic, rehabilitative and restorative objectives of such sanctions (Bottoms, 1983; Raynor and Vanstone, 2002). Nevertheless, events in the development of alternatives to punishment, particularly community-based sentences, appear to substantiate Cohen's ideas about the dispersal of discipline from formal penal settings to the wider community. For example, when community service was introduced in England and Wales by the Criminal Justice Act 1972, it was meant to serve as a tough alternative for people who would have received a custodial sentence. However, studies indicate that shortly after it was introduced, almost 50% of those sentenced to community service would not have received a custodial sentence (Pease et al, 1975). These people received a high-tariff punishment (albeit one that is based in the community) that placed them at risk of a custodial sentence if they violated the order or if they were reconvicted. Studies continue to suggest that high-tariff sanctions are being imposed on people convicted of first-time minor offences who would have received lower-tariff orders if the higher-tariff orders had not been introduced. In addition, it is argued that alternatives to imprisonment have failed to fulfil their objective of decarceration. According to Mair (2009: 179), 'If alternatives to custody are aimed at cutting the prison population, then their history is one of complete failure' (see also Mair et al, 2008). Mair's study of the impact of community-based alternatives to custody has found that 'There is no evidence that the orders are acting as alternatives to custody' (Mair, 2011: 229) and their failure to have a 'significant impact on reducing short-term custody and in tackling uptariffing is a major disappointment' (Mair and Mills, 2009: 49).

Abolitionists have been criticised for being idealistic and for advocating a transformative agenda that is perhaps almost impossible to translate into practical crime prevention strategies. There is also the argument that abolitionists are not able to provide an adequate account of how the public may be protected from people whose offending behaviour poses considerable risks. In addition, even advocates of penal abolitionism recognise that the radical penal reforms that they propose have to be accompanied by fundamental change to the dominant culture that shapes understandings of crime and justice in society. From this perspective, in order to actualise the abolitionists' agenda, it is necessary to move away from traditional notions of crime, punishment and justice as constructed within criminology and within the existing political and cultural order (see, generally, Tierney, 2009; De Haan, 2010).

Convict criminology has also attracted some criticisms. Newbold and Ross (2013) cite several limitations that, in their view, undermine the viability of convict criminology as a scholarly endeavour. They point out that of the two key areas of study convict criminologists engage in, which are activism and scholarly work to reform criminal justice, the former has been pursued more vigorously, almost to the detriment of the scholarly dimension. According to Newbold and Ross (2013), if convict criminology is to impact on academia and on policy, it is necessary to develop the scholarly dimension. That said, they do acknowledge that a small but growing number of PhD-educated convict criminologists are beginning to conduct high-quality ethnographic work that is not based solely on prison experience. Their work is bolstered by strong social science research methods.

Conclusion

Apart from convict criminology, which focuses mainly on the impact of imprisonment on those who have experienced the sanction, the critical perspectives that we have encountered in this chapter generally provide useful insights into wider structural factors that may shape punishment in Western societies. Their accounts differ on several grounds but, collectively, they suggest that punishment serves as a mechanism of control. It is used to control those whose actions are deemed to threaten the prevailing social and economic order. The Marx-inspired penal theorists go further to argue that punishment operates as a means of transforming target populations, particularly the lower classes, into productive workers. Some critical writers, such as Foucault, Garland, Wacquant and others, move their analyses of punishment away from primarily economic explanations. Nevertheless, they identify links between the socio-economic conditions of capitalist societies and punishment.

SUMMARY

- Scholars who examined the political economy of punishment in industrial capitalist societies argued that in capitalist societies, punishment helps to sustain the capitalist mode of production.
- Other writers who have explored the nature and form of punishment in contemporary Western societies have not focused exclusively on economic imperatives. Notwithstanding this, some espouse an instrumental view of punishment. They argue that punishment is used to control target populations in order to maintain the existing social order. The groups targeted for punishment are typically the poor and the dispossessed.
- Convict criminologists focus more closely on the impact of imprisonment. They reject traditional penal interventions, and propose alternative perspectives that take into account the lived reality of those who have experienced penal intervention, particularly imprisonment.

SAMPLE QUESTIONS

1. Do you agree that in capitalist societies, punishment serves as a means of controlling target populations?
2. Critically assess the claim that 'Every system of production tends to discover punishments, which correspond to its productive relationships' (Rusche and Kirchheimer, 2009: 5).

Notes

[1] Foucault (1977: 136/138) states that 'A body is docile that may be subjected, used, transformed and improved', and 'discipline produces subjected and practiced bodies, docile bodies'.

[2] We shall encounter the work of both penal theorists later in this chapter.

[3] Foucault's work on penal development has also been described variously as structuralist by some (Milovanovic, 2011a: 151).

[4] For Foucault, power can be viewed as the ability of one to use non-violent means to make an individual behave in a particular way (see also Downes and Rock, 2007).

[5] Foucault described discourse as the accepted knowledge or 'truth' of any area of life.

[6] Foucault appeared to be quite critical of criminology. He did not consider criminology to be a social science discipline that improves understandings of crime. He described criminology, as a discourse that bolsters surveillance and control. Indeed, Foucault avers that criminology grew as part of the human science disciplines that helped to organise and expand surveillance as a means of control (Carrabine et al, 2009). Alongside other disciplines, criminology was said to be central to the rise of the modern prison as an

instrument that can be used to monitor and discipline individuals whose behaviour was deemed to have deviated from the established norm.

[7] Foucault maintained that the role of discipline as an instrument of control was not restricted to the context of the prison. Discipline was subsequently deemed to be a useful means of controlling the masses in order to maintain the existing order.

[8] This concept is borrowed from Nietzsche's work on genealogical analysis, which opposes the idea of linear logic and embraces instead a route to knowledge that is marked by uncertainty, and the effort to unravel the dynamics that shape the exercise of power, including the power to construct dominant discourses, and the power to punish. Foucault (1977 : 23) described one of the aims of the text *Discipline and Punish* as 'a genealogy of the present scientificolegal complex from which the power to punish derives its bases, justifications and rules'.

[9] Foucault (1977) used Jeremy Bentham's panoptic prison design (the panopticon) as a metaphor for strategies that facilitate the constant but discreet observation of the subjects of control.

[10] Some scholars who do not subscribe to postmodernist thought have rejected the idea that there has been a shift towards a postmodern era, and argue instead that what has, in fact, occurred has been a continuation of the process of modernisation that began in the modern era (Cavadino, 2010). Therefore, for these scholars, the term 'late modernity' (not 'postmodernity') more accurately captures the period that has succeeded the modern period. These scholars have incorporated into their analyses of crime causation (Young, 1999) and penal developments (Garland, 2001) ideas about the impact of late-modern conditions, including the fall of expansionary Keynesian policies, and the emergence of an exclusionary free-market economy.

[11] Young (2009) considered the social and economic conditions of late modernity to be quite different. The emergence of neo-liberalism, or free-market liberalisation, the advent of globalisation, the rise of the finance industry, and the fall of the manufacturing industry have combined to create large swathes of socio-economically marginalised populations, particularly among the working class (Young, 2009).

[12] In his account of the advent of a culture of control, Garland acknowledged the impact of free-market ideology (neo-liberalism) on punishment. However, unlike Wacquant and others who have theorised the impact of neo-liberal policies on crime and punishment, Garland focused his account on the conditions of late modernity (see also Brown, 2011).

[13] Some point out that the emphasis on 'race', the demonisation of welfare dependants by the media and the constant publicity given to criminal offenders are all 'symbolic and ideological' dimensions of the penal regulation of the poor (Squires and Lea, 2012: 2). It is part of the effort to responsibilise the poor by inducing them to believe that they are

responsible for the condition they are in. It is also part of the effort to convince the 'middle classes and the powerful elites' that neo-liberalism promotes their safety and wellbeing (Squires and Lea, 2012). The poor are reconstituted (typically in racialised terms) as the threatening or dangerous 'other', who should be contained. It is argued that the state employs liberal strategies to secure the consent of the 'middle classes and upper classes' but uses coercive measures to secure the conformity of the precariat (Squires and Lea, 2012: 2). In Wacquant's (2010: 217) words:

> With the advent of the neoliberal government of social insecurity mating restrictive workfare and expansive prisonfare, however, it is not just the policies of the state that are illiberal but its very architecture. Tracking the coming and workings of America's punitive politics of poverty after the dissolution of the Fordist–Keynesian order and the implosion of the black ghetto reveals that neoliberalism brings about not the shrinking of government, but the erection of a centaur state, liberal at the top and paternalistic at the bottom, which presents radically different faces at the two ends of the social hierarchy: a comely and caring visage toward the middle and upper classes, and a fearsome and frowning mug toward the lower class.

[14] For Cavadino and Dignan (2006), the concept of political economy does not incorporate only economic policy. It includes cultural dimensions, political conflicts and institutions, and the individual- and group-level factors that shape experiences in society (Reiner, 2012b).

[15] These include measurable practices and quantifiable outputs (such as reconviction rates).

[16] Some British criminologists have also come together to discuss how to establish a convict criminology group in the UK (Aresti et al, 2011). Convict criminology generally has a longer history in the US than in Europe, where it still remains an emerging perspective (Richards, 2013).

[17] It has been argued that a fundamental consequence of neo-liberal ideals of enhanced criminal justice intervention and reduced social welfare provision in order to promote economic goals in an increasingly globalised world has been to create a precariat class. The precariat has been described as a group that is economically marginalised and constantly unemployed, or engaged in sporadic, insecure and very low-paid employment. They are described as the 'underclass' or the 'socially excluded', and they are typically the target and, indeed, the focus of 'penal and social policy' (Squires and Lea, 2012: 1–2).

Part Five
Conclusions

THIRTEEN

Future directions in critical criminology

Advanced Western societies, such as the US and the UK, have undergone several changes since the 1970s, when critical criminology became popular in the field of criminology. As mentioned earlier, some theorists argue that a shift has occurred towards what is variously conceptualised as postmodernity, high modernity or late modernity. Proponents of this view insist that the shift has been accompanied by social, economic and cultural conditions that have given rise to new forms of crime and crime control (see Garland, 1996, 2001; Young, 1999; Downes and Rock, 2011). As we saw in Chapter Twelve, the advent of neo-liberalism is a key feature of some contemporary Western societies, and several critical criminologists believe that it has had a profound impact on crime control. We have also observed (in Chapter Twelve) how critical scholars have responded to this shift and its alleged impact on crime control.

In addition, some argue that developments such as the 'war on drugs' in the US, the 'war on terror' on both sides of the Atlantic and the advent of globalisation now pose novel implications for crime and its control. Critical criminologists and others believe that the 'war on drugs', which began during the Reagan era, has contributed to the phenomenal expansion of the US prison population. They also aver that it has facilitated the selective mass incarceration of target populations, particularly young black men accused and convicted of non-violent drugs-related offences (Ross, 2009). Some have gone as far as to describe the 'war on drugs' as the new Jim Crow[1] (Alexander, 2010).

The 'war on terror' is the product of the 11 September 2001 ('9/11') attacks on the World Trade Centre in New York and '7/7' bombings in the UK. These and other acts have been linked to terrorism. They have provided the basis for the introduction of policies that, according to some, threaten to erode the rights traditionally preserved for accused persons and expose target populations to excessive policing and criminal justice intervention (Rose, 2004; Welch, 2012). Critical criminologists have responded to the 'war on terror' agenda by engaging in debates about human rights and the activities of the state (Cohen, 2001, 2006; Welch, 2012).

The advent of globalisation[2] is yet another factor that has been identified as a novel feature of contemporary societies. In response to the advent of globalisation, critical criminologists have addressed several key themes, including the rise of new forms of crime and new technologies of surveillance and control. For example, the phenomenal ascent of fast-speed internet access across the world has given rise to new forms of behaviour, such as cyber-bullying, cyber-racism and cybercrime (Jensen, 2007, cited in DeKeseredy and Dragiewicz, 2012). These are new forms of behaviour that can victimise large swathes of the population. However, developments in cyber-technology have increased not only rates of cyber-victimisation, but also the ease with which state governments are able to conduct electronic surveillance of citizens and others. Thus, critical criminologists maintain that the advent of globalisation has created new technologies of surveillance, communication and other forms of virtual interaction (DeKeseredy and Dragiewicz, 2012). Governments and large corporations access these new technologies for surveillance and control purposes. In addition, Nelken (2012) points out that crime has become more of an international or transnational problem than a local problem. Human trafficking (of illegal immigrants, children and body parts), the illegal dumping of waste, computer crime, money-laundering and tax evasion represent examples of crimes that occur, in large part, because of the increasing ease with which information and people traverse an increasingly globalised world. Collaborative international agencies have been established to manage the penal regulation of cross-border crimes, particularly cross-border organised crimes and the trafficking of women and children. These developments have opened up new areas of study for critical criminologists.

Critical criminology has evolved in different directions. However, one is inclined to agree with Downes and Rock (2011) that much of what is presented as 'new developments' in critical criminology appears to rehash the earlier theories. This is not to say that the more recent theories are theoretically useless. Far from it, the recent theories succeed in reviving increasingly marginalised narratives and in directing attention to new areas of concern in the field of critical criminology. Thus, although the foundational perspectives in critical criminology may have lost the popularity that they enjoyed in the 1970s, critical criminologists continue to expand on and theorise several themes they alluded to. These themes include the relative impunity that powerful groups who cause harm to others enjoy, and the relative vulnerability of the less powerful to criminalisation. Criminologists who study crimes of the powerful, and Zemiologists who highlight the harms that the powerful cause, cite significant statistics to highlight these issues. Green criminologists alert us to the impact of the harms that the powerful inflict on the environment and on less-powerful communities. Critical race theorists emphasise the embeddedness of power in what they consider to be socially constructed racial categories that disadvantage minority ethnic groups and render them more vulnerable to criminalisation. Feminist criminologists continue to draw attention to societal structures that confine women who offend, and women who are victimised, to positions of relative powerlessness. Cultural criminologists have revived labelling arguments, including the notion of media-generated moral panics about the activities of mainly less-powerful groups or subcultures. They have also revived earlier arguments that deviance and crime are infused with meaning. They emphasise that labelled deviants and legal authorities contribute to the social construction of crime. Therefore, they argue that to understand crime, it is important to study the meanings that give crime its existence. Critical criminologists who study the structural dimensions of punishment also alert us to the interrelatedness of structural factors and the nature of punishment. They assert that groups who suffer structural disadvantage because they experience social, economic and political marginalisation are the typical targets of surveillance and control by a penal system that seeks to maintain the existing order.

It is clear from the foregoing that, as noted earlier, contemporary Western societies have witnessed events that have created conditions that are rather different from the conditions of the 1960s, when the labelling tradition laid the foundations of critical criminology. However, this is not to say that these events and subsequent theories or ideas have 'outpaced' the theories of deviance (Downes and Rock, 2011: 346). Moreover, there appears to be limited evidence of attempts to innovate the field by developing new theories that can take these significant developments into account. As such, it is perhaps accurate to assert with Downes and Rock (2007) that critical criminology has not been 'overthrown or eclipsed' (as some critics will have it); rather, it 'is in the process of metamorphosis'. Therefore, it could be argued that although the contemporary perspectives restate several themes that were covered by the foundational perspectives, critical criminology has continued to flourish, expanding the themes introduced by the foundational perspectives and borrowing from key European thinkers along the way.

Notes

[1] As the conflict theorist George Vold observes, the so-called Jim Crow laws of the southern states were created (after the abolishment of slavery) in the 19th century to maintain racial segregation and a racial hierarchical structure that disadvantaged black people. Added to the formal oppressive control mechanisms embodied in Jim Crow laws were also informal control mechanisms that operated through a system of brutal repression. This found greatest expression in the activities of the white supremacist group known as the Ku Klux Klan. Sherman (2010: 380) aptly states that 'the rise of "Jim Crow" laws created an American Apartheid… Criminal law-making repressed black rights. Disenfranchisement flourished along with lynchings.'

[2] There are many definitions of globalisation. Broadly, it refers to a decrease in levels of physical and virtual distance among people across the world. Several means of maintaining close social, economic and political ties have proliferated in the face of widespread internet access and increased ease of travel across continents.

References

Adler, F. (1975) *Sisters in Crime: The Rise of the New Female Criminal*. New York, NY: McGraw-Hill. Akers, R. L. (1968) 'Problems in the Sociology of Deviance: Social Definitions and Behaviour'. *Social Forces*, 46, 455–465.

Akers, R. and Jennings, W. (2009) 'Social Learning Theory', in J. Miller (ed) *21st Century Criminology: A Reference Handbook*. Thousand Oaks, CA: Sage.

Akers, R.L. and Sellers, C.S. (2009) *Criminological Theories: Introduction, Evaluation, and Application* (5th edn). New York, NY: Oxford University Press.

Alexander, C. (2008) *(Re)thinking Gangs*. London: Runnymede Trust.

Alexander, M. (2010) *The New Jim Crow: Mass Incarceration in the Age of Colorblindness*. New York, NY: The New Press.

Almond, P. (2013) *Corporate Manslaughter and Regulatory Reform*. Basingstoke: Palgrave Macmillan.

Almond, P. and Colover, S. (2012) 'The Criminalization of Work-Related Death', *British Journal of Criminology* 52: 997–1016.

Alvesalo, A. and Tombs, S. (2002) 'Working for Criminalization of Economic Offending: Contradictions for Critical Criminology?', *Critical Criminology* 11(1): 21–40.

American Civil Liberties Union (2003) 'Inadequate Representation'. Available at: https://www.aclu.org/capital-punishment/inadequate-representation (accessed November 2013).

American Friends Service Committee (1971) *Struggle for Justice*. New York: Hill and Wang.

Anthony, A. (2011) 'Rewind TV: Shameless; Episodes; Kidnap and Ransom; Human Planet – Review', *The Telegraph Newspaper*. Available at: http://www.theguardian.com/tv-and-radio/2011/jan/16/episodes-matt-leblanc-tamsin-greig (accessed February 2011).

Aresti, A., Earle, R. and Darke, S. (2011) 'Convict Criminology in the United Kingdom: The Emergence of British Convict Criminology'. Available at: http://www.convictcriminology.org/pdf/CONVICTCRIMINOLOGY_UK.pdf (accessed July 2013).

Arrigo, B.A. (2001) 'Theoretical Concepts "Deconstruction" and "Praxis"', in E. McLaughlin and J. Muncie (eds) *The Sage Dictionary of Criminology*. London: Sage.

Ayres, I. and Braithwaite, J. (1992) *Responsive Regulation: Transcending the Deregulation Debate*. Oxford: Oxford University Press.

Bandura, A. (1977) *Social Learning Theory*. Englewood Cliffs, NJ: Prentice Hall.

Barak, G. (ed) (1991) *Crimes by the Capitalist State: An Introduction to State Criminality*. Albany, NY: State University of New York.

Barak, G. (2009) *Criminology: An Integrated Approach*. Lanham: Maryland: Rowman & Littlefield Publishers.

BBC News (2003) 'Minister Attacks Rap Lyrics'. Available at: http://news.bbc.co.uk/1/hi/wales/2752681.stm (accessed 14 March 2013).

Beck, U. (1992) *Risk Society: Towards a New Modernity*. London: Sage.

Becker, H. (1963) *Outsiders: Studies in the Sociology of Deviance*. New York, NY: The Free Press.

Becker, H. (1967) 'Whose Side Are We On?', *Social Problems* 14(3): 234–47.

Beckett, K. (1997) *Making Crime Pay: Law and Order in Contemporary American Politics*. Oxford: Oxford University Press.

Beirne, P. (2009) *Confronting Animal Abuse*. Plymouth: Rowman and Littlefield Publishers.

Bell, D. A. (2004) *Silent Covenants: Brown v Board of Education and the Unfulfilled Hopes for Social Reform Racial Justice*. New York: Oxford University Press.

Bernard, T.J. (1981) 'The Distinction between Conflict and Radical Criminology', *The Journal of Criminal Law and Criminology* 72(1): 362–79.

Bernburg, J.G., Krohn, M.D. and Rivera, C.J. (2006) 'Official Labelling, Criminal Embeddedness, and Subsequent Delinquency: A Longitudinal test of Labelling Theory', *Journal of Research in Crime and Delinquency* 43: 67–88.

Blau, J.R. and Blau, P.M. (1982) 'The Cost of Inequality: Metropolitan Structure and Violent Crime', *American Sociological Review* 47: 114–29.

Blumer, H.G. (1966) 'Sociological Implications of the Thought of George Herbert Mead'. *American Journal of Sociology*, 71(5): 535–44.

Blumer, H. (1969) *Symbolic Interactionism: Perspective and Method*. New Jersey, NJ: Prentice-Hall, Inc.

Blumstein, A., Cohen, J. and Nagin, D. (1978) *Deterrence and Incapacitation: Estimating the Effects of Criminal Sanctions on Crime Rates*, Washington DC, National Academy of Sciences.

Bonger, W.A. (1916) *Criminality and Economic Conditions*. Boston, MA: Little, Brown.

Bonger, W. A. (1969) *Criminality and Economic Conditions*. Bloomington: Indiana University Press. (Originally published in 1916).

Booth, D.E. (1978) 'Karl Marx on State Regulation of the Labour Process: The English Factory Acts', *Review of Social Economy* 36(2): 137.

Bottoms, A.E. (1983) 'Neglected Features of Contemporary Penal Systems', in D. Garland and P. Young (eds) *The Power to Punish*. London: Heinemann.

Bottoms, A.E. (1995) 'The Philosophy and Politics of Punishment and Sentencing', in C. Clarkson and R. Morgan (eds) *The Politics of Sentencing Reform*. Oxford: Oxford University Press.

Bottoms, A.E. (2012) 'Developing Socio-Spatial Criminology', in M. Maguire, R. Morgan and R. Reiner (eds) *Oxford Handbook of Criminology* (5th edn). Oxford: Oxford University Press.

Bowling, B. (1999) 'The Rise and Fall of New York Murder: Zero-Tolerance or Crack's Decline?', *British Journal of Criminology* 39(4): 531–54.

Bowling, B. and Phillips, C. (2012) 'Ethnicities, Racism, Crime and Criminal Justice', in M. Maguire, R. Morgan and R. Reiner (eds) *Oxford Handbook of Criminology* (5th edn). Oxford: Oxford University Press.

Box, S. (1983) *Power, Crime, and Mystification*. London: Tavistock.

Box, S. (1987) *Recession, Crime and Punishment.* London: Macmillan.

Braithwaite, J. (2003) 'What's Wrong with the Sociology of Punishment?'. *Theoretical Criminology.* 7, 1, 5–28.

Braithwaite, J. (1989) *Crime, Shame and Reintegration.* Cambridge: Cambridge University Press.

Braswell, M., Fuller, J., & Lozoff, B. (2001) *Corrections, Peacemaking, and Restorative Justice: Transforming Individuals and Institutions.* Cincinnati: Anderson Publishing.

Brightman, H. (2009) *Today's White-Collar Crime: Legal, Investigative, and Theoretical Perspectives.* New York, NY: Routledge.

Brisman, A. and South, N. (2013) 'Introduction: Horizons, Issues and Relationships in Green Criminology', in N. South and A. Brisman (eds) *The Routledge International Handbook of Green Criminology.* London: Routledge.

Brody, S.R. (1976) *The Effectiveness of Sentencing.* London: HMSO.

Brown, D. (2002) '"Losing My Religion": Reflections on Critical Criminology in Australia', in K. Carrington and R. Hogg (eds) *Critical Criminology.* London: Routledge.

Brown, D. (2011) 'The Global Financial Crisis: Neo-Liberalism, Social Democracy and Criminology', in M. Bosworth and C. Hoyle (eds) *What is Criminology?* Oxford: Oxford University Press.

Burgess, E. W. (1925) 'The Growth of the City: An Introduction to a Research Project', in R.E. Park, E. W. Burgess, R. D. McKenzie (eds) *The City.* Chicago: University of Chicago Press.

Burgess-Proctor, A. (2006) 'Intersections of Race, Class, Gender and Crime', *Feminist Criminology* 1: 27–47.

Burke, R. (2009) *An Introduction to Criminological Theory* (3rd edn). Cullompton: Willan.

Burns, J. H. and Hart, H. L. A. (2008) *A Comment on the Commentaries and A Fragment on Government (The Collected Works of Jeremy Bentham)* (reissue edn). Oxford: Oxford University Press.

Cain, M. (1990) 'Realist Philosophy and Standpoint Epistemologies or Feminist Criminology as a Successor Science', in L. Gelsthorpe and A. Morris (eds) *Feminist Perspectives in Criminology.* Milton Keynes: Open University Press.

Carlen, P. (1983) *Women's Imprisonment.* London: Routledge and Kegan Paul.

Carlen, P. (ed) (1985) *Criminal Women: Autobiographical Accounts.* Cambridge: Polity Press.

Carlen, P. (1988) *Women, Crime and Poverty.* Milton Keynes: Open University Press.

Carrabine, B., Iganski, P., Lee, M., Plummer, K. and South, N. (2009) *Criminology: A Sociological Introduction*, 2nd edn. London: Routledge.

Carrington, K. (2008) 'Critical Reflections in Feminist Criminologies', in T. Anthony and C. Cunneen (eds) *The Critical Criminology Companion.* Sydney: Hawkins Press.

Cavadino, M. (2010) 'Penology', in E. McLaughlin and T. Newburn (eds) *The Sage Handbook of Criminological Theory.* London: Sage.

Cavadino, M. and Dignan, J. (2006) *Penal Systems: A Comparative Approach*. London: Sage.

Cavadino, M. and Dignan, J. (2007) *The Penal System: An Introduction* (4th edn). London: Sage.

Chambliss, W.J. (1975) 'Toward a Political Economy of Crime', *Theory and Society* 2(1): 149–70.

Chambliss, W.J. (1989) 'State-Organised Crime', *Criminology* 27(2): 183–208.

Chambliss, W.J. and Seidman, R. (1971) *Law, Order, and Power*. Reading, MA: Addison-Wesley.

Cheliotis, L.K. and Liebling, A. (2006) 'Race Matters in British Prisons: Towards a Research Agenda', *British Journal of Criminology* 46(2): 286–317.

Chesney-Lind, M. and Morash, M. (2013) 'Transformative Feminist Criminology: A Critical Re-thinking of a Discipline', *Critical Criminology* 21: 287–304.

Christie, N. (1981) *Limits to Pain*. Oxford: Martin Robertson.

Christie, N. (2000) *Crime Control as Industry: Towards Gulags, Western Style* (3rd edn). London: Routledge.

Christie, N. (2004) *A Suitable Amount of Crime*. London: Routledge.

Clarke, J., Hall, S., Jefferson, S. and Roberts, B. (1976) 'Subcultures, Cultures and Class: A Theoretical Overview', in S. Hall and T. Jefferson (eds) *Resistance Through Rituals: Youth Subcultures in Post-War Britain*. London: Routledge.

Clarke, R. (1980) 'Situational Crime Prevention: Theory and Practice', *British Journal of Criminology* 20: 136–47.

Clarke, R. (1992) *Situational Crime Prevention*. New York: Harrow and Heston.

Cohen, A.K. (1955) *Delinquent Boys: The Culture of the Gang*. New York, NY: Free Press.

Cohen, L. and Felson, M. (1979) 'Social Change and Crime Rate Trends: A Routine Activity Approach', *American Sociological Review* 44(4): 588–608.

Cohen, S. (1971) 'Introduction', in S. Cohen (ed) *Images of Deviance*. Harmondsworth: Penguin.

Cohen, S. (1973) *Folk Devils and Moral Panics: The Creation of the Mods and Rockers*. Abingdon: Routledge.

Cohen, S. (1979) 'The Punitive City: Notes on the Dispersal of Social Control', *Contemporary Crisis* 3, 8, 339–63.

Cohen, S. (1985) *Visions of Social Control: Crime, Punishment and Classification*. Cambridge: Polity.

Cohen, S. (1988) *Against Criminology*. New Brunswick: Transaction Publishers.

Cohen, S. (1993) 'Human Rights and the Crimes of the State: The Culture of Denial', *Australian and New Zealand Journal of Criminal Justice* 26(2): 97–115.

Cohen, S. (1995) 'State Crimes of Previous Regimes: Knowledge, Accountability and the Policing of the Past', *Law and Social Enquiry* 20(1): 7–50.

Cohen, S. (2001) *States of Denial: Knowing about Atrocities and Suffering*. Cambridge: Polity.

Cohen, S. (2006) 'Neither Honesty nor Hypocrisy: The Legal Reconstruction of Torture', in T. Newburn and P. Rock (eds) *Politics of Crime Control: Essays in Honour of David Downes*. Oxford: Oxford University Press.

Cohen, L. and Felson, M. (1979) 'Social Change and Crime Rate Trends: A Routine Activity Approach'. *American Sociological Review*. 44, 588-608.

Cohen, S. and Young, J. (1973) *The Manufacture of News: Deviance, Social Problems and the Mass Media*. Reprinted Edition. London: Constable.

Coleman, R., Sim, J., Tombs, S. and Whyte, D. (2009) 'Introduction: State, Power and Crime', in R. Coleman, J. Sim, S. Tombs and D. Whyte (eds) *State Power and Crime*. London: Sage.

Comack, E. (1999) 'Producing Feminist Knowledge: Lessons from Women in Trouble', *Theoretical Criminology* 3(3): 287–306.

Connell, R.W. (1995) *Masculinities*. Berkeley, CA: University of California Press.

Connell, R. (2000) *The Men and the Boys*. Cambridge: Polity.

Cook, P.J. (1980) 'Research in Criminal Deterrence: Laying the groundwork for the Second Decade', in N. Morris and M. Tonry, *Crime and Justice: An Annual Review of Research*, 2, 211-268.

Cooper, A.D., Durose, M.R. and Synder, H.N. (2014) 'Recidivism of Prisoners Released in 30 States in 2005: Patterns from 2005 to 2010', Bureau of Justice Statistics. Available at: http://www.bjs.gov/index.cfm?ty=pbdetail&iid=4987

Corston Report (2007) *Review of Women with Particular Vulnerabilities in the Criminal Justice System*. London: Home Office.

Crawford, A. and Evans, K. (2012) 'Crime Prevention and Community Safety', in M. Maguire, R. Morgan and R. Reiner (eds) *Oxford Handbook of Criminology* (5th edn). Oxford: Oxford University Press.

Craine, S. (1997) 'The "Black Magic Roundabout"', in R. Macdonald (ed) *Youth, The Underclass and Social Exclusion*. London: Routledge.

Crawford, A., Jones, T., Woodhouse, T. and Young, J. (1990) *The Second Islington Crime Survey*. London: Middlesex Polytechnic.

Crenshaw, K., Gotanda, N., Peller, G. and Thomas, K. (1995) 'Introduction', in K. Crenshaw, N. Gotanda, G. Peller, and K. Thomas (eds) *Critical Race Theory: the Key Writings that Formed the Movement*. New York: Free Press.

Critcher, C. (1993) 'Structures, Cultures and Biographies', in S. Hall and T. Jefferson (eds) *Resistance Through Rituals: Youth Subcultures in Post-War Britain*. London: Routledge.

Croall, H. (1989) 'Who is the White-Collar Criminal?'. *British Society of Criminology*. 29, 2, 157-174.

Croall, H. (2001) *Understanding White-Collar Crime*. Buckingham: Open University Press.

Cullen, F.T. and Agnew, R. (2011) *Criminological Theory: Past to Present* (4th edn). Oxford: Oxford University Press.

Currie, D. H. (1991) 'Confronting Woman Abuse: A Brief Overview of the Left Realist Approach', in B.D. MacLean and D. Milovanovic (eds) *New Directions in Critical Criminology: Left Realism, Feminism, Postmodernism and Peacemaking*. Vancouver: The Collective Press.

Currie, E. (2009) *The Roots of Danger: Violent Crime in Global Perspective*. Harlow: Prentice Hall.

Currie, E. (2005) *The Road to Whatever: Middle-Class Culture and the Crisis of Adolescence*. New York: Metropolitan Book.

Currie, E. (2010) 'Plain Left Realism: An Appreciation and Some Thoughts for the Future', *Crime, Law and Social Change* 54: 111–24.

Daly, K. (1994) 'Gender and Punishment Disparity', in M. Myers and G. Bridges (eds) *Inequality, Crime, and Social Control*. Boulder, CO: Westview.

Daly, K. (2010) 'Feminist Perspectives in Criminology: A Review with Gen Y in Mind', in E. McLaughlin and T. Newburn (eds) *The Sage Handbook of Criminological Theory*. London: Sage.

Daly, K. and Chesney-Lind, M. (1988) 'Feminism and Criminology', *Justice Quarterly* 5: 497–538.

Daly, K. and Stephens, D.J. (1995) 'The "Dark Figure" of Criminology: Towards a Black and Multi-Ethnic Feminist Agenda for Theory and Research', in N. Hahn Rafter and F. Heidensohn (eds), *International Feminist Perspectives in Criminology: Engendering a Discipline*. Milton Keynes: Open University Press.

Davies, P.A. (2014) 'Green Crime and Victimization: Tensions between Social and Environmental Justice', *Theoretical Criminology* 8, 3: 300–16.

De Giorgi, A. (2007) 'Toward a Political Economy of Post-Fordist Punishment', *Critical Criminology* 15: 243–65.

De Giorgi, A. (2010) 'Immigration Control, Post-Fordism, and Less Eligibility. A Materialist Critique of the Criminalization of Immigrants Across Europe'. *Punishment and Society*. 12, 2, 147-167.

De Haan, W. (1990) *The Politics of Redress: Crime, Punishment and Penal Abolition*. London: Unwin Hyman.

De Haan, W. (1991) '"Abolitionism and Crime Control": A Contradiction in Terms', in K. Stenson and D. Cowell (eds) *The Politics of Crime Control*. London: Sage.

De Haan, W. (2010) 'Abolition and Crime Control'. Available at: http://nomoreprison.blogspot.co.uk/2010/12/abolition-and-crime-control-willem-de.html

DeKeseredy, W.S. (2010) *Contemporary Critical Criminology*. Abingdon: Routledge.

DeKeseredy, W.S. and Dragiewicz, M. (2012) 'Criminology: Past, Present, and Future', in W.S. DeKeseredy and M. Dragiewicz (eds) *The Routledge Handbook of Critical Criminology*. Abingdon: Routledge.

DeKeseredy, W.S. and Schwartz, M.D. (2010) 'Friedman Economic Policies, Social Exclusion, and Crime: Toward a Gendered Left Realist Subcultural Theory', *Crime, Law and Social Change* 54: 159–70.

DeKeseredy, W.S. and Schwartz, M.D. (2012) 'Left Realism', in W.S. DeKeseredy and M. Dragiewicz (eds) *The Routledge Handbook of Critical Criminology*. Abingdon: Routledge.

Delgado, R. and Stefancic, J. (2012) *Critical Race Theory: An Introduction*. New York, NY: New York University Press.

Denzin, N.K. (1992) *Symbolic Interactionism and Cultural Studies: The Politics of Interpretation*. Oxford and Cambridge, MA: Blackwell Publishers.

Dobash, R.E. (1979) *Violence Against Wives: A Case against the Patriarchy*. Free Press.

Dobash, R.E. and Dobash, R.P. (1998) *Rethinking Violence against Women*. Thousand Oaks, CA: Sage Publications.

Dobash, R.E. and Dobash, R.P (2004) 'Women's Violence to Men in Intimate Relationships: Working on a Puzzle. *British Journal of Criminology*, 44, 3, 324–349.

Doob A.N. and Webster, C.M. (2003) 'Sentence Severity and Crime: Accepting the Null Hypothesis', *Crime and Justice: A Review of Research*, Vol 30, 143–195.

Downes, D. and Rock, P. (2007) *Understanding Deviance* (5th edn). Oxford: Oxford University Press.

Downes, D. and Rock, P. (2011) *Understanding Deviance* (6th edn). Oxford: Oxford University Press.

Dutton, D.G. (2006) *Rethinking Domestic Violence*. Vancouver, British Columbia: University of British Columbia Press.

Eaton, M. (1986) *Justice for Women?* Milton Keynes: Open University Press. Edgar, K and Martin, C (2004) *Perceptions of Race and Conflict: Home Office Online Study 11/04*. London: Home Office.

Emsley, C. (1997) 'Crime and Crime Control', in M. Maguire, R. Morgan and R. Reiner (eds) *The Oxford Handbook of Criminology*. Oxford: Oxford University Press.

Engels, F. (1845/1975) '*The Conditions of the Working Class in England,*' in K. Marx and F. Engels (eds) *Collected Works, Volume 4*. London: Lawrence and Wishart.

Ericson, R.V. and Haggerty, K.D. (1997) *Policing the Risk Society*. Oxford: Clarendon Press.

Erikson, K. (1962) 'Notes on the Sociology of Deviance'. Available at: https://www.soc.umn.edu/~uggen/Erikson_SP_63.pdf (accessed June 2013).

Faber, D.A. and Sherry, S. (1997) *Beyond all Reason: The Radical Assault on Truth in American Law*. New York: Oxford University Press.

Feeley, M. and Simon, J. (1992) 'The New Penology: Emerging Strategy of Corrections and its Implications', *Criminology* 30(4): 449–74.

Feilzer, M. and Hood, R. (2004) *Differences or Discrimination – Minority Ethnic Young People in the Youth Justice System*. London: Youth Justice Board.

Felson, M. and Clarke, R. (1998) *Opportunity Makes the Thief: Practical Theory for Crime Prevention*. Police Research Series, Paper 98, Policing and Reducing Crime Unit. London: Home Office.

Ferrell, J. (1996) *Crimes of Style: Urban Graffiti and the Politics of Criminality*. Boston, MA: Northeastern.

Ferrell, J. (1998) 'Against the Law: Anarchist Criminology', *Social Anarchism* 25: 5–23.

Ferrell, J. (1999) 'Cultural Criminology', *Annual Review of Sociology* 25: 395–418.

Ferrell, J. (2005) 'Crime and Culture', in C. Hale, K. Hayward, A. Wahidin and E. Wincup (eds) *Criminology*. Oxford: Oxford University Press.

Ferrel, J. (2006) 'Cultural Criminology', in G. Ritzer (ed) *Blackwell Encyclopaedia of Sociology*, London: Blackwell.

Ferrell, J. (2010) 'Cultural Criminology: The Loose Cannon', in E. McLaughlin and T. Newburn (eds) *The Sage Handbook of Criminological Theory*. London: Sage.

Ferrell, J. (2013) 'Cultural Criminology and the Politics of Meaning', *Critical Criminology* 21: 257–71.

Ferrell, J., Hayward, K. and Young, J. (2008) *Cultural Criminology: An Invitation*. London: Sage.

Ferri, E. (1901) *The Positive School of Criminology* (English edn, published in 1908 by C.H. Kerr and Co, Chicago).

Field, S. and Nelken, D. (2010) 'Reading and Writing Youth Justice in Italy and (England and) Wales'. *Punishment and Society* 12, 3: 287–308.

Fionda, J. (2000) 'New Managerialism, Credibility and the Sanitisation of Criminal Justice', in P. Green and A. Rutherford (eds) *Criminal Policy in Transition*. Oxford: Hart Publishing.

Flavin, J. (2001) 'Feminism for the Mainstream Criminologist: An Invitation', *Journal of Criminal Justice* 29: 271–85.

Foucault, M. (1977) *Discipline and Punish: The Birth of the Prison*. London: Allen lane.

Friedrichs, D.O. (1991) 'Introduction: Peacemaking Criminology in a World Filled with Conflict', in B. MacLean and D. Milovanovic (eds) *New Directions in Critical Criminology: Left Realism, Feminism, Postmodernism and Peacemaking*. Vancouver: The Collective Press.

Friedrichs, D.O. (2002) 'Occupational Crime, Occupational Deviance, and Workplace Crime: Sorting Out the Difference', *Criminology and Criminal Justice* 2, 3: 243–55.

Friedrichs, D.O. (2009) Critical Criminology', in J.M. Miller (ed) *21st Century Criminology: A Reference Handbook, Volume 1*. London: Sage.

Friedrichs, D.O. and Rothe, D.L. (2012) 'Crimes of the Powerful: White-Collar Crime and Beyond', in W.S. DeKeseredy and M. Dragiewicz (eds) *The Routledge Handbook of Critical Criminology*. Abingdon: Routledge.

Garfinkel, H. (1991) *Studies in Ethnomethodology*. Cambridge, Polity Press.

Garland, D. (2003) 'Penal Modernism and Post-Modernism', in T.G. Bloomberg and S. Cohen (eds) *Punishment and Social Control* (2nd edn). New York: Aldine de Gruyter, pp 181–209.

Garland, D. (1996) 'The Limits of the Sovereign State: Strategies of Crime Control in Contemporary Society', *British Journal of Criminology* 36(4): 445–71.

Garland, D. (2001) *The Culture of Control: Crime and Social Order in Contemporary Society*. Oxford: Oxford University Press.

Gelsthorpe, G. 1997) 'Feminism and Criminology', in M. Maguire, R. Morgan and R. Reiner (eds) *The Oxford Handbook of Criminology* (2nd edn). Oxford: Oxford University Press.

Gelsthorpe, G. (2002) 'Feminism and Criminology', in M. Maguire, R. Morgan and R. Reiner (eds) *The Oxford Handbook of Criminology* (3rd edn). Oxford: Oxford University Press.

Gelsthorpe, L. (2004) 'Female Offending: A Theoretical Overview', in G. McIvor (ed) *Women Who Offend*. London: Jessica Kingsley.

Gelsthorpe, L. (2006) 'Women and Criminal Justice: Saying it Again, Again and Again', *Howard Journal of Criminal Justice* 45(4): 421–4.

Gelsthorpe, L. and Morris, A. (1988) 'Feminism and Criminology in Britain', *British Journal of Criminology* 28, 2: 93–110.

Genders, E. and Player, E. (1989) *Race Relations in Prisons*. Oxford: Clarendon Press.

Gibbs, J. P. (1966) 'Conceptions of Deviant Behaviour: The Old and the New'. Pacific Sociological Review, 9, 1, 9-14.

Gibbs, C., Gore, M.L., McGarrell, E.F. and Rivers, L. (2010) '"Introducing Conservation Criminology": Towards Interdisciplinary Scholarship on Environmental Crimes and Risks', *British Journal of Criminology* 50(1): 124–44.

Gibson, M. (2002) *Born to Crime: Cesare Lombroso and the Origins of Biological Criminology*. Santa Barbara, CA: Praeger.

Giddens, A. (1991) *Modernity and Self-Identity: Self and Society in the Late Modern Age*. Stanford, CA: Stanford University Press.

Glueck, S. and Glueck, E. (1950) *Unravelling Juvenile Delinquency*. New York, NY: Harper and Row.

Godfrey, L. (2012) 'Foucault's Interpretation of Modernity, October 26, 2012', e-*international relations*. http://www.e-ir.info/2012/10/26/foucaults-interpretation-of-modernity/ (accessed June 2014).

Goffman, E. (1959) *The Presentation of Self in Everyday Life*. Garden City, NY: Doubleday.

Goffman, E. (1961) *Asylums: Essays on the Social Situation of Mental Patients and Other Inmates*. Harmondsworth: Penguin.

Goode, E. and Ben-Yehuda, N. (1994) *Moral Panics: The Social Construction of Deviance*. Cambridge, MA: Blackwell.

Gordon, D. (1973) 'Capitalism, Class, and Crime in America'. *Crime and Delinquency*. 19, 2, 163–86.

Gottfredson, M. and Hirschi, T. (1990) *A General Theory of Crime*. Stanford, CA: Stanford University Press.

Gouldner, A. (1973) 'The Sociologist as Partisan: Sociology and the Welfare State', in A. Gouldner (ed) *For Sociology*. London: Allen Lane (essay first published in *The American Sociologist* [May 1968] 3: 103–16).

Gramsci, A. (1971) *Selections from the Prison Notebooks of Antonio Gramsci*. New York: International.

Green, P. and Ward, T. (2004) *State Crime*. London: Pluto Press.

Greenberg, D.F. (ed) (1993) *Crime and Capitalism: Readings in Marxist Criminology* (2nd edn). Philadelphia, PA: Temple University Press.

Greer, C. and Reiner, R. (2012) 'Mediated Mayhem: Media, Crime, Criminal Justice', in M. Maguire, R. Morgan and R. Reiner (eds) *The Oxford Handbook of Criminology* (5th edn). Oxford: Oxford University Press.

Groves, C. (1991) 'Us and Them: Reflections on the Dialectics of Moral Hate', in B. D. Maclean and D. Milovanovic (eds) *New Directions in Critical Criminology*. Vancouver: Collective Press.

Guardian Newspaper (2005) 50 Cent Film Posters Withdrawn'. Available at: http://www.theguardian.com/film/2005/oct/31/news1 (accessed 14 March 2013).

Hale, C. (2005) 'Economic Marginalisation and Social Exclusion', in C. Hale, K. Hayward, A. Wahidin, and E. Wincup (eds) *Criminology*. Oxford: Oxford University Press.

Hall, S. (1988) *The Hard Road to Renewal: Thatcherism and the Crisis of the Left*. London: Verso.

Hall, S., Critcher, C., Jefferson, T., Clarke, J. and Roberts, B. (1978) *Policing the Crisis: Mugging the State and Law and Order* (Critical Social Studies). London: Macmillan.

Hall, S. and Winlow, S. (2007) 'Cultural Criminology and Primitive Accumulation: A Formal Introduction for Two Strangers who should really become more Intimate'. *Crime, Media, Culture*. 3, 82-90.

Halsey M. (2004) 'Against "Green" Criminology. *British Journal of Criminology*. 44, 833-853.

Harcourt, B. E. and Ludwig, J. (2006) 'Broken Windows: New Evidence from New York City and a Five-City Social Experiment'. *University of Chicago Law Review*. 73, 271-320.

Harding, S. (1986) *The Science Question in Feminism*. Milton Keynes: Open University Press.

Harding, S. (1987) *Feminism and Methodology*. Milton Keynes: Open University Press.

Harding, S. (1991) *Whose Science? Whose Knowledge?* Ithaca, NY: Cornell University Press.

Harding, S. (1993) 'Rethinking Standpoint Epistemology: What is "Strong Objectivity"?', in L. Alcoff and E. Potter (eds) *Feminist Epistemologies*. London: Routledge.

Hartmann, H. (1981) 'The Unhappy Marriage of Marxism and Feminism: Towards a More Progressive Union', in V.D. Lippit (ed) *Radical Political Economy: Explorations in Alternative Economic Analysis*. M.E. Sharpe.

Hawkins, K. (1984) *Environment and Enforcement: Regulation and the Social Definition of Pollution*. Oxford: Oxford University Press and Clarendon.

Hayward, K.J. (2004) *City Limits: Crime, Consumer Culture and the Urban Experience*. London: Glasshouse Press.

Hayward, K.J. and Young, J. (2004) 'Cultural Criminology: Some Notes on the Script', Special Edition of the *International Journal Theoretical Criminology* 8(3): 259–85.

Hayward, K.J. and Young, J. (2012) 'Cultural Criminology', in M. Maguire, R. Morgan and R. Reiner (eds) *The Oxford Handbook of Criminology* (5th edn). Oxford: Oxford University Press.

Heidensohn, F. (1992) *Women in Control? The Role of Women in Law Enforcement*. Oxford: Oxford University Press.

Heidensohn, F. (1996) *Women and Crime* (2nd edn). Basingstoke: Macmillan.

Heidensohn, F. (2012) 'The Future of Feminist Criminology', *Crime, Media and Culture* 8(2): 123–34.

Heidensohn, F. and Silvestri, M. (2012) 'Gender and Crime', in M. Maguire, R. Morgan and R. Reiner (eds) *Oxford Handbook of Criminology* (5th edn). Oxford: Oxford University Press.

Hernstein, and Murray, C. (1994) *The Bell Curve: Intelligence and Class Structure n American Society*. New York: Simon and Schuster.

Her Majesty's Inspectorate of Constabulary (2014) *Everyone's Business: Improving the Police Response to Domestic Abuse*. Available at: https://www.justiceinspectorates. gov.uk/hmic/wp-content/uploads/2014/04/improving-the-police-response-to-domestic-abuse.pdf (accessed July 2014).

Henry, S. and Einstadter, W.J. (2006) *Criminological Theory: An Analysis of its Underlying Assumptions* (2nd edn). Lanham: Maryland: Rowman & Littlefield Publishers.

Hester (2013) 'From Report to Court: Rape Cases and the Criminal Justice System in the North East', Centre for Gender and Violence Research, School for Policy Studies, University of Bristol and Northern Rock Foundation.

Hillyard, P., Pantazis, C., Tombs S. and Gordon, D. (2004) *Beyond Criminology: Taking Crime Seriously*. London: Pluto Books.

Hillyard, P. and Tombs, S. (2005) 'Beyond Criminology?', in P. Hillyard, C. Pantazis, S. Tombs, D. Gordon and D. Dorling (eds) *Criminal Obsessions: Why Harm Matters More than Crime* (2nd edn). London: Centre for Crime and Justice Studies.

Hillyard, P. and Tombs, S. (2007) 'From Crime to Social Harm', *Crime, Law and Social Change* 48: 9–25.

Hirsch, T. (1969) *The Causes of Delinquency*. Berkeley, CA: University of California Press.

Hirst, P. (1975) 'Marx and Engels on Law, Crime and Morality', in I. Taylor, P. Walton and J. Young (eds) *Critical Criminology*. London: Routledge and Kegan Paul.

Hollin, C.R. (1989) *Psychology and Crime. An Introduction to Criminological Psychology*. London: Routledge.

Hood, R. (1992) *Race and Sentencing: A Study in the Crown Court*. Oxford: Clarendon Press.

Hooker, E. (1957) 'The Adjustment of the Male Overt Homosexual', *Journal of Projective Techniques*. XXI, 18–31.

Hooker, E. (1963) 'Male homosexuality', in N.L. Farberow (ed.), *Taboo Topics*. New York: Atherton.

hooks, b. (1981) *Ain't I a Woman: Black Women and Feminism*. Cambridge Massachusetts: South End Press.

Hoare, Q. and Nowell–Smith G. (2005) *Selections from the Prison Notebooks of Antonio Gramsci*. Norfolk: Biddles Ltd.

Hudson, B. (1989) 'Discrimination and Disparity: The Influence of Race on Sentencing', *New Community* 16: 23–34.

Hudson, B. (2003) *Justice in the Risk Society*. London: Sage.

Hudson, B. and Bramhall, G. (2005) 'Assessing the "Other": Constructions of "Asianness" in Risk Assessments by Probation Officers', *British Journal of Criminology* 45: 721–40.

Hulsman, L. (1986) 'Critical Criminology and the Concept of Crime', *Contemporary Crises* 10(2): 62–80.

Hutter, B. (2001) *Regulation and Risk: Occupational Health and Safety on the Railways*. Oxford: Oxford University Press.

Ignatieff, M. (1978) *A Just Measure of Pain: Penitentiaries in the Industrial Revolution, 1750–1850*. New York: Pantheon Books.

International Labour Organisation (n.d.) http://ilo.org/global/topics/safety-and-health-at-work/lang--en/index.htm (accessed February 2014).

Jefferson, T. (1975) 'Cultural Responses of the Teds: The Defence of Space and Status', in S. Hall and T. Jefferson (eds) *Resistance Through Rituals*. London: Hutchinson.

Jones, T., Maclean, B. and Young, J. (1986) *The Islington Crime Survey*. Aldershot: Gower.

Katz, J. (1988) *Seductions of Crime: Moral and Sensual Attractions in Doing Evil*. New York: Basic Books.

Kelling, G.L. and Coles, C. (1996) *Fixing Broken Windows: Restoring Order and Reducing Crime in Our Communities*. New York: Free Press.

Kelling, G.L. and Wilson, J.Q. (1982) 'Broken Windows: The Police and Neighborhood Safety'. Available at: http://www.theatlantic.com/magazine/archive/1982/03/broken-windows/304465/ (accessed January 2011).

Kinsey, R., Lea, J. and Young, J. (1986) *Losing the Fight against Crime*. Oxford: Blackwell.

Kitsuse, J. (1962) 'Societal Reaction to Deviant Behaviour', *Social Problems* 9: 247–56.

Klinefelter, H.F., Reifenstein, E.C. and Albright, F. (1942) 'Syndrome Characterized by Gynecomastia Aspermatogenesis without A-Leydigism and Increased Excretion of Follicle Stimulating Hormone', *Journal of Clinical Endocrinology & Metabolism* 2: 615–27.

Kramer, R., Michalowski, R. and Kauzlarich, D. (2002) 'The Origins and Development of the Concept and Theory of State-Corporate Crime', *Crime and Delinquency* 48(2): 263–82.

Kretschmer, E. (1936) *Physique and Character: An Investigation of the Nature of Constitution and the Theory of Temperament.* Abingdon: Routledge.

Lacey, N. (2008) *The Prisoner's Dilemma: Political Economy and Punishment in Contemporary Democracies.* Cambridge: Cambridge University Press.

Ladson-Billings, G. (1998) 'Just What is Critical Race Theory and what's it Doing in a Nice Field like Education?', *International Journal of Qualitative Studies in Education,* 11, 1, 7–24.

Ladson-Billings, G. and Tate, W. F. (2006) 'Towards a Critical Race Theory of Education' in Dixson, A and Rousseau, C. (eds) *Critical Race Theory in Education: All God's Children Got a Song.* New York: Routledge

Lea, J. and Young, J. (1984) *What Is To Be Done About Law and Order: Crisis in the Eighties.* Harmondsworth: Penguin.

Lea, J. and Young, J. (1993) *What Is To Be Done About Law and Order: Crisis in the Eighties* (revised edn). London: Pluto Press.

Lea, J. and Young, J. (1996) 'Relative Deprivation', in J. Muncie, E. MacLaughlin and M. Langan (eds) *Criminological Perspectives – A Reader.* London: Sage Publications.

Lemert, E. (1951) *Social Pathology: A Systematic Approach to the Study of Sociopathic Behavior.* New York, NY: McGraw-Hill.

Lemert, E. (1972) *Human Deviance, Social Problems and Social Control* (2nd edn). Englewood Cliffs, NJ: Prentice Hall.

Levit, N. (1999) 'Critical of Race Theory: Race, Reason, Merit and Civility', *Georgetown Law Journal* 87(3): 795–822.

Liazos, A. (1972) 'The Poverty of the Sociology of Deviance: Nuts, Sluts, and Perverts', *Social Problems* 20(1): 103–20.

Liebling, A. and Crewe, B. (2012) Prison Life, Penal Power and Prison Effects', in in M. Maguire, R. Morgan and R. Reiner (eds) *Oxford Handbook of Criminology.* Oxford: Oxford University Press.

Lynch, M.J. (1990) 'The Greening of Criminology: A Perspective on the 1990s', *Critical Criminology* 2(3/4): 11–12.

Lynch, M.J. (2011) *Critical Criminology: Oxford Bibliographies Online Research Guide.* Oxford: Oxford University Press.

Lynch, M.J. (2013) 'Reflections on Green Criminology and its Boundaries: Comparing Environmental and Criminal Victimization and Considering Crime from an Eco-City Perspective', in N. South and A. Brisman (eds) *The Routledge International Handbook of Green Criminology.* Abingdon: Routledge.

Lynch, M.J. and Groves, W.B. (1986) *A Primer in Radical Criminology.* Albany, NY: Harrow and Heston.

Lynch, M.J. and Stretesky, P.B. (2003) 'The Meaning of Green: Contrasting Criminological Perspectives', *Theoretical Criminology* 7(2): 217–38.

Lynch, M.J. and Stretesky, P.B. (2007) 'Green Criminology in the United States', in P. Beirne and N. South (eds) *Issues in Green Criminology: Confronting Harms against Environments, Humanity and other Animals.* Cullompton: Willan.

Lynch, M.J., Burns, R. and Stretesky, P. (2010) 'Global Warming and State-Corporate Crime: The Politicalization of Global Warming under the Bush Administration', *Crime, Law and Social Change* 54: 213–39.

Lynch, M.J., Long, M.A, Barrett, K.I. and Stretesky, P.B. (2013) 'Is it a Crime to Produce Ecological Disorganization?', *British Journal of Criminology* 53: 997–1016.

Macdonald, R. (1997) 'Youth, Social Exclusion and the Millennium', in R. Macdonald (ed) *Youth, The Underclass and Social Exclusion*. London: Routledge.

Macdonald, R. (2008) *Disconnected Youth? Social Exclusion, the 'Underclass' and Economic Marginality'*. Social Work and Society. 6, 2, 236-248.

MacKinnon, C.A. (1991) 'Difference and Dominance: On Sex Discrimination', in K.T. Bartlett and R. Kennedy (eds), *Feminist Legal Theory*. Boulder, CO: Westview.

Macpherson, W. (1999) 'The Stephen Lawrence Inquiry. Report of an Inquiry by Sir William Macpherson of Cluny (Macpherson Report)', Cm. 4262-I.

Maidment, M.R. (2006) 'Feminist Perspectives in Criminology', in W.S. DeKeseredy and B. Perry (eds) *Advancing Critical Criminology: Theory and Application*. Lanham, Maryland: Lexington Books.

Mair, G. (2009) 'Community Sentences', in Hucklesby, A. and Wahidin, A. (eds) *Criminal Justice*. Oxford: Oxford University Press.

Mair, G. (2011) 'The Community Order in England and Wales: Policy and Practice', *Probation Journal* 58: 215–32.

Mair, G. and Mills, H. (2009) *The Community Order and the Suspended Sentence Order Three Years On: The Views and Experiences of Probation Officers and Offenders.* London: Kings College, Centre for Crime and Justice Studies.

Mair, G., Cross, N. and Taylor, S. (2008) *The Community Order and the Suspended Sentence Order*. London: Centre for Crime and Justice Studies.

Manis, J.G. and Meltzer, B.N. (1972) *Symbolic Interaction: A Reader in Social Psychology* (2nd edn). Boston: Allyn & Bacon.

Mann, K. (1992) *The Making of an English Underclass? The Social Divisions of Welfare and Labour*. Milton Keynes: Open University Press.

Martin, J., Kautt, P. and Gelsthorpe, L. (2009) 'What Works for Women? A Comparison of Community-Based General Offending Programme Completion'. *British Journal of Criminology*, 49, 879-899.

Martinson, R. (1974) 'What Works? Questions and Answers about Prison Reform', *The Public Interest* 35: 22–54.

Marx, K. (1842/1975) 'Debates on the Law of Theft of Wood', in K. Marx and F. Engels (eds) *Collected Works, Volume 1*. London: Lawrence and Wishart.

Matczak, A., Hatzidimitriadou, E. and Lindsay, J. (2011). *Review of Domestic Violence Policies in England and Wales*. London: Kingston University and St George's, University of London.

Mathiesen, T. (1974) *The Politics of Abolition*. London: Martin Robertson.

Mathiesen, T. (1990) *Prison on Trial*. London: Sage.

Mathiesen, T. (1997) 'The Viewer Society: Michel Foucault's 'Panopticon' Revisited', *Theoretical Criminology* 1(2): 215–34.

Matsuda, M., Lawrence III., Charles, R., Delgado, R. and Crenshaw, K.W. (1993) *Words That Wound*. Boulder, CO: Westview Press.

Matthews, R. (2005) 'The Myth of Punitiveness'. *Theoretical Criminology* 9(2): 175–201.

Matthews, R. (2009) 'Beyond "So What?" Criminology'. *Theoretical Criminology*. 13, 341–362.

Matthews, R. (2012) 'Marxist Criminology,' in W. DeKeseredy and M. Dragiewicz (eds) *Handbook of Critical Criminology*. Abingdon: Routledge.

Matthews, R. (2014) *Realist Criminology*. Abingdon: Routledge.

Matthews, R. and Young, J. (1986) 'Introduction', in R. Matthews and J. Young (eds) *Confronting Crime*. London: Sage.

Mawby, R. and Walklate, S. (1994) *Critical Victimology*. London: Sage.

McRobbie, A. and Thornton, S.L. (1995) 'Rethinking "Moral Panic" for Multi-Mediated Social Worlds', *The British Journal of Sociology* 46(4): 559–74.

Mednick, S.A. (1987) 'Biological Factors in Crime Causation: The Reactions of Social Scientists', in S.A. Mednick, T.E. Moffitt and S.A. Stack (eds) *The Causes of Crime: New Biological Approaches*. New York, NY: Cambridge University Press.

Melossi, D. and Pavarini, M. (1981) *The Prison and the Factory: Origins of the Penitentiary System* (trans. G. Cousin). London: Macmillan.

Menzies, R. (1992) 'Beyond Realist Criminology', in J. Lowman and B.D. Maclean (eds) *Realist Criminology: Crime Control and Policing in the 1990s*. Toronto: University of Toronto Press.

Merton, R.K. (1938) 'Social Structure and Anomie', *American Sociological Review* 3: 672–82.

Merton, R.K. (1968) *Social Theory and Social Structure*. New York, NY: New York Press.

Messerschmidt, J.W. (1986) *Capitalism, Patriarchy, and Crime*. Totowa, NJ: Rowman and Littlefield.

Messerschmidt, J.W. (1993) *Masculinities and Crime: Critique and Reconceptualization*. Lanham, MD: Rowman and Littlefield.

Messerschmidt, J.W. and Tomsen, S. (2012) 'Masculinities', in W. DeKeseredy and M. Dragiewicz (eds) *Routledge Handbook of Critical Criminology*. Abingdon: Routledge.

Milovanovic, D. (2011b) 'Critical Perspectives on Law', in W. Dekeseredy and M. Dragiewicz (eds) *Routledge Handbook of Critical Criminology*. Abingdon: Routledge.

Ministry of Justice (2013a) *Statistics on Race and the Criminal Justice System 2012: A Ministry of Justice publication under Section 95 of the Criminal Justice Act 1991*. London: Ministry of Justice.

Ministry of Justice (2013b) *Proven Re-Offending Quarterly July to June 2011*. London: Ministry of Justice.

Minkes, J. (2010) 'Corporate Financial Crimes', in F. Brookman, M. Maguire, H. Pierpoint and T. Bennett (eds) *Handbook on Crime*. Devon: Willan.

Mooney, J. (2012) 'Finding a Political Voice: the Emergence of Critical Criminology in Britain', in W. DeKeseredy and M. Dragiewicz (eds) *Routledge Handbook of Critical Criminology*. Abingdon: Routledge.

Mooney, J. (2000) *Gender, Violence and the Social Order*. New York, NY: Palgrave.

Moxon, D. (1988) *Sentencing Practice in the Crown Court*, Home Office Research Study No 103. London: HMSO.

Muncie, J. (2000) '"Decriminalizing Criminology", British Criminology Conference: Selected Proceedings. Volume 3. Available at: http://britsoccrim. org/volume3/010.pdf (accessed September 2013).

Muncie, J. (2010) 'Labelling, Social Reaction and Social Constructionism', in E. McLaughlin and T. Newburn (eds) *The Sage Handbook of Criminological Theory*. London: Sage.

Murray, C. (1990a) 'The Emerging British Underclass', Institute of Economic Affairs Health and Welfare Unit, Choice in Welfare Series, No 23. Available at: http://www.civitas.org.uk/pdf/cw33.pdf (accessed November 2009).

Murray, C. (1990b) 'Charles Murray and the Underclass: The Developing Debate'. Available at: http://www.civitas.org.uk/pdf/cw33.pdf (accessed November 2009).

Murray, C. (1999) 'The Underclass Revisited', American Enterprise Institution for Public Policy Research: Studies in Social Welfare Policy. Available at: http:// www.aei.org/papers/society-and-culture/poverty/the-underclass-revisited-paper/ (accessed November 2009).

Murray, C. (2001) *Underclass + 10: Charles Murray and the British Underclass 1990–2000*. London: Civitas – Institute for the Study of Civil Society in Association with *The Sunday Times*.

Murray, C. (2012) *Coming Apart: The State of White America, 1960–2010*. New York, NY: Crown Forum.

Muzzatti, S.L. (2012) 'Cultural Criminology: Burning up Capitalism, Consumer Culture', in W. S. DeKeseredy and M. Dragiewicz (eds), *Routledge Handbook of Critical Criminology* London: Routledge.

Naffine, N. (1997) *Feminism and Criminology*. St Leonards: Allen and Unwin.

Nelken, D. (2007) 'White Collar Crime', in M. Maguire, R. Morgan and R. Reiner (eds) *Oxford Handbook of Criminology*. Oxford: Oxford University Press.

Nelken, D. (2012) 'Comparing Criminal Justice', in M. Maguire, R. Morgan and R. Reiner (eds) *Oxford Handbook of Criminology*. Oxford: Oxford University Press.

Newbold, G. and Ross, J. (2013) 'Convict Criminology at the Crossroads: Research Note', *The Prison Journal* 93(1): 3–10.

O'Brien, M. (2005) 'What Is Cultural About Cultural Criminology?', *British Journal of Criminology* 45: 599–612.

O'Malley, P. (2010) *Crime and Risk*. London: Sage.

Painter, K. (1991) 'Wife, Rape, Marriage and the Law', Survey Report, Department of Social Policy and Social Work, University of Manchester.

Park, R.E. and Burgess, E.W. (1966 [1921]) *Introduction to the Science of Sociology* (3rd edn). Chicago, IL: University of Chicago Press.

Parmar, A. (2011) 'Counter-Terrorist of Counter-Productive', *Policing and Society* 43(2): 207–23.

Patel, R. and Tyrer, D. (2011) *Race, Crime and Resistance*. London: Sage.

Pearce, F. (1976) *Crimes of the Powerful: Marxism, Crime and Deviance*. London: Pluto Press.

Pearce, F. and Tombs, S. (1998) *Toxic Capitalism: Corporate Crime and the Chemical Industry*. Aldershot: Dartmouth.

Pease, K., Durkin, P., Earnshaw, I., Payne, D. and Thorpe, J. (1975) *Community Service Orders*, HORS 29. London: HMSO.

Pepinsky, H. (1978) 'Communist Anarchism as an Alternative to the Rule of Criminal Law', *Contemporary Crises* 2: 315–34.

Pepinsky, H. (2012) 'Peacemaking Criminology', in W. DeKeseredy and M. Dragiewicz (eds) *The Routledge Handbook of Critical Criminology*. New York, NY: Routledge.

Pepinsky, H. (2013) 'Peacemaking Criminology'. *Critical Criminology*. 21, 319-339.

Pepinsky, H. and Quinney, R. (1991) *Criminology as Peacemaking*. Bloomington, IN: Indiana University Press.

Pfohl, S.J. (1994) *Images of Deviance and Social Control: A Sociological History*. New York, NY: McGraw Hill.

Piliavin, I. and Briar, S. (1964) 'Police Encounters with Juveniles.' *American Journal of Sociology* 70: 206–14.

Plummer, K. (2000) 'Symbolic Interactionism in the Twentieth Century', in B. Turner (ed) *The Blackwell Companion to Social Theory* (2nd edn). London: Blackwell.

Pontell, H.N., Black, W.K. and Geis, G. (2014) 'Too Big to Fail, too Powerful to Jail? On the Absence of Criminal Prosecutions after the 2008 Financial Meltdown.' *Crime, Law and Social Change* 61, 1–13.

Potter, H. (2006) 'An Argument for Black Feminist Criminology: Understanding African American Women's Experiences with Intimate Partner Abuse using an Integrated Approach', *Feminist Criminology* 1: 106–24.

Pratt, T., Gau, J.M. and Franklin, T.W. (2011) *Key Ideas in Criminology and Criminal Justice*. London: Sage.

Presdee, M. (2000) *Cultural Criminology and the Carnival of Crime*. Abingdon: Routledge.

Presdee, M. (2004) 'Cultural Criminology: The Long and Winding Road'. *Theoretical Criminology* 8, 3: 275–85.

Prison Reform Trust (2013) *Prison: The Facts – Bromley Briefings Summer 2013*. London: Prison Reform Trust.

Quninney, R. (1974) *Critique of the Legal Order: Crime Control in Capitalist Society*. New Jersey: Little Brown.

Quinney, R. (1975) 'Crime Control in Capitalist Society: A Critical Philosophy of Legal Order', in I. Taylor, P. Walton and J. Young (eds) *Critical Criminology*. London: Routledge and Kegan Paul.

Quinney, R. (1980 [1977]) *Class, State, and Crime: On the Theory and Practice of Criminal Justice*. New York, NY: Longman.

Quinney, R. (2000) *Bearing Witness to Crime and Social Justice* (SUNNY series in Deviance and Social Control). New York: State University of New York.

Quinney, R. (2008 [1970]) *Social Reality of Crime*. New Brunswick, NJ: Transaction Publishers.

Raynor, P. and Lewis, S. (2011) 'Risk–Need Assessment, Sentencing and Minority Ethnic Offenders in Britain', *British Journal of Social Work* 41: 1357–71.

Raynor, P. and Vanstone, M. (2002) *Understanding Community Penalties: Probation, Policy and Social Change*. Buckingham: Open University Press.

Rigakos, G. S. (1996) 'New Right, New Left, New Challenges: Understanding and Responding to Neoconservatism in Contemporary Criminology'. *Critical Criminology* 7, 2, 75-91.

Reckless, W. (1933) *Vice in Chicago*. Chicago, IL: Chicago University Press.

Reckless, W. (1961) *The Crime Problem* (3rd edn). New York: Appleton-Century-Crofts.

Reiman, J.H. (1979) *The Rich get Richer and the Poor get Prison: Ideology, Class and Criminal Justice*. New York: Wiley.

Reiman, J.H. and Leighton, P. (2013) *The Rich get Richer and the Poor get Prison: Ideology, Class and Criminal Justice*. Cambridge: Pearson.

Reiner, R. (2012a) 'Political Economy and Criminology: The Return of the Repressed', in S. Hall and S. Winlow (eds) *New Directions in Criminological Theory*. Abingdon: Routledge.

Reiner, R. (2012b) 'Casino Capital's Crime: Political Economy, Crime and Criminal Justice', in M. Maguire, R. Morgan and R. Reiner (eds) *Oxford Handbook of Criminology* (5th edn). Oxford: Oxford University Press.

Reiss, A.J. (1951) 'Delinquency as the Failure of Personal and Social Controls'. *American Sociological Review*. 16: 196-207.

Renzetti, C.M. (2012) 'Feminist Perspectives in Criminology', in W. DeKeseredy and M. Dragiewicz (eds) *The Routledge Handbook of Critical Criminology*. New York, NY: Routledge.

Richards, S.C. (2013) 'The New School of Convict Criminology Thrives and Matures', *Critical Criminology* 21: 375–87.

Richards, S.C. and Ross, J. I. (2001) 'Introducing the New School of Convict Criminology'. Social Justice. 28, 1: 177- 190.

Richards, S.C. and Ross, J.I. (2001) 'The New School of Convict Criminology', *Social Justice* 28(1): 177–90.

Rock, P. (2012) 'Sociological Theories of Crime', in M. Maguire, R. Morgan and R. Reiner (eds) *Oxford Handbook of Criminology* (5th edn). Oxford: Oxford University Press.

Rose, N. (1999) *Powers of Freedom: Reframing Political Thought*. Cambridge: Cambridge University Press.

Rose, N. (2000) 'Government and Control'. *British Journal of Criminology*. 40, 321–39.

Rose, N. and Miller, P. (1992) 'Political Power beyond the State: Problematics of Government'. *British Journal of Sociology*. 43, 2, 173–205.

Rose, D. (2004) *Guantánamo: America's War on Human Rights*. London: Faber and Faber.

Ross, J.I. (ed) (2009) 'Introduction to the Second Edition', in J. I. Ross (ed) *Cutting the Edge: Current Perspectives in Radical/Critical Criminology and Criminal Justice*. New Brunswick, New Jersey: Transaction Publishers.

Ross, L.E. (2010) 'A Vision of Race, Crime and Justice Through the Lens of Critical Race Theory', in E. McLaughlin and T. Newburn (eds) *The Sage Handbook of Criminological Theory*. London: Sage.

Rothe, D. and David Friedrichs (2006) 'The State of the Criminology of State Crime'. *Social Justice* 33, 1, 147–161.

Rothe, D., Ross J.I., Mullins, C.W., Friedrichs, D., Barak, G. Kramer, R.C., Kauzlarich, D. and Michalowski, R. (2009) 'That Was Then, This is Now, What About Tomorrow? Future Directions in State Crime Studies'. *Critical Criminology*. 17, 3–13.

Ruggiero, V. (2013) 'The Environment and the Crimes of the Economy', in N. South and A. Brisman (eds) *The Routledge International Handbook of Green Criminology*. London: Routledge.

Ruggiero, V. and South, N. (2010) 'Green Criminology and Dirty Collar Crime', *Critical Criminology* 18: 251–62.

Ruggiero, V. and South, N. (2013a) 'Green Criminology and Crimes of the Economy: Theory, Research and Praxis', *Critical Criminology* 21: 359–73.

Ruggiero, V. and South, N. (2013b) 'Toxic State–Corporate Crimes, Neo-Liberalism and Green Criminology: The Hazards and Legacies of the Oil, Chemical and Mineral Industries', *International Journal for Crime, Justice and Social Democracy* 2(2): 12–26.

Runciman, W.G. (1966) *Relative Deprivation and Social Justice: A Study of Attitudes to Social Inequality in Twentieth Century England*. Berkeley, CA: University of California Press.

Rusche, G. and Kircheimer, O. (1939) *Punishment and Social Structure*. New Brunswick, Jersey: Transaction Publishers.

Russell, S. (2002) 'The Continuing Relevance of Marxism to Critical Criminology', *Critical Criminology* 11: 113–35.

Ryan, M. and Sim. J. (2007) 'Campaigning for and Campaigning Against Prisons: Excavating and Re-Affirming the Case for Prison Abolition', in Y. Jewkes (ed) *Handbook on Prisons*. Cullompton: Willan.

Sampson, R. J. and Wilson, W. J. (1995) 'Toward a Theory of Race, Crime, and Urban Inequality', in J. Hagan and R. D. Peterson (eds.), *Crime and Inequality*. Stanford, CA: Stanford University Press.

Scarman Report (1981) *The Brixton Disorders: Report of an Inquiry by the Rt Hon Lord Scarman, OBE*. London: HMSO.

Scheerer, S. (2000) 'Three Trends into the New Millennium: The Populist and the Road Towards Global Justice', in A. Rutherford and P. Green (eds) *Criminal Policy in Transition*. Oxford: Hart Publishing.

Scheff, T. (1974) 'The Labelling Theory of Mental Illness'. *American Sociological Review*, 39, 3, 444-452.

Schneider, C.J. (2003) 'Integrating Critical Race Theory and Postmodernism Implications of Race, Class, and Gender', *Critical Criminology* 12: 87–103.

Schur, E. (1963) *Narcotic Addiction in Britain and America. The Impact of Public Policy*. London: Tavistock Publications.

Schur, E. (1965) *Crimes without Victims: Deviant Behaviour and Public Policy—Abortion, Homosexuality, Drug Addiction*. Englewood Cliffs, NJ: Prentice-Hall.

Schur, E.M. (1973) *Radical Non-Intervention: Rethinking the Delinquency Problem*. Englewood Cliffs, NJ: Prentice Hall.

Schwartz, M.D. and DeKeseredy, W.S. (1991) 'Left Realist Criminology: Strengths, Weaknesses, and the Feminist Critique', *Crime, Law and Social Change* 15: 51–72.

Schwendinger, H. and Schwendinger, J. (1970) 'Defenders of Order or Guardians of Human Rights?', *Issues in Criminology* 5: 123–57.

Schwendinger, H. and Schwendinger, J. (1972) 'The Continuing Debate on the Legalistic Approach to the Definition of Crime', *Issues in Criminology* 7(1): 70–81.

Schwendinger, H. and Schwendinger, J. (1977) 'Social Class and the Definition of Crime', *Crime and Social Justice* 7: 4–13.

Schwendinger, H., Schwendinger, J.R. and Lynch, M.J. (2008) 'Critical Criminology in the United States: The Berkeley School and Theoretical Trajectories', in K. Carrington and R. Hogg (eds) *Critical Criminology: Issues, Debates, Challenges*. Devon: Willan.

Sellin, T. (1938a) 'Conflict and Crime', *American Journal of Sociology* 44(1): 97–103.

Sellin, T. (1938b) 'Culture, Conflict and Crime', *The Social Science Research Council Bulletin* 41: 63–70.

Senior, P., Crowther-Dowey, C. and Long, M. (2007) *Understanding the Modernisation of Criminal Justice*. Milton Keynes: Open University Press.

Shaw, C. and Mackay, H. (1942) *Juvenile Delinquency and Urban Areas*. Chicago, IL: University of Chicago Press.

Sherman, L.W. (2010) 'Defiance, Compliance and Consilience: A General Theory of Criminology', in E. McLaughlin and T. Newburn (eds) *The SAGE Handbook of Criminological Theory*. London: SAGE.

Sherman, L.W. (2011) 'Criminology as Invention', in M. Bosworth and C. Hoyle (eds) *What is Criminology?* Oxford: Oxford University Press.

Shichor, D. (1980) 'Some Problems of Credibility in Radical Criminology', in J.A. Inciardi (ed) *Radical Criminology: The Coming Crises*. Vol 23, Sage Focus Editions Series.

Shildrick, T., MacDonald, R., Furlong, A., Roden, J. and Crow, R. (2012) *Are 'Cultures of Worklessness' Passed Down the Generations?*, York: Joseph Rowntree Foundation.

Sim, J. (1994) 'The Abolitionist Approach: A British Perspective', in A. Duff, S. Marshall, R.E. Dobash and R.P. Dobash (eds) *Penal Theory and Penal Practice: Tradition and Innovation in Criminal Justice*. Manchester: Manchester University Press.

Sim, J. (2009) *Punishment and Prisons: Power and the Carceral State*. London: Sage.

Sim, J., Scraton, P. and Gordon, P. (1987) 'Introduction: Crime, the State and Critical Analysis', in P. Scraton (ed) *Law, Order and the Authoritarian State*. Milton Keynes: Open University Press.

Simon, J. (2007) *Governing Through Crime: How the War on Crime Transformed American Democracy and Created a Culture of Fear*. New York, NY: Oxford University Press.

Skinner, B.F. (1938) *The Behavior of Organisms: An Experimental Analysis*. New York, NY: Appleton-Century.

Slapper, G. and Tombs, S. (1999) *Corporate Crime*. Harlow: Longman.

Smart, C. (1976) *Women, Crime and Criminology*. Abingdon: Routledge.

Smart, C. (1995) *Law, Crime and Sexuality: Essays in Feminism*. London: Sage.

Smith, D. (1995) 'Black People, Crime and Social Control', in D. Smith (ed) *Criminology for Social Work*. London: BASW.

Snider, L. (1993) *Bad Business: Corporate Crime in Canada*. Scarborough, Ontario: Nelson.

Snider, L. (1998) 'Towards Safer Societies', *British Journal of Criminology* 38(1): 1–38.

South, N. (1998) 'A Green Field for Criminology? A Proposal for a Perspective', *Theoretical Criminology* 2(2): 211–33.

South, N. and Beirne, P. (eds) (2006) *Green Criminology*. Aldershot: Ashgate.

South, N., Brisman, A. and Beirne, P. (2013) 'A Guide to a Green Criminology', in N. South and A. Brisman (eds) *The Routledge International Handbook of Green Criminology*. Abingdon: Routledge.

Spalek, B. (2007) *Knowledgeable Consumers? Corporate Fraud and its Devastating Impacts*. Centre for Crime and Justice, Briefing 4, August 2007.

Spencer, D. (2011) 'Cultural Criminology: An Invitation … to What?', *Critical Criminology* 19: 197–212.

Spencer, D. and Fitzgerald, A. (2013) 'Three Ecologies, Transversality and Victimization: The Case of the British Petroleum Oil Spill', *Crime, Law and Social Change* 59(2): 209–23.

Spitzer, S. (1975) 'Towards a Marxian Theory of Deviance', *Social Problems* 22: 638–51.

Squires, P. and Lea, J. (2012) 'Introduction: Reading Loic Wacquant – Opening Questions', in P. Squires and J. Lea (eds) *Criminalisation and Advanced Marginality: Critically Exploring the Work of Loic Wacquant*. Bristol: The Policy Press.

Stretesky, P.B. and Lynch, M.J. (2002) 'Environmental Hazards and School Segregation in Hillsborough, 1987–1999'. *The Sociological Quarterly*. 43, 4: 553–573.

Stretesky, P.B., Long, M.A. and Lynch, M.J. (2013) *The Treadmill of Crime: Political Economy and Green Criminology*. Abingdon: Routledge.

Sumner, C.S. (1976) 'Marxism and Deviance Theory', in P.Wiles (ed) *The Sociology of Crime and Delinquency in Britain: Volume 2, The New Criminologies*. Oxford: Martin Robertson.

Sutherland, E.H. (1939) *Principles of Criminology* (3rd edn). Philadelphia, PA: Lippincott.

Sutherland, E.H. (1949) *White-Collar Crime*. New York, NY: Holt, Reinhart and Winston.

Sykes, G. and Matza, D. (1957) 'Techniques of Neutralization: A Theory of Delinquency', *American Sociological Review* 22: 664–70.

Tannenbaum, F. (1938) *Crime and the Community*. New York, NY: Ginn.

Taylor, I., Walton, P. and Young, J. (1973) *The New Criminology for a Social Theory of Deviance* (International Library of Sociology). London: Routledge.

Taylor, I., Walton, P. and Young, J. (2013) *The New Criminology for a Social Theory of Deviance* (40th Anniversary Edition). London: Routledge.

Thomas, W. I. (1907) 'The Mind of Woman and the Lower Races'. *American Journal of Sociology, 12*, 4, 435-469.

Thomas, W.I. and Thomas, D.S. (1928) *The Child in America: Behavior Problems and Programs*. New York, NY: Alfred A. Knopf.

Thomas, W. I. and Znaniecki, F. (1918–1920) *The Polish Immigrant in Europe and America. Monograph of an Immigrant Group,* (Volumes 1 to 5) Chicago: University of Chicago Press and Boston: Gorham Press. n.Vol. 1, 1918-1920

Thrasher, F. (1927) *The Gang: A Study of 1,313 Gangs in Chicago*. Chicago, IL: University of Chicago Press.

Tierney, J. (2009) *Key Perspectives in Criminology*. Maidenhead: Open University Press.

Tifft, L. and Sullivan, D. (1980) *The Struggle to be Human: Crime, Criminology, and Anarchism*. Orkney: Cienfeugos.

Tombs, S. (2007) '"Violence", Safety Crimes and Criminology', *British Journal of Criminology* 47(4): 531–50.

Tombs, S. (2013) 'Corporate Crime', in C. Hale, K. Hayward, A. Wahidin and E. Wincup (eds) *Criminology*. Oxford: Oxford University Press.

Tombs, S. and Whyte, D. (2007) *Safety Crimes*. Cullompton: Willan.

Tombs, S. and Whyte, D. (2010) 'A Deadly Consensus: Worker Safety and Regulatory Degradation under New Labour'. *British Journal of Criminology*, 50: 46–65.

Tombs, S. and Whyte, D. (2013) 'The Myths and Realities of Deterrence in Workplace Safety Regulation', *British Journal of Criminology* 53: 746–63.

Turk, A.T. (1966) 'Conflict and Criminality', *American Sociological Review* 31(3): 338–52.

Turk, A.T. (1969) *Criminality and the Legal Order*. Chicago, IL: Rand McNally.

Tushnet, M. (2005) 'Critical Legal Theory', in M. P. Golding and W.A. Edmundson (eds) *The Blackwell Guide to the Philosophy of Law and Legal Theory*. Oxford: Blackwell.

van Swaaningen, R. (2000) 'Back to the "Iron Cage": The Example of the Dutch Probation Service', in A. Rutherford and P. Green (eds) *Criminal Policy in Transition*. Oxford: Hart Publishing.

van Swaaningen, R. (1997) *Critical Criminology: Visions from Europe*. London: Sage.

van Swaaningen, R. (1999) 'Reclaiming Critical Criminology: Social Justice and the European Tradition', *Theoretical Criminology* 3: 5.

Vold, G.B. (1958) *Theoretical Criminology*. New York, NY: Oxford University Press.

Vold, G.B. and Bernard, T.J. (1986) *Theoretical Criminology*. New York, NY: Oxford University Press.

Von Hirsch, A. (1976) *Doing Justice: The Choice of Punishments. Report of the Committee for the Study of Incarceration*. New York: Hill and Wang.

Von Hirsch, A., Bottoms, A., Burney, E. and Wikstrom, P. (1999) *Criminal Deterrence and Sentence Severity: An Analysis of Recent Research, Summary of Findings*. London: Home Office.

Wacquant, L. (2009) *Punishing the Poor: The Neoliberal Government of Social Insecurity (Politics, History, & Culture)*. Durham, NC: Duke University Press.

Wacquant, L. (2010) 'Crafting the Neoliberal State: Workfare, Prisonfare, and Social Insecurity', *Sociological Forum* 25(2): 197–220.

Walklate, S. (2005) *Criminology the Basics*. London: Routledge

Walklate, S. (2011) *Criminology the Basics* (2nd edn). London: Routledge.

Watson, J.B. (1913) 'Psychology as the Behaviorist Views It', *Psychological Review* 20: 158–77.

Webber, C. (2007) 'Background, Foreground, Foresight: The Third Dimension of Cultural Criminology?', *Crime, Media, Culture* 3: 139–57.

Weisburd, D., Waring, E. and Piquero, N. (2008) 'Getting Beyond the Moral Drama of Crime: What We Learn from Studying White-Collar Criminal Careers', in J. Minkes and L. Minkes (eds) *Corporate and White-Collar Crime*. London: Sage.

Welch, M.F. (2004) *Ironies of Imprisonment*. London: Sage.

Welch, M.F. (2011) 'Counterveillance: How Foucault and the Groupe d'Information sur les Prisons Reversed the Optics', *Theoretical Criminology* 15: 301–13.

Welch, M.F. (2012) 'War on Terror, Human Rights, and Critical Criminology', in W. DeKeseredy and M. Dragiewicz (eds) *The Routledge Handbook of Critical Criminology*. New York, NY: Routledge.

White, R. (2010a) 'A Green Criminology Perspective', in E. McLaughlin and T. Newburn (eds) *The SAGE Handbook of Criminological Theory*. London: SAGE.

White, R. (2010b) 'Globalisation and Environmental Harm', in R. White (ed) *Global Environmental Harm: Criminological Perspectives*. Cullompton: Willan.

White, R. (2013) 'Eco-Global Criminology and the Political Economy of Environmental Harm', in N. South and A. Brisman (eds) *The Routledge International Handbook of Green Criminology*. London: Routledge.

Wilkins, L. (1964) *Social Deviance*. London: Tavistock.

Wilkinson, R. and Pickett, K. (2009) *The Spirit Level: Why More Equal Societies Almost Always Do Better*. London: Allen Lane.

Wilson, J.Q. (1975) *Thinking About Crime*. New York, NY: Basic Books.

Wilson, J. and Hernstein, R. (1985) *Crime and Human Nature: The Definitive Study of the Causes of Crime*. New York, NY: Simon and Schuster.

Wilson, J.Q. and Kelling, G.L. (1982) 'Broken Windows: The Police and Neighbourhood Safety', in E. McLaughlin, J. Muncie and G. Hughes (eds) *Criminological Perspectives: Essential Readings*. London: Sage.

Worrall, A. (2004) 'Twisted Sisters, Ladettes, and the New Penology', in C. Adler and A. Worrall (eds) *Girls' Violence: Myths and Realities*. New York: State University of New York Press.

Young, J. (1971a) *The Drugtakers: The Social Meaning of Drug Use*. London: McGibbon and Kee.

Young, J. (1971b) 'The Role of the Police as Amplifiers of Deviancy, Negotiators of Reality and Translators of Fantasy: Some Consequences of Our Present System of Drug Control as seen in Notting Hill', in S. Cohen (ed) *Images of Deviance*. Harmondsworth: Penguin Books,.

Young, J. (1975) 'Working-Class Criminology', in I. Taylor, P. Walton, and J. Young (eds) *Critical Criminology*. London: Routledge.

Young, J. (1986) 'The Failure of Criminology: The Need for Radical Realism', in R. Matthews and J. Young (eds) *Confronting Crime*. London: Sage.

Young, J. (1988) 'Radical Criminology in Britain: The Emergence of a Competing Paradigm', *British Journal of Criminology* 28(2): 159–83.

Young, J. (1991) 'Asking Question of Left Realism', in B.D. MacLean and D. Milovanovic (eds) *New Directions in Critical Criminology: Left Realism, Feminism, Postmodernism and Peacemaking*. Vancouver: The Collective Press.

Young, J. (1994) 'Incessant Chatter: Current Paradigms in Criminology', in M. Maguire, R. Morgan and R. Reiner (eds) *The Oxford Handbook of Criminology*. Oxford: Oxford University Press.

Young, J. (1997) 'Left Realist Criminology: Radical in Its Analysis, Realist in Its Policy', in M. Maguire, R. Morgan and R. Reiner (eds) *The Oxford Handbook of Criminology*. Oxford: Oxford University Press.

Young, J. (1999) *The Exclusive Society*. London: Sage.

Young, J. (2002) 'Critical Criminology in the Twenty-First Century: Critique, Irony and the Always Unfinished', in K. Carrington and R. Hogg (eds) *Critical Criminology: Issues Debates, Challenges*. Cullompton: Willan.

Young, J. (2007) *The Vertigo of Late Modernity*. London: SAGE.

Young, J. (2009) 'Moral Panics: Its Origins in Resistance, Resentment and the Translation of Fantasy into Reality', *British Journal of Criminology* 49(1): 4–16.

Young, J. (2010) *The Criminological Imagination*. Chichester: Wiley.

Young, J. (2012) 'Working-Class Criminology', in I. Taylor, P. Walton, and J. Young (eds) *Critical Criminology* (Routledge Revivals). London: Routledge.

Young, J. (2013) 'Introduction to the 40th Anniversary Edition', in I. Taylor, P. Walton and J. Young (eds) *The New Criminology for a Social Theory of Deviance* (40th anniversary edn). Abingdon: Routledge.

Yosso, T. J. (2005) 'Whose Culture has Capital? A Critical Race Theory Discussion of Community Cultural Wealth'. *Race Ethnicity and Education*. 8, 1: 69–91.

Index